ONE OF OUR OWN

MEMOIRS OF CHANGE

by

H U G H   W E I R

with mainly his own illustrations

BALLINAKELLA PRESS

First published in 2001 by Ballinakella Press,
Whitegate, Co. Clare

ISBN 0946538 38 7

Copyright © 2001 Hugh W.L. Weir

A CIP record of this file
is available from the British
Library

Editing: Sonia Schorman
Typing: Grania Weir
Typesetting: Don Harper, Artwerk Ltd

Illustrations, Hugh Weir, Oak House, Malcolm and Ingrid Ross MacDonald
David and Veronica Rowe

Cover photo: Philip Sides

Printing: ColourBooks Ltd.

*This book is dedicated to all those
who have touched my life, especially
to my parents and Grania, my wife.
I also acknowledge with thanks,
those who have helped it to maturity,
and who have given encouragement
including editor Sonia Schorman,
Grania O'Brien Weir, Tomás Porcell,
P.J. Kenny, The Chief Officer – Church of
Ireland R.B., Malcolm and Ingrid
Ross MacDonald, Claire Besnyö
(Oak House), David and Veronica Rowe,
Philip Sides, Ann Jones, Don Harper,
Adrienne Foran and Colour Books*

*In no way has it been my intention to
offend anyone herein mentioned. I
unreservedly apologise if I have, and beg
forgiveness. I hope, however, that all my
readers will enjoy these pages.*

PROLOGUE

Recollection and reflections which spurred me to write this book. A chronological taste of an interesting and active, if unusual life.

I have always loved Ireland; the background which has influenced me most is my Irish one. As I travel the Slieve Aughty mountains behind our west of Ireland home, I often dream of my past. Little glimpses of my life's many paths come to mind.

Catching crabs in a muddy Essex tidal estuary or crayfish in the river Suir, playing sandcastles on the beach at Tynemouth with my cousin, incendiary bombs being dropped by German aircraft beside the road my mother and I were travelling and the 'Crunchy' bars given me by friends in Cashel when there was rationing, are early memories. The people who have befriended me, my first brush with sexual innuendo, the horses I rode, the dogs shared, and Polish airmen who taught me boxing all helped to mould my life.

Sometimes I feel vulnerable and alone as I reflect on those who have gone before me, and the happy times they created. The polio that I contracted when I was six has since displayed itself with the Post Polio Syndrome, a crippling and tiresome affliction, but I have led and still live a very full and active life.

Many twentieth century Irish biographers have exposed experiences of poverty, abused childhood and travel, and their armchair journeys delight many a contemporary reader. Usually they have written up activities that have happened at one or two homes. They follow a particular, usually steadily developing, pattern. I offer something different. I have attempted to recollect a variety of activities which have happened in very different places.

* * * * * * * * * *

Born to an Irish family of landed gentry, I have been reluctant to rely on the achievements of my ancestors, of many of whom I am immensely proud. I feel them to be my friends and mentors. I have my own achievements, often experienced as a loner. This may have been a disadvantage, but my story is my own.

My parents gave me a good start. Their friends and relations were very much part of an ascendancy which, although on the wane during my formative years, was still alive. There were extremes of wealth and poverty. The big houses and their demesnes, although many inhabited by their original owners, were falling into disrepair through a lack of income and the burden of property taxes. The Second World War saw an almost final massacre of a society which had been unable to recover from the First; there had also been the Irish Troubles and the Civil War. Yet gentry still lived as gentry; there was an air of pretence that circumstances would recover and that butlers, housemaids and farmhands would rally to their employers' call even if the latter could afford a mere pittance. Times weren't good. Some cut down on their sport, others took over the running of their estates from their agents while many hoped their gamekeepers would take different jobs. It was an era of change.

Even during the war, or the 'Emergency' as it was known in Ireland, clothes were important. In spite of shortages and the handing down from parents of already well-worn items of apparel, there was an emphasis on them being well tailored. Ridiculous customs included leaving the bottom waistcoat button undone in deference to British monarch Edward VII's inability to keep his stomach in. 'Brothel creepers' - shoes with thick soft soles were out.

As for eating, there was a perpetuation of the Victorian obsession with minor etiquettes, such as the leaving of a little food on one's plate for 'Mr. Manners' - what a ridiculous waste. Fish was eaten with a fork to let it be known, I presume, that one understood the anatomy of the slab of pink or white flesh placed before one. Elbows were not permitted to rest on a table and afternoon tea was accompanied by thin slices of over-buttered bread, or cucumber sandwiches cut into tiny delicate squares. I loathed my mother's fashionable caraway seed cake. Butter knives, fish or cake slicers, and cruets were all taboo to indicate, in our case, that the Weirs were old gentry, not nouveaux riches. Of course, during the war, valuables such as silver were professionally stored.

In my young days, education was less important than schooling. The preparatory school for young gentlemen was followed by a 'good' public school and then perhaps Cambridge or Trinity College, Dublin. With great difficulty large sums were procured to pay for one to become a 'Little Lord Fontleroy'. As each term began, hours would be spent listing the obligatory school clothes which were packed in large timber-bound trunks - sweets and toys were shoved into wooden 'tuck' boxes.

On arrival at school, snobbish bullies who had experienced one or two previous terms would boast about their friends and possessions. Girls were out; they went to other schools. Aged about twelve, boys sought acceptance to their public schools, preferably Eton or Harrow, or Cheltenham as in my father's case. Failure was unacceptable and in some cases 'pull' was used, especially for the children of well-known or financially comfortable parents. Boys should also excel at sport, and become friendly with 'acceptable' young men in the company of whom they were likely to spend the rest of their days. Many of my friends became employed in stockbroking, Lloyds Insurance, rubber planting in the Colonies or as army officers.

I was lucky to escape a lot of pomposity and arrogance by going to Portora at Enniskillen. My comrades came from all walks of life and there was an easily acceptable and genuine Christian bias. Money and station were less important than honesty and integrity, generosity and consideration for others. The subjects were made interesting. We were encouraged to achieve in our own chosen fields and if not keen on games or military cadetships, were channelled into cycling or exploring.

In the decade following the war the prospects for employment in Ireland were almost nil. Most of us accepted that we would have to emigrate. Canada embraced most of my colleagues while I also considered New Zealand. As my parents had to pay for my brother's education, and being no scholar, I had to leave Portora early - a pity as I was belatedly beginning to make use of my parents' investment in my future.

From an early age, I got to know people like my father's friends author Henry Williamson *(Tarka the Otter, Salar the Salmon* etc.), John Betjeman the poet, and artist Sir Alfred Munnings. Aunt Lilian had hoped I would take on her South African estate and cousin Edith Collison regularly corresponded. My grandparents often looked after me during the war years and I especially enjoyed my times with my mother's father on Lough Derg, the southernmost of the Shannon lakes.

My father encouraged me to read classics such as Thackery and Surtees, and even Maurice O'Sullivan's *Twenty Years a Growing* - still a favourite. He had extensive interests and shared his variety of hobbies. He abhorred socialism, although he was comfortable with individuals of all classes and backgrounds. His efforts to impose his ways on me were not successful. I was determined to do my own thing, much to his disappointment. Still, he was tolerant enough to accept that.

My mother has never understood my reluctance to tie myself to her ambitions of hunting and painting. My birth, fathered by a divorcee of whom her family disapproved, although both parents' families were friends, curtailed her social activities; she was attractive and popular. Although no longer able to do as she pleased, and in spite of my father's small income at the time, she could escape to Ireland to hunt and socialise.

The Second World War denied many their childhood, as most parents were actively involved. For my part, I was left increasingly to my own devices. I was sent to board, aged seven, at Glebe House in Norfolk where pupils were expected to emulate their brave fathers. There were air-raid warnings, even raids. Everything was controlled, there was rationing, and we had crocodile walks to cold windswept beaches. I made my first solo journey to Ireland only a little later, and loved it. I was insecure though, for I missed my parents and worried terribly when I learnt that bombs had been dropped where they might have been. I cannot recall them visiting me at prep school – my pals would often greet their gift-bearing and loving families. The warmth experienced from the people of Ireland was always a comfort.

Unable to enjoy many of my family's traditional activities such as riding and hunting, I preferred carpentry, mechanics, farming and art. I am thankful for all my parents did for me. There was, though, little sensitivity to my incapacities. Although they didn't display it there was affection and I was, for my early years, my parent's only son and heir.

*   *   *   *   *   *   *   *   *   *   *

Following the war, my father played his role in healing the problems of war-torn Britain and we lived in Essex. My brother Guy's birth took place when I was almost twelve. Although attention was lavished on the new-born, I accepted the situation and anyway, I was now interested in archaeology and history and here was Roman and Saxon Britain with tales of Old King Cole and the Celtic Queen, Boadicea. I began to get out and about and to explore, help with archaeological digs, catch fish in the local rivers and whistle my new-found freedom. A friend across the road advanced my interest in genealogy. A Dublin cleric encouraged my fasination with history and gave me items from his collection I still treasure. I wasn't, however, allowed to go down one part of the road; there lived a 'naughty lady' with over twelve children. I didn't understand why she was called such, but eventually my bombardment of questions elicited an answer. I now understood what prostitution was.

Sharing my parents' excitement of my brother, I proudly boasted to my pals at school. Arriving home for holidays, though, I found that he had been given my most treasured book and had scribbled over it. I think my parents sensed my hurt.

Whilst I was at my second English prep school in Sussex, my Gibson grandfather transferred his house in Tipperary to my mother. He had moved to County Clare. I recall my excitement as I caught the Holyhead boat train from London. This was the beginning of a new life, a different history, real country.

My first political awareness followed my return to school at Newells in Sussex. Punished for contradicting a teacher as he told my class that the Irish lived in hovels alongside their pigs, my end of term report recorded me as "rebellious and sullen". My time at Portora was different. Due to my family's Fermanagh roots, I could identify with the locality and its people. Fermanagh was Weir country and my family had evolved here. Gone was an education fraught with bullying, fear and insecurity. There were, of course, the comparisons between each side of the Irish border, but there were many exciting new experiences.

As I had no Certificate of Education when I left school, no money, and was unable to matriculate to university, I helped my parents before working on a farm in Kildare, and later with friends a few miles from home. I spent my spare time selling my hand-drawn Christmas cards. The Korean war had started and rumour was that Communism would overcome the world, so I joined the British Army to support the United Nations against the prospect. My service in the Far and Middle East gave me a chance to see the world. Although there was boredom when garrisoned in England, exciting times included being chased by a tank on Salisbury plain during very realistic military exercises.

While I was working for a London publisher and studying theology, following my military service, my parents decided to sell Ardmaylebeg, our Tipperary home. They felt my brother would do better at school in England and could see no long-term future in Ireland. At their new Suffolk property they continued to farm, but my rug, of belonging and security, was pulled from under me.

Health problems saw me back in Ireland for I had been 'burning the candle at both ends'. I found accommodation in the early fifties in Cork where I continued my studies. Welcomed by just about everyone I met, I was given a sense of being wanted as never before and was able to earn pocket money teaching, cataloguing a library and even co-producing postcards. I also became involved in chaplaincy and taking Church services, radio and the theatre. I grew to love this characterful city. While I was there, my father died and my mother re-married. I also leased a small hut beside Lough Derg from whence I fished and explored, and later purchased the ruins of a nearby cottage which was to become a home and 'root place'. However, finding it difficult to survive financially, eventually I had to move.

There were few grants for religious education and Dublin offered more opportunities to earn living expenses. I got a residential teaching job in Bray, Co. Wicklow from whence I travelled to Trinity

College. Aravon was very different to Cork Grammar and more like an English prep school. In the end I gave up my studies and after posts at two more central Dublin schools, St. Stephen's and Brook House, decided to discontinue teaching and move to Clare. My base was the small cottage I had reconstructed and from which I sought agencies for machinery to sell throughout Ireland. I missed teaching but continued to run the English language centre I had established during previous summer holidays. Many of my pupils, often with their parents, would visit and share happy recollections.

A countryman at heart, I was content where I had settled. Not only did I set up my machinery company, but gradually involved myself in my community and church. An Ireland I had hardly known opened up as I travelled with my wares and continued to experience social life. Later I erected a new store and shop which enabled me to employ an assistant and to expand. I sold quality products, and gave good service to my tractor, mower and DIY customers. Two bank strikes, though, were devastating. A friend came to my rescue by suggesting I take on his job with Barnardo's children's charity - a house in Clondalkin was part of the deal and the salary was good. This and a legacy from my South African aunt helped me recover.

I could now feather a nest. A girl I had met in my teens was the local Chairman of An Taisce, an organisation of which I was also on the committee. We were attracted to each other. The purchase of a lakeside site and the erection of a new house at Whitegate were the foundations of our present home.

Our wedding was elaborate as Grania was popular and had been brought up in her father's O'Brien family castle. Having worked abroad and in London, she could speak Spanish and French. Intelligent, widely read and considerate, she was back in Ireland to help her parents transfer to a smaller house. I fell for her. Family squabbles and the education of two orphaned girls to sort out followed our marriage in 1973. However, we enjoyed two honeymoons and travelled to Britain, Europe, and throughout Ireland. We substituted my machinery business for publishing, partly through a book on houses for which I had had difficulty in finding a publisher. Today I produce postcards, write regular environmental and historical columns for the press, and Grania and I have compiled a number of our own books. As well as being an author, artist and publisher, I was Irish Heritage Historian, sponsored by government agencies. This enabled me to travel throughout the United States and Canada to promote tourism amongst the descendants of Irish emigrants, and to help them understand the history and contemporary circumstances of Ireland.

A dedicated Christian, I am by no means 'saintly'. Membership of the Church of Ireland has involved me in preaching and taking services, themselves a source of anecdotes. Once my sermon slipped behind a wooden panel, and a mental patient elsewhere shouted at me during my address. I have helped organise seminars, served on church councils, Diocesan radio programmes and Bishops' selection conferences for aspiring ordinands. Today I am less active or forthright but I have received spiritual fulfilment through such activities.

More than a decade of my married life was devoted to the Clare Young Environmentalists, voluntarily promoting what was then a greenfield concept. The group was necessary at a time when citizens were only just becoming aware of the natural and man-made world with which we are entrusted. I still write a reputedly influential weekly environmental column in the *Clare Champion*.

Travel, whether for work or play, has been an exciting facet of my life. My early experiences of train and boat journeys to and from school and my military service in the Far and Middle East enabled me to experience the culture, people and places of areas I would never otherwise have been able to visit. Some events were unpleasant such as a sleety winter half-day wait on Rosslare pier, but others were thrilling. My marathon journey round Kerry on a 50cc. motorbike and my first drive to the north of Scotland were memorable. Since marriage, I have driven throughout Europe, usually sleeping in the back of a van, and have been to such destinations as China and Bermuda with Grania. I have even had wildlife experiences with my vehicle in Kosovo, been unjustly detained in a Yugoslav police station, and nearly drowned in a Swedish bog.

My stamina has kept me going but physical discomfort has curtailed an ability to undertake activities about which I now only dream.

CHAPTER ONE

Those who preceded me: my forebears, my parents and their interests and activities, my birth and those who have influenced my life.

Until his comparatively early death, I was influenced by my father's bravery, his travels and his interest in nature and history; he wrote for the Countryman and was an avid reader. My mother's love of horses and of hunting was encouraged by her father, especially as he was Master of the Thurles and Kilshane Hounds in Co. Tipperary. She was also keen on painting and did some very professional work - mainly in oils.

An old County Fermanagh family, the Weirs descend from Baltredus de Vere who left France around 1165. They inter-married with Norman and Gaelic families before settling in Magheraboy where their neighbours were their kinsfolk the Hamiltons, Croziers, Somervilles and Dunbars. Amongst those forebears who have fascinated me are the children of Alexander Weir of Tullymargy Castle and of his wife Anne, daughter of Sir John Dunbar, founder of the village of Derrygonnelly.

During the 1641 civil war, with their widowed mother Anne, his younger brother Alexander (Sandy), his sister Jane, and about fifty others, John took refuge in Lisgoole Abbey south of Enniskillen. A 'numerous body of rebels' surrounded the thatched building and prepared to burn it. As the refugees had few arms and little ammunition, John accepted enemy terms. He would surrender in return for his and his party's safe passage to Enniskillen. Taking over the abbey, however, the invaders seized John and with others, "tied them two together back to back with gads and then cut their throats". Anne, Jane and the then nine year old Alexander escaped, rescued by one of the Maguires, possibly Rory - a "person of consequence

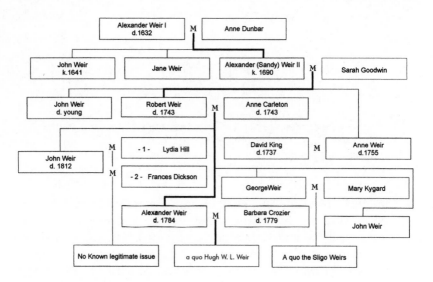

amongst the rebels". This chivalrous gentleman who knew the family sent the three of them by boat down-river to Enniskillen where they remained until the end of the troubles.

Alexander's experience in one so young must have been traumatic. Ten years later, in 1651, he served in the Battle of Worcester. He had possibly already fought Cromwell at Drogheda and Wexford in 1649. Charles, proclaimed King of Scotland and Ireland, had invaded England expecting to receive more assistance there. This was not forthcoming; the Royalist army was defeated and Sandy escaped to Scotland.

Staying with relations and awaiting news from Ireland, Sandy was informed that he 'Alexander Weir of Monaghan' had been attainted and his estate forfeited for carrying arms in support of Charles Stuart (King Charles II). This news did not expedite his return and he remained in Scotland for two or three years. In Ireland his friends pleaded with the Provost Marshall, emphasising his minority, as a result of which he returned home and peaceably repossessed his property. For most of the next thirty years, he developed orchards and mills, and enjoyed a reasonably tranquil rural life. His first wife, from whom I descend, was Sarah Goodwin whose father Robert of

County Derry was First Chamberlain of the city. Her mother was a daughter of Captain Mansfield, a County Donegal landlord. They had two sons, John and Robert whose story is similarly fascinating. On Sarah's death, her husband married Elizabeth, daughter of Sir Paul Gore, who died in 1674.

In November 1688 Sandy Weir raised a two hundred man independent troop of horse with Sir John Hume's eldest son, James. Following James's death, Williamite Captain Weir routed King James' soldiers at Ballyshannon and played a significant role in the victory of Newtown Butler. After their success, his cavalry became the Inniskilling Dragoons. Weir was ordered to Boyle in Co. Roscommon where, the following October, there were squirmishes before the opposing forces were dispelled. He was to stay in the town and send information about the movements of General Sarsfield's forces to Colonel Lloyd at Sligo. When Sandy told Lloyd he needed re-enforcements, the Colonel showed little concern and in effect told him: "soldier on - no re-enforcements available". In command at Boyle, Sandy received intelligence that Sarsfield and his army were approaching. He marched towards Sligo, but the enemy were dug in at the foot of the Curlew mountains. Sandy successfully attacked but was severely wounded and died within twenty-four hours, having been carried back to the town. Lord Kingston, arranged for him to be buried in the latter's family plot in Boyle Abbey. A monument was erected at the spot where he fell.

In 1676, when this Captain Alexander Weir was forty-four, his surviving son, Robert, was brought into the world. Robert enrolled in his father's troop at Boyle when he was aged fourteen. He lost his left arm on service (my father also lost an arm) and was twice wounded. Reported as killed, he failed to get his brigadier's nomination for a commission. He returned to his mother when the stump had healed, and rejoined his regiment the following spring. Having fought at Athlone, Aughrim and Limerick, he went to England in 1694, intending to serve in Flanders on the recommendation of the Duke of Ormonde. He was well received and soldiered for three years in Sir Henry Bellassis' Infantry Regiment. Like his father, he regained possession of his property but in February 1713, his "strong house of stone and loopholed" was accidentally burned to the ground together with irreplaceable family manuscripts, silver and furniture. It was eight years before he and his wife Anne, daughter of Captain Carleton, and of a 'Monea Castle' Hamilton, built the present Hall Craig.

Hall Craig is a tall three-storey, three bay double pile house with a delightful door-case. There is a spectacular view over the Sillies river towards the distant mountains to the south. The yard and foundations of the original house are a short distance to the north-west. The house was sold on the death of Gerald Weir at the beginning of the twentieth century. It is now a well maintained, listed building loved by the Scotts whose family have owned it since. When at school at Portora, I was always welcome at my family's one-time home.

*   *   *   *   *   *   *   *   *   *

The Gibsons, my mother's family, were a mixture of Unionists and Nationalists. The 'Pope' O'Mahony, clan historian and genealogist, once told me that they descended from an illegitimate son of Lord 'Somebody'. Unfortunately at the time I had little interest and so forgot which 'somebody', but recent searches indicate perhaps a Plunket. Most became lawyers and did well both in finance and marriage.

My great great grandfather William, Taxing Master of the Irish Court of Chancery, was a son of William Gibson of Lodge Park, Co. Meath, and of Marianne Bagnall. He married Louisa, daughter of barrister Joseph Grant, and set up home at Rockforest, a rambling old house near Roscrea which he rebuilt and surrounded with magnificent parklands and an ornamental lake. A dower house, gatelodges and fine farm buildings were erected on his five thousand acre estate.

I only learnt about the Taxing Master's cousin when doing research. I was intrigued as to a possible family connection with the Reverend C. B. Gibson, author of the *History of the County and City of Cork*, published in 1861. Records in Cork historical and archeological journals confirmed the relationship. Born in Dublin in 1807, Charles Bernard Gibson became a non-conformist pastor of the Irish Evangelical Society at Mallow when aged twenty-seven. He married Margaret, a daughter of Dr. Justice - the now ruined Duarrigal Castle, in her family's hands since Elizabethan times, overhangs the river near Millstreet.

At Mallow, the clergyman had a printing press he used to promote the repeal of the Union. In 1845, Thomas Davis was told that Gibson thought there was room for a more popular and cheaper publication than *The Nation*. Two thousand copies weekly would yield a profit of £300 per annum and the editor would be offered £100 a year. Gavin Duffy, in his *Life of Davis*, says the support was welcome; "he was delighted when the nonconformist Minister of his own town believed in the Parliamentary party". Gibson wrote ". . . . and may God bless you, for you labour for the country that you love." The output from the press included small paperbacks distributed to adults and children. In November, Gibson was supported for the post of Cork University College Librarian by Mallow Town Council. I am not sure if he got the job but books he wrote include *The Last Earl of Desmond* based on Mallow, and *Dearforgil,* following which his Presbytery censored him for expressions "inconsistent with his position as minister". Although his opus was his history of Cork, he was also author of *Beyond the Orange River; Life Amongst the Convicts* (1863), *Historical Portraits of Anglo Irish Chieftains and Anglo-Norman Knights* (1871) and *Philosophy, Science and Revelation* three years later.

In 1846, the Mallow Congregation abandoned his independent church for the Presbyterians and two years later he had become chaplain to convicts on Spike Island. Difficulties led him to publish a pamphlet entitled *The Spike Island Chaplaincy and the Mallow Congregation* which endeared him to neither cause. During this chaplaincy, he resided across Cork harbour at Monkstown. He doesn't appear to have served out his time at the prison for to have done so would have entitled him to a substantial pension. Instead he went to London where, having taken Church of England orders, he was appointed lecturer at St. John's, Hoxton and chaplain to Shoreditch Workhouse where he was loved for his kindness and attention. He lived in fashionable Charlotte Street where he died in August 1885, aged seventy-seven.

*   *   *   *   *   *   *   *   *   *   *

William and Louisa Gibson had five sons, and a daughter Elizabeth whose husband Francis Martley of Co. Meath was drowned on the Lusitania. Three years after Louisa's death, William married Charlotte Hare of Deer Park, Cashel to whom Fanny was born; she died unmarried in 1914. The elder of William and Louisa's sons, my great grandfather Captain William Gibson, was a High Sheriff for County Tipperary and a Justice of the Peace. His first spouse, the artistically talented Emily Rachel was a daughter of Admiral John Jervis Tucker of Trematon Castle. When widowed, he married as his second wife Sophia Charlotte White of Charleville, near Roscrea.

William's brother Edward Gibson, my great grand uncle was born in 1837. A Judge of Dublin's Kings Inns in 1877, and Member of Parliament for Dublin University, he became Attorney General. In 1885 he was appointed Lord Chancellor of Ireland with a seat in the Cabinet, and was created Baron Ashbourne of Ashbourne, Co. Meath. A Privy Councillor, he was also Chairman of the Brehon Law Commission and author of the definitive *Pitt, Some Chapters of his Life and Times*.

When the future King George V visited Ireland in 1897 Ashbourne, along with his wife Frances Maria Adelaide – daughter of barrister H. Johnathan Cope Colles – entertained him at Howth

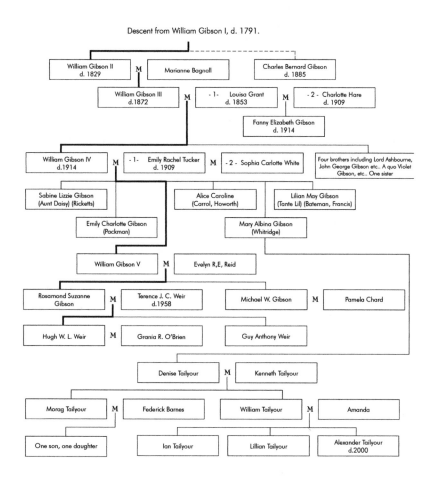

Descent from William Gibson I, d. 1791.

Castle. Edward is mainly remembered for the Irish Land Act of 1886, which quashed absentee landlordism. A man of integrity, he was a fair if strong Judge. Although the Gibsons intermarried and intercommunicated with influential legal and political colleagues, Ashbourne was a loner and preferred the company of his wife and eight children, often at his Chateau at Boulogne. One strong personal relationship he formed was with the Viceroy Lord Cadogan which, however, impaired his friendship with his fellow Irish lawyers, kinsman David Plunket, and Gerald Fitzgibbon. On his death aged seventy-six, his ashes were interred in Dublin's Mount Jerome cemetery and capped by a handsome monument.

William and Louisa Gibson's fifth son, John George was a High Court Justice, Solicitor General, a Member of Parliament and Attorney General in 1887. Sergeant Sullivan in *Old Ireland: Reminiscences of an Irish K.C.* wrote: "John Gibson was a brother of Lord Ashbourne who looked after his relations well . . . . His people and his people in law held many high positions in the courts. . . . . No one was ever offended. Ashbourne's jobs moreover, had the extraordinary facility of justifying themselves on their merits, and John Gibson was one of the best . . . . He bombarded counsel with the titles of reported decisions." This was the era of Lord Peter (The Packer) O'Brien, a Gibson in-law through the Hares (O'Hehirs).

Lord Ashbourne's eldest son William was an eccentric. The first modern noble to speak Irish in the House of Lords, he took delight in delaying the proceedings by having an interpreter. He spoke perfect English, of course, as well as Irish and French, the tongue of his wife Marianne Conquerré. He was President of the London branch of the Gaelic League and a considerable financial supporter. Amongst the books he wrote were *The Abbé Lamennais and the Liberal Catholic Movement in France* (1896) and *L'Eglise Libre dans l'Etat Libre* published in 1907. In my youth, Dubliners recalled him wearing his traditional saffron kilt, green jacket and large beret.

One of William's sisters was the notorious and eccentric Honourable Violet Albina Gibson. Modern history could have taken a significantly different course had she been successful in her 'mission'. Born in 1876, she was well educated and cultured. Although baptised in the Church of Ireland - her uncle John George was Lay Chancellor of Killaloe Diocese – she became a Roman Catholic, the ceremony and ritual attracting her. When her brother Ernest Victor died, either by his own hand or someone else's, she became secretive and suspicious. Following a nervous breakdown, she travelled to Rome for the 1925 Holy Year Festivities and initially stayed with French nuns.

Violet carried a pistol; foreign men were such that ladies took no chances! The Italian Fascists had, on a Sunday, celebrated their anniversary parade. Amongst those there, observed Doctor Ugo Taviani, was a lady resembling Miss Gibson. She held a bouquet of flowers in her left hand, while she concealed her right in her pocket. She tried to approach Mussolini as he addressed the crowd, but the doctor restrained her. The incident seemed of little consequence until, later in 1926, Violet was out walking. Another vast assembly cheered as Mussolini exited, having opened the International Surgical Congress. He looked smug, and was wallowing in popular support. Suddenly, the impetuous Irishwoman forced her way through the crowd and up to the Dictator, drew her revolver, thrust it into his face, and squeezed the trigger.

Mussolini was shot through the nose - another few centimetres and he would have died. She was heard to exclaim "I've missed him, I've failed my mission." At first the crowd was silent, speechless. Suddenly there was a roar in Italian: "kill her. . . . lynch her . . . . get rid of her . . . . " . Violet stood petrified as hands stretched to scratch her, punch her and rip her clothes. The great Benito, humiliated, held his handkerchief up to his bloody nose. Miss Gibson was manhandled to the nearby police station by 'Black Shirts' and Guards. That evening she was interrogated at the local prison, but denied she had ever seen 'El Duce' before. Generously, the dictator ordered that there be no reprisals. The world's newspapers were full of such headlines as "Mad Irishwoman shoots Mussolini". Telegrams from world leaders, including Britain's King George V, congratulated the socialist dictator on his escape. Violet was never brought to trial as she was considered unfit. Had she been a better shot she could have changed the course of the Second World War.

Although I don't personally remember these forebears, they are my past.

*   *   *   *   *   *   *   *   *   *   *

My father's father, Octavius Weir, died when I was a babe in arms but I remember my grandmother Flora quite well. Her daughter Bryda had erected a large aviary where I used to delight in watching the birds outside a window at the end of her drawingroom at Abberton in Essex. In her youth she had travelled throughout

Descent from Robert Weir (d.1818) and Mary (nee Rynd) (d.1820)

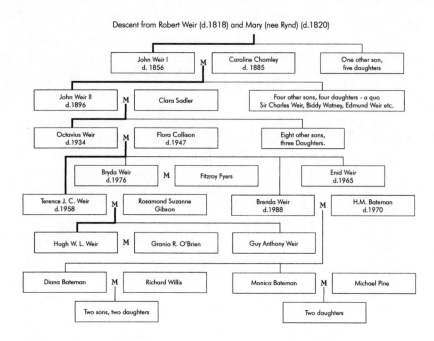

Europe, usually accompanied by a Mrs. De Vesci or another companion, and servants. The Collisons were wealthy and owned property in the city of London as well as lands in Norfolk. There is a family tradition that two brothers with adjoining lands took court action over a tree common to both, and that each lost £40,000. Maybe that is why little of their money filtered down to my father. His cousin Edith Collison though, who lived near Cork, travelled daily by train into the city to collect the *Financial Times* - having studied the stock-market during the return journey, she would telephone her broker. Due to Irish tax laws, and in spite of her relationship with the nearby Grove-Whites, she moved to South Africa. Her fortune was left to Irish societies for animal welfare.

Flora Weir became incapacitated in later years, having only one leg. Aunt Bryda, who married my mother's cousin Fitzroy Fyers, one-time equerry to the Duke of Connaught, looked after her mother even as she participated in the war effort. Brenda, another of my father's sisters, married Australian caricaturist H.M. Bateman. I cannot remember him as they parted when I was quite young. He went to live at St. Ives in Cornwall where he died, and Brenda moved to London's Kensington. Their daughters became accomplished artists, Monica being awarded the 'Beaux Arts' in Paris twice and Diana, the elder, having a wide accomplishment. Diana married Richard Willis, the sculptor and marine artist and now lives in their beautiful old Elizabethan house in Somerset. Their children have also become well-known in arts, one of Lucy's pictures being used by the Royal Academy for publicity. Monica married architect Michael Pine. Their two daughters have done well in Canada where Monica, now separated, designs stained glass from her base at Ottawa.

I only learnt about another aunt, Enid, when in my twenties. Very popular and a good horsewoman, she fell for and married somebody considered unsuitable by the family. Her brother and sisters corresponded with her but family loyalty and embarrassment tragically kept them apart. I would love to have known her and recall with sadness the hurt when family relationships get strained. Enid died sometime around 1950, I think.

* * * * * * * * * *

Collison Descent from Nicholas Cobb Collison (d. 1841) and Elizabeth Stoughton (d. 1847).

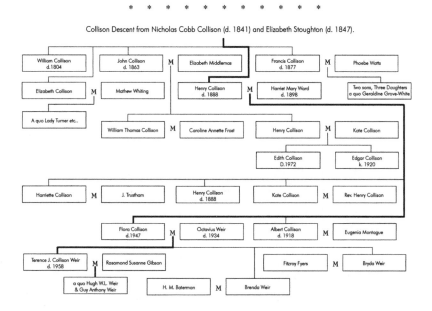

Terence John Collison Weir, my father, was a strong character. Much of his youth was spent in East Anglia, but he made frequent visits to friends and relations in County Fermanagh and to Fivemiletown in County Tyrone where his cousin Edmund Weir lived. Their ages and interests were similar although Edmund later became an alcoholic. He had set his house in apartments and moved into the gate lodge when I visited him from school after his dog had bitten off his finger. He told me to wait for him at Gillespies where he was permitted a daily bottle of whiskey.

Father was educated at Cheltenham Military College after being crammed by a Mr. Campbell, the custom with aspiring young officers. After a time at the Royal Military College at Sandhurst, he was commissioned with the Royal Norfolk Regiment and served on the Somme, in Belgium and in Italy during the First World War and on the Indian North-West Frontier. He was awarded the Military Cross in 1918. Three years previously, he had spent two years in Mesopotamia. He used to tell me how he tied his boat to the ancient Biblical tree in the 'garden of Eden' at the confluence of the Tigris and Euphrates. The following year he was in Aden. A keen sportsman, he loved polo and hunting and was Master of the Eastern Counties Otter Hounds. He was also involved in stag-hunting on Exmoor, and in beagling. In spite of having lost one arm in India, he was a good shot and loved rough shooting. I find it a little difficult to reconcile his shooting and hunting prowess with his love of animals - he kept tame badgers and otters which he had rescued. He never seemed to take to fishing. As was usual in the period prior to the Second World War, he shared right-wing politics with many of his friends.

A fine upstanding man with fixed opinions, Terry, as Father was known, was reputedly destined for senior rank in the British Army. This was denied him by his incapacity. He loved soldiering and liked to live dangerously. At the beginning of the Second World War, he didn't hesitate to present himself for service. Responsible for the camouflage and defence of airfields, he was transferred from base to base, mainly in southern Britain. He was popular amongst both his brother officers, who included David Niven the actor, and his men. There are many stories about him but I recall one which took place in Wales. Not one to sport expensive jewellery or utensils, he was on

manoeuvres when he lost his favourite cigarette case which he liked
due to its comfortable shape and ease of opening with his one hand.
His company, perhaps his regiment, was commanded to search for
it. After an hour, a junior officer asked him its exact measurements.
On being told, he replied that the only case of this size seen was a
very worn 'first aid tin', over which they had passed several times.
"That's it", roared my father excitedly. The subaltern had, no doubt,
at least expected one of silver, if not of gold.

Later in the war, my father found himself in an East Anglian pub
at a secret conference of senior army officers. They were discussing
the seriousness of the atom bomb around a large wooden table. A
storm was raging outside. Lightning and thunder struck the building
and in seconds the experienced officers had dived between the stout
wooden legs. After some minutes, they sheepishly surfaced.

The 'Major', as my father was called in Co. Tipperary, in the same
way as his father-in-law, was keen on Weir and Collison family
histories. He compiled a book with genealogical trees and which he
illustrated with photographs, coats of arms and memorabilia. He also
liked good furniture, ornaments and paintings and had a useful
knowledge of antiques. He scorned contemporary music, publicly
anyway, but I recall Sunday evenings when the household had to be
silent while, using the latest valved wireless (radio was a word one
didn't use) with its plywood front, he listened to the Palm Court
Orchestra from the B.B.C. The reception was crackly – 'news' came
from Athlone, but Radio Eireann was similarly difficult to scan into.

Reading, for my father, was a mixture of sentimental poetry such
as Masefield, Kipling, or Lear whose nonsense rhymes he loved, and
prose such as Surtees whose 'Jorrocks' books were fed to me from
an early age. Henry Williamson gave him each of his books as they
appeared. Pepys, Chaucer and Thackarey were as contemporaneous
as were the living novelists and others he also avidly read, such as
Dorothea Conyers, Iris Murdock, M.J. Farrell, and Honor Treacy. He
was also keen on Chaucer, the Knyvet and Clopton letters and other
diaries which had family connections. He loved all books. *The Field,
Country Life, Horse and Hound* and *Dublin Opinion* were taken
regularly and the *Irish Times* perused for national or international
news, 'hatches, matches and dispatches'. He collected stamps,

cigarette cards, snuff boxes and sporting prints, and cut out illustrations of anything from Stubb's horse paintings to old English game fowl, which he stuck into scrapbooks.

Of course, he also loved dogs, particularly Staffordshire bull terriers. I don't, on reflection, think that there was anything for which he didn't hold some interest or strong opinion. Sometimes he overdid his efforts to encourage me to indulge in his hobbies such as ornithology: "Quick, what's that bird over there?" "A blackbird?" "No, you idiot, that brown one with yellow spots". I wish he hadn't, for nowadays I'd love to know more about them.

Papa was loyal to his friends. He also had a subtle sense of humour and would occasionally roar with laughter at some little thing he had read or heard. Quite often dinner or drinks parties were held - the Bakers of Lismacue or the Harrises of Golden (both veterinary families on whom we called for service), the de Wiltons of Clonoulty, the nearby Grubbs, the Russells of Cashel and the Phillips of Gail, being amongst those friends invited to meet others from further afield, at Ardmaylebeg.

My mother, as strong a character as my father if not more so, was supported in her interest with horses and the production of quality milk from our herd of Ayrshire cows. She enjoyed *Horse and Hound*, Rupert Brook, and a Pandora's box of mainly equine reading. She was endearingly known by her father and friends as 'Fuzzy' or 'Scut'. As her parents, William and Evelyn Gibson, were amicably separated for most of her life, she spent holidays in both Tipperary and Essex.

My grandmother's Feering Bury, a delightful Elizabethan Manor in Essex, was leased to the Catchpools by the Church Commissioners a couple of hundred years back. Rosa Jane, heiress daughter of Quakers Edward and Rebecca Catchpool, married brewer Percy Reid. Rebecca had improved the pleasure area by adding a bowls lawn, a shrub garden and borders, and while they were levelling the lawn workmen found Roman pottery. My grandmother added a tennis court. Those who lived at Feering Bury, except for Rebecca who didn't approve, enjoyed hunting and shooting; cricket, tennis and hockey were also played. Mama loved 'the Bury' where she spent much of her youth riding her pony. She was devastated when the family left for a smaller house, her last surviving uncle having been killed in 1915.

My maternal grandfather, William Gibson, born in 1874, had met his wife in India where, as an infantry officer and sportsman, he had a large bungalow with furniture and artifacts from Rockforest, his North Tipperary home. He had gone to meet a train for his colleague Captain Hugh Reid, on which the Captain's sister, Evelyn, was due to arrive.

My grandparents were married at Feering following their return from India in early 1906. William, a Captain in the Durham Light Infantry, served on the North-West Frontier with the Tirah Expeditionary Force. Before retiring in 1911, possibly to devote more time to his family, he had been involved with mapping Upper Burma, been master of his own bobbery pack of hounds, hunted big game and with his spouse, the first woman to actually stick a wild boar, gone pig-sticking. I was brought up with shields of pigs' tusks, wild cat skins, and silver trophies and, at our County Tipperary home, a large brass Buddha, Indian brass trays and gongs. As well as being a keen horseman, my grandfather enjoyed motoring.

There is a legend that Grandfather brought the first car into Ireland; certainly he had to stop and back someone else's which couldn't make a now cut-away hill on the main Dublin to Cork road at Urlingford. He also drove the first car into Galway where he was welcomed at the County Club in Eyre Square. Martin Lynch of Ballinasloe, who later lived at Mountshannon, remembered the event. Grandfather had several vehicles which he loved, including a Delage. When Henry Ford introduced 'Model Ts', he was amongst the first to purchase. Spares could be a problem so, as these mass-produced machines were cheap, he bought two.

I remember well Grandfather's comfortable Opel which he purchased for £200 just before the war; Hitler needed sterling at the time and so subsidised the price of these excellent German six cylinder cars with their stainless steel bars above the back of each seat. The remains of this vehicle lie in a Galway farmyard. During the Troubles, he would carry boards tied alongside his cars which, if a road had been blown up, he placed across the hole and drove over.

There is a story of when, having been fishing the Mulcair - which he developed into a successful salmon river - he made his way towards his car for the journey home. The engine had to be cranked with a handle inserted under the radiator, the other option being for the vehicle to be parked on a hill or to be pushed so that when it gained momentum, it would be put into gear and start. As the handle gave a nasty kick-back when the engine fired, my grandfather usually opted for the latter. This day, he had parked on a hump bridge over the river. As he approached, a number of men, some of whom he knew, greeted him. "Hello Major; I'm afraid we want your car". As the Civil war was in full swing, he had, as a matter of course, disconnected the ignition.

"Well, I suppose you'd better take it", retorted the fisherman.

"But Major, we can't start it".

"Right so; you're strong men. Give me a shove so that she'll run down-hill."

As it reached the appropriate speed, he put the car into gear; nothing happened.

"I'm afraid she's sulky. Give me another push and she should get going."

The four or five hefty men pushed away and the exercise was repeated: my grandfather got out, fiddled with some wires, and returned to his driving seat. After several such 'pushes', the men were getting breathless and even considered reneging on their orders.

"Just this time and she should go", said the Major. After another lengthy fiddle and a final shove, the engine roared, and away went my grandfather with the exhausted men flushed and speechless as he rapidly disappeared.

I was told this story in a local pub many years later. The general consensus was that he deserved to keep his car. There was respect for such wiliness amongst the country people of those days, especially for someone who had accepted that they meant him no harm and who understood, as a fellow Irishman, their cause.

* * * * * * * * * * *

Minnie, as my maternal grandmother was known by me, was a keen gardener and loved her English homes. Grandfather, however, preferred the sporting life and wildness of his own country. Both went their mutually separate ways. My mother, born in September

1913, spent most of her early years at her mother's rambling manor. Her eldest uncle, Captain Hugh Edward Reid of the Royal Scots Regiment, had died of cholera when returning from India in 1911, leaving a daughter Hughie Thelma Reid who, although three years older, was her lifelong friend and companion. A keen yachtswoman, Hughie married three times. Major J. Williams, an Indian army officer from Co. Cork killed on the North-West Frontier in 1936, was the father of their daughter Patricia (Healy), and by Colonel David Hunter Blair she was the mother of Neil, now a Buddhist monk in Thailand. Her third husband was Admiral Sir Walter Couchman from Co. Carlow. In her young days, she had been engaged to Peter Anderton, later to become my godfather. She died in 1972.

When my mother was two, devastating news was received by Percy Charles and Rosa Jane Reid, my great grandparents. Their only remaining son and twenty-seven year old heir, Geoffrey Percy Neville Reid, was killed in action.

Geoffrey's father, Percy Charles Reid, born in 1857, had moved from the family's Hertfordshire home, the Node, to Feering Bury on

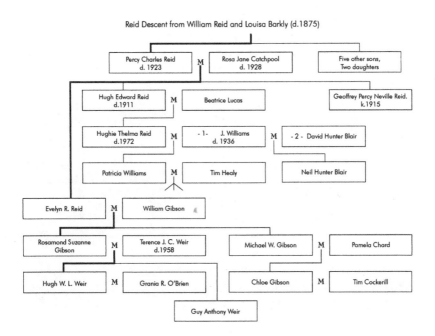

Reid Descent from William Reid and Louisa Barkly (d.1875)

his marriage to Rosa Catchpool. Educated at Harrow, where at least seventeen other Reids were schooled, he had joined the 15th Huzzars. He travelled extensively and was Managing Director of Hatfield and Harpenden Breweries. This family business was later absorbed by Watney-Mann whose Director Sandy Watney married my father's cousin Biddy, daughter of Sir Charles Weir. No doubt devastated following the death of his surviving son, Percy died when my mother was nine. His widow lived another five years.

Rosamund Suzanne Gibson, my mother, had a brother Michael William Gibson, born in 1916. Married to Pamela Chard in 1946, he was a keen landscape gardener. Their daughter Chloë, recipient of the M.B.E. for her Citizens Advice Bureau work, is married to lawyer Tim Cockerill. In her teens my mother was encouraged to ride and was introduced to the social life of close-to-London Essex. She loved Feering Bury, but she was also devoted to her father's Brittas in County Tipperary and, of course, the horsy worlds of steeplechasing, hunting, hacking and talking of horses. Mick, her brother, had other interests and, like his mother, preferred England. Mama, an attractive teenager, also made many contacts at her Lausanne school .

Between the wars, my father, born in 1898, ran a riding school. He regularly visited East Anglia, calling into friends at Stratford St. Mary, Langham and Bilney, and used to stay at Carlisle House, London home of his Collison cousin, Lady Turner. In the early thirties he made his first marriage, to Katherine, daughter of Colonel Lennox of the Suffolk Regiment, which ended in divorce. He never spoke about this period except for admitting that he had doffed his hat to an attractive lady at a race meeting before realizing that she was his estranged wife. She had gone off with, and later married, one of his friends.

In December 1933, my parents eloped. My mother lowered her suitcase from an upper window, crept downstairs and joined a large horse in my father's trailer for the journey to Hastings where he had taken over a riding school. They stayed in different houses until they were married in a Colchester registry office, my father's previous wedding having been in church.

I was born on the twenty-ninth of August, 1934 at Lexden Nursing Home, not far from my parents' temporary Mile-End quarters. At my baptism, I was given the names Hugh (possibly after my deceased uncle), William, probably after my grandfather, and Lindsay, after a Weir forbear. My godparents were my mother's Gibson cousin Denise Tailyour, her aunt Millie Whitridge's daughter, Polish friend Dick de Valda and Peter Anderton who, a friend of my mother's and fiancé of her cousin Hughie, lived near Nenagh, with his second wife Sheila (Dwyer), until his death in 1999. This is my background; my story now begins.

CHAPTER TWO

Early days in England and Ireland. My first solo international
journey, wartime Britain – escapades in Norwich, near Cardiff
and in Cornwall – a supernateral encounter.

One of my earliest memories is of the
garden and stables of the redbrick Mill
House at Peldon on the way to Mersea Island
in Essex. It was to be my parents' next home
after Mile End. Alongside the road, to the west
of the building, was an orchard where I recall
my father balancing me on his knee, the smell
and feel of the summer grass and the sound
of bees. On the other side of the house were
the half-doored horse boxes where I was
encouraged to ride almost before I walked.
There were lots of visitors but I had to go to
bed early. Initially fenced in by the wooden
pillars of a large cot, I would later slip over to
the window to see who was coming, and

Father's knee,
Peldon, 1936

strain to hear what they were saying. I was given a German tin
Schuco model car. Many of my father's friends such as Sir Oswald
Moseley, had fascist, if British and patriotic, tendencies. This is
possibly why I received this product of Hitler's National Socialist
industries.

While being looked after by my nursemaid Ivy at my grandmother
Minnie's Park House, my father preparing for war, I found myself
unable to climb the rather steep stairs. My mother, hunting with her
father in Ireland, had her visit curtailed by being summoned home;
my father, Minnie and Elsie were alarmed. "Come back, please. We
are concerned about Hugh", read the telegram. I was taken to
London's Harley Street, where a specialist diagnosed that I had had

a mild attack of infantile paralysis or polio. An epidemic was raging at the time. My mother was not to worry. It was only in later life that I was to realise how, in fact, this disease had affected me and still does in its manifestation as the Post Polio Syndrome. About this time I developed a habit of rolling about the bed building up a rhythm to induce sleep which was hindered due to physical discomfort.

The real enjoyment of Peldon was the walks with my parents or nanny to the tidal mudflats bordering the causeway that led to Mersea Island. Here I studied crabs and other creatures in the rancid saline mud. From that early age I gained my first insight into history, for the area reeked in Roman and Saxon, Viking and Norman remains and legends. Count de Mamby, across the Strood, as the causeway was known, had a Roman centurion's tomb beside his island residence. He had identified it as such due to having observed three bands of men, possibly a hundred each, the central group carrying a casket. They were traversing treacherous tidal marshland as he watched them make their way towards where he lived. There they faded. Apparently, as the Colchester Museum authorities suggested, he had witnessed the ghostly scene of a Roman centurion's funeral. Archeologists probed the mound, found it to be hollow and excavated it. Inside a vaulted chamber was a Roman urn containing ashes. Another time, de Manby heard what he thought to be the dashing of milk cans. Was this the phantom re-enaction of a Roman battle?

Just up the road from Mill House was the Peldon Rose, a quaint but typical sixteenth century East Anglian pub owned by the Pullens. Here my parents would meet local inhabitants and bring their friends. Having sold Feering Bury my grandmother was now living at Berechurch, close to West Lodge where my paternal grandfather Octavius had died when I was one. For school holidays, I would later stay with her at Park House, a pseudo-Elizabethan residence surrounded by her extensive garden. My father's mother was also to move nearby to a house at Abberton known as the Maltings.

When the Second World War started, my father volunteered for his old regiment while my mother helped to make bandages and served in various American canteens. We stayed near Royal Air Force bases such as Swanton Morley, where we were paying guests of the

*Swanton Morley
– early war years*

Reverend Mr. Ussher at his attractive red brick Georgian Rectory. I remember the delightful gardens, cared for by this descendant of the Irish Archbishop, and the sycamores and other trees. Someone bought me a packet of pear drops; I can even now recall the taste as I relished them, strolling along a nearby road. A little later, while my parents were attending a fête at the modern Crafer family house, I bought a pickled newt encased in a glass dome on a crystal paperweight. Only recently did my wife Grania encourage me to dispose of it. From Swanton Morley I attended my first school where I learnt copperplate writing and basic English.

*   *   *   *   *   *   *   *   *   *   *

Almost from the year I was born, I regularly accompanied my mother back to her old Cashel haunts in Ireland. Ardmaylebeg permitted an element of freedom for even the smallest youngster. I was welcomed and mollycoddled as only Irish people treat their young. In October

1937, I was already being introduced to my grandfather's Thurles and Kilshane Foxhounds - I was blooded on the sixteenth at Rahilty despite being only three. The journeys across England and the excitement at Fishguard and Holyhead, where identity cards were scrutinised and customs officials went to town on the luggage, I only slightly recall. I must have slept a lot; certainly I was usually tired. There was little if any air travel and the only ferries were the Mail boats between Holyhead and Dun Laoghaire or Fishguard and Rosslare. Usually we took the former. Often there were long delays between London's Euston station and Holyhead. The carriages were dimly lit and the blinds drawn. It seemed to be always dark when we reached Crewe, a major junction. Apart from the slamming doors, the odd shout, and the hissing of escaping steam, there being no diesel or electric trains, people whispered to one another as to what was happening. Passengers got to know each other and shared experiences. Sometimes there was a breakdown and we would be transferred to another train. We huddled under rugs, newspapers or greatcoats to keep warm, and to avoid the noise and lights. The journey was never comfortable and we rolled our clothes to cushion our bodies from the knobbly cloth-covered arms between each seat.

When the train arrived at the Welsh port, there was a mad scramble to join a queue. Women and children were given preference and got ushered towards the gang plank, although those with excessive luggage often had problems getting porters, the latter speaking to each other in Welsh. Travelling with my mother meant that we shared a cabin as she was a bad sailor; I prefered to sleep on the upper bunk. Sometimes the crossing was stormy, no fun in those pre-stabiliser days. There was a foul sweet smell caused by the inability of passengers to hold their food. Once a German torpedo had scored a hit as we were about to depart from port - there was tremendous activity and a long delay. When we arrived in Dun Laoghaire harbour, we were sometimes met by my grandfather - if he wasn't able to make it, we would catch a taxi or a cab into the city. There were plenty of these horse-drawn vehicles in wartime Dublin as petrol was difficult to get, or rationed. Some cars had big bags attached to their roofs which contained gas, an acceptable substitute. "The Hibernian, please," my mother would tell the driver as we drove or trotted through a city almost unharmed by war. The situation was known as the 'Emergency' in the Irish Free State, or Saorstat Éireann, as the country was then called. When we got to our bedroom at the Royal Hibernian Hotel which faced up Molesworth Street towards Leinster House, I would jump on the bed and smell the starched pillowcases. I was back in Ireland - deep down, I was 'home'. The Hibernian was a family hotel. Not quite in the same category as the Gresham or Shelbourne, it was a top quality intimate establishment where we were greeted by name and with concern for our well-being. From here we would take the excursions. Sometimes my mother, or more usually my grandfather, would be molested by beggars. Once Grandfather had no change and a woman with a babe in arms cursed him down the street. I was upset at this episode which I felt unjustified - Willie Gibson never denied a reasonable cause.

On arrival at Ardmaylebeg, we got great greetings. I had my own bedroom overlooking the porch. Mrs. Meskell (Molly) and Meskell, as Batt Meskell, my grandfather's head groom was called and Mick and Dan Kinane joined Dolly O'Neill in asking questions as to our welfare and recent activities. In winter, I would be taken tobogganing up the Motte with my mother's Swiss sledge if it snowed. There would be riding and trips in the dog car, an open pony-drawn trap with a seat facing to the front across it, which was used when petrol for the Opel was unavailable. In the kitchen Mrs. Meskell would teach me Irish dancing. The smell of my grandfather's pipe permeated the house. Bosun, his springer spaniel, also smelt.

With Dolly O'Neil and the Kinanes, the Motte, 1937

Quite often, either due to a shortage of petrol or for the mere fun of it, we would take the Cashel train from Ardmayle. Our

local station was close to Mrs. Meskell's house on the ten kilometre branch from Goolds Cross, a junction on the main Cork to Dublin line. Sometimes I would be invited into the engine driver's cab to 'drive' the train. Because turf and timber produced less heat than coal, difficulty was experienced in building steampower to negotiate a couple of rises. I particularly enjoyed crossing the big metal bridge over the river Suir, and passing Cashel racecourse.

My first solo trip was when I was very young. No doubt I was put on the train in London, but it wasn't until I landed at Rosslare harbour that memorable events happened. In those days the pier with its open Victorian shelter was linked to the mainland by a railway bridge and the only way for a pedestrian to cross was by a wooden catwalk. As the ship berthed on the stormy winter's evening, the passengers alighted, but there was no train. The biting wind hurled hail stones at us and it was bitterly cold. There were screams of complaint and bitter arguments with the railway and port staff. Eventually there was a surge to the edge of the platform as in the distance appeared a loudly chuffing engine. It hooted and there were cheers as we prepared to board. The number of carriages was inadequate. Those who were able pushed and shoved their way aboard, but I had luggage and, like perhaps a hundred others, was forced to stay behind. The bursting trainful puffed its way into the distance with a promise that the situation would soon be rectified. It wasn't, and we spent seven hours with nothing more than cups of tea brewed by a sparse staff who took pity on us. I remember sitting on my case, almost weeping with the cold. Now and again I would, like the others, take an arm-slapping stroll. But we couldn't cross the dangerous catwalk - there was little to cross for anyway.

What a relief it was when we eventually boarded a second train, bound for Cork, which had come from Waterford. It conveyed us to the junction at Rosslare itself where some carriages were separated to be destined for Wexford and on to Dublin, while ours continued through Waterford to Limerick Junction. As this was wartime, Britain was almost totally in darkness. The contrast around Carrick on Suir was impressive for night had set in and little stars of light were visible over the hillsides above the Suir valley. Although there were regulations in Ireland, there was a semblance of civilisation.

*   *   *   *   *   *   *   *   *   *   *

On another journey, early in 1945, I was met at Dun Laoghaire by Pat and Mavis Hunt, then in their twenties. They were the attractive daughters of Vere Robert Vere Hunt of Ardmayle House, across the river from Ardmaylebeg. Their Dublin apartment was in or close to the Gibson town house in Merrion Square. They were driving a most exciting vehicle. I had only seen pictures of the advanced-designed baby Fiat. It was a tiny car and the bonnet contained a two-part heart-shaped grille under which were headlights. A canvas hood extended from the windscreen to the boot and, immediately behind the two front seats was a small bench seat on which I perched. It was a thrilling experience and, obviously showing delight, I was taken all over Dublin. In spite of our age difference, Pat and Mavis were extremely kind. I must have been an awful bore to them, really. They even took me to Clerys Stores which, in those days, was a delightfully chaotic shop full of interesting goods unobtainable in England.

My bedroom faced the park in the centre of the square over a main tram route. The electric two-deck vehicles, with their curved outside staircases at the rear, gave out a peculiar whining noise from their electric motors. This was not unlike that hummed by a small boy imitating the revving of the engines of his toy car, but with regular "cling clings" every few seconds as the wheels crossed rail joints. Above each were twin 'feelers' which linked the motor with overhead electric cables.

Another year, having travelled from Dublin to Ballybrophy, the nearest station to Grandfather's old Tipperary home, I was welcomed and taken to meet long-standing friends of his in Roscrea. In the hotel bar, I was impressed when he was greeted with cheers and a memorable welcome. We continued to Williamstown, his County Clare retreat, for this holiday. He and Dolly were in the wooden bungalow he leased from Mrs. 'Lotty' Studdert of Cullane near Sixmilebridge. The arrangement had its ups and downs - once I put perch fry in the water tank and was severely reprimanded because the action could cause friction. The old lady found out, but took it in good part. On our arrival this time, just after sunset, we entered the bungalow where I dumped my luggage. I then returned to the kitchen to talk with Dolly. The bathroom being occupied and nature calling, I went and stood in the tree-surrounded ruins of Williamstown house a few yards from the back door. As I relieved myself, I could hear loud snoring. Embarrassed and nervous, doing up my flies en route, I rushed back to Dolly and related my experience. She laughed her head off, as also did my grandfather who appeared in the doorway. "Did ye never hear an owl snore?"

The cedar-wood bungalow at Williamstown had been imported, completely knocked down, from Canada. This single storey building which faced Lough Derg had a large central room off which almost all the others led. It was appallingly draughty if a door was left open. At the front was a well-proportioned verandah which ended, at each end, in the bay windows of the two front

Grandfather Willie Gibson, Pat Hunt and myself with Bosun, Williamstown, c. 1946.

bedrooms. It was approached from the road through the small garden and up a flight of brick steps. One of the front rooms was my grandfather's, while the small one in the centre of the south-west side, which looked onto a grass tennis court, was mine.

I liked to sleep with my window open but one morning I was rudely awakened by the braying of Jackie Tuohy's ass. It put its head through the open window, thereby exacerbating the chillingly loud sound. I was careful afterwards to close it, if I was to expect a full night's sleep. Taking up the west corner was Dolly O'Neill's room, and a little lobby led to the kitchen and utility room at the back. The opposite front room to my grandfather's was, on a later visit, given to me, but it was usually a spare room, or used for tying flies. It was always bright and well-lit. In those days, the nearest neighbours were the Tuohys, one of whom my grandfather christened 'the Teapot' due to her preparing tea when there were visitors. Jackie lived in the delightful lakeside cottage a couple of hundred metres up the road. Fred and Nancy Holland, from whom we got our milk and eggs, resided in a two storey farmhouse behind the hill above. Nancy was the organist in Mountshannon church. Fred's cousins, also Hollands, lived nearby in a cosy old farmhouse called Nutgrove with an orchard in front and two storey farm buildings beside. On the lakeshore was their corrugated-iron fisherman's lodge.

Further up the road, Cappaghbeg, later to be mine, was inhabited by the Whites, many children and their parents - previously it had belonged to a character, Socey Mugovan. A kilometre south west of the wooden bungalow lived the Sampsons in Williamstadt House, one of the largest in the area. Other neighbours were Willie Hogan, a bodhran player and maker, who was, on and off, my grandfather's gardener, the Burkes of Dromaan, whose senior member was the local politician, the Leahys, John Tuohy, and Paddy and Delia O'Brien. The O'Briens lived in Reinskea, another large residence above the lake, and had a farming background. Their claim to fame was Paddy's niece, his brother Michael's daughter, Edna O'Brien. Spoken of in whispers, her first book *The Country Girls* disclosed riské thoughts on church and sexuality. It was, for many years, banned. That was the best boost any author could wish for, as hundreds of copies were smuggled in by returning emigrants. I used to spend a lot of time with the childless Paddy and Delia, while my grandfather was pre-occupied or needed a respite from the pestering questions of my inquiring mind. Hours were spent on the lake with Grandfather and his springer spaniel Bosun, who used to sit in the bow of the boat. Usually we were powered by an Evinrude outboard imported from America. We would go shooting on the Tipperary shore around Luska or on the Corrikeen islands. Sometimes the targets were, as around the 'Twenty Islands' where they habitually nested, cormorants. Trout fishing was in Church bay or other inlets beyond Hare Island but the best pike were located round the buoy beside it, where Lough Derg bent its axis. Different winds would meet here and the water could be quite choppy. I was usually told not to fish out of sight and, in deference to Grandfather and Dolly's wishes and fearful of being sent home, I seldom ventured further. One of the first times I was on my own, I hooked and landed a massive 23 lb. pike in the bay outside Williamstown Harbour. It played like a salmon and I was terrified that I wouldn't get it into the boat. Eventually, by using the gunnel as a fulcrum for the gaff, I made it. I was about eleven at the time.

Williamstown Harbour, across the road from the wooden bungalow, was mostly built during the Famine. Constructed as a relief exercise, it had at one stage been used by Bianconi, the Italian who introduced public transport to Ireland. His passengers were accommodated at Williamstown House, then a hotel. There was a long pier, a short distance down which was a bridged channel to allow boats into the deep inner harbour. On the outer edge of this inner shelter was a path through rough vegetation which I considered to be my 'jungle'. I constructed a small stone pier on the lake side of the isthmus. Mrs. Studdert berthed her beautifully varnished wooden cabin cruiser, the 'Antoinette', under a specially constructed open boathouse in the corner between the pier and the lower quay during the Emergency; the Hodsons, of Holybrooke in County Wicklow, their larger 'Fortuna' beside the opposite bank.

In the larger or outer harbour area sheltered by the pier was the tie-buoy, a frame of huge black wooden beams bolted to enormous posts set in the mud. Here Guinness barges pulled in on stormy nights. Some of the porter being transported never reached its official destination. Whitegate pubs were just too far away for most of these hard-drinking and tough bargees as they navigated the Shannon to Limerick, and the canals to Dublin. Sometimes larger tug-barges, the St. James and St. Brigid, came pulling several of the standard boats. Their diesel engines had a memorable "tug, tug, tug" sound and could be heard from a long distance. For some reason they were eventually banned from using all but the largest harbours on the Shannon.

My grandfather's boatman and friend, on whom he progressively relied, was John Tiernan. John resided in an attractive old two storey house facing a white-washed courtyard opposite the Protestant church in Mountshannon. There was always a roasting fire when we called. A cup of tea and brown bread would be proffered by Mrs. Tiernan in the kitchen, the walls of which were covered with mementos of fishing expeditions, and knick-knacks. John's family were traditional eel fishermen, mainly from Athlone but also along the Shannon where they put out lines of several kilometers containing thousands of hooks. With the Shannon scheme of rural electrification in and after 1928, the government took over this lucrative fishery.

John's brother, James Tiernan, and other members of the family lived on Illaunmore, a seventy-five acre island in the middle of the lake. It was one of my favourite places for I was already developing my craze for areas of water-surrounded land. James' house, above a small well-constructed harbour built to take cattle cots, was a slated single-storey building. Several rods hung in the cosy, fire-warmed kitchen where there was no mains electricity. Tea always tasted better here; water was either from a nearby well or, in those days, the lake itself. Leading from James' was a crudely cobbled path bordered by stone walls which meandered between the ruins of a stone schoolhouse and other buildings - in my imagination, 'my village' - and on to O'Meara's neat thatched farmhouse. Mrs. Holland of Nutgrove, once an O'Meara herself, had been brought up here. The track continued west round part of the island, on the summit of which was a copse and nearby the ruin of an ancient church.

*   *   *   *   *   *   *   *   *   *

My days at Williamstown, especially when on holiday from across the Irish Sea, were exciting and always fun. I loved being outdoors and free. Even on stormy days, there were friends to visit or the stories, about man-eating tigers or his early years at Rockforest, which my grandfather would relate.

During the war my father was stationed in different parts of south Wales, the south-west of England and in East Anglia - my mother accompanied him and I was usually brought along when on school holidays. At some places we spent several months, at others shorter periods.

St. Helen's guest house in Norwich, a beige brick townhouse was below my father's hilltop regimental headquarters, Britannia Barracks, and beside the river Wensum. This was a deep and rather treacherous slow-flowing river at the end of a long shrub and tree-full garden of snowberry bushes, black-barked laurels and gloomy trees. I was terrified of the 'Dracula' which, to prevent me from drowning, my parents told me inhabited the river's banks. I hadn't heard of Bram Stoker and so had no idea what the intimidating creature was. I do remember having been encouraged to go into the bushes by a similarly aged small girl who lowered her panties in a bout of exhibitionism. When a bush rustled in the wind nearby, we both ran, I having innocently reciprocated by beginning to display my future manhood. At the street-side of the garden was the 'Adam and Eve' where a hatch at the back permitted after-hours drinkers to purchase their alcohol from behind the scrub. There were stories about illicit happenings amongst my parents and their friends who included the designer Oliver Messel, then local camouflage officer.

In wartime Norwich, as in most British towns and cities, we were reminded of our proximity to Germany by air-raid sirens similar to present-day fire alarms. These gas warnings had an intermittent soft and then louder rythm to warn us to run for cover.Uniformed wardens ushered everyone to special shelters. We wore uncomfortable Miss Piggy-like gas masks difficult to breathe through. When all was clear, the siren would give a long even blast, and nervous women and children would re-appear from their shelters like fledglings from a nest. Sometimes bombs had been dropped with disastrous consequences. Usually people continued their routine.

Our apartments included a second storey drawingroom with a bay window at the river end. I recall, when dreamingly gazing through it, an enemy fighter plane flying straight towards me, firing as it continued over our roof. Told later that I was brave, I feel that in fact I was probably frozen to the floor in terror.

While in my bedroom, I had another frightening experience when my mother had gone to post a letter in the nearby Cathedral Close. I heard a bomb explode and, as I looked in the direction of the blast, saw that it had landed where I knew the letterbox to be. It was a wonderful relief when, some minutes later, my mother appeared unscathed. She had had a miraculous escape; the area was devastated.

When we first arrived at St. Helen's guest house, an extraordinary thing happened. Our white Staffordshire Bull Terrier travelled with us wherever we went. On arrival at a new destination, we had to register for security reasons so, once the luggage had been unloaded, my mother drove us to the imposing City Hall. As we got out, Sally was left to guard the car. On our return there was no sign of our beloved dog. The window had been accidentally left open, and she had escaped. Police were alerted and a search put in motion. Late in the evening, exhausted, worried and dog-less, we returned to the guesthouse. "Eureka!" - there was Sally sitting on the doorstep. The only time she had been there before was the few minutes it took to unload our luggage earlier in the day.

Although terrified of the river Wensum and its murky waters, one of my favourite walks from St. Helen's was to Pulls Ferry, an old watergate up-river. Occasionally I was taken by Miss Chaston, who ran the school I attended, to visit her red-brick home beside the Broads. It was rather a bleak site, but her kindness and warmth introduced me to the remnants of English Victorian rural life. I remember, too, visiting the Gurneys, a banker family whose house was near Wroxham Hall, my father's cousin Edith Collison's place. I was so enchanted by a caged budgerigar that they offered it to me. My father was furious, having deduced that I had hoped to be given it. About this time numerous Polish refugees had fled to England to help free their country by serving with the Royal Air Force. Many befriended me; no doubt they had young families whom they missed. One of them taught me to box.

Norwich Castle, a huge Norman keep on a strategic summit close to the city centre was, and still is, an interesting museum. For a youngster interested in history, to what better place could I have been taken than to meander over its ramparts. Surrounded by high land beyond the river plain itself, the fortress is susceptible to high winds. I was a reasonably light boy and my mother was no heavyweight. One walkabout, a gale gust lifted and re-located me close to a dangerous drop. I wasn't ever brought up to the castle ramparts again when there was a likelihood of wind.

*   *   *   *   *   *   *   *   *   *   *

In 1939, when I was five, my parents had leased a pleasant modernish one-time rectory at Pentyrch, not far from Cardiff. In a rich Welsh coal-mining area, there were deep unprotected mine-holes in the surrounding woods, of which I was a little nervous. That autumn, I was taken hunting with the Pentyrch Foxhounds. It was here that we possibly encountered the supernatural although I was too young to remember much about it. My mother was preparing to attend a welcoming party given by my father's Commanding Officer when, at around five in the evening, the dogs barked. Gwen, our maid, helping me to bed, called from the landing: "Would you like me to see who's at the door?" My mother indicated that she would investigate and, reaching the front door, was greeted by an air-raid warden. "Are you all right Mrs. Weir?" As he was persistent and obviously concerned, my mother felt impelled, at the party, to commend him to the officer concerned. Following questions as to his identity, the officer turned white. That particular warden had been killed in an air-raid on Cardiff at three o'clock that afternoon.

The house had a long glass porch which stretched along the wall from the front door. Another time Mama was sure she heard a North of England voice but there was nobody there. The local Master of Foxhounds paid a visit a little later and commented that the previous owner must have left some of his pictures. "Not at all" replied both my parents. The sporting prints which were on the porch wall were theirs. The visitor insisted that the same pictures had hung there before. He explained that the house's previous occupant was an ardent North of England collector. This also sent a shiver down my mother's spine.

*   *   *   *   *   *   *   *   *   *

Another sojourn in Wales was spent at Little Haven with a family of Davies at their pleasant farmhouse. I used to catch newts in a boggy area of springs in the dip below. I was here introduced to the clear waters, rocks and sand of the Irish Sea as it meets the Atlantic. Torbenny, his Pembrokeshire base, was one of my father's favourite postings for he was able to partake of his hobby as a naturalist and ornithologist. His interest in islands led me, possibly at a later stage, to treasure R.M. Lockley's *I Know an Island* and Maurice O'Sullivan's *Twenty Years a-growing*.

In Cornwall, where my father was stationed at Davidstow on Bodmin Moor, we were boarded in the county's highest inhabited house, run by a family called Coffin. Here I secretly smoked my first cigarette. My father told me that, on my vehement denial, hair would grow on my hands if I had. Of course, like everyone else, I looked. What he didn't know was that I had been violently sick before he and my mother had returned from a party. Boscastle and Tintagel weren't far and we would walk along the craggy shore. King Arthur's castle fascinated me and I was introduced to the 'Round Table' era of legend, and possible fact. Cornwall was like Ireland; a Celtic country, it had that sense of mystery, legend and history particularly found in Sligo and northern areas of the Emerald Isle. The countryside was similar too, with its stonefaced banks and stone walls, its bogs and its heather.

One evening my father returned from duty with another creepy story. The area around the airfield was treacherous bogland. If a person ventured onto it, they could easily disappear into one of its 'bottomless' bogholes. As they were returning to base along the public road, several airmen had observed people dressed in 'medieval-looking' costume taking a particular zig-zag route across the bog. Suspicious that these could be enemy spies, the servicemen reported the event. The circumstances were investigated and, as a last resort, the men were asked to define the exact route. Although it was a treacherous spot, long staves were driven down at intervals through the wet turf. As they did so, those delegated to record the depths began to realise that a pattern was forming sixty or seventy centimetres below the surface. A trackway taking the same zig-zag course across the bog had, over centuries, been grown over with sphagnum moss, and forgotten. I recall the excitement and the discussion as to whether the phantoms had been of King Arthur's men, perhaps the legendary figure himself.

Returning from Cornwall to East Anglia in our tiny Austin Seven, my mother and I together with the dogs and a vast loadful of luggage had an eventful time. I don't think we could do more than thirty miles an hour as the trip took two days. To ensure that the enemy didn't spot the trends of traffic or target the few moving vehicles, headlights were covered with metal plates; in the centre of these were horizontal slits, the metal cut in 'U shape' from the space being bent up to create 'eyebrows'. The light emanating from the simple six volt filament bulbs was poor in normal conditions, but dangerous under these. In darkness, the road could hardly be discerned.

On the first night we arrived at Honiton, a pleasant Devon market town east of Exeter. No bookings had been made and my mother was concerned that there would be 'no room at the inn'. Eventually, she located a pub known as the Angel. "Never fear, Ma'm. If you're stuck, any Angel will find a place for you to rest your head!" We had a wonderful night's sleep in a deliciously warm atmosphere. Later on the same journey, I think somewhere in Wiltshire, we were driving along a straight treeless road bordered by cornfields. It was daylight. Suddenly, out of the blue sky from the rear, a German Messersmidt zoomed alongside us to our left, dropping incendiary bombs. The fields were aflame. My mother, extremely brave especially under such circumstances, continued driving. It is not easy nowadays to recall the tremendous difficulties when travelling during the war. It was nearly always exciting. That little old Austin Seven wasn't much more than a toy - I loved it.

* * * * * * * * * *

The south-west of England holds other fleeting memories from this time. 'Aunt Daisy', my grandfather William Gibson's eldest sister lived at Paignton. In 1895 she had married Captain Theophilus Ricketts of the Leinster Regiment but their only son had been killed in action. Her comfortable two storey Devonshire house had a small triangular garden which she enjoyed showing us.

A few miles north was Shaldon, another Devonshire resort. I have a report from Hill View School at nearby Ringmore, dated Summer 1940; I seemed to be quite good at all subjects. Miss Radley, my form mistress said I enjoyed my work and was making good progress. Headmistress Hughes indicated that, although I had improved, a little more concentration would have been welcome. Now married to Doctor Tim Healy, my mother's first cousin Hughie Reid's daughter, Patricia Williams, joined us for a holiday. Bessy Hardy or Bobby, my mother's family's nanny, and Hughie herself were also staying at the same small Edwardian two storey terraced house with its boxlike front garden. Entered through a wooden gate, it faced a quiet road to the beach where Patricia and I paddled and played sand castles. It was a hot, sunny year and I got badly sunburnt with blisters on my shoulders.

At another stage during the war Hughie had leased the Orangery at Felix Hall, an enormous fourteen bay classical house at Kelvedon, near Feering Bury. We stayed there with Hughie, her second husband David Hunter-Blair and Jacqueline, as Patricia was now named. There was a large, long drawingroom with enormous windows. In the basement of another part of the house Richard Chopping, whose book I still have, was painting illustrations for a Puffin picture book on British butterflies. Drawing directly on to the printing plate, he made me aware of the techniques necessary for this art-form. The Hunter Blairs later lived at Clonakilty in County Cork, near the home of Hughie's first husband. As a teenager I visited them at their pleasant Georgian house overlooking one of the many inlets of the Atlantic.

The last time I saw Hughie was in Suffolk when she was married to Sir Walter Couchman. My mother was with me. I joined the party in the drawingroom late, having been to the bathroom. The only vacant chair was a reasonably comfortable-looking stool with a long wooden handle on each side, and an embroidered seat. I sat down, naturally taking care with an antique piece of furniture. The look of horror and disgust from my mother almost had me springing back to my feet. Only later did she disclose to me that I had sat in Admiral Nelson's favourite chair, a treasured family possession. Although Hughie died some years ago, Patricia and I correspond at Christmas and meet at the occasional wedding or funeral. I would like to see more of her, especially as there has been hardship in her own family circle. One of her sons, a doctor, came to a tragic end some years ago. As I have already mentioned, her half-brother Neil, who was at Gordonstoun, is now a Buddhist monk in Thailand.

*   *   *   *   *   *   *   *   *   *   *

Returning to times spent in the south-west of England, it is probably due to their mother coming from Trematon Castle that not only did Aunt Daisy settle in Devonshire, but Alice, my grandfather's third eldest sister, had a house at Barnstable. In 1896, she had married Egerton Carrol of Lissenhall near Nenagh. As June O'Carroll Robertson says in her book *A Long way from Tipperary*, their wedding was "a fashionable affair, with diminutive bride in a billowing white dress, and six delightful bridesmaids". Apparently Alice had been cajoled into marrying Egerton rather than the man she really loved, Henry Howorth. The marriage lasted four months for Egerton died suddenly, perhaps of appendicitis. Two years later, she wedded Henry, eldest son of Sir Henry Hoyle Howorth. There were two sons, Peter who married Val Morris and was a Colonel in the Royal Artillery, and Henry; there was also a daughter Kathleen, Mrs. Druce. Egerton's niece, Rosaleen Angus, remained a family friend and I often visited her and her Austrian husband Paul Tausch. She was the main beneficiary of the Carrol Trust and when she died, her furniture went to the Irish Georgian Society for display at Castletown, in County Kildare. I can recall Alice's house overlooking the river Taw with its Raleigh and New World associations; I can also remember that I found her a little intimidating.

Trematon Castle was a different sort of residence. When Emily Tucker left it in 1868, it was a vibrant family home. Her father,

Admiral John Jervis Tucker, had married another admiral's daughter, her mother Sabine Young. The Tuckers had the freehold of the castle from the then Prince of Wales, later George IV, as a reward for service in 1807 - John Jervis' father Benjamin having been Naval Secretary to Lords St. Vincent and Grenville, as well as to Charles Fox and William Pitt. As Surveyor General, John Jervis Tucker considerably improved the Duchy of Cornwall estate. He sold his London mansion and moved to Cornwall. The residence he built beside the castle is a delightful two storey building with large sash windows, surrounded by attractive gardens and woods and overlooking an inlet of the Tamar estuary.

The circular medieval tower was made into a music room in which was placed an organ originally made for the Empress of Russia; the walls were hung with Goblin tapestry. Later, due to dampness, the organ was moved to the drawingroom in the main house and the tower converted to a museum. Shortly after this was done, the Prince of Wales, later William IV, enjoyed a grand lunch with the Tuckers. After the repast, his host took him to see the display. The future king admired the tapestry and, as was the custom, was presented with it. A Naval Man of War sailed to Plymouth to receive it. The prince also admired a little Brazilian gold cup; on Tucker's saying "Sire, its yours", he promptly pocketed it. Most of these Tuckers lie buried in the family vault at St. Stephen's nearby Anglican church where Aunt Alice was married for the second time by the Reverend Charles Edward Gibson, another cousin.

A stunning story is told about Tucker's brother-in-law. It seems that one night he had a remarkable dream. The following morning, while the family were having breakfast at Trematon Castle in 1812, a chaise drove up. Mr. Williams asked Tucker to immediately accompany him to London; he had had a dream concerning the Right Honourable Spencer Percival, a leading Tory politician, and couldn't rest. 'He was in the House of Commons when he saw Mr. Percival walk across the Lobby; from the other side of the House appeared Bellamy (Bellingham), dressed in a striped waistcoat, when he raised his hand and shot Mr. Percival, who fell dead.' Tucker and Williams proceeded at once to the House of Commons and related the dream to one of the ushers. "Why, Sir, you must have been present, it has occurred just as you relate it." This creepy story has possibly re-enforced me in my acceptance of ghostly appearances.

* * * * * * * * * * *

I was not particularly happy when I was sent to my first boarding school. The Glebe House at Hunstanton was a huge dark red-brick or sandstone purpose-built pile bleakly situated on the edge of the north-west Norfolk seaside town of Hunstanton. The fact that I was a boarder for the first time at the age of seven wasn't a concern but the bullying 'macho' outlook of the English preparatory school system, and of those who volunteered to teach wartime scholars was.

The school was run by two Coghill brothers who were extremely fair. I can visualise the billiards room with its fading photos of past pupils in sports pullovers, the corrugated iron building in which we were taught French and drama, and one of the dormitories. There was bullying amongst the boys, and that of some staff members responsible for sport is indelible. I wasn't really fit and used to wander off the cricket pitch to examine the huge caterpillars which munched their way through the leaves of the young poplar trees which bordered the bleak playing field. We froze in the bitter East Anglian winds between the Wash and the North Sea. A good deal of our time was spent being chivvied round the school buildings as we were forced to run like Buchenwald prisoners. "Come on, hurry up . . . . don't dither, boy. . . ." At one stage I got housewife's knee, an extraordinary complaint for a young boy. The school doctor drew the liquid off with a large-needled syringe. He was watched by the kindly matron in front of a rather dingy window from which I observed my pals as they speedily jogged past.

In the school basement was a comprehensive library containing *Jane's Military Ships, Punch,* interesting history books and the *London Illustrated News.* On the ground floor above, beside the Headmaster's quarters, was a large high-ceilinged recreation room with pictures of the galaxies, Red Indians and New World Aborigines and with a huge bay window. Here I wrote my first book, *The Haunted House of Hornton* consisting of fourteen pages of quite an exciting ghost story; it was based on Borley Rectory, reputedly England's most haunted house, where my father had once stayed. I created this, my first effort at book production, from end to end; it had a brown cover and I still use the stapler with which I bound the pages. I kept my story until about thirty years ago.

While at Glebe House, I was privy to one of the twentieth century's epoque-changing events before it actually occurred. One of my school friends told me that in a few days, Britain was going to mount a major offensive to end the war. His father, a senior army officer, had obviously hoped that his son would have been more discreet. Luckily those with whom he shared his shattering secret were loyal – 'D' day was an outstanding success! Amongst other close friends were, we only used surnames, Rowse, Hampson, and a boy called Pull the son of a nearby farming family. On Sundays we went to the latter's church at Old Hunstanton, in the tower of which was an unpopular loudspeaker chime. The real bronze bells had been dismantled and stored for safekeeping. On Wednesday afternoons I used to take the bus to the Heacham where I was taught riding. The head groom was Mr. Howlett. The stables were just below the Georgian house where the Red Indian Princess Pocohontas lived - a thought provoking deviation at this dull seaside resort with its suburban bungalows. The Norfolk Downs, inland from the school, with their grassy valleys and scattered trees, where we walked, were pleasantly rural. I also enjoyed beachcombing on the shore of the Wash. We marched in orderly organised groups through the town but when we arrived, we were let loose on the stony strand. There were lots of black 'H' shaped empty sharks egg containers and bits of flotsom and jetsom; the sandstone cliffs above were in multicoloured layers of mainly brown sandstone. Across the Wash was Boston Stump, the huge high tower of that town's medieval church which reared conspicuously above the Lincolnshire Fens; the place gave its name to the American city.

During these war years most consumer goods were rationed. Petrol was almost unavailable which is why my grandmother Minnie Gibson's recently acquired Hillman Minx was permanently left on blocks in her garage; she had to start the engine occasionally to ensure that the motor didn't seize. Food and clothes coupons were provided to permit a minimum share for each individual. Food parcels from Ireland, where there was comparatively plenty, South Africa and more peaceful zones, were welcome. They contained sweets, fruit, meat and even soap.

School food at Glebe House included such nutritious tidbits as the slightly fish-tasting but acceptable, oily and bloodful whale-meat steaks, sweet tasting horse flesh, and rather unpleasant ham and potato croquettes. Cremola, a delicious creamy custard, was occasionally substituted for the interminable starchy suet and custard or rice puddings. Powdered egg which, when scrambled, was sliced and served as wobbly solid blocks, or little solid lumps like loose expanded polystyrene, was often on the breakfast menu. Some boys were able to supplement their diet from their parcels, many from tropically based relatives. One boy got a parcel from Africa. We didn't understand the shape or texture of something called a 'green banana' which had been stolen from him. Following major interrogation, we assumed it to be something very special, even valuable. Most of us had never even seen a banana, let alone a green one. We were quite deflated when we learnt what the thing was.

We had educational excursions. One day we were taken over a printing works; it was particularly interesting and influenced me to buy my little Adana letterpress many years later. Judging by my reports before I left in December 1945, my time here did little for me, nor for my parents who were scrimping to send me to this well-recommended school.

During a geography class when we were supposedly being taught about Ireland, the master told us that Irish people shared their houses with cattle and pigs. When I protested that my family and friends did not, I was severely reprimanded: "How dare you interrupt the class and question what you are taught!" Afterwards, those who were not my friends taunted me with "We-er lives in a pig stye". Such arrogant manipulation of the facts by members of the teaching profession harmed my future acceptance of school education and discipline. While at Glebe House, I was initially quite good at arithmetic and came top of the class. My drawing was "Very Fair". Headmaster Coghill considered my conduct "Very Good", my industry "Good" and my progress "Very Satisfactory. . . . He will go ahead well". By the end of often unhappy, uncomfortable, even painful years only my English grammar and literature, English History, Geography and Natural Science were "Good". My overall progress was only fair and I was "lacking in energy and initiative".

While I was at Glebe House, my mother's American friend and keen horsewoman, Barbara Harcourt-Wood, leased a house on the Sandringham estate. We visited and even stayed with her. I recall the excitement and pride I was able to share by telling my friends that I had been staying in the 'King's house'.

*   *   *   *   *   *   *   *   *   *   *

At war's end, my father's first cousin, his aunt Ella Weir's son, Peter Hope-Lang bought a school at Lower Beeding just south of Horsham. The establishment had been returned to the area from the south-west, to where it had been evacuated. Peter, whose father was the Anglican rector of the Sussex resort of Hove, was searching for extra pupils to help the venture's viability. Naturally he contacted relatives who had sons of school-going age. As I had not been doing well at Glebe House, my parents thought change could be beneficial. Besides, my father was no longer stationed in Norfolk and I was well able to travel by myself. I had already experienced journeying on my own, mainly on trains, and had never come to harm, perhaps because there was so much security or because of greater moral responsibility. Liverpool Street, Paddington and Euston stations were all familiar to me, my worst fears being that I'd lose the huge trunks and tuckboxes I had to lug or that I'd overshoot my destination, some stations being ignored by certain trains.

Off I was packed to Newells. This preparatory school, once a private house, was a large stone mock-tudor building surrounded by grey-squirrel inhabited woodlands and with terraces leading downhill to the south. On a distant hill was Cowfold Monastery. Newells was approached by a longish drive from the north, to the side of which were games fields. "Thank God", I thought to myself, "there doesn't seem to be the same emphasis on games". If we didn't feel like being involved in cricket or football, we were permitted to undertake other occupations either physical or mental. I had a

Newells School

knowledgeable interest in motor cars. One of the masters, Mr. Collier, had a pre-war Austin 10 of the latest design which he used to discuss with me. He was a considerate, delightful and excellent teacher, as also was Major Cavan who had a large house near my aunt Alice's Barnstable. These two, often on supervisory duties, encouraged us to create model forts in the clay provided for the purpose; Collier also introduced me to photography with his ancient glass-plate camera.

* * * * * * * * * *

Even though the destination could be school, travel for me was usually fun. Initially, to arrive at Newells meant being put on the London train at Colchester. As the carriages pulled in to the platform at Liverpool Street station there would be crowds awaiting passengers. Billows of steam would shush up from under the train as doors would be opened and closed, each with a loud clunk. There were plenty of blue-uniformed porters to carry heavy luggage but they preferred to offer their services to the adults who they knew would give a decent tip. "Porter! . . . . porter! . . . ." Eventually there were a few unable to locate wealthier clients. They would load up different people's luggage onto one huge trolley and lead the owners towards the open gate from the platform and on to the taxi ranks. If there was a delay, I would visit the W.H. Smith kiosk and purchase such magazines as *Everybody's* with its mixture of light stories and pictures, *Picture Post* or *The Illustrated London News*. My favourite was *The Wide World*, a young man's periodical which contained weird, mysterious and supposedly true stories. Throughout the station passengers were bombarded with the hollow echoes of tannoy announcements of train departures and arrivals. Often nobody could make out what was being said due to the muffled and crackling sound from the loudspeakers. There were calls for lost children, even warnings. On reaching the taxi rank I would, possibly by preordination, meet fellow pupils who had come in on the same train. We would be sharing the rest of the journey. The others would be a little distant and rather embarrassed as they were kissed and hugged by weepy mothers, brothers and sisters: "It won't be long to half term . . . . have you got your handkerchief ? . . . . be sure to write when you arrive . . . . tell Matron I'll be sending on one more pair of underpants. . . . " When our trunks were being packed, a clothes list had to be filled according to the items needed; there was always fear that something would be missing, and that we would be reprimanded. The list was then placed in the trunk, on top of the clothes.

As one reached the front of the queue for transport, a typical London taxi with its noisy engine would pull up beside the trolleyfull. "Now mate, where are you going?" "Waterloo please". "O.K. mate, hop in". I was always nervous that every piece of luggage was loaded. Even presented with a reasonable tip, the porters looked scornful before pocketing it. On arrival at Waterloo the taximen would also comment on the meagerness of the ten per cent we added to the fare. The latter was clocked up on a meter with extras which we youngsters dared not question.

At Waterloo we would be met by more porters and escorted either to the cloakroom where we left our luggage for later collection, or to the departure platform. People were running in all directions as they arrived late, or had lost connections. Eventually, having seen our trunks on to the luggage van, we would climb aboard, lower the window on its graded strap in the platform door and wave. The seats were upholstered in carpety cloth. I was warned not to rest my head against the stuff, even if there was a linen antimacassar, for fear of getting nits or hair lice. The three or four passengers on each side of a compartment faced each other. Above each seat was a framed scene of some touristic part of the country, in this case the south-east, served by the railway company concerned. Over them was a steel-framed rack with netting strung between the bars, on which small suitcases and bags were placed. Beneath the seats was steam heating supplied from the engine. Sometimes it wasn't turned on and one froze. Beyond the inner door a corridor ran the length of the carriage, at the ends of which were minute toilets and queer concertina-like mini-passages linking the rest of that train. There were often queues for the lavatory and prospective occupants would shift from leg to leg. One could hear the metallic clicking sound as the 'vacant' or 'occupied' sign on the handle was changed.

Fellow passengers were a motley crowd. Some ventured a conversation while others held tightly on to their book or the newspaper they were reading without as much as an acknowledgment or even a smile. A few would innocently offer a sandwich or fruit but we were warned to be wary of strangers offering gifts. Often fellow occupants of a compartment would be asked to mind someone's property while the owner answered nature's call. As we pulled into our destination, there were large white signs with the name in bold black capitals; the stationmaster or his delegate would shout the name "Horsham . . . . , Horsham Station . . . . " as he made his way down the length of the platform. Uncomfortable places on my travels were the junctions where "Change here for . . . . " was called. I was never quite sure whether the carriage I occupied would continue to my destination or whether I had to change.

At Horsham, the nearest station, those destined for Newells would disembark. Trunks and cases were collected into a common pile, separate from those of the local Mercer's Hospital public school. Scholars who met up with friends would swap stories - most were conspicuously quiet. New boys and old, everybody was loaded into taxis or a bus which took us to the tree-surrounded school gates, down the longish drive, and eventually deposited us at the front door.

We would be greeted by the duty staff, told which dormitory we would be in and where to meet. Later we were to unpack but most would spend their time showing off their latest Dinky toys or boasting about their holiday activities. New boys were usually ignored, except by the few sympathetic students who were either unpopular or simply kind. There was regimentation and organisation to the extreme.

I never enjoyed the first evening's tea. Most of the food was probably wasted. The noise of chattering nervousness was only quelled by the incursion of the headmaster who would give a welcoming speech, during which there would be utter silence. Afterwards the youngest went to bed, followed by the next youngest and so on; the routine had started. The dormitories were in the care of the matron, a large uniformed woman with a nunnish headdress who came from Waterford. Even though she lived and worked in England, she had strong nationalist sympathies and was a devout Roman Catholic. "You're not Irish" she'd tell me, implying that the son of a British Army Officer, a Protestant at that, could never aspire to Irish nationality. She would ignore my protests. As she doled out concentrated orange juice or malt each night and saw to the wounds of impetuous young heroes, B.B.C. radio broadcast 'Dick Barton, Special Agent', to which we listened enthusiastically. As we had to go to bed early, especially in the summer, we would get up to antics in our dormitories such as placing a pillow above a half open door, so that the duty master would get it on his head on entering - sometimes there would be a container of water. Once we stopped a sleepwalker stepping out of a low-silled dormitory window.

Except for classes taken by Mr. Collier or Major Cavan, and perhaps the headmaster, lessons were boring. Not all members of staff were suitable to be in close contact with young boys; there was, however, a whispered 'caveat' so that we knew what was going on amongst those who were susceptible. As far as I know, nobody reported the goings on which were pretty rampant both in the class and the changing rooms. I don't think anyone liked the perpetrators. As regards the standard of education, it may have been because of my dislike of Glebe House where Latin and mathematics were forced on us parrot fashion, that my development in most subjects was stymied. I liked English, geography and history, however. Apart from evening services in the rather over-decorated school chapel, the occasional readings of interesting books given by the headmaster in his drawingroom, and the black and white films of such characters as Laurel and Hardy, there is little about which I am nostalgic. During rest periods, we sometimes watched military activities on the minute screen of an early television set in the front hall. Peter's wife, Nan, acted as a sort of assistant matron, firm but kind. Their son Keith Hope Lang, was treated like everyone else. Amongst my friends were several from the south-west of England such as Fetherstonhaugh, Forbes about whom we created crude 'latin' poems, Selwood who went into military law and is a major general, Pearson, Grey whose father was Governor of Gambia, Curry, Melbourne who was a cricket fanatic and Pertwee who was half Dutch. The school burned down some years after I had left, an event which broke Peter Hope-Lang's heart. He died a short while later.

*   *   *   *   *   *   *   *   *   *

During my education in England, my holidays were spent either at Park House, at Little Paddocks, at Ardmaylebeg, or at Williamstown near Whitegate in County Clare where my grandfather Willie Gibson enjoyed fishing and shooting.

Park House at Berechurch, a few kilometers from the garrison town of Colchester, was a modern mock-tudor residence with a large garden which extended alongside a minor road. Bordering the road was coniferous woodland. On the other side of the lawn, with its sunk heather garden which my grandmother, a keen gardener, had created, was a field used for military manoeuvres. Beyond were delightful deciduous woodlands with bluebells, and purple loosestrife in the open areas where trees had been felled.

The house was 'L' shaped with a two roomed kitchen area, off which was a pantry. The sliding doors to protect storage shelves were on ball bearings which made a ratchetty sound. In the hall, from which the stairs to the bedrooms rose, was a giraffe's head on which were hung hats, whips and dog leads. The drawingroom was furnished with delightful oil paintings, a large what-not and good furniture, beautiful china and porcelain, and a crystal wind-chime on my grandmother's desk. There was always a smell of hyacinths or other flowers. The diningroom had a different but distinctive smell. At breakfast there was always freshly ground coffee which permeated its atmosphere throughout the day. In the middle of the circular table, the dumb waiter was fun - easily turned, it could do several rounds before stopping. One corner had a cupboard on which was a telephone and lots of directories. My grandmother Minnie's number was Layer de la Haye 'two double two'. Upstairs there were four bedrooms. Mine was narrow with a window at the end opposite the door. The bed took up about half the length. I remember having a nightmare when I dreamed that uniformed Germans were climbing through the window to attack me. I often heard their 'doodlebugs', early guided missiles, stop over our heads. Frightening as it may have seemed, when the engine stopped, they continued to glide on for a few kilometres. Then one heard the bang. The house wasn't far from the coast where I remember seeing, across the Channel, the faint puffs of smoke as the larger German 'V-2' rockets were launched from the coast of Holland or Belgium.

My Uncle Mick, three years younger than my mother, had his base at Park House. He died in the early 1990s, but his wife Pam lives on at their Coggershall home. Mick was also a keen gardener and wrote on landscaping. He had also been involved in tea planting in Assam and in the production of Christmas cards. Their daughter Chloë and her husband Tim Cockerell near Cambridge are fascinated by family, church and local history.

I was happy at Park House. Life there was a mixture of walks through the distant woods and shopping expeditions into Colchester. I knew the town well, its history, from Roman times, being fascinating. There was Saint Botolph's ancient part-Saxon church, and the remaining lower part of the castle in which was an excellent museum. Colchester Castle had a special association with my grandmother too, for in 1909, she performed the part of Boadicea, Queen of the ancient Britons, in a centenary pageant. There were also the port, the town wall, and a picture by the artist George Moreland in the local 'Cups' hotel. Opposite was Neal and Robarts' teashop, a particular favourite with my grandmother and her friends. Off the High Street were smaller shops. I was horrified when told that the huge queue of old ladies outside a purveyor of dog meat ate the stuff themselves; they couldn't afford the meat sold for human consumption. At the bottom of the hill was the railway station, a departure point for school.

* * * * * * * * * *

A smallish but comfortable two storey house on the Long Road at Dedham, north of Colchester, was for sale after the war. My parents bought it and, because it had two tiny fields, called it Little Paddocks. I had a small bedrooom at the back which overlooked a yard and outbuildings. In one of these lived my two white rats, Aneurin and Clementina, named after parliamentarians Aneurin Bevin and Clement Attlee. Opposite lived Mr. Shepherd who, a keen genealogist, enjoyed painting intricate coats of arm. Another resident was the Reverend Mr. Baynham. A Dubliner retired from active ministry, he was interested in history and collected fascinating curios. I still have a stone axehead and some unrefined gold which he gave me. He was a kind and loving man, a dedicated clergymen.

Following his military service, and while living at Little Paddocks, my father was liaison officer between prisoners of war camps and the British authorities. One day, however, he was taken ill. He was brought home under the care of a German prison doctor, guarded by two soldiers. At Ipswich hospital, it was assumed that he might also have contracted polio. He couldn't move, but had had a stroke. Due to his determination, he recovered and soon returned to work.

When I was eleven my brother Guy appeared. I am told that I was jealous but I can't remember having any grudge except that I did feel a little hurt at being suddenly neglected. Certainly a few years later, when I returned from school, I was horrified to find that my Arthur Mee's *Children's Encyclopedia*, which I had treasured, had been given to him; its pages torn and scribbled over. He told me later that it helped him to establish his artistic career. There was a tremendous age difference between us and, due to my being at boarding school, we didn't see a great deal of each other. At Dedham, I was at an age of budding independence. I used to take my bicycle down to the river Stour and fish, explore, join archeological digs or visit old churches. Sometimes on my trips I would meet up with Lady Munnings who rode side-saddle and kept a pekinese called Black Knight in her large jacket pocket. Her husband, the artist Sir Alfred, was an old friend of the family - he drew a characterful pen and ink drawing of my grandfather and composed a poem to my Aunt Bryda about her pony.

*   *   *   *   *   *   *   *   *   *   *

From the age of about two, I had spent regular periods at my grandfather's home near Cashel. Each time I visited Ireland, there were new excitements and a sense of freedom. Irish people love children and I was always drooled over, getting attention seldom afforded me in Britain. In Cashel, the owner of a shop where my grandfather often called presented me with delicious 'Crunchies' in their metallic wrapping. These milk chocolate and honeycomb bars were not available across the water. Similarly, in Whitegate, Mick Treacy who owned the general stores on the hill which his son Mike continues, used to keep boiled sweets for the 'Major's grandson'. Everywhere, I would be taken to look at animals or castles, and into people's homes. "Be certain and call down, now", Mrs. Ryan 'the Moat' at Ardmayle and her daughter Peg would say. When I visited them, a warm loaf of brown bread straight from the griddle would be placed on the table together with a glass of fresh milk or later, a cup of tea.

I was brought into the kitchen rather than the musty and rather uncomfortable parlour with its Papal picture and dark Victorian furnishings. Kitchens were the centre of domestic activity. The open hearths had their black cranes on which hung heavy soot-covered iron kettles or skillets over smouldering turf fires. Beside the fireplaces were small wooden or stone benches on which people sat to keep warm. The stone-flagged kitchens had large unvarnished and well-scrubbed wooden tables surrounded by sugán or wheelback chairs. On one side would be a tall dresser with displays of china intermixed with pieces of twine, jars of small change or tools for every-day use. Other items would include a bucket of spring water, perhaps a churn, a coop for clucking hens, and a broom. By the outer door hung a Holy Water font into which those entering or departing would dip their fingers before crossing themselves.

Denis Ryan, manager of the Boherlahan Co-operative Society stores at Ardmayle always greeted me. A little dour, he had a stock of 'peggy's legs' at an 'old' pre 1972 penny each. These were long cylindrical brown bars of crunchy sweet rock. There were the Kinanes and Jimmy Devane, the Hennessys, Wallaces and Delanys, across from the front gates the Albert Mahers and behind us, another family of Mahers. One of the latter, our good friend T.J. who cut our grass with his small Ford Ferguson tractors, was to become President of the National Farmers' Association and a member of the European Parliament. Everybody knew everyone and an innocent youngster was unaware of any intrigues, politics or enmities.

My grandfather William Gibson, colloquially known as 'the Major', returned to Ireland after my mother was born. During the War of Independence he was Brigade Major at Queenstown, or Cobh. He then stayed as a paying guest with his friends the Pattons at Fethard Rectory and at Bill Hanley's Lanespark near Littleton. While leasing Brittas, a largish three bay house owned by the Devitts near Cashel, he learnt that the rectory at Ardmayle was for sale. Canon Hardy, who sported a beard and side whiskers and who bred spaniels, hadn't been replaced and the Thompsons, now owners of 'The Beeches', were selling it. Grandfather bought it, on twenty-three acres. He also had a grá for his boyhood haunts on Lough Derg and made regular visits to Mountshannon and Williamstown.

*   *   *   *   *   *   *   *   *   *   *

During my time at Newells my parents moved to Ardmaylebeg, which my grandfather had transferred to my mother. My journeys home would now start from London's Euston Station, that grandiose classical building north of the Thames which I had already experienced many times. From here the trains left for Holyhead. The atmosphere was different. There was the excited chatter of returning emigrants, some drunk, others with newly acquired families or wealth. People knew each other and passengers chatted to other travellers, even if they didn't. There was an air of excitement . . . . and nearly always a bar and dining-car.

The junction at Crewe was the first major stop although there were often delays. We were joined by passengers from Manchester and other Midland centres. Trolleys would be wheeled along the platform with tea and minerals, sandwiches or revoltingly sweet cakes. Some passengers dared to take advantage of the ten minute stop to slip into the station restaurant. I never took the risk.

At Holyhead, we were herded onto one of the rather spartan mail boats. The 'Princess Maude' was the worst. She had no stabilizers and we who travelled 'third class' were treated like cattle. At Dun Laoghaire, the train to Westland Row, now Pearse, station in central Dublin was ancient. We were locked into each compartment, there being no passage and no W.C. I always had an urge to urinate but had to hold on, often in extreme discomfort. Sometimes a carriage which, linked to another engine, continued to Kingsbridge (Heuston) station, but more often I took a taxi or bus. From here the green Coras Iompair Eireann Cork-bound trains left for Goolds Cross. Well experienced with this journey both accompanied and unaccompanied, I would get really excited as the train rattled through the rich cow-scattered Kildare farmland beyond Sallins. I was homebound . . . . really homebound.

CHAPTER THREE

The family returns to Ireland - Ardmaylebeg, my Irish home described; our neighbours and my activities. The social whirl of the post war rural south west.

Real life for me began in 1947 when my grandfather Willie Gibson offered my parents his house. He, together with his friend and faithful housekeeper, Dolly O'Neill, would move to Williamstown on Lough Derg, where he would take over and convert the old Canal Company stores across the road from the wooden bungalow where I had spent my holidays. The financial consideration was minute and there was the least possible hassle. The two or three grooms and Mrs. Meskell, the headgroom's wife, would be kept on. The furniture that Grandfather didn't need could stay, together with the big game trophies and Gibson family portraits. It was ideal for all. My mother could continue her way of living. My father could return to an Ireland which was little changed and where he could enjoy the activities of a country gentleman, then being rapidly denied to residents of Britain. Guy would benefit from the country air and rural pursuits. I was to be among friends.

*   *   *   *   *   *   *   *   *   *   *

Ardmaylebeg in County Tipperary was a typical rectory, the residence of the rectors of Ardmayle, a medieval parish of which chief family were once the Butlers. Like many early nineteenth century glebe houses, it was designed by a Church of Ireland architect as a two bay two storey hip-roofed house with a small two storey return. The entrance was through a porch to one side. This led into a longish hall with the diningroom to the left, and the drawingroom ahead - on the right was the staircase.

A circular inlaid ship's table surrounded by Irish Chippendale chairs, and a large Georgian sideboard stood in the diningroom, the walls of which were hung with sporting prints and family portraits. Under the stairs, in the hall, was a huge bog-oak sideboard on which polished silver candlesticks and oil lamps were ready to be collected at bedtime. Underneath was reputedly the last pine marten in Ireland, stuffed and in a glass case, but even today the creature is by no means extinct. On the wall over the stairs were large 'shields' containing pigs' tusks, and a leopard skin. There was also a brass gong, probably Indian, used to summon us to meals.

The drawingroom, with its bay window near which he sat at his desk, was enlarged by my father. The wall of the almost redundant pantry was knocked, and the two made into one large room. As Grandfather had lowered the bath into the floor above the pantry, this necessitated boxing off its depth, causing that part of the ceiling to be lower. The fireplace was enhanced by blue tiles of Lipizzaner horses from the Spanish Riding School in Vienna. There were comfortable chairs and a sofa, a whatnot, a delightful Dutch marquetry chest of drawers, a Potter landscape and a little portrait of Skittles, a famous courtesan and horsewoman.

A small flight of steps, illuminated by a little red oil lamp, led from the timber floored front of the house down a dark passage to the flag-floored kitchen area. On the left was the larder where perishable foods were stored. The dark room opposite the larder, once the rector's study, merely had a shuttered sash window which looked north over the yard. When it became my bedroom, a large steel-framed window was inserted to face the front drive. My bed was under it.

A steep back stairs led to my father's room over the kitchen, and to my old bedroom. By the back door was a scullery where my father fed the dogs and, later, his cat. The kitchen was a warm low-ceilinged room in which was a huge plate rack, possibly from Rockforest, containing the remnants of a crested family dinner service. The big scrubbed multipurpose deal table was surrounded by kitchen chairs which grated on the stone floor. A large window faced over the yard and on the opposite wall was a dresser with blue delph meat dishes, and more Gibson family plates. An ancient tin-cased alarm clock sat on the mantlepiece; I repaired it once and gave it a new lease of life. Various receptacles contained the odd seed, money, shopping list or promissory note. A door, under the back stairs, opened into a veritable Pandora's box, a darkened cupboard where there were all sorts of things to attract a small boy. At the far end of the room was an Aga-style 'A.B.' cooker where Mrs. Meskell and my mother baked bread, scones or potato cakes. The kitchen had a particular smell from cooking food, the scrubbing of the stone floor with carbolic soap, and burning turf.

Parts of Ardmaylebeg smelt musty. At the front of the house, off a banistered landing upstairs, were two bedrooms. One was used by my mother, the other for guests. The bathroom with its low-set bath was narrow. Above the bath was a shallow water tank under which was an improvised shower, and opposite was a large hot press. Over the bathroom door, in the landing, hung a chipped and possibly worthless Chinese plate I still treasure. Also upstairs, what was for many years my room had a ceiling which sloped downwards to the left. Beside my bed a small table supported my silver candlestick and snuffer. In daylight, I would look out of the window to the kitchen garden; in the winter a fire in the small black iron art nouveau grate kept me warm. My bookshelf contained 'island' books, historical and topographical works. My treasures were in a box on the far side of the bed where the ceiling was lowest. When the window was open, the loose lace curtain would billow in the wind. In the winter, the faded yellow flecked lined curtains would be tightly drawn. I would read until all hours by the light of a flickering candle, for there was always a draught. On cold nights, I would have a stoneware jar. These could be agony if touched when newly filled with boiling water, so I would wrap mine in a spare pillow or a pullover.

When I got up in the early morning, Papa would be in the bathroom, so I had to wait. Shaving incurred great difficulty for him. He seldom complained - life was a challenge which he readily accepted. After I became ill, I was moved downstairs. Supi Youlet, our Siamese cat, would jump on to the bed from the new window's open top and deposit her little gift for my recovery. This was usually a mouse or occasionally a small bird, although once or twice the offering was rat.

*   *   *   *   *   *   *   *   *   *   *

Approached by a long drive through a small tree-scattered park bounded with a sunken fence or 'ha-ha', Ardmaylebeg had a flower garden in front of the house. In a corner was a large Wellingtonia at the top of which was a wind-charger linked to a bank of batteries. This supplied us with weak slightly shimmering electricity. We also had Calor gas which hissed as it produced its cold white light. Our pressurised Aladdin table lamp produced the best results.

Between each of the bow windows which lit the reception rooms was a verandah to which a rock garden with colourful blue, mauve and white aubretias crept up steps. Two Thuya trees opposite the hall door protected a secluded garden with a small circular pond containing goldfish, water hyacinths and fairy moss. Slightly left was the entrance to the kitchen garden. This quarter acre was fenced by a beech hedge; my father, with his one arm, managed to keep it trimmed using sheep shears. Peas, reputedly descended from seeds buried with an Egyptian mummy, and wineberries were amongst the more unusual plants.

The yard was spacious. Between the kitchen and the dairy block was a hand pump used to raise water to the tank above the bath from a concrete rain-water reservoir. We had to take our turn as this was the only water supply. It often had to be augmented by river water drawn in butts by horse and car from the river. There was no main supply. The garage ope was closed by a sliding door. Beneath its loft, where old pictures and oddments were stored, was a well stocked workshop. Opposite the pump was a saddleroom, the groom's quarters, and looseboxes.

A back gateway, beside an outdoor kennel for the working dogs, led to the farmyard in which was a corrugated iron haybarn and a vast manure heap which steamed on frosty days. Between the two was the long open cow parlour with its Simplex milking machine. The adjoining haggard where cabbages and potatoes, some of which had survived from Famine times, were grown was larger than the kitchen garden. Three large level fields were used mainly for rotated crops. There were also two small coniferous copses, one in a disused quarry.

Opposite our gate was Fort Donough, the home of Albert Maher and his family. Albert used to transport our cattle in his American Ford truck. Fort Donough was a taller house than ours and more in keeping with others in an area where the land was good, and where Cromwell had settled his new landlord race. Facing it was Ardmayle Church. The three bay gothic edifice with its large medieval tower and surrounding graveyard was approached by a short tree-lined drive bordered by stone walls.

Ardmayle Church

The trees surrounding the church were home to masses of cawing rooks. There was seldom a substantial congregation which must have been very disheartening for the Dundrum-based rector.

*   *   *   *   *   *   *   *   *   *   *

In the field next to our lawn stood the Norman Castlemoyle, once surrounded by a medieval town. This tower was in Butler hands until 1652, when most of the area was granted to the Earl of Ormonde, and a portion allocated to Isaac Walton, author of *The Compleat Angler*. For fourteen years until 1872, the rector of Ardmayle was the Reverend William Carson, once a medical doctor and surgeon, who dispensed free medical treatment. His nephew was Dublin-born Edward Carson who would study at the top of the tower when visiting his uncle. Probably due to his links with Tipperary, a great hurling county, the future peer promoted this national Gaelic game at Trinity College, Dublin, drew up rules and organised the sport. A Unionist lawyer and politician, he helped establish the Ulster Volunteers and led the separation of the six northern counties from the then Free State.

Less distinguished, I also enjoyed the serenity of Castlemoyle. I often clambered up the stone stairs within the massive outer walls. As the timber floors had rotted away, when each door was reached there was merely a gaping hole. Cattle sheltered in the ground-level hall, in winter a mushy quagmire. Near the top were several small rooms, including a garderobe or toilet with its stone seat; some of the ceilings still had their original plasterwork with the imprint of their wattle reinforcement. The vaulted upper storey had become a grassy area open to the sky. In the surrounding field were humps indicating the one-time walls of houses and other buildings – adjoining it was a large quarry from which the stone used for the tower's construction was mined. Duckweed covered its stagnant water.

* * * * * * * * * *

The Grubbs, a once Quaker family, owned the parish's biggest house, known simply as Ardmayle. It was a large two storey residence over a basement, facing the river with imposing steps to the front door. Sam and Phyllis had sold the place and were living near Fethard for most of my time - but they still loved it and loyally attended our small church. Their eldest son Louis now runs the farm at Beechmount where, with his wife Jane, he produces 'Cashel Blue' cheese. Brian, the next, is an architect and lives in Co. Clare – there is also Clodagh, and her younger sister, Petronelle Clifton-Brown who lives at the old Murphy estate near Cashel with her husband and family; Sam's widow, Phyllis lived with them for much of the time until her death in 2001.

Beside the road from Ardmayle to Cashel were the Delanys, Hacketts and other farmers, and at the Arglo Bridge lived the Barrys, one of whom helped my mother in the kitchen and on the milk round. In the other direction, the road wended downhill to the old bridge over the river Suir. In front of the nineteenth century woollen mill beside the bridge was Ardmayle Stores. I used to buy sweets in this shop, but there were also bushman saws, wellington boots and most things that country people needed. Behind the mill was the ruined Tudor Butler manor house, protected by high walls.

Opposite the Stores was a grassy triangle which sloped to a shallow ford. Here I used to back our horse and car and fill water butts by bucket. In the bordering wall were the blocked-up windows and doors of single storey houses, remnants of the once populous township. Cromwell, or one of his officers, reputedly put his horse to graze outside one, and the occupant offered to hold it. Another story was that he nursed an injured Cromwellian soldier. Certainly a Mr. Murphy was allocated the extensive lands at Ballinamona a few miles away. The family, represented by Eddie and his sister, was still there in my day. The house now belongs to the Clifton-Browns.

The river at Ardmayle Bridge was shallow but rock-strewn. Catching crayfish involved straddling a large rock and gently prising it up so as not to create a mud cloud. Placing my forefinger and thumb on either side of its body, I would carefully lift each of these miniature lobsters and deposit it in a water-filled bucket. Crayfish salad was particularly popular with my father; another of his favourites was trout.

My grandfather founded the Holy Cross Fishing Club which nurtured the river between Thurles to the north and Camas, a few miles downstream. He caught some hefty fish, though he did leave some for me. He was an outstanding fly-fisherman, and I could never match his expertise. In fact, I preferred to wet-fly the mountain streams in the hills around Upperchurch. As the river had some very deep pools, there were also good-sized pike. Often I'd take a heavy spoon or plug bait, even with a light rod and line, to catch one. My largest was about twelve pounds. Fishing and shooting in the Suir valley, or even just walking, permitted me to dream; at home there was work and other more meaningful activities to be undertaken.

Across Ardmayle Bridge, past the creamery, the straight road faced up a hill to our out-farm. The two storey house with its breakfront and fanlit doorway was once a police barracks. Behind it were fourteen acres of rough grazing from which we harvested hay and silage. It had been bought by my parents in the early 'fifties.

On the road to the left, leading to and past the railway station, lived the Meskells, Connollys, and the Ryans of Bawnmore who shared my mother's interest in horses. Beyond lived Tommy Wade, later a successful show jumping champion on his little horse, Dundrum.

In the other direction were the ruins of a small house on a bend of the road. The lower part was of stone while above, the walls were of clay. Whether by pony and trap, car or bicycle, a noise such as bushes being caught underneath or a binding brake would start and continue until we got to the rear of Bianconi's Longfield House where inevitably it would stop. Reputedly Charles Bianconi had mistreated the occupant of the then inhabited cottage, who placed a curse on him and his vehicles. It was near the site of a Norman fortified gateway. The road continued past Longfield, and the attractive Woodford, the house where Lord and Lady Ashtown resided. Beyond Goolds Cross our friends the de Wiltons lived at Clonoulty Rectory, the Pennefathers at Marlowe and, a little further, the Kemmises at Moyaliffe and the Ryans at Inch, the Commander being Grandfather's great friend.

* * * * * * * * * *

A right turn from our gate would bring us to another junction, beside which was one of my favourite haunts. The Motte and Bailey's grass-covered earthworks were also constructed by the Normans; on the thirty metre summit grew an almost hollow-trunked sycamore. From it was a wide view of the river valley. Ardmayle House where the

Our outfarm house, Ardmayle.

Hunts lived and Longfield, then the home of Molly O'Connell Bianconi Watson, faced from the other side. The slopes of the Motte were often bared and in the clay were bones and sherds of pottery thrown from the top by feasting Norman barons or their servants.

Along the Nodstown road, one of the last to be tarred, I could visit the Ryans 'the Motte' whose monkey-puzzle trees shaded their large thatched half-hipped farmhouse. Further on were Jimmy Devane, in another thatched house, and the O'Dwyers of Nodstown Castle. Leaving the Motte Cross towards Boherlahan were the Hennessys, the Wallaces, several families of Ryans and the Sheehans.

At Boherlahan was the Italianate Bianconi chapel. For centuries, people from around used to gather at the Motte cross on summer evenings and dance to traditional music on the stone and mud-metalled roadway; gossip and porter flowed freely. Around 1820, a twenty year old Lombardy boy, apprenticed to a fellow-Italian picture and holy medal salesman, was touring Munster. As he approached from Boherlahan with his wares, he was jeered. "Look at the poor Italian, come to rob us of our few coppers . . . . ye won't get far in this country, boy . . . . " With presence of mind Carlo Bianconi called some of them to the brow beside the Motte. Pointing to the then ninety-year old Georgian house owned by the Longs, he told them: "Mark my word, you'll be the foolish ones when I'm living in that castle". He was soon to establish the first regular transport system in Ireland and by the 1860s, Bianconi side-cars covered four thousand miles of routes. Having accumulated enough to purchase Longfield in 1846, he lived there comfortably for his remaining thirty years. His youngest daughter wedded Daniel O'Connell's nephew, from whom Molly Watson descended. Molly, delightful and interesting, wrote a comprehensive biography of her forebear. We used to visit her for tea in front of a roaring log fire in the rather dilapidated drawingroom at Longfield, a house on which she doted and which she left to the Irish Georgian Society in the 1960s.

*   *   *   *   *   *   *   *   *   *   *

Although our closest neighbours were those with whom we came into contact most, friendships follow patterns. My parents shared an interest in horses and cattle with those of like mind. Field sports also had a strong impact and even if they had little money, many stayed bound to their traditional pursuits. The twentieth century European transition from landlordism hadn't yet reached Co. Tipperary. Money did count, however, and new settlers, mainly English with a spattering of Americans, were welcomed into the dwindling society of 'old families'. The Craik-Whites had settled near Caher and, nearer home, the Evan Williamses had come for the hunting. Topics of conversation included the incursion of socialism, the spiraling cost of living, and the settlers and their backgrounds; also discussed were those who had emigrated from Ireland or had died, and of course, hunting, racing, shooting and farming.

When the last remaining member of an old established family died and left her property to her butler, there was stunned horror. The reasons were less to do with class than that another Irish 'old gentry' family had gone. There was one less of 'us'. Religion, although in this case Roman Catholic, may have also been a concern. Most landed families were members of the Church of Ireland and due to diminishing numbers, places of worship were being closed and de-roofed by SPAC, the Sparsely Populated Areas Commission. Nobody wished to witness the end of their church which was a comforting symbol, not only of God, but of their Irish heritage.

Events throughout Ireland brought people together such as the Steeplechases at Punchestown in Co. Kildare with which my grandfather had been closely identified. Limerick Show, held around my birthday in late August on the Greenpark racetrack south of the city, attracted participants from the surrounding counties. Jumping and horse judging events took place in front of the huge stand overlooking the track. Behind this were halls and tents with butter, flowers, wool, crafts and a host of small exhibits. Over the open grassland were crude machinery and industrial stands interspersed with bars and untidily parked vehicles. Somewhere in this area, my parents with their then twelve or fourteen year old eldest son, chatted with Lord and Lady Inchiquin. I was impressed and can still vividly remember eyeing their younger daughter, Grania O'Brien. Donough and Anne were eventually to become my parents-in-law. Clonmel horseshow was the venue for meeting with those who lived in and around the lower Suir Valley such as the Smiths of Caher who were millers, the Wyses, Carrigans, two O'Brien families, the Cleeves, Murray Moores, Bagwells, Donoughmores and a host of equine and agricultural devotees.

The Royal Dublin Society's similar but larger event took place in early August. More fashionable than the Spring Show, there was an air of dignity and tradition. Most families had been members of the Society for generations. Those admitted to the members' stand at the northern short-end of the ring puffed superiority, while those without ceded grudging respect. The Aga Khan trophy was presented by the President of the new state. To shake his hand was almost as significant as a bow or a curtsey to the Queen of England. Those who hadn't lost their young men to the First World War, or who hadn't left during the 'Troubles', were beginning to accept the majority will for an independent republic. It may not have been easy, but a small dapper gentleman in tails and top hat helped. Séan T. O'Kelly made a significant impact, by his impartiality and his perpetuation of tradition; a statesman, he was popularly ensconsed in Aras An Uachtaran, once the Vice-regal Lodge. As in South Africa more recently, Séan T. wasn't into upsetting those who had to undergo drastic change. Douglas Hyde, his predecessor, had also been positive; a Gaelic scholar, historian, a Protestant and a gentleman, he had a foot in both camps. Eamonn de Valera, although very different, also had a statesmanly approach which enabled him to calm the fears of those who disapproved of him and to initiate a new pluralist state. There evolved a subconscious blending of the aspirations of politicians, even revolutionaries, with those of landed gentry. This continues today.

*   *   *   *   *   *   *   *   *   *   *

Meets of hounds were social gatherings especially when held on supporters' lawns. Whiskey would be proffered as the excitement of the day's prospects gathered momentum. This was as significant a part of the event as the chase and chat would often continue even as the first covert was drawn.

At gymkhanas, we would meet local friends; my parents would occasionally be involved in organising or judging. We would drive to the edge of the ring, often beside someone we knew, and unload a rug on which the picnic was shared with hopeful dogs. My young brother was usually the only one who actually sat on the rug - Father used his shooting stick.

There were several point-to-points in the county. We would patronise the bookies and I once won ten pounds for my two shillings and sixpence. Some of the jockeys we knew gave us first-hand tips. Following the final race, there were long queues as the cars were guided to the exits for the journey home. In wet weather, the mud caused many of them to get stuck. 'Spot Tobacco' from Cashel would be at such meetings and would doff his cap hopefully, usually receiving generous rewards for assisting people to park or to get out on to the highway. A few times we went flat-racing, to Thurles or the Curragh. En route we would speculate as to whether the car-loads of men, women and children or the posh Bentleys, Citroens or Rovers were making for the same destination.

Winter would find me rough shooting often with George Russell and his son who lived on the edge of Cashel, or other close neighbours. Snipe was the popular target, but duck and woodcock were also prized. Organised shoots took place at Killenure Castle (Coopers'), Marlowe (Pennefathers') and at such more distant venues as Noan where the Armitages lived. With my 410 shotgun, and later a Cogswell & Harrison 12 bore weapon, I was not a bad shot.

Church services and functions were also meeting places. My parents were not regular church attenders - I think the fact that Papa had been divorced made them feel proscribed in days when termination of marriage was abhorred. I, however, was packed off on Sunday mornings to boost the tiny congregation. "Hugh, you go to church this morning and represent the family". There were some dreadfully boring preachers but Canon Hogg from Dundrum, later Archdeacon, introduced a bit of life to his services. From a rural North Tipperary background, he understood country living. Sometimes the preacher, or members of the congregation would join us at home after a service for 'elevenses' or lunch.

Every now and again the Dean of Cashel or the rector of Dundrum would organise a 'social'. The object was to bring Church of Ireland parishioners together in sparsely populated areas in hopes that they would marry within their community, for these were 'Ne Temere' days. In Cashel they took place in the long paraffin-stove-heated parish hall which had been constructed in the upper half of a large building beside the Queen Anne Deanery. Having been dropped off by my mother, for my father seldom drove, I would climb the steps and shyly enter. The din of gossiping parishioners was deafening. Elderly people sat on benches or chairs around the edge, middle aged ladies organised meals and games, and children rushed from corner to corner. They often bumped into adults bearing cups of tea on saucers, on which they also rested their food. Curate Burke, who had been in the parish for decades, wore old fashioned black clerical garb and a flat-topped hat. The Dean, for most of my time Robert Wyse-Jackson, and his wife would be busily organising, he also in his gaiters and black suit. There would sometimes be dancing, although most of us were too embarrassed to take the floor, and a lot of speeches. Before departure, thanks were publically expressed, almost everyone being mentioned.

Sales of work were different and my mother would be more inclined to involve herself ; Guy, I recall, was usually left with my father at home. Participants could be categorised as a Protestant and a Roman Catholic gentry, farmfolk, professionals such as clergy, teachers and doctors, parents of school children, country people and townsfolk. There was more intermixing or interrelationship than is nowadays accredited though due to 'Ne Temere', Roman Catholics couldn't marry members of other denominations without having their partners agreeing to bind their offspring to that faith. A lot of parents would chat at school when they went to deliver or collect their children. Guy's organised education started in 1953 at the numerically small Deanery School whose headmistress, Mrs. Black, lived in the gate lodge.

Dinner parties were usually black tie events in the 1950s. Guests from different parts would expect to meet strangers - being Ireland, this was seldom the case. "Oh, hello. Welcome . . . . this is Mary and Michael Verygood from Back-of-beyond . . . . " "Hello Mick, hello Viv; how did you do at Clonmel last week?" Often host and hostess were disappointed and stunned, especially the new English or American settlers, that most invitees knew each other.

Children's parties were also held, often at rectories, as clergy gave dances for the younger members of their families. I particularly enjoyed visiting Thurles Rectory where Canon and Mrs. Palmer's daughter Mary lived. I had quite a crush on her and occasionally asked her home. The only thing which spoiled our friendship, however, was the taunting of my parents: "Mary Palmer, Mary Palmer, how I'd love to throw my arms around you". Hopefully Mary, slightly older than I, was never aware of this.

Contemporaries, male or female, were few and far between. Mariquita, the gorgeous daughter of Harry Cleeve, of the Limerick Dairy-product and toffee family, and of his glamorous American wife Olive, lived on the edge of Clonmel. Audrey O'Brien whose religious denomination, even at that early age, precluded me from developing too close a relationship, and Iva Keane from near Fethard were also close. Iva was to marry Geoffrey, the son of String and Han de Wilton of Clonoulty.

One winter, Harry Ponsonby of Grove near Fethard gave a large party. The main excitement was a game of 'Squashed Sardines' where one or two of us would hide until located by other guests who would silently squash beside or on top of us. One of the participants was a delightful English girl whose family came from Co. Meath. Gill and I spent longer than was considered appropriate in our successful hiding place. We became good friends, but the mileage between us was too large to overcome. Although there were quite a few girls I used to dream about, relationships often only got as far as cuddles of my pillow. As most of my school holidays were taken up with helping on the farm, I had few male friends. Those companions that I did have were mainly from school. Some shared two domains such as Ricky Jackson, son of the Dean of Cashel, Bobby Harris, and John Pocock who hailed from near Clonmel.

Other winter events were the hunt balls. Each pack of hounds sponsored their own to raise funds. 'The Scarteen' or 'Black and Tan' gathering took place at the Ryan's pleasantly unpretentious house. This was always an enjoyable and intimate event. That of the Tipperary hounds was very different. I usually joined the pre-ball dinner party which Lord and Lady Donoughmore held at their delightful house near Clonmel. Mark Hely Hutchinson, their second son, more recently Governor of the Bank of Ireland, was born the same year as myself. The Donoughmores, later to be kidnapped by subversives, were family friends, he being master of the hounds. I was made to feel at home and there were usually attractive female guests. From Knocklofty we would proceed to Hearnes Hotel where Mick Delahunty and his band would play the latest dance tunes loudly enough to keep the town awake. Cloaks were deposited before we entered the ballroom. Around the periphery clusters of tables and chairs would be set, so we would 'bag'several for our own use. I was always given enough money for drinks, so I usually stood our own table of four or six guests what they desired at the start - not the most sensible strategy. Amongst friends, I lost some of my shyness although I didn't do much dancing. Come the early hours of the morning, I would share the return journey, sometimes to Knocklofty, before continuing home or, at other times, to different destinations.

Our Weir and O'Brien (Grania being a 'Heraldic Heiress') arms, parted per pale.

CHAPTER FOUR

Farming days, milk deliveries, creameries, horse cars and changing times. Cashel, her shops and businesses, the Convent laundry and her churches. Visits to Limerick.

L iving at Ardmaylebeg was by no means all recreation or a social whirl. There was work to be done and a living to be made. Even the annual three months spent during the different seasons at home from school were no real holiday. When my father retired, after years of military service, he was left with an inadequate pension. We had less than, albeit the best, twenty-five acres of agricultural land. Even in 1947 this was not enough to produce an income which could support two adults in the way to which they were accustomed, as well as two children of school-going age who had to board. My grandfather had dealt in horses and had kept a cow or two for his own domestic use, but he had an income from inherited investments. How would my handicapped professional ex-soldier father, countryman and naturalist, and my mother Rosamund Suzanne Weir, keen horsewoman and artist, produce an income?

The answer obviously lay in the land even though, under normal farming conditions, there was too little of it. That meant either purchasing more, which was nigh impossible, or going into intensification. They initially chose the latter. Pure-bred long-horned brown and white Ayrshire cattle were acquired, mainly from the McCormick farm on the edge of Belfast. A bull, Silver Sprig, which Albert Maher and I collected in his truck from the Camolin herd in Co. Wexford was the foundation of our significant Grade 'A' dairy herd. Fencing round the fields was duplicate - strange beasts would not be permitted to rub noses with our regularly tested tuberculosis-free animals. The disease was rampant in Ireland at the time and there were several specifically dedicated hospitals for those unfortunate people who contracted it. Everything, especially in the dairy, had to be extra carefully sterilised. Along with the herd, a bottled milk round was organised. This meant costly capital expenditure; bank managers were visited and there were associated worries. The grooms, including Batt Meskell who had all but retired, were replaced with herdsmen such as John Sheehan, Billy Carter, Counihan, and a young Boherlahan boy named Barrett. While I was abroad, a popular Finnish girl, Toyni Alamaki, helped in return for accommodation and the opportunity to perfect her English.

A routine was established. Each morning my father would be up at five o'clock. I would hear him in the kitchen making tea for my mother and himself. Although 'right-handed' and now with only his left arm, he managed an amount of tasks. He would feed the dogs, put on the hot water for washing the cows' udders before they were milked, prepare for and do the manual filling of each bottle from a special cooler after milking, heat the dairy if it was winter, and help bringing in the herd.

A cowman was employed to do the milking. Naturally, when on holidays, I would help at home. While the herd was being milked and having achieved his earlier tasks, my father would finish his ablutions and, between seven and eight, call me; my mother would already be up. I never liked getting up and, too often for my father's liking, took a long time to dress. I couldn't understand his dislike of paying big money for my education. I hadn't asked for the investment and besides, being at home should have been a restful holiday. Most of my school pals boasted of lovely worry and work-free vacations.

"Come on, boy . . . . hurry up . . . . you've been hogging that bed long enough . . . . come on . . . . !" He was still at heart a military man and I was treated like one of his troops. Downstairs, however, he would offer me a 'cuppa' and was disarmingly civil. My mother would already be in the dairy as I made my way to the milking parlour. There I would take responsibility for one or two of the sets of teat cups and wash down the next cow's udder to stop dirt from contaminating the milk. I would then dry it so that the animal wouldn't feel cold and hold back, and place a sucking cup on each of her four teats. The machine did the rest. The bucket would fill with warm steamy milk. When each was finished, the cups were removed but we still had to squeeze out any few drops of milk left in an udder for fear of mastitis infection. When the machine broke down we had to milk by hand.

The buckets of milk were carried from the byre to where my father would be waiting in front of the cooler. The bucket was hoisted head-high and the milk tipped into a large stainless steel vat. Below this was a sort of corrugated hollow radiator; within it passed a flow of cold water to cool the warm milk which flowed down the outside into an open-topped trough with automatic taps. My father would pull up his stool and stretch into the bottle crate beside him. Sitting there, he would fill each glass bottle and replace it. My mother or I would then, with our thumbs, press down the sides of the waxed cardboard discs so that the bottles were capped. Aluminium foil was later introduced, and a differently shaped bottle. A special tool did the job then, although still by hand.

When the crates were filled, they were loaded into the back of our delivery vehicle. Lists of who would receive how many bottles were consulted, amended, and placed on the passenger seat ready for the milk round. My mother, usually, would be delivering each bottle to our customers in Cashel and the surrounding area.

The cows would be released. After leaving their concrete-floored stalls they would, much to our frustration, deliver their excrement between the milking parlour and the gate to the fields. Once the last cow, well fed with silage, dairy nuts or hay, was herded to the appropriate pasture, the gate would be closed. One of my tasks was to bucket gallons of water to their troughs so that they had plenty to drink; dairy cows producing four or five gallons of milk a day need a lot of liquid.

When all was prepared for the morning delivery, my father, my mother and I joined Guy, who by then would also be up, for a quick breakfast in the diningroom, or in the kitchen if we were by ourselves. The cowman, who had already had his, would be brushing out the milking parlour and cleaning up the machine. He would also fill the racks in the stalls with fodder for the evening. Sometimes, I would accompany my mother and do the actual delivering to each door while she drove the vehicle and kept the record of each sale. Normally she undertook this onerous task by herself. She did, however, enjoy meeting customers and learning the latest news.

Characters amongst our customers included Joe Buckley who kept a shop in the island of buildings in the centre of Cashel's divided main street. He had a stock of huge cabbages, and was the first in town to have a juke box; this ghetto-blaster was so loud that it would be heard throughout the town. Michael Burke, whose family runs his stationers shop since his retirement, had a good voice and played a leading role in the Cashel Opera Society's annual performance in the City Hall. He was considered a worthy and supportable rival to Anew MacMaster who performed Othello in the same building, and put on other mainly Shakespearean plays. Anew McMaster's repertory company drew large audiences throughout Ireland. There were also the draper Daverns, the MacDonalds, the MacMathunas - then calling themselves O'Mahony - and Dowlings to whose garage we took our vehicles for repair.

There were problems for our milk deliveries if it snowed. Somewhere at Ardmaylebeg there were chains, but they could seldom be located when they were needed. One particular hill near Hacket's farmhouse always presented a problem, but it was seldom long before someone would appear and offer help.

Fair days were troublesome whatever the season. Until Marts were introduced when cattle were organised into pens by local auctioneers and then auctioned, cattle, horses, sheep and other domestic animals were driven, usually on foot, to the Main Street. Specific days for fairs were allocated to different towns and villages and recorded in *Old Moore's Almanac*, an ancient tradition. Afraid that cattle or horses would push up against them and break them, shopkeepers would barricade their windows. Their doors would be open, for trade was brisk if sales of farm animals were taking place. Most grocery shops were pubs; most pubs had shops. Farmers would leave a list of requirements to the person behind the counter, while they went into the bar beyond for their 'pint'. The assistant, usually a young girl from 'out the country' would then process the groceries orders. The concept was a sensible one, though it could lead to erratically driven journeys home and some difficult family situations.

Tourists were now visiting Ireland and her 'Acropolis', the Rock of Cashel, was on many of their itineraries. One day an English couple in an immaculate Jaguar pulled up as I was about to distribute a crateful of bottles. "Hoch, begorra, could ye tell me am I right for Cork?" said the driver with a pseudo Irish accent. I was delighted to tell him that he was in my best, albeit over-emphasised, Oxford English. Flummoxed, he stuttered an apology before continuing on his way.

Another time, an individual with a carload of family members was driving through the crowded main street on Fair day. Nobody had warned him to keep his windows closed. As he passed a cluster of cattle, one pressed its rear against the open window of the front passenger door and squirted its message over the occupants. Mortified, he and his passenger stopped their car, jumped out and wiped themselves as clean as they could. Nobody took much heed - I suppose it was natural. I felt terribly sorry for them, but I couldn't just drop the milk round to help.

Each afternoon, the delivery vehicle would return with the empty bottles. If it was early enough, essential tasks would be undertaken, otherwise we'd have lunch. This was a light repast of perhaps chicken noodle or tomato soup followed by biscuits and soapy cheese. My parents usually had a regulated hour's break. Guy, now aged three or four years, could be in the house playing in the drawingroom, unless the day was particularly sunny when my father would have him in the garden.

Following the after-lunch siesta, each member of the household would undertake their specific task. My mother would rinse the bottles, some of which contained the remnants of aged sour milk which stank. Having been used for storing anything from paint to food stuffs others had to be discarded. Beside the large vat of cold water used for rinsing was the sink containing hot water and detergent. Each bottle was immersed and carefully washed with a special bottle brush; any spec of dirt could contaminate the next fill. After the bottles were washed, they'd be rinsed and stored upside down to dry. Occasionally I undertook this chore but Mama, a perfectionist, preferred to do it herself. My afternoon tasks included mucking out horseboxes and cleaning the kennels. In winter I took the steaming farmyard manure by horse and car to the fields and forked it in heaps for distribution. In summer there would be hay and silage making and later, harvesting of the cash crops.

* * * * * * * * * *

My parents, as T.J. Maher reminded viewers of a television programme many years later, were very advanced in their methods and introduced new ideas. This put some of the more traditional farmers' noses out of joint as they saw these new 'book' farmers succeed. We were amongst the first to introduce open-pit silage, and excavated drained hollows with sloping entrances and exits, between built-up banks. This meant that a tractor could be driven in and, as it progressed, tip its buckrake-load of fresh grass before continuing out from the other end. There is a story from when silage was made in concrete circular towers and horses were used to trample the fresh grass down. One of the first farmers to save it led his animal through the ground level door and started to press the grass which was already in the seven or eight metre tower. As new greenery was fed from the top, so the compacted silage rose. When the pit was full, he had the unforeseen problem of getting the horse down. I believe that a specially erected ramp was put in place while he nervously held the excited horse, for fear it would jump to the ground and break its legs.

'Procter's' tripods were another innovation my parents introduced. Normal haymaking meant that the grass was dried in the sun, collected, and built into cocks like Christmas puddings. These were then tied with binder twine to prevent them disintegrating. To stop the cock going mouldy in damp weather 'Procters System' meant that we would erect three wooden poles joined at the top like wigwams. At the bottom of each sloping shaft was fitted a wooden frame like a miniature roof but open at each end and facing outward. The hay would be built over the tripods to form the cocks and when the frames were removed, a hole leading into a central hollow enabled air to circulate. The result was better hay with almost as much nutritional value as silage, but it took an awful lot of extra work.

During the summer we employed extra help; there was one regular, Larry Regan, a Trojan worker. When the 6 p.m. Angelus rang Larry always knelt and prayed the Rosary before standing and returning his large cap to his head. He spent his last days in sheltered accommodation for the elderly, which had once been the Cashel workhouse.

At harvest time, as with the grape harvest in France and similar crop gatherings, neighbours would rally. A vast feast of bacon and cabbage, or ham and salad would be provided and plenty of liquor, mainly Guinness' stout. Those who were non-drinking'Pioneers' had strong tea. Pitching sheaves of corn from the trailer to the top of the steam-traction engined threshing machine, I was expected to set an example by working twice as hard as our helpers. I enjoyed the challenge but once overdid it; how I suffered when I went to bed. Occasionally, we would harvest hay or corn in our out-farm or on lands leased by the con-acre or 'eleven-month' system. Sometimes we saved hay at Graan or Clonoulty, seven or eight kilometres away. At home or away my mother or one of the girls would bring out a flagon of hot tea, scones which my mother excelled at making, or sodabread and butter. We would sit or lie about the grass to the lee side of a recently made tram or haycock as we devoured our snack. Before the winter, the hay would be brought in on a buckrake linked to the hydraulic lift of T.J's. tractor. It was then forked into the high corrugated-iron haybarn. Sometimes, in a wet year, we couldn't do this for fear the dampness would cause overheating and fire or, in spite of the tripods, that the crop would go mouldy and be unacceptable by the animals to whom it was proffered. In such conditions, the seeds would begin to sprout. We had to wait as long as it took for dry sunny weather to appear.

*   *   *   *   *   *   *   *   *   *

As I have said, we kept our own bull as there were no local Ayshires to cover our cows. Milk breeds seemed to produce the most dangerous beasts and we had to be extremely careful. The huge males, with rings through their tender noses, would be loosely chained from these to a larger ring on the wall of their loosebox. In order to move or exercise them, we would use a rigid bull-stick. This two metre broom-handle like tool had a gapped hollow metal circle attached to its top, inside which a sprung part could slide, causing the gap to be opened and closed. Atttached to a tiny ring welded to it was a cord which, when pulled, caused the gap to open; the cord released, it would automatically close. The bull handler, usually my mother or I, would slip the gap in the circle over the bull's nose ring and close it. We would then release the chain to the wall-fitting and lead the bull, keeping it at the handle's length.

One day I was cleaning out the bull's loosebox when a cold shudder came about me. The creature was facing me, its worn ring disintegrated from its nose. Presence of mind caused me to calmly creep over to it, stick my thumb and forefinger where the ring had been, and yell for help. It seemed like hours before I was rescued.

Occasionally, for those milking cattle we kept to boost our butterfat content such as Kerrys, Dexters or Jerseys, we would call for AI. Artificial Insemination was new and the sperm of only a few breeds was available. We would hold the cow while the officer donned his elongated rubber gloves before entering his arm to inject the womb. A tale told at the time brings a smile to my face! A smallholder had a cow ready for service and called the AI Centre. In due course, a smartly suited official arrived. He had difficulty in getting his hands into the animal's vagina and exasperatedly commented to her owner; "By God, this is a devil of a cow; she won't even let me in". The owner, watching from an appropriate distance retorted 'Faith and I'll tell you one thing. T'is the first time she's ever had a bull with a bowler hat."

Although my parents were advanced as regards livestock and crop production, farm machinery was out. This was partly due to the capital cost involved in the purchase of a tractor. Having a mechanical bent, this was a disappointment for me. I could see the advantage of having our own rather than to be beholden to T.J. or contractors. I just had to accept the status quo. Often my father would pay me the compliment of asking me what I thought. Sadly though, that was as far as it went. Young boys, or even young men, were there to 'be seen and not heard'.

When I received pocket money or perhaps a ten shilling note from Aunt Daisy, I would often spend it on an excellent American magazine called *Popular Mechanics* which had illustrations and articles on machines and innovative ideas, or on *Popular Farming* which was similar. There were also other mainly English farming and machinery publications. In my mid teens, during school holidays from Portora, I took pen to paper. In an English periodical, I had read about a new tractor, the Trusty Steed, which had one rib-tyred wheel at each corner of its frame. Until now, few conventional tractors had hydraulic systems. Here was a machine where the tools, such as a harrow or plough, were centrally mounted and driven by a low slung water-cooled engine. It was a simple machine and reasonably priced.

I wrote to the Trusty Company. I knew that they were unlikely to have an Irish representative as they were a new business, so I offered to act as their agent. At the time I owned a comprehensive box of rubber lettering which, fitted into a multi-channelled holder and pressed into an ink pad, produced professional-looking letter headings. The manufacturers must have been impressed, for I received an envelope in the post; rushing to my room I opened it. "Dear Sir, we are delighted that you have expressed confidence in the success of . . . . As a consequence, we would be happy to supply you with . . . .(I think four) Trusty Steeds at a special trade discount." In my reply I suggested that, as I was taking a risk, I would initially take one machine pro rata. Unfortunately, my father firmly queried me about this correspondence and made me refuse their offer, explaining that I was merely a young boy.

A little later, to earn some pocket money, I made a rather crude but successful tractor trailer. I procured an axle and wheels with leaf springs to which I fitted a heavy wooden sub-frame using carriage bolts and attached a thick timber floor, mudguards and a towbar made by the local forge. Although we had no tractor with which to test it, I advertised it in the *Nationalist* and got, as far as I recall, fifteen pounds. This was a lot in the early fifties and gave me a useful profit, perhaps two pounds. In 1987, when Peter Meskell's parish history was being launched, a one-time neighbour approached me and told me that the trailer I had made was still being used.

For a mainly chivalrous military and landed family, 'trade' was not acceptable. My parents did, however, appreciate my amateur attempts to earn money - in fact, my father encouraged me. I also designed and sold Christmas cards. These usually had an Irish motive. Possibly they encapsulated my future interests in the design and publishing of postcards, in Irish archaeology and history, and in the Celtic church. Before Christmas, during my school holidays or when, later, I had left school, I would peddle my products to local

On Peggy, Ardmaylebeg, 1950.

retailers. The shopkeepers were supportive and nearly always made a purchase. I will never know if this was out of kindness, or if they really liked them and thought they would sell. I still have a letter-headed sheet of paper which I got printed, "Hugh Weir's Cards, Cashel", it says. I also entered book dustjacket design competitions, for one of which I received an award at Limerick Show when I was fourteen; I had chosen to cover Seán O'Faolain's *The Story of Ireland* then recently published. It had as its theme a Round Tower with a backdrop of lakes and mountains.

* * * * * * * * * *

Those of us who spent our formative years in nineteen-fifties Ireland underwent a unique period which paved the way for huge changes. Rural electrification, initiated with the 1928 Siemens Generating Station on the Shannon, was underway. Every house which requested the facility was soon to be supplied with power. Electric lighting enabled people to read more and to extend their hours of work. Television was to introduce the outside world to almost every home. Electric cookers and heaters meant cleaner rooms while those who could afford them purchased washing machines, refrigerators, dryers, dishwashers and mixers. Farmers benefitted by having housing for their animals lit; angle grinders, circular and chain saws and electric drills were introduced. Industry was brought into the twentieth century as darkness no longer denied the possibility of night-time manufacture.

Although we had no telephone at Ardmaylebeg, telephonic links were being provided to clergy and doctors, creameries, garda stations, factories and to some private houses. Although I had experience of telephoning from England, I rarely did so in Ireland. Once, however, making a call from Cashel post office to my cousins at Clonakilty, I became third party to an animated bargain between two farmers.

"Is that Clonakilty XYZ?", says I .

". . . . , no I'm not delivering them to Clonakilty . . . . " replied an anonymous Tipperary accent;

"I didn't ask you to . . . .", said another.

"Why did you mention Clonakilty then?"

"I didn't . . . . "

"I'll give you no more than what I already offered . . . ."

Those were handle-turning and request-to-operator days which were to continue in parts of rural Ireland until the 1970s. The increase in telecommunication that began at that time has been incredible.

The creamery was on the road from Cashel to Goolds Cross so that farmers bringing milk from Nodstown or Boherlahan would pass along the beech-lined avenue below our house. It wasn't tarred and the main transport for milk until the fifties was the horse and car with its iron clad wheels. Their long shafts were extended to the rear enabling them to be rested at a 45 degree angle, thus making it easier to lower them onto the waiting animal when harnessing. Churns of milk would be loaded at the farmers homes, or collected from where neighbours had clustered them by the roadside. The drivers would hop backwards onto the flat platform and dangle their legs over the near front corner, shake the reins over the horses' back and give the command "Gowon, glick glick . . . ." Confident young men stood as they drove, using the reins to help them balance.

The churn-rattling and ground-crunching noise of the iron tyres, combined with that of the trotting horses and their harness, as the farmers passed in convoys at around ten every morning welcomed me home each school holiday. One visit, however, was eerily different. The sound of the iron-clad horse drawn vehicles was diminished - instead there was the drone of Henry Ford's early 'Prefects' and the less frequent sound of the metal churns as they rattled against each other on the rubber-tyred trailers.

Although cars had occasionally been owned by wealthy farmers, clergy or doctors, others who could afford them now began to buy. The most popular Fords were quite cheap, had leather covered seats in front and a bench behind. They looked modern with pointed fronts, streamlined silver radiators, and sloping backs. Most also had four doors and their chassis' were capable of taking tow bars. They were black. Sometimes a less wealthy farmer had the smaller Ford 'Anglia'. In no time the sounds of the old creamery cars were history, those that continued having had their wooden spoked wheels changed for rubber tyred car wheels and leaf springs.

When the suppliers arrived at the creamery, there would be two long queues, one coming from our side, and the other from across the river. The slow progress of each would be a time for gossip. As each supplier came to his turn, he would pull up below a large suction tube from under the roof of a covered bay, and have his milk siphoned from the churns; a sample would be scooped to record butter-fat content, and if the farmer had calves or pigs, he would get a similar quantity of skimmed milk to bring home. Records of quantity and quality having been taken, he would make his way to the Stores for the 'messages' ordered by his wife, such as salt bacon or cigarettes. He would usually be home for dinner.

The production process started as the milk was piped into huge wooden rotary churns. Eventually rectangles of slightly salted full cream butter would be disgorged on to a conveyer belt. These were machine-wrapped with grease-proof papers informing in print that they came from the "Boherlahan Co-operative Creamery Company" and that they weighed one pound 'avoir du pois'. They would be placed in carefully made wooden boxes which often eventually became wastepaper bins; when the latter happened, dried rushes from the river would be woven over them and varnished. Later, the butter was placed in cardboard cartons. Cheese was reserved for Fridays when most people fasted. Only available were a mild cheddar from convents in Co. Limerick and, I think, Co. Roscommon, 'Manderville', 'Three Counties' processed triangles, and a rather soapy Edam with a red wax coating.

Unlike poorer parts of Ireland, our community ate well. Breakfast was usually a hearty eggs and bacon with rounds of brown bread and butter, washed down with plenty of strong tea. Sometimes there were sausages and black or white pudding. On Sundays we nearly always had a roast. For dinners Mr. O'Connor, our butcher, provided us with vast legs of beef to last the household throughout the week; his account was always larger than expected. Monday would be a day for cold beef and chutney, Tuesday perhaps curried chunks, Wednesday more cold beef or shepherd's pie and so on until the meat was finished and another week loomed ahead. In their gardens, most people grew potatoes, usually cooked in their skins, carrots, turnips and cabbage; so did we for winter, but in summer as each crop matured, we had peas, broad beans, parsnips and a variety of interesting vegetables.

*   *   *   *   *   *   *   *   *   *   *

Retailers didn't really modernise in Co. Tipperary until the nineteen-sixties. Grocers' shops were still in two parts. As one entered, stocks were displayed on shelves behind long wooden counters. Tinned 'Heinz' baked beans and processed peas, 'Nestlés' condensed sweetened and unsweetened milk, boxes of 'Maguire & Paterson's Friendly' or 'Safety' matches and packets of 'Players' and 'Woodbine' cigarettes, were often 'growing' dust. At arms level would be containers of loose tea and sugar, currants, prunes and 'Jacob's Marietta' or 'Jersey Cream' biscuits, the latter being amongst the earliest products to be packaged. Also in the often glass-topped containers would be scoops used for filling the brown paper bags. The bags, sometimes printed with the shop's name, would be placed on the counter scales and a pound, two pounds or a stone of goods accurately weighed. The bags would be folded over at the top, and the end neatly tucked in. On the counter would also be huge glass jars of loose sweets; white bags were used for these. To seal them, the two top corners were held, one in each hand, between which the bag would be swivelled. My favourites included multicoloured boiled sweets, 'bulls eyes', bars of Limerick-made 'Cleeves' toffee, 'peggys legs' and, because they were cheap, 'macaroon' bars. 'Lemon's malt and cream' toffees wrapped in white greaseproof with red lettering also became popular. On hooks above the counter would be flitches of salty bacon or pairs of Wellington boots. The differentiation between groceries and hardware blurred.

Usually there was a wooden partition with frosted glass panels between the grocery and the bar. This enabled anonymity for those enjoying a quiet 'pint' unbeknown to wife, family or friends. The main drinks stocked were different versions of Irish whiskey such as 'Powers' or 'Jamiesons', and 'Guinness'; occasionally these would be supplemented by 'Tullamore Dew', ancient bottles of cognac and 'Gordons' or 'Cork Dry Gin', even older half empty bottles of port and sherry, and unusual liqueurs, donated by returned or vacation-taking emigrants. The maximum comfort in these smokey drinking areas was often a few tall four-legged wooden stools with hard circular tops which would be drawn up to the counter until disarrayed by customers. On the opposite wall there could be benches and plain wooden tables on which were scattered little glass-mats made of thick absorbant board printed with the name of a brewery or distillery. 'Spearmans', where we bought our groceries, was different; a 'Protestant' shop, they didn't have a bar. Their products often bore superior brand-names and they had a greater variety of imports.

Drapers shops, although dark, were different; they had artistic window displays. The posher ones, like 'Davern's', incorporated men's wear on hangers and strategically placed shirts. Women's clothes could be intermixed with them, but never bras or knickers. When one entered, the owner or an assistant - with a tapemeasure over his or her shoulder - would approach across the wooden floor. These emporia were likely to be more open and one could walk around examing the wares, although there was still the inevitable counter. Round the walls shelves contained shirtboxes, folded lengths of cloth, shoe boxes, folded trousers and other essentials. High fashion in the form of ladies dresses and coats and skirts, men's suits and ties, ladies' hats and gentlemen's hats and caps (at that time very much in vogue), great coats and mackintoshes, would be hanging by coathangers on racks or hooks around the premises, space permitting. Everyone spoke softly in such places.

"Good morning Sir, can I help you?"

"Yes, I'd like a good warm working shirt, please."

"Certainly Sir . . . . these have just come in from England, Sir.

They're first class quality." On our examination of the exorbitant price, the self-trained 'psychologists' would note our expression of horror.

"Of course, Sir, we do have these ones made in Ireland by Portico. They're not bad". In fact, Irish manufacturers produced extremely high quality clothes at very fair prices.

"Yes please, I'll take this one." "And a tie to go with it?"

"No thanks"

"Oh and we do have a new range of . . . . " Parcels would be carefully wrapped in brown paper taken from a roll attached to the counter, and string. Drapers were helpful, but it was sometimes difficult to leave the shop only having bought essentials. The onus, of course, was on the salesman.

'Mullins' hardware shop in Main Street, and 'Feehan's', in the central block between the City Hall and 'Buckleys', were fascinating places for the tool-minded. The term DIY hadn't entered the vernacular, so everything was pretty basic. Items sold were essentials, service was often slow. Sometimes we would wait until the previous customer had finished imparting local news in exchange for further tidbits.

"Hello, Master Hugh. How's things out in Ardmayle? Are ye home for the holidays? . . . . and how's the Major and Dolly, did ye hear ? . . . . Is that so, by Gor, what can I do for ye?" Matty Dunne, and most hardware people, wore plain brown denim work coats.

"I'm looking for a good rough-toothed Bushman saw"

"Sure, I have them over here". I would be led over to where a variety of brands at different prices would be hanging from a hook.

"How much is this one?"

"Twelve and eight pence".

"I'll take it, so . . . . and I want a pound of six inch nails and a half pound of one and a half inch ovals. . . . "

Hardware shops, of their nature, were untidy. If one wanted a bargain, it would often be found under a pile of other things which hadn't been disturbed for months. There were no electric tools, but hammers, pliers and spanners would be tied in bunches and precariously hung on strings. Hinges, screws, bolts and handles would be in boxes stacked on roughly constructed shelving. Screwdrivers, chisels, gimlets and planes would rest casually where space permitted. Often they would fall and be replaced in the wrong section. Large wooden vats contained wire nails, galvanised nails, steel nails and other objects of percussion which were scooped out and weighed according to the customers' needs. Forks, spades, shovels, pitchforks and rakes would be lent up against blank walls both inside and out, and there were piles of galvanised buckets, churns and other items. Rolls of barbed wire were painful if one walked into them. Due to the amount of different items, their shapes and the way they were stored, one had to undergo contortions to avoid bumping into them.

One of my most popular shops in Cashel was 'Burke's' stationery shop; a misnomer, for this emporium sold everything from the daily papers to 'Claddagh' rings and 'Beleek' china. Michael Burke and his wife would quickly lay hands on anything demanded which wasn't displayed. From here I bought much of my collection of postcards. These were affordable and I tried to purchase each new one as it was published. Burkes also stocked local histories, particularly about the 'Rock'. *The Irish Times, the Irish Press, the Irish Independent, the Tipperary Star* and the *Farmers' Journal* would, together with the *Nationalist*, be neatly spread over the counter. Reserved or specially ordered copies of *the Field, the Irish Field, Country Life, Horse and Hound, Dublin Opinion* and the *Irish Digest* would be kept behind. Watches were displayed in special glass-fronted cabinets, the choice ranging from the cheap Scottish 'Timex' to the more expensive Swiss models, there being no digital time pieces. Other items stocked would be school exercise books, 'Royal Irish Vellum'and 'Basildon Bond' writing paper which were both in pad form and in boxes with heavily-lined sheets for those who couldn't write straight, fountain pens, pencils, cigarette lighters and their miniature rubbery balloon-like petrol refill cartridges, the odd book, pencil cases and looseleaf folders. The Burkes also bought our milk.

There were, in every town, quite a few butchers. Animals were often killed in the yards to the rear and brought into the shops where they were cut into joints. Sometimes a whole lamb would be hung from the ceiling. Offal was thrown out or given to dogs - only the best steaks or legs of lamb seemed to be sold. There were no steak and kidney pies or sausage rolls on display, just unprocessed meat.

Pork came from pork butchers. They were slightly more adventurous and displayed their pigs' heads, shanks, legs of pork, crubeens, black and white puddings and sausages. Smoked bacon or ham was usually bought from groceries.

Philomena was a girl behind the counter of the sweet shop in Quirkes Old Castle. Usually great fun, one day she was quite downhearted. Bernadette, another assistant, told me that her name-saint had been struck off the official list of saints from whom Roman Catholic parents could draw names with which to have their children baptised. I was horrified; I think she considered herself a 'non-person'.

Other 'non-persons', in the eyes of some anyway, were the unfortunate girls who had got themselves into trouble. The nuns who greeted us with our rolls of dirty laundry at the Convent door inculcated kindness and politeness. I couldn't help feeling that the 'naughty' girls in the background shadows, only mentioned by my parents and a few others in almost whispered undertones, bore an air of mystery. I craved to actually see them. I knew they were there; they did the laundry work. Like so many, I had no idea of the undignified treatment of these often innocent and sexually uneducated girls. In the eyes of their 'carers' and of their 'disgraced' families, they were the dregs of the earth, 'sluts, unclean, easy-living whores, unworthy of the task of bringing up their own children'. It is horrifying, in our more enlightened age, to realise the trauma experienced; these teenagers were denied the children which should have been God's greatest gift to them and which were given to 'more responsible' foster or adoptive parents. The work endured at the Convent no doubt took their minds off their fate. Later I began to identify some of them. They were usually attractive unsophisticated and innocent girls who would make ideal wives.

Garages combined mechanical repairs with the selling of petrol and diesel oil. Mainly petrol was dispensed, as diesel was only gradually being introduced for large trucks and for agricultural use. New cars or tins of lubricating oil were seldom prominently displayed, there being few smart grey-suited salesmen. One had to ask for a make and number of tyre or for a specific brand of oil. Mechanics weren't afraid to dirty their hands and new tins of oil bore their oily finger marks. We would be a little nervous that the grime

off their hand-wiped overalls would mess-up our leather car seats -
my mother and other women didn't appreciate the dark smudges on
their clothes as they went to parties or dances. The staff at Dowling's
were always obliging and helpful as were most of the four or five
garage owners throughout the town.

The post office was a neat purpose-built showpiece of state
support for modern architecture and craftsmanship. Near the
courthouse, it symbolised the officialdom of early twentieth century
Ireland with its mahogany counter and dividers.

Cashel has been a cathedral city for fifteen hundred years. I spent
many happy hours exploring a then toll-free Rock, hopping from
wall-top to dangerous wall-top, exploring within-wall passages and
acting an Archbishop chanting down its nave. There was no-one to
hear me. Mr. Minogue, who kept the keys and lived near the bottom
of the hill, was always obliging and informative. The Church of
Ireland St. John the Baptist's Cathedral in the town was a Georgian
edifice with a balcony and interesting wooden stalls and misericords.
Dean Jackson who recognised my embryonic interest in the Church,
made the place alive - he also shared his devotional awareness of the
Creator. He would take me on the pillion of his hefty motor bike to
such places as Knockaney in Co. Limerick where archaeologist John
Hunt was to prove that the Normans often constructed their mottes
and baileys on earlier raths. We stayed at the Rectory with Canon
Dobbin and his Indian wife. Once we made a terrifying trip to St.
Canice's cathedral in Kilkenny on the icy surface of the twisty and
dangerous road. Boney, as he was known, used to subtly suggest
that I consider a religious life.

Dedicated to St. Patrick's Rock, the Cathedral faced down John
Street, Cashel's version of London's Harley Street. Doctors and dentists
had their practices in its tall and spacious Georgian houses. St. John
the Baptist's Roman Catholic church, not the diocesan Cathedral which
was now in the more populous Thurles, was an ornate classical
building with a mosaic frieze of the rising Christ in its pedimented
front. Consecrated in 1795, it is one of the earliest Catholic churches
in the country. Below its tripartite east window is an ornate marble
altar piece and there are balconies on each side. I was never inside it
when I was young, only 'anomously' venturing some years later.

Rows of new and second-hand cycles would be stacked outside Hannigan's bicycle shop. Ryans Hotel, later burned down, was where one expected the menu to include brown 'packet' soup, overdone meat with semi-mashed potatoes, cabbage and processed peas, followed by custard and jelly trifle. I still recall the old cinema on the hill in Ladyswell street (now a fashionable restaurant), Mr. Grant who cut my hair for sixpence, the one-time workhouse on the Dublin road and the bakery run by Caldwells. In a secluded town house lived Miss Ethel Corby, a generous bridge-playing lady who rode side saddle to the Tipperary Hounds. Mrs. Cooper occupied Maryville, now the Deanery, Surgeon and Mrs. Kennedy lived on Gallows Hill and the Russells in Rock Abbey. Mrs. Shine, whose daughter Eileen and my mother shared a lifelong friendship, and who was later to build Camasbeg on the Cork road, lived outside the town. Behind this new house was the new hospital where my life was saved from blood poisoning. My left thumb, which I had cut, went septic and swelled like an egg. The poison had reached my armpit, so a tube was inserted to syphon the stuff.

Cashel was typical of any midland Irish town. Limerick, however, was our local city. Every now and then milk filters had to be purchased from the dairy shop in Roches Street or tools and gardening equipment from Boyds. Roches Stores was not that popular, but there was an excellent grocery shop in O'Connell Street, Leverett and Fry's. There my father could buy his favourite Patum Peperium, or 'Gentleman's Relish' which would be indulged sparingly on buttered toast. Todds was considered a posh shop and although my mother enjoyed buying the odd coat and skirt there, she couldn't be extravagant - in the early post-war years coupons as well as money were needed. The Stella café in O'Connell Street, to which we would go for tea, was where we all enjoyed creamy cakes. Embarrassingly for me my father, with a naughty twinkle in his eye, would mockingly raise his little finger when his cup reached his mouth, as was the wont with some of the genteel Limerick ladies. There were bookshops in Limerick, too, such as the A.P.C.K. and O'Mahonys. As the journey home was considered long there was little time to browse; besides, the milking had to be done

CHAPTER FIVE

My last term at Newells. An evolving Ireland. My dispersed family following the war years. Portora, a new educational experience – Dublin, and travels by Irish railways. Weir family people and places.

I only just passed my Common Entrance Exam. I would be leaving my preparatory school for a public school. But where was I to be sent? Harrow, where most of the Reids were educated, Wellington College, the alma mater of my uncle Mick, and my father's Cheltenham College were all discussed. Eventually, my father recalled the Weir family connections with Portora, a seventeenth century 'Royal' public school in County Fermanagh.

My last term at Newells was uneventful, the staff probably being glad to see the end of me. I can't remember what I had done wrong, but I do recall receiving the severest form of punishment, bar being expelled. Perhaps the staff were trying to force me into submission - maybe they felt that by beating me, my stupid lazy brain would function. Small offences got four or six slaps of a slipper as we bent over a special chair in the headmaster's study, slightly worse cases would be similar but with one's trousers down, and bad behaviour would mean four or six cane lashes with trousers up. If one was really bold, six of the best meant six severe strokes on one's bare behind with a thin bendy cane. This type of punishment was similar to that at Glebe House. Occasionally blood was drawn but this meant being a hero for the day as we showed off our bare buttocks in the dormitory. Because of my relationship to the headmaster and due to his desire to be impartial, I felt that the punishment was particularly harsh. I don't think it did me any harm - on the other hand, it didn't do much good. In spring 1948, when I was thirteen, those of us who were leaving were summoned to Peter's drawingroom. Nan, his wife, was also in the room as we were offered refreshments. "I suppose you know why I've called you in here?" There were three or four of us. "You are going out into the world to your respective public schools. We hope that you've been happy and that what we've taught you will be a good basis for you . . . . "

In those days, small boys didn't answer - they weren't given the chance. Some of us no doubt would have welcomed the opportunity to say "no" to much that went on. I held no feelings of resentment - Peter, Nan and many of their staff had tried their best. They were basically kind, considerate and conscientious.

Beside Peter's armchair was a pile of books. Each of us was given one. Mine, which I still have, was *Ski Patrol* by M.M. Atwater, a North American adventure published by Faber in 1945. It was inscribed "Hugh Weir with all best wishes, Peter Hope Lang, Newells 1946 - March '48" It was years before I read it, but it was a kind gesture. Peter must have known that I was particularly keen on history and travel books, and on hobbies other than ski-ing or North American wildlife, but there was little encouragement for us to further our own interests. Sports and adventure books were imposed on us and *Ski Patrol* incorporated both. The school staff didn't really sympathise with or understand the children. Disability would only be recognised if it manifested itself obviously and visually. My polio wasn't bad enough and didn't. After the presentation Nan left the room.

"Now boys, I want to tell you a few things . . . . "

The talk frightened the lives out of us. We'd never had the 'birds and the bees' before. We were so embarrassed that we hardly listened. Public school life sounded terrifying too. When we had been shaken by the hand and allowed to go, we gathered outside and discussed what we had been told. Leaving another place I had known, even if the experience wasn't wonderful, was unsettling. I was glad, a few days later, to have said my last goodbyes and be on my way.

For many years, I kept up with friends, some of whom I continued to meet when I was in London. I returned for an Old Boys re-union once and sat under the Felix Topolski etching which hung in the diningroom. But now I was facing a new life; I wanted to forget the past. I would be spending my time in Ireland where I had always been treated for what I was. Maybe I was too old to be mollycoddled, but those I knew there listened to what I had to say.

*   *   *   *   *   *   *   *   *   *   *

Members of the Church of Ireland and Protestants are encouraged to support the administration of the day, irrespective of how it has achieved its position. The rule of law is a Divine gift. Their authority comes from God and is guaranteed by the Head of State. Church members have therefore accepted the administration of British rulers in Ireland, even if they protest against malpractice and maladministration. Roman Catholics, though, have a different loyalty. Their primary rules against which they have also been known to rebel, come from Rome.

Shortly after the Normans came to Ireland in the twelfth century, King Henry II obtained a bull from Pope Adrian IV granting him the overall Lordship of the island. Celtic Ireland had gradually begun to accept religious authority and monks and clergy interchanged with continental Europeans. The religious figurehead of the Church became greater than the temporal ruler. Each was responsible to the other but in England, the Pope's authoritarianism rivalled that of the King. The Church was a well-established vehicle not only for the promulgation of religion but also of authority. So we have a divided society with no longer the misty differentiation of the past, but rather a strong core of black and white; those who accept the authority of the earthly administration and those who deny it.

In early twentieth century Ireland, those who accepted the order imposed by the Head of State were rewarded with the better positions. Those with a different outlook rebelled. When the administration was ousted, many Protestants felt neglected, in a vacuum and lost, so they left. Having for centuries accepted the unity of Great Britain and Ireland, they had intermarried throughout these islands and so had cross-insular relations and connections. Many had served in India or the colonies where, in the main, Protestants were given the responsible positions. Linked, too, with this acceptance of the status quo, was the offering of military service. Although Roman Catholics numbered those who felt the same way, many of them who rallied did so because they were unemployed. They were, however, often considered less trustworthy to the government and its supporters, even if permitted to carry weaponry. There were, of course, plenty of nationalist Protestants and many Roman Catholic Unionists. Mainly members of the Church of Ireland, most of my Irish extended family either found themselves in British Dominions, or earthbound around the Somme in wartime France. There were also both my grandmothers' mainly English kin.

* * * * * * * * * * *

In 1926, my father's sister, Brenda, married the cartoonist H.M. Bateman, to whom she gave two daughters, Diana and Monica. From 1934 they lived at Newbury. I remember staying at the house they later had at Bognor Regis on the English south coast. It was too cold to swim so we spent a lot of time in the garden. In 1948, Diana Bateman married Naval officer and artist Richard Willis, whose family home was Ayot Place in Hertfordshire, and Brenda moved to Kensington's Stafford Terrace. I was often to visit her here and met many of her distinguished friends. She had a spacious apartment round the corner from that of Cousin Margot, widow of Sir Charles Weir. Her comfortable drawingroom contained pictures by her artist friends whose work was becoming popular. One of these was Maurice Codner who had painted a portrait of my future father-in-law. Brenda also had a significant collection of netsuke. My aunt was good fun but once she embarrassed me while we were walking in the district. She had no garden of her own but loved flowers and foliage. Stopping below a 'For Sale' sign outside a select terrace house, she led me into their garden where there were flowers. "Now Hugh, lets get a few sprigs of this . . . ." said she, breaking off large blossomful branches. " . . . . its such a pity to see them go to waste".

Another time, Brenda organised a drinks party. Basically shy and not a little sensitive to the pomposity of London society, I asked her if I could act as butler. I played my role impeccably, and enjoyed my anonymity. As I proffered drinks or dishes of neatly arranged tidbits, I got little acknowledgment, let alone thanks. "Another gin and lime please. . . .", "I'd love a scotch and soda . . . . " After an hour, I changed to my suit, as suggested by Brenda. She introduced me to some of the guests she felt I should meet. "This is my nephew Hugh, over from Ireland . . . ." "Good Lord, haven't we met somewhere before?" "I've seen someone very like you recently . . . . I can't remember where". I don't think that I let more than one or two into the secret. They wouldn't have been interested. Besides visits to Margot, Brenda gave me a tremendous introduction to London. She took me to the Royal Academy where she was well known, the theatre, the zoo and to parties given by her friends.

At Stafford Terrace where Brenda lived, I would often meet Monica, her daughter. Following her marriage to her since separated husband, Barbara Hepworth's architect and sculptor colleague Michael Pine, she lived in a studio apartment overlooking Hampstead Heath. It was a privilege to be introduced to such leading artists and experts in their field. Michael, and Monica who had been awarded the 'Beaux Arts' in Paris twice, were amongst their number.

Brenda's sister Bryda, born in 1904, moved to Peldon after her mother's death in 1947. She was a keen sailor and horsewoman. At the Maltings she had cared for her mother Flora, who besides her extensive travels, drove a coach and four horses. Bryda's bungalow had a large garden which stretched towards the Mersea mudflats. Her future husband, Fitzroy Fyers had been billeted at the Abberton Maltings during the war. His Irish connections included Lord Templemore, the Marquess of Donegall, and the Percivals.

After Fitzroy and Bryda were married, they lived in a tall corner house in London's fashionable Langham Place. I remember going there. At our own wedding Fitzroy was to wear his kilt. Some years later we visited them at Strathpeffer in Scotland. Following Bryda's death in 1976, he came to stay at Ballinakella. We left him up to his relatives at Temple House in Co. Sligo. He died five years later.

Godmother Denise, daughter of my grandfather Willie Gibson's Whitridge sister in Africa, had married Kenneth Tailyour, a Colonel in the Royal Artillery. Their first child Morag was born a year after me; William came a short while later. Denise had spent a lot of her youth with my mother in Ireland. The war brought the Tailyours to the Middle and Far East, so I didn't see a lot of them until Kenneth commanded the Territorial Army in Glasgow. After 1945, they settled in Essex.

Mick and Pam Gibson, my uncle and aunt who married in 1946, were often at Park House. Chloë was two years younger than my brother. Although living near Cork, my father's cousin Edith Collison's links were mainly through correspondence. Aunt Daisy Ricketts sent me a white dotted red handkerchief every Christmas and ten shillings for my birthday, while Aunt Lilian wrote long descriptive letters from South Africa. She was to be one of the most important people in my life.

'Tante Lil' as she signed her correspondence, was William Gibson's youngest sister. With her surveyor husband, she had committed herself to a 7,000 acre South African farm named Wilton Valley. She hoped that I would succeed to her property and to an exciting life in the Transvaal; however, I wasn't happy with apartheid and my spiritual home was Ireland. I had had enough changes and needed stability. I was bored with family stories of lions and tigers but Aunt Lilian was special. She had left Rockforest against the wishes of her parents and had created her own exciting life. The thought of following in her footsteps was enticing, but I was falling on my own feet. Eventually Tante Lil sold Wilton Valley and moved to Bothas Hill in Natal. There she finished, on my thirty-fifth birthday, her autobiography *A Lion to Market* which was published in Capetown two years later. My mother, my brother and I would each receive a third of the proceeds.

* *

Portora was different to my previous schools. I can't remember my first journey there. I presume that, as he was about the only other boy from our area, I joined Ricky Jackson, the Dean of Cashel's son. I do recall, however, being taken to my dormitory in the moated Redoubt, a sixteenth century hilltop battery which had also been a military hospital. It was about one kilometre from the school itself and necessitated a surburban walk early every morning and late at night.

I was made feel at home by those there since the beginning of the school year. Wilfred McOstrich hailed from Cork where his family had for generations special privileges at St. Anne's, Shandon; P.D.

Portora Royal School, Enniskillen

Warrington and McKenna were, I think, from Dublin and A J. Mitchel from the North. I had known none of them before but they made me welcome. Indeed, apart from a few minor circumstances, I was accepted by Portorans as an equal, one of their own.

Boys at Portora Royal School were divided into four houses: Ulster, Leinster, Connaught and my own Munster. The school had been established at Lisnaskea on the Upper Erne. James I gave it a charter in 1618, and it was moved to Schoolhouse Lane in Enniskillen twenty-five years later. In 1777, the substantial present building was erected facing over the town from the summit of a high drumlin above the river. At the end of the hilly point facing north over Lower Lough Erne was Portora Castle, built by the then Governor of Enniskillen, Sir William Cole.

The earliest students were members of local families and included several of my Weir forebears: George, William and Lancelot Carleton, a number of Hamiltons and the Reverend Thomas King who was given the living of Swords, Co. Dublin by his kinsman Archbishop King. Amongst later scholars were Henry Francis Lyte who wrote the hymn *Abide with Me* and Oscar Wilde, whose name was seldom mentioned. Sam Beckett the playwright was also an Old Portoran.

Many of my contemporaries emigrated to Canada. Of members of the Old Portora Union whose addresses are recorded, about thirty percent are now in Northern Ireland, fifteen in different parts of the South, twenty five percent in Canada, Australia and the New World, and a considerable twenty two percent in Great Britain; this must be due to poor work opportunities, rather than a lack of patriotism. However, at least ten of my contemporaries have become senior army officers, four are bishops, at least seven work as medical doctors and two or three are professors of academia, not a bad record for one of Europe's westernmost secondary schools. As the establishment was absorbed into the Grammar School system to help overcome running costs, and due to political circumstances, there are now few southerners; it seems that nearly all come from the west of Northern Ireland. This is a great pity as it denies these young people the opportunity to live with those from another jurisdiction and the lightening of their politically-influenced lives. There is, however, a useful twinning with the Roman Catholic Clongowes Wood College in Co. Kildare.

The school buildings at Portora are approached through the magnificent war memorial gates erected to the memory of the Rea brothers at the end of Willoughby Place to the north west of Enniskillen. I was present when the Governor of Northern Ireland, Lord Wakehurst, undertook the symbolic opening. The four Corinthian columns had originally been part of the front portico of Innismore Hall on Upper Lough Erne. The poor Governor was castigated by staff, the more snobbish or traditional boys, and some citizens of the town for having the audacity to do the task in his shirt sleeves, even though it was a roasting day. As a uniformed member of the Combined Cadet Force Guard of Honour, I understood.

The tree scattered drive looped to the top of Portora Hill where there was a cannon-protected terrace in front of the main buildings. Here, in the centre, is the original seven bay three storey block with its basement. The ground floor windows were huge while those at the top were quite small; the latter threw light into what was to become my dormitory when I was moved from the Redoubt.

On each side of the main building, wings were added in the 1830s with indentations fronted by colonnades. Behind, approached by steps, were the main entrance doors to the school. On the right was the headmaster's house - not a part of the school where one wanted to be, or to be seen although Douglas Graham was not intimidating. The other vast pannelled door led into the main hall. Newspapers would be laid out on a long sloping desk to the right, behind which the banisters indicated a stairs to the basement. The front rooms of the main building, also accessed from here, included an office and the well-stocked library. There were fascinating books about Fermanagh, many of which contained references to my family. There was also a copy of Laurence Sterne's *Tristam Shandy* which I recall struggling through with a determination to finish. Across the hall was the music room and to the left, down some steps, the diningroom at the near end of which was the Head's table and, at the far end, the kitchen. Walls of these rooms bore rolls of honour and portraits of previous headmasters, some of whom looked terrifyingly stern. Inside the hall to the left and through another door was the narrow locker room where I kept my valuables.

The Steele Hall was named after the Rector of Monea's father. This is where we assembled for our morning and evening prayers, for plays and entertainment. I remember Mrs. Trimble, a great school supporter whose husband owned the *Imperial Reporter,* clapping and calling "bravo" at the appropriate times. It also had its Rolls of Honour and a monument to hymn-writer Lyte. Under the Steele Hall were classrooms which I associate with prep, as we termed homework, and adjoining them the tuck shop, changing rooms and a gymnasium. Behind the school was a large separate classroom block and, at an awkward angle to the other building, the since demolished Leinster House. Towards the castle, the top of the hill was levelled as a games field. It overlooked the Narrows where the river Erne entered the lower lake. Below the other side, a flat mud plain was used for playing rugger. The boat club was down a steep incline below the headmaster's house.

The main road to South Donegal curved round the school hill past the twentieth century preparatory school, Gloucester House. I never saw the establishment's inside but a lot of my friends had studied there before moving up to the main school.

Only a short distance beyond it and on the other side of the road was Lovers' Lane, on the right of which was a delightful cottage known as The Orchard. We would buy apples from Mrs. Maguire and her daughter. They were a link with the outside world. Manus' Quarry and Kinarla Lough to which we used to walk, family friends and haunts such as Dunbar House where my great-great-great-grandmother had spent her youth, and Hall Craig were beyond.

Portora was in the parish of Rossorry. The hilltop cruciform nineteenth century parish church was quite a distance from the school and few enjoyed the Sunday walks to Morning Prayer. There was, though, the consolation of knowing that the afternoon would be free. We dreaded Archdeacon Pratt's extended sermons, but the monuments on the walls were interesting. Little did I then know that, thanks to the then rector's successor Canon Howe, I would be invited to preach from that pulpit myself one Sunday in the 1970s.

Often we would go to St. Macartin's Cathedral in the town centre. This was more fun as it meant passing through the nationalist area where we bought the Irish Sunday papers. On arrival at the church, we would join the queue behind the congregation as they slowly shuffled in.

The pinnacled and buttressed gothic Cathedral was really a parish church, the Bishop's main throne (Cathedra) being in Clogher. It was built in 1842 on the site of an earlier eight hundred seat edifice. Close by, an ancient stone tablet had been erected to the memory of one of my Rynd ancestors. The largish six bay nave with its side aisles and delicate spire was entered through the tower from the west door. We would make our way to the front of the left aisle where a block of pews was reserved. Above us was the gallery, held up by cast iron columns, which encircled three sides. In the nave beside us sat significant members of the parish including, quite often, the then Prime Minister of Northern Ireland, Lord Brookeborough - he tried hard to ignore the traditional misbehavings of bored young boys. There were few smiles from the smart and usually suited members of the congregation.

If the sermon went on too long, one book would be dropped, and then another until it was obvious to the preacher that the pattern was orchestrated. Dean Macmanaway was a kindly soul and I don't think we were ever reprimanded. On our return walk, Headmaster Douglas Graham who was an ex rugby cap for Ireland and a distant cousin, would give a lift to four or five of us in his newly acquired American-style Ford. This was usually after we had purchased our papers. No doubt he had been chatting with members of the congregation. Only a very small number of us boarders were left for weekends. The others were either day boys or those whose homes were near enough for them to be weekly boarders.

*   *   *   *   *   *   *   *   *   *   *

Getting to Portora was an adventure. As with my previous schools, clothes were carefully recorded and neatly packed into our trunks, and although tuck boxes weren't compulsory, as I still had mine, I used it. Sweets and chocolates being rationed, we would be purchasing Ovaltine or Horlicks tablets in the tuck shop. The confections we imported each term didn't last long. Other necessities were books, collections and hobbies. We would swap our surplus stamps or cigarette cards.

When trunk, tuckbox and small case were fully packed, I would haul them to the porch at Ardmaylebeg. Papa would ensure that I had enough pocket money. He and Mama would expect a letter as soon as I arrived at school; remember, we had no telephone. The car would be driven to the front of the house and I'd load up. The dogs, Cronk the raven, the horses and even some of the cattle got a pat and a promise that I'd soon be back. As my father stayed to look after my young brother, I would bid a tearful farewell. I was on my way, my mother at the wheel.

At Goolds Cross station, vehicles would be parked in front of the neatly kept grey stone station house. Some of the occupants we would know. Occasionally Ricky Jackson would join us, though others such as the Harrises of Golden or the Pococks of Clonmel would probably have boarded at Limerick Junction. The entrance hall echoed as my mother asked for my ticket to Dublin. "A single half-fare to Kingsbridge station, please. What time does it get in?" "Eleven thirty-five, Ma'am". Waiting on the platform, lower than those in England, we experienced an eerie silence. People muttered to each other, while others walked up and down, and looked at the time.

As we began to be slightly more relaxed, we would hear the distant rumble of the approaching train before it slowed to a stop with a squeal of metal brakes. Steam would hiss from under and around the huge engine. "Goolds Cross . . . . Goolds Cross Station . . . . passengers for Thurles, Ballybrophy, Maryborough, Sallins and Dublin aboard . . . ." A station master or railwayman would walk the length of the platform calling "Goolds Cross . . . . Goolds Cross, Goolds Cross station . . . ." Very few people got off the train coming from the south for most were on their way to the capital, or to Dun Laoghaire as emigrants travelling for the mail boat to Holyhead or Liverpool.

My family was not into embracing - there would be no hug or even a kiss at times of parting. Manliness, especially as regards young boys, dictated a wave and perhaps a hand kiss. Having ensured that my luggage was loaded, I'd locate a seat, at a window if possible. I'd then unhook the strap in the door, let down the heavy wood-framed window, lean out, and call "good-bye Mummy. . . . see you soon!" She would reply "don't forget to write . . . . have a safe journey. Did Daddy give you pocket money? . . . . Good . . . ." There would be a loud whistle and several blasts of steam as the train gathered its slow momentum. My mother, waving from the platform, faded into the distance. I would heave the window up and sit, if possible facing forwards.

Looking out of the train window, I'd recall my visits to or descriptions I had read about places I recognised as we rattled through the Tipperary countryside. The same jargon as at Goods Cross would be repeated at other stations - Thurles was always particularly busy. At Ballybrophy junction, anxious fellow passengers would ask each other ". . . . are we on the right train for Dublin?"

Here the main line from Cork joined another for Nenagh, Birdhill
and Limerick, and carriages could be separated ". . . . Passengers for
Roscrea, Nenagh . . . . change here . . . . Dublin passengers stay on
the train."

Reaching Kingsbridge, as Heuston Station was known, was a mad
scramble as everybody rose to put on their coats and don their hats
well before disembarking. Suitcases, paper bags, fishing rods and an
assortment of other items were lowered from the netting racks above
the seats. Some were accidentally dropped on the heads of
unsuspecting passengers who hadn't yet vacated their seats: "oops,
so sorry . . . . " "ah, don't worry . . . . can I give you a hand . . . . "
Travel on Irish trains was always friendly and passengers co-
operated with each other and chatted. Sometimes the train hit the
buffers at a faster rate than the engine driver had no doubt intended.
The queue for the door would tumble into each other with the jolt
and young children would be almost squashed in the meleé.

Kingsbridge station had a crackly loud speaker. Everybody knew
where the latest leviathon to arrive had come from but almost every
station was called out: "The train now standing in platform one is the
eight o'clock train from Cork, Mallow, Limerick Junction, Thurles,
Ballybrophy, Sallins . . . ." The arriving passengers, some of them
screeching in delight as they hugged girlfriends or fiancées, would
make their way towards the gate at the end of the platform, some
walking quickly or running, few ambling at a slower pace. I had to
get a porter to transfer my luggage to the taxi rank. Most Dublin taxi-
cabs were old American saloons rather than the squat London
vehicles, but some of the drivers weren't particularly friendly. I used
to wonder how reliable their rather bashed looking meters were, if
they had had them installed at all. Luggage loaded, I would hop into
the spacious back seat. The driver would slam the door as he made
his way round to the front.

"Where to, Sir?" "Amiens Street, please". "Are you'se catching the
Belfast train?" "Yes, as far as Dundalk . . . ." "You've plenty of time
then." We would pass the Guinness breweries on our right - often
one of the trains delivering their stout would be leaving through a
'hole' in their wall to cross the street and join the main line at
Kingsbridge. " . . . . cursed nuisance, them things . . . .are you on the

way to school?" "I am, yes". "God, I don't envy you. Used to hate it
myself . . . . Brothers . . . . Christian Brothers . . . ." We would
continue along the south bank and - there were no one-way streets
- cross O'Connell bridge before turning right up the straight Amiens
Street to the station, now known as Connolly, which was visible
ahead. I would thank and pay the driver and struggle up the steps
for the cloakroom where I'd leave my luggage. Having obtained a
ticket, I would descend to the street.

Dublin was safe, even for a 'culchie' public school boy dressed in
blazer and trousers who didn't know the city that well. Soon though,
I got to know and love the characterful Dublin that still was Joyce,
or O'Casey or Yeats or O'Connell, or Parnell, or O'Brien whose
statues graced the area, a concoction of just about anyone who had
written about it or been associated with it. Dublin was 'Anna Livia',
the dirty Liffey that held it together and yet divided it north and
south. It was exciting. Men, women, children, bicycles, paperboys,
taxis, buses, trams, fruit and vegetable sellers, and 'religious' jostled
as one. Now and again friends or acquaintances would meet, chat,
and then part as if refuelled; it was life, real life, Dublin life. The
variety of shops was staggering. Untidy and dirty many may have
been, but they were full of all sorts of things, some items unsold
since before the Emergency. Even looking in the windows could be
fascinating - that's often all I did as I hadn't the money to buy.
Although the city looked somewhat drab and devoid of today's
multicoloured advertising, its people made it vibrant and colourful.

I hadn't more than a few shillings of pocket money but there was
one place I always visited. Cafola's Icecream Parlour between the
General Post Office and the Liffey bridge, had a downstairs. There I
would join the many patrons, often sharing a table, and order a
'Knickerbocker Glory'. These multi-layered ice creams in slender
glasses were huge. There was one glamourous waitress who used to
squeeze my shoulder as she passed, having delivered their 'specials'
to other customers. She would call me "Love". There were antique
shops and bookshops to visit. Climbing to the top of Nelson's Pillar,
little was I to know that years later I would hear the explosion of its
destruction by subversives. From the top of the stone monument
with its tiny circular staircase, with friends and unaware of the

possible dangers to pedestrians below, we dropped pennies narrow side downwards. We then went down to see if they had penetrated the pavement. Later visits, when I was a little braver and able to judge the time it took to get back to the station, I'd go to the Savoy and see most of, if not all, a matinée film. It was a luxurious cinema with carpety seats. The one at Cashel, being rural, and those at school, were merely assembly halls.

Back at Amiens Street Station, Dublin boys and those from the south and east would be gathering near the ticket gate with their parents. In Ireland, a generally more family orientated attitude to that which I had previously experienced meant a closeness of my pals to their parents which I envied. Sometimes I would be called over. "Hey Ma, hey Pa, this is Weir. He's in Munster and is related to Mr. Steele. . . . " "Good to meet you; maybe you'll keep an eye on Joe for the journey?" was a usual request. "Of course, I'd be delighted." I was usually very content to share their company. Eventually we'd board the carriages which would be separated from the 'Enterprise' Express at Dundalk, most Portorans finding themselves together.

Slowly the long Great Northern Railway's or Corás Iompair Eireann train, the two companies sharing the line, would start 'chumphing' out of the station. There had been hasty last minute embraces, hand shakes and shouted messages before we were on our way. The backs of north Dublin houses, factories, shops and warehouses, clotheslines and waving housewives were shared as the train rattled over rivers and canals. The sea faded into the distance on the right, beyond the shingly Portmarnock' and Skerries' beaches. Drogheda necessitated locating small change for, as we crossed the river Boyne, we'd throw coins into the river over the high iron bridge.

When the train reached Dundalk, our carriages would be disconnected and linked to a small locomotive for one of the most fascinating train experiences. The north-western line passed through drumlin country. Travelling in and out of South Armagh's border country, our first stop was Innishkeen, a few metres into the North. Cullaville, although north of the border had its station in the south, whereas the first major stop at Castleblayney was well into County Monaghan.

The journey onwards through Ballybay and Newbliss to Clones took us around each of the hundreds of drumlins, little round glacial hills. As we leant out of the windows we often became quite close to the engine as it manoeuvered each particular loop. In the carriages there would occasionally be chickens, even pigs and calves. There were whole families too, housewives, farmers or children in all types of apparel.

Once I boarded a compartment already occupied by one person, most likely a local farmer's wife. She had embarked at Dundalk but we had said little to each other. When the train pulled into Innishkeen station, another woman got in. The conversation was riveting.

"Hi!"

"Hi . . . are ye goin far?"

"Aye".

"Were ye in town?"

"Aye".

"Cold enough isn't it . . . ."

"Aye". "They don't heat these trains enough."

"Aye".

There was silence for some minutes. "Are ye's gettin off at 'Blayney?"

"Aye".

They did. No further conversation was shared as they dispersed.

The southern border station at Clones was exciting for, although Dundalk was also a customs station and we were sometimes questioned and searched there, this was the last town before crossing into County Fermanagh. There were long delays as identification papers were scrutinised, especially if there were strangers. Customs officials boarded each compartment, searched under the seats and looked into selected luggage from the racks above our heads. There were no corridors, so they left each compartment the way they had entered. Mainly for the devilment, we southerners smuggled things then unobtainable in the north such as sweets. Cigarettes and whiskey were also on our 'dares' list.

One year, somebody came up with a clever idea. As the train pulled into the station and before the customs search, items such as cigarettes would be hung on the outer handles of the doors away from the platform, and the windows closed. It was 'years' before an official happened to observe the other side of the train from the outside. Each handle was occupied by a well wrapped item of contraband. Clones was also a junction for Monaghan, and Belfast through Armagh. There would be loud cheers, whichever direction we were travelling, as we crossed the border. The next station north was Newtown Butler. Here the customs people were equally dedicated to their task. "Anything to declare, Sir? May I see in that suitcase please?" "Would you mind removing your jacket please, Sir" The police would also seek proof of identity; we youngsters were usually ignored, but some travellers got a gruelling. Arriving at Enniskillen station, there would be bustle and an air of efficiency.

*   *   *   *   *   *   *   *   *   *

A normal day at Portora was like that at any other public school. Sundays, for me were different, and half terms also special. As my parents had to work the farm and look after Guy, it was all but impossible for them to visit me. My father, however, did come one half term. It was wonderful to share friends and to show him family haunts. He also took me to places he had known in his youth. He stayed in Enniskillen's most popular commercial hotel and we met each day for trips to Monea, Hall Craig, and to Fivemiletown where his only close cousin remaining in the area, Edmund Weir, still owned Corcreevy House, now a sad ruin on the edge of the town. He also got on well with the Reverend W.B. Steele, and his cousins Mrs. Steele and Miss Reade at Castletown. We spent quite a lot of time with Mr. Kerr at the Enniskillen Club - he was interested in the Weirs and associated families and was delighted to meet Papa. My mother never managed the journey. One half term, though, Percy Harris took the boys who came from Tipperary to Bundoran where we dined at the Great Northern Hotel on its promentary beyond the town.

Most Sunday afternoons, those of us who stayed at school would gang up for walks or, in the summer, cycle rides. Quite often we would involve ourselves in harmless mischief. Once, a group of us were walking around the shore of a nearby lake when we spotted a rowing boat which looked as though it was no longer in use. After bailing the water out, we embarked and soon found ourselves in the middle of the lake. Somebody saw us from a nearby bridge and reported us. At lunch the following day, Douglas Graham requested the name of the boy wearing a dark raincoat who was standing in the boat and giving orders. Would this offender report to his study. The sensible and apt punishment was that I would lead the party down town and personally apologise to the boat-owner, a citizen of some significance and a friend of the school. Another time several of us got cut off from the mainland on an island. We had scrambled over a vegetation-covered quaking bog and couldn't find our way back. It was a most uncomfortable experience.

One summer Sunday, three of us cycled to Ballyshannon and into Co. Donegal. It was a roasting day and on the return journey we became exhausted. Somewhere along the southern shore of Lower Lough Erne we decided to stop and, as we had no money, ask for a drink of water. Each took a different house. The single storey thatched farmhouse I chose was that of a wonderful couple. I knocked on the door: "Good evening, I'm sorry to bother you but . . . . " "Of course ye may, son. Come in . . . . " The kitchen table was laid for two. In its centre was an enormous bowl of floury potatoes and a large jug of skimmed milk. "Will ye's join us for a wee bit to eat?" I refused, but it took little pressure to change my mind. "Well, maybe just a small bit". My hostess dished me an enormous plateful of potatoes, semi-mashing them as she did. In the dip she formed, a large pat of homemade butter was dropped. My glass was filled to the brim. "Get that down now, dear. That should help to get ye's going again." That meal was the best I ever indulged in; it is still a vivid recollection. I was unable to finish my repast for my pals, having also been offered and having accepted similar snacks, appeared at the door. Thanking my kind hosts, I took leave as the three of us embarked on our stimulated return.

Blacklion is a small village across the Cavan border from its Fermanagh twin, Belcoo. Situated between the Upper and Lower Loughs MacNean, it was a smugglers paradise. We thought so anyway. Because it was only about twenty kilometres from

Enniskillen, we would often cycle our way to the first shop and pub over the border. Here we would replenish our stocks of sweets and items not available in the North. One day, as we returned, our pockets bulging with contraband, we suddenly got wind that the customs were following. Whether they were targeting us or not, we slipped up a bye-road and hid in a graveyard until all was clear.

No way nowadays could we do some of the things we got up to. A short distance from the school was Manus' Quarry. It was a great place for fossils and I had quite a collection. In its centre, away from its towering cliffs, was a store house for explosives used to blast the rock. Beneath it was a drain big enough for a young person to squeeze through and into the locked building. Inside were sticks of gelagnite and boxes of small detonators. Each of us who had joined up for the day dared the others to steal a detonator. We all did. Within weeks one boy blew up part of a wall near the castle and others destroyed the lock on mathematics master 'Bottle' Barnes' desk by detonating his keyhole. We were by no means perfect.

One of my favourite weekend occupations was the fishing trips I made to a railway bridge over the Sillies river. The Sligo, Leitrim and Manorhamilton railway train would signal its approach by the narrow guage lines which would rattle well before it came into sight. I caught quite a few small trout and coarse fish.

Many Sundays and half terms were spent at Castletown, a large plain house overlooking Monea Castle. The castle, built by a Hamilton forebear, was owned by Weir kinsfolk, the Kings and, in the eighteenth century, John Brien whose daughter Wilhelmina Ruth Brien married Robert Weir in 1857. Two years previously Mrs. Weir's nephew, Rev. Arthur George Reade had wed Mary Weir. In 1919, her step grand-daughter Elinor married the Reverend William Babington Steele, Rector of Devenish. The Steeles and Elinor's younger sister Constance lived in the house.

Mr. and Mrs. Steele and Miss Reade were wonderful and I was welcome at any time. Their house was a significant repository of Weir family items, Hall Craig being no longer in family hands. I would arrive by bicycle usually early on a Sunday morning. There was always a routine. The ancient open-topped car, with or without its hood, would be brought round to the front of the house by Mr.

Steele himself. I would open the little carriage-style doors as the ladies embarked and then climb in myself. We would then slowly drive down 'the Long Shot' to St. Molaise's Church at the bottom of the hill. As we pulled in to the car-park in front of the gate, the men of the parish would stand as a guard of honour. The car doors would be opened by the bystanders and we'd all make our way into the building with the men following. Most of the women would already be inside. I was always put in the Weir family pew up front. Afterwards we would return to the house for lunch.

Mr. Steele was personally restoring the castle for it hadn't yet been taken over by the government. He undertook a lot of excavating and was rebuilding some of the interior walls. Apparently those of the bawn had been removed and used to construct Hall Craig farm buildings. He shared his project with me and often asked for 'advice'. I was also consulted about the trading in of his old car. I suggested an Austin A.30 and, the next visit, was proudly greeted with the new vehicle with which he was delighted. I wish I had taken in more of

St. Molaise's Church, Monea

what this well read and kindly clergyman had told me. He hoped
that I would consider the church or become a historian. His *History
of the Parish of Devenish,* the last copy of which, beside his own, he
gave me is a mine of information. He knew even more in his head.

*   *   *   *   *   *   *   *   *   *   *

Over the hills from Castletown was Hall Craig. The Scotts were also
welcoming and would invite me in. Kenneth who had a heavy 500
c.c motor bike, and Hazel enjoyed showing me the place to which
they, too, were devoted. They had taken over the property after my
great uncle had died not that long before.

I had hated school before Portora. However, for the first time in
my educational life I was acknowledged for who I am. I just wasn't
able to catch up with my work, partly due to previous experiences.
There were some great teachers such as 'Buddy' Halpin who taught
geography as I had never before experienced, Michael Murfet a
classicist, L.S. Breadon, Frankie Rowlette and Mr. Butler, the Bursar,
who enjoyed explaining the mundanities of running the place to
those who were interested. Of course, there were others too. The
food was also good. Breakfast was porridge followed by rashers or
eggs or beans but nearly always with triangular potato cakes. Lunch
was not soaked in gravy or custard as I had previously experienced,
and high tea was a filling Northern Irish meal. I tried my best at
Rugby and was selected for house competitions. There wasn't that
compulsion to play team games I had previously experienced. As
long as we were meaningfully occupied, we could indulge in
boating, running, walking, physical training or cycling. Douglas
Graham's suggestion that I organise a pack of beagles would have
come off, had I continued at school. I was also a member of the
Combined Cadet Force, once going to camp at Ballykinlar in Co.
Down where Eamonn de Valera had been imprisoned.

As I was no longer forced to exert my physical functions, the
effects of polio were negligible and so I was usually able to keep up
with the others. My parents were convinced that any of my problems
were due to laziness. Perhaps some were.

When the end of my last term at Portora came, I suddenly felt terribly sad, albeit lonely and insecure. My contemporaries, and friends such as B.K. Glover, Colin Dunlop, Ricky Jackson, Brian Kidd, Timothy Webb, the Todds of Coleraine, R.J.B. Palmer, Nigel Umfreville-Moore and Mitchell would all be staying on. The 'club' stayed and it was only I who was leaving, the rest continuing their bonds of friendship. Only two of us were departing, as far as I can recall, the other being the more senior Jimmy Moore who retired as Church of Ireland Bishop of Conner in 2001. I had no idea what was ahead and I didn't think I was wanted at home, but home was my only base and I loved my parents, my brother, our dogs and animals, the house and farm and the general locality. Fear, however, was the predominant sensation.

"Good-bye, Hugh". "Good-bye, Weir". "If I'm down your way I'll look you up". "You're welcome to stay anytime". "We'll miss you". For the first time when leaving school, tears began to well up in my eyes. I did see a few old Portorans again, especially those who lived nearby, but it wasn't until I returned to Ireland in the late fifties that I was able to catch up with those I meet today. Mr. Butler continued to correspond from his new school in the English Lake District and Douglas Graham from the more southerly public school he took over shortly after I'd gone. Other teachers, acquaintances and friends took an interest in my future, too.

Monea Castle

CHAPTER SIX

Ireland , my first employment. Military service - Britain, the Far East and Cyprus. My twenty-first birthday, and demobilisation.

As I was not a successful student, my parents were concerned about my future. Suggestions as to what I should do were presented. "What about going to New Zealand as a potential sheep farmer or trainee dairy farm manager; you could always contact your relations?" "Look, Hugh. Here's an advertisement; the Australians are subsidising the fare to those wishing to emigrate there." "What about taking up that offer to study for the Church in Saskatchewan?" I don't think I was ever asked what I would like to do; would I care to manage the farm or even join the family team. When I suggested that I take on the out-farm and set up a business there to help our ailing finances, the idea was rapidly crushed. I liked farming but both my father and my mother felt there was no future in Ireland. I should emigrate.

The situation at home was getting strained; I didn't want to take up the various parental suggestions. Quite keen to go to New Zealand or, though at the time I had no real vocation, to be trained for the Ministry in Canada, most of my own submissions such as greeting card production, writing, archaeology or agricultural machinery sales and maintenance were condemned. "Our family has never been in trade. The army's what you should be in, my boy. . . . or what about the navy?"

From the time I left Portora, I had been working hard to relieve the workload at home. We were now shortstaffed with an increasingly large herd and a larger milkround, but there was no suggestion of taking me in as a partner.

Fred Kennedy of Limerick, a nephew of Mrs. Studdert of Cullane, had a brother who had just bought a farm at Rathmore near Naas, Daffy Lodge. Would I be interested in helping him, and learning farm management? I jumped at the opportunity, especially as I had just been wrongly accused of smashing iron guttering which could have been re-utilised. The lengths were already cracked and leaking.

Soon I was on the bus to Naas. We had a breakdown on the Curragh and I was worried because Basil Kennedy, my boss to be, would be expecting my arrival. I didn't want to keep him waiting. Thankfully he had been in touch with Coras Iompair Eireann, the bus company, before setting out and so we arrived about the same time.

Daffy Lodge was a pleasant, rural, tree-surrounded two storey farmhouse approached by a short drive from Rathmore village with its church, St. Colmcilles, and Giltrap's shop. It was almost equidistant from Naas, Rathcoole and Blessington. The farm, although not large, stretched from reasonably good roadside land around the house to reclaimed bog. Basil Kennedy's mother Rose Mary Studdert and his brother Fred, whose wife Bin was always elegant as she rode side-saddle, were friends of my parents. He introduced me to interesting people such as Baron de Roebeck, and the Cornwalls who lived towards Rathcoole.

After work sometimes, Basil would collect a neighbour and we would proceed to rather boring Macra na Feirme meetings at Blessington. One weekend I went home to Ardmaylebeg and returned with my bicycle which enabled me to explore. I received the princely sum of fifteen shillings a week (ninety-five euros) and my keep. However, even in those days I felt I should have been doing better. Eventually it was mutually agreed that, although the experience had been beneficial to both parties, I would return home and re-organise my life. I was not leaving my employer without help for he already had a young Macnamara from O'Briensbridge who had been with him for some time. Basil Kennedy now lives in Arizona.

* * * * * * * * * * *

It was no time before our neighbour and fellow dairy-farmer, 'String' de Wilton, asked if I would help him. I readily agreed and spent some months milking and generally assisting him and his wife, Han, on their farm at Clonoulty. This gave me an opportunity to think out my future and weigh up my various options.

Talk of events in Korea and the fears of Communist domination of the world were rampant. It was natural that I would be caught up in the sentiments expressed so forthrightly by my father and his friends. They were deeply and sincerely concerned about the future. A threatening and evil philosophy seemed to be just as dangerous as Nazi-ism and was getting wholesale support from the politically uneducated, just as Adolf Hitler's 'National Socialism' had in so very recent times. "Hugh, your future is at stake now more than ever; have you really considered an army career? Remember, the Weirs have always been chivalrous. I, your father, was in the army and nearly all your ancestors have fought for their country. . . . " " But . . . ." " . . . . or, of course . . . . what is right for the world." I was caught. There were no other job opportunities ahead. I passionately wanted to stay in Ireland but the work just wasn't there. As the situation was the same throughout the country and even in neighbouring Britain, it was narrowed down to two real options. I would either have to emigrate to the New World like many of my schoolmates or else – if I did not get posted to a Malay rubber plantation – join one of the forces. British and American troops were both serving the United Nations Organisation in Korea. The temptation to join the Americans was over-ruled in favour of my father's old regiment, The Royal Norfolks or Ninth of Foot. I could either sign on for two years as a national serviceman – there was no national service in Ireland, but it was compulsory for citizens or residents of Britain – or join the regular army for an initial three. Because the prospects of promotion would be better, due to the higher pay, and because I could have a greater chance of choosing my unit, I opted for the latter; most of the regiment was already in the Far East. In 1952, after my eighteenth birthday, I departed for Norwich.

*   *   *   *   *   *   *   *   *   *   *

Troops marched hither and thither on the huge parade ground of the Royal Norfolk Regiment's red brick Britannia Barracks when I arrived at the similarly built guard house, having struggled up the hill. "Good afternoon, Sir. . . . " "Don't call me bloody 'Sir', can't you see I'm only a sergeant, mate". I had received my introduction to the most significant rank in the British Army. Sergeants ran the show. "My name's Weir. I've been in touch . . . ." "You're the bloody rookie from Ireland, right?" "Yes, Sergeant". Shown in to the guard commander's office, I signed the necessary forms. I was to proceed to the Quartermaster's Store to be togged out with my uniform. From there, a corporal would show me to my designated barrack-room. I was to be in 'C' Company of the First Battalion. My eight digit number for use on all occasions was mine exclusively.

The barrack room was a huge nineteenth century high-ceilinged hall with a wooden floor. Heated by an enormous pot-bellied solid fuel stove, it had rows of neatly organised beds on either side, like those in a hospital. Each soldier had, almost ridiculously, laid out his blankets and kit to conform with the standard. Clothes, kitbags and backpacks were meticulously clean and pressed, and spare black boots shone with the spit and polish used to embellish them. Hours were spent dipping rags into Kiwi or Nugget tins of polish, spitting on the toe caps, and then softly rubbing the black polish in small circles until it had stuck to the surface, a softer rag being used to buff the results. "O.K. mate," said the Corporal, "it won't be long till the others get back, so I'll leave you here to sort your kit out".

I was on my own. The prospect of being confronted, a stranger, by thirty or forty men already acquaintanced with each other was daunting. Even the language would be difficult, people here speaking broad Norfolk interspersed with four letter words. Conscious of my plummy accent, I recalled my father's condemnation of the Fermanagh lilt I had at Portora, even though his mother had commented that her father-in-law used to say "ut" rather than "it" when referring to, say, the weather.

I didn't have much time for contemplation, for beyond the open windows could be heard the march of hobnailed boots. "Compnaaay . . . halt . . . . diss . . . . miss". Within seconds the wooden floor reverberated like a thousand hammers as the rest of 'C' Company each made for their own space. There was no time for idle chatter as supper was about to be served, so I nervously joined my future mates at the canteen. Gradually we got to know each other as we shared army life and I participated in the simple conversations of similarly-aged young men from all walks. Some, possibly due to the circumstances of war, couldn't even sign their names, using a cross, even for legal purposes. The early weeks were spent at drill, hours of marching from one end of the parade ground to the other. "Come on Smith, you f - g idiot, keep in step. . . . left . . . . left . . . . left, ... right, left . . . ." "Keep your arms up, Baxendale . . . . " Luckily, there were other Irishmen along with me, mostly from Dublin or Belfast. We were automatically branded as 'Paddies'.

Soon, after a number of interviews with my commanding officer and others, I was distinguished as an O.R.1. As an 'Other Ranks One', I was considered potential officer material. I had to prove myself, though. Somewhere in the south of England, I think Aldershot, I was put through assault courses, drill tests, leadership tests and generally assessed. One interviewer was a Scotsman. ". . . . Name. . . .?" "Weir, Sir", "from . . . .?" "Ireland, Sir . . . ." "That's enough. Another of you bloody Irish over because you can't live in your own country". Unfortunately I hadn't the guts to reply in the way I'd liked to have done, and should have done. My attitude, I discovered later, was recorded as "capable of dumb insolence."

On my return to Norwich, I was sent to Brigade Headquarters at Victoria Barracks in nearby Bury St. Edmund's. Here I joined like-minded O.R.Is with whom, because they were more aware of the world and were educated to a similar standard, I could converse and share life more easily. Thorne - who was to become a senior staff officer, Bosanquet who later excelled in the communications field, and Paddy Forde - an Irish student doctor - were amongst my companions. The latter had an ancient open canvas-hooded 'Austin 7' which had its bonnet tied down with straps - several of us would join him on the town, imbibing the local Greene King's beer, barley wine or strong cider. Here, too, I was to purchase my own Triumph which had belonged to a comrade posted abroad. It was cheap and I had to keep up small regular payments for some time, our pay being minimal. I overshot an unsigned 'T' junction and the vehicle disintegrated over a felled tree stump. I don't think I ever received full payment when I sold what was left.

Apart from the lengthy route marches along miles of dull main roads through flat East Anglian countryside, experiencing stinking blasts of pig slurry spread on adjoining fields, I enjoyed Bury. Some of the nearby villages had Irish connections. Bartons, Wingfields, Blennerhasetts and Dennys were amongst those families who came from these parts. While stationed here, we undertook exercises such as on the Thetford Battle Area, a huge wilderness devoted to army manoeuvres.

Having finished 'playing' active-service soldiers one day, we were to gather at a huge Nissan-hut style building somewhere near the centre. Waiting for the open trucks to collect us, two of us decided to investigate the building. The huge sliding door was slightly ajar. Imagine our surprise when we discovered inside an Armstrong Siddeley car with its ignition still on, as indicated by the red light on the wooden dashboard. From the exhaust, a flexible pipe led through the slightly open rear window and under an open newspaper. Horror-struck, we realised that beneath it rested the bald head of a middle-aged man. He was dead, but rigor mortis hadn't yet set in. We shouted urgently to the radio operator outside to call the police. They, informed of our location, said we were to hang on; they'd be with us shortly. As we waited, our own vehicles arrived and we loaded our packs. Those of us involved couldn't, however, leave the scene. The others returned to barracks.

An hour later, in the distance, we could discern a lone cyclist. Eventually a uniformed constable dismounted his bike and asked who was in charge. "I am", said I. "What's this about a corpse?" "Its over here, Constable". The policeman heaved the sliding door to shed more light, opened the car's rear door and lifted the newspaper. I'd not seen a cadaver before, especially one which had taken his or her own life. "He's dead, all right. Better tell them back at the station.You can go, lads".

* * * * * * * * * *

Eventually, a fully trained non commissioned officer, I left with my company to join our battalion in the Far East. From Liverpool we sailed on the 'Devonshire', a luxury liner converted into a troopship. Biscay, Gibraltar, Port Said, Aden, Socotra where we hit a storm, Colombo, Singapore and Hong Kong were new to me and exciting.

I enjoyed learning basic words of Hindustani and observing the Indian crew's eating habits. "Nihirbani", I would practice when in receipt of a gift or assistance. We slept in hammocks and took turns at watch, an exercise in discipline rather than a military necessity.

The Suez Canal was my first thrill. Here ships appeared to glide through the sand beside us as they sailed along a parallel channel in the opposite direction. When stopping at Port Said or Ismailia, we would be besieged by hundreds of 'bumboats' and 'gully gully' boys holding up leather wallets, poofs, fêzes and other items to be bargained for. One magician managed to get aboard. How he made his assortment of birds appear and disappear, I still find it hard to understand. "You buy this from me and I only charge you half what I ask . . . . real value. . . . ." I recalled my vague attempts at bargaining at Cashel fair. These were the experts.

Although Suez days were hot and balmy, it got extremely cold at night. I know, having been on deck duty. The Red Sea was flat calm. In the distance, we could make out the reddy-brown coastlines of Africa or Saudi Arabia in the heat haze. In Aden, fascinating varieties of fish basked in the dirty-blue harbour water. Little boats scurried about propelled by noisy diesel engines ". . . . tub, tub, tub, tub". Soon we disembarked, but not without warnings: "Mind your wallets. . . . remember, the Rolexes aren't genuine . . . . ". Of course, we succumbed. We also accepted suggestions that we had seen the ghostly 'Flying Dutchman' as we crossed the Indian Ocean. Certainly there were flying fish, some of which landed on deck. At Colombo, a few gullable troops were encouraged to view sexually explicit spectacles. Others purchased precious stones from sinister-looking traders as they proferred their 'sparklers' from behind curtains. I bought garnets, moonstones and an amethyst.

The Korean war was pretty well 'old hat' when we reached the FARELF Active Service Theatre. Our regiment had made a major contribution to ensure a peaceful outcome, but killing people, even 'enemies', disgusted and disturbed me in spite of the commitments for which I had volunteered.

My battalion's next station was to be Hong Kong where I enjoyed being stationed in the New Territories, near the then border with Communist China. I was able to travel to such nearby destinations as

Macao, the Portuguese Colony across the Pearl river, and gain an insight into the Far East. Our headquarters at Bea's Stables was near Fanling, a bustling town of traders and prostitutes where I often went just to enjoy chatting, and picking up the local Chinese dialects.

There was always something new at Fanling. I would catch the train from the border at Lo Wu or from Fanling to Kowloon. Third class seats were plain benches while those in the first class were, I think, upholstered in moulded leatherette. I chose second class where the slatted seats permitted a degree of comfort but where one was unlikely to have to share one's lap with a basketted pig, or a cage-full of brightly coloured fowl. Signs at the station indicated "no hawking" - it took me some time to realise that this was an instruction not to cough up and spit out phlegm. To get to the station we often hired a 'parcicol', a bicycle pedalled by a strong man behind whom one uncomfortably balanced. This was the cheapest form of transport.

Bea's Stables had been just that; the long blocks with their overhanging roofs once housed horses. They had been converted into barrack rooms or dormitories. Being in charge of one of them, I had a small room at the end to myself - in it was a bed with its large mosquito net, and a basic war-office wardrobe of plywood. The windows were always open. When newcomers arrived, their mosquito nets would be covered with weird insects and lizards. Once I tucked my net around my mattress with my knees up. When I lowered them, I became aware of something cold and solid. The snake was harmless and long dead but, dressed as Adam, I leaped out of bed and fled through my door into the open, to be surrounded by gleeful and amused comrades.

The area around was delightful mountainy countryside, quite different to Ireland but bearing enough similarity for me to enjoy exploring. This I did to tremendous ends and there was little of the New Territories which I didn't cover including a jungle where there were still, reputedly, tigers. Just below our headquarters, was a village. Thrilled by the antics of its population as they acted - supported with weird music - their traditional ceremonies, I would silently watch them, camouflaged by trees, from the hill above.

My duties included border protection with the Hong Kong Police. Loc Ma Chau Station was above the wide paddy-field-covered esturial plain through which flowed the sluggish river dividing the British Colony from Communist China. On our roof was a searchlight which we carefully directed only over our own territory. Even a slight incursion by its beam across the river could have disastrous consequences, the huge unit's glass being badly cracked and almost totally covered in bullet-holes. One day, when I had just taken up duty, our Chinese policemen guided a struggling and protesting, rather elderly, man towards me. "Don't go near . . . . keep your distance", they warned me. "He's a leper". "So?" said I. "He's been sent over by the Commies for us to handle . . . . or to infect us". The unfortunate man remonstrated to let him stay. He had come by boat. If sent back, he'd be shot. "We'd better get in touch with the authorities. Maybe he'd be given a place in the colony's leper colony". Every effort to get a positive response to our request elicited a repeated "No" - a precedent could be established. The poor man, hunched in the corner of his cell, quietly sobbed. Told that he'd have to be returned, he went berserk and grabbed my hand. Terrified that I might contract the disease, I rushed to wash and disinfect my hands. Meanwhile, the man was escorted to his boat and forced to return to the Communist bank. A short while later, we heard two shots. He wouldn't be returning.

In Hong Kong we often carried out practice manoeuvres, especially on the then remote Sek Kong peninsula. Patrol commanders were expected to lead their men in formation, one of which was the 'arrowhead' where they were at the forwardmost point with troops spaced out at an ever increasing lateral distance from each other behind them. One day I was leading my patrol up a dry scrub and rock-strewn river valley. As I clambered over the huge boulders of the river bed, I slipped into a hollow between them. Coming to my senses, I realised that half a metre in front of my chin, a small greeny snake had woken and was staring at me as though to strike. I was petrified lest someone would frighten it into action. Luckily, I was calmly asked if I was all right. Through clenched teeth, I explained the situation and ordered the others to wait till it was resolved. Eventually I managed to steal away. Later I was told that the reptile was quite harmless. In spite of joining snake hunts where we pinned the unsuspecting creatures with forked sticks, I was not at the time to know. In fact, I have never been comfortable with them. At Dublin Zoo a keeper had wrapped a boa constrictor round Guy's willing shoulders before turning to me to repeat the action in front of the assembled crowd, a challenge I had accepted reluctantly.

The following circumstances, therefore, still bring a smile to my face. Even in sub-tropical areas, winter nights can be cold and I liked my comfort. I was, though, considerate of the welfare of those in my charge. After spending a February day in a battle area, I chose an old farmstead to bed down for the night. The deserted house was a typical Chinese dwelling consisting of the main room and, at one end, a kind of porch. This took up the width of the house, had its outer and inner doors in the middle of the gable and central walls respectively and was perhaps two metres deep. As one peered through the gable door from outside there was a two metre long niche on either side. I told my second in command to take the one on the left while I would sleep in the other, my troops having pitched under trees of the adjoining orchard. At my head was a pile of kindling I would use as a pillow. I placed my poncho and blankets on the earthen ground, having checked that all was well, and lay down. Eventually quelling the comments and chatter of the orchardeers, I dozed towards sleep. However, I was soon disturbed by something moving on the sticks behind me. The slight sound made on the pile by a creature of weight reminded me of the many different kinds of snakes. Was this a venomous serpent? I felt the sensation of movement over my poncho-covered upper chest and towards my stomach. Would the creature curl up there and take advantage of my body-warmth on this cold star-lit night? If I moved it could strike and I'd be dead. I was rigid with fear. Maybe some unsuspecting comrade would try and wake me, and cause the thing to sink its fangs into my juicy flesh. Minutes, more like lengthy hours, passed until I heard the welcome noise of a preferable, but to some equally nasty, horror. At home I had witnessed the sound of chewing rodents. My relief that it wasn't a venomous snake permitted me to rapidly shove the thing off. The huge rat scuttled back into its hole behind me. My neighbour grunted but he couldn't begin to sense my trauma.

*   *   *   *   *   *   *   *   *   *

Journeys in the New Territories and Hong Kong in the 1950s could be hazardous. Roads were constructed mainly for military transport such as that which led to the Sek Kong Peninsula. Army trucks were the responsibility of the drivers and nobody else could drive them, even the transport officer in charge, without their 'O.K'. The route to Sek Kong was, for some kilometres, a narrow steeply declining one-way road constructed into the mountainside. No way could two vehicles pass, so it was regulated by traffic lights, alternatively one hour or so one way and the next, the opposite direction. In the valley below were the remnants of vehicles which had gone over the edge.

This day, my driver was fearful that the brakes of his truck wouldn't hold. I couldn't order him on, though we were to rally at a specific point at a designated time. In the end he agreed that he'd sign over the vehicle to me so that I'd be fully responsible. He and a number of the soldiers aboard disembarked to follow by foot while I boarded the driving seat and started. The lights were green but it was true, the brakes were almost non-existent. First gear was so slow that I pressed the clutch to free-wheel a number of times. This was not wise as I built up too much speed and without power steering the manipulation of the wheel was heavy. As we gathered momentum, sweat poured from the pores of my body and of those brave enough to accompany me. At the bottom was a sharp corner as the road veered right over a narrow parapetless concrete bridge. We slowly came to a halt, disembarked, weak at the knees, and thanked our lucky stars.

On manoeuvres later, in the same area, we were to disembark from a landing craft but a steep wedge of sand and a nasty current prevented us. The only option was to dive in and make for the shore. I checked that the others could swim and ordered them overboard. I had never learned and so, terrified, asked a corporal to watch out for me as I leapt from the craft. Drawn downwards beside the almost solid wall of sand, somehow my flailing limbs enabled me to surface, and I made it and joined the others. From then on I was able to swim.

Hong Kong waters were full of interesting sea creatures including giant octopi whose tentacles could be seen under large boulders. Sometimes I would join friends for a trip in a sampan, a small open boat. Once I was with a fisherman pal. "What are those jugs and pots strung out on that line for?" "I don't know. . . . have a look". I did, into several of them. I began to habitually put my hand into each, presuming them to be empty. As I thrust my hand into one pot with a fairly small collar, something sucked hold of it. Struggling to free it, I whipped my hand out and shook the thing away. We were horrorstruck as a small octopus landed fully over my companion's face to which it clung, albeit for seconds. Not only did he scream, but his language included threats to test my recently gained swimming prowess.

* * * * * * * * * * *

Typhoons often struck Hong Kong, when even huge ships would be blown ashore. With the monsoons, all sorts of frogs and reptiles appeared, the cool rain being welcomed not only by the plants and creatures but by us.

Each free weekend I would travel to the main conurbations of Kowloon or Victoria. There was bustle and bargains as retailers provided anything from pickled snake to silk paintings. I made many Chinese friends and had a couple of intimate relationships. My study of Cantonese helped me to converse and, to an extent, read. These all enabled me to understand and enjoy this wonderful city and its cultured international population from hundreds of different tribes and districts. Hong Kong was perpetually exciting.

No longer a virgin, perhaps the first really comfortable relationship I experienced came to a frustrating end. Hurt on learning that money and family ties often had a stronger influence than love, I was devastated and lonely when my beloved half-Chinese partner of some months was forced to return to Manila. Her parents had a wealthy banker earmarked for her future. More sadness from this relationship was to come.

* * * * * * * * * * *

Perhaps it was through God's intervention that shortly after my trauma, I was walking along Nathan Road, Kowloon's long main

thoroughfare, gazing vacantly into shop windows. Reaching an
emporium selling Bibles and religious books, I realised that a man
leaning in the doorway was watching me. A well-built European with
broken English, he asked me if I was interested in books. I told him
I was and we discussed reading material. About to move on, I was
verbally waylaid: "If you're free on Sunday, we convert the
bookshop inside and hold a service here. You'll be welcome if you'd
feel like joining us". I had avoided church parades by stating my
religious denomination as 'Church of Ireland'. As nobody questioned
me, perhaps it was assumed that I belonged to some queer Irish Sect.
Military authorities weren't concerned that we were Anglicans, if
members of an independent church, and at that time my faith was
undeveloped. "Yes, I'd like to". The sentence left my mouth before I
could check it, but I kept my word.

The following Sunday, having witnessed sixty thousand refugees
fleeing for their lives as fire ravaged their shanty town of cardboard
boxes and bits of discarded timber on the edge of the Gau Loong or
Nine Dragon Mountains, I took the train to Kowloon. When I arrived
at the bookshop door, my 'friend' was there. "So you've come", said
he. "Yes, I've kept my promise". "Come on in". The place was
transformed. Although books were still on their shelves, a lectern
faced rows of chairs. By the door were two or three tables, behind
which were chairs. I joined the queue of people as they located their
seats. In front of mine, in the fifth row, was a vast man wearing a
black cylindrical Indonesian-style fêz. Some of the astonishing variety
of nationalities also wore hats, others their national costumes – many
were Cantonese but there were other Chinese. Imagine my
astonishment when the Irish preacher at this non-denominational
gathering was introduced. The name of Father Woods had been given
me, but as yet I hadn't had the courage to contact him. The Service
was inspired, with plenty of singing - it didn't matter if those present
made mistakes, or what religious persuasion they were. God was
surely here. Friend and stranger chatted as, following worship, I found
myself facing the tables inside the door, the chairs behind them
occupied by pen and paper touting members of the congregation.
"Would you like to help us do something for the refugees at Seung
Shui Po?" Although my action was probably disapproved by army

bosses, I joined them to distribute watery soup and help restore estranged children to distraught parents. For the first time I had encountered large-scale civilian suffering. A little later I was to witness a starving mother weighting down the baby she was unable to feed, on the railway. She was pushed away and the toddler rescued as the lines began to rattle and the sound of the oncoming train increased.

These insights to man's inhumanity to man, and to suffering in general were to have a profound effect on my future. I became aware of my Christian tradition. More than that, I felt I had to do something positive. My life was now to have three main dimensions, each inextricably linked: work to bring food to my mouth and sustenance to my dependents, and recreation such as my interest in archaeology, cars and collecting would continue but there was a new spiritual motivation. I gained a deeper understanding of others, which also encouraged me to survey population movements in South-East Asia, later recognised by the Royal Geographical Society.

It was not long before I was on my way to Aberdeen. Father Jack Woods, a native of Cashel, was expecting me. Having crossed to Hong Kong on the Yaumati Ferry, I boarded the number seven bus which skirted the west end of the island. The conductor's Cantonese wasn't easy to understand. Presuming me to be having linguistic difficulties an elderly gentleman in Manderin's clothes and a little skull-cap tapped me from behind. "Excuse me, can I help you?" He spoke perfect English. Having sorted the fare with the conductor, he told me he had been educated at Oxford. Jolted, I hadn't expected such beautiful English from such a very Chinese gentleman. I was beginning to learn of life's many anomalies, too.

Reaching the Seminary, a delightful garden-surrounded complex on a peninsula, I was entertained by a gentle Austrian giant of a cleric until Father Woods was free. Young refugee students in groups were scattered under shading trees on the slopes above the gently lapping harbour waters. Secular instructors or monitors were teaching them how to propagate the Gospel. Several times I revisited these delightful and dedicated 'religious' and had an opportunity to chat with novitiates. Here was a broadminded and generous faith that I had not previously witnessed. On later visits, I was always profusely welcomed.

Below the Seminary floated three large two storey purpose-built restaurants which, tied to moorings on the shore, were surrounded by junks and sampans. Inside, on the lower decks, were tanks of fish, from which to select one's meal, eaten in the crowded upper floor. I came here a couple of times. I loved Chinese food. Whether it was Sechuan, Cantonese or Pekinese, the variety was incredible. Once, however, I agreed to take a couple of new arrivals to eat on Lam Tau, a nearby island slightly larger than that of Hong Kong. Showing off, I suggested that they order the simple rice 'chowfan' while I would try something new. Imagine my horror when, they having almost finished, I was with great ceremony presented with snake-meat. As I delicately devoured a bit of the soft chicken-like coil with the confidence of a know-all, I could sense the wry smiles of my guests. I don't think I ever made a similar mistake again. Hong Kong helped me to mature.

The Reverend Mark Green, an understanding, kindly and efficient chaplain to the Forces, gained a new friend in me. He understood my recent calling and, without pushing, encouraged my participation in spiritual activities. At Easter, as a member of the Norfolk Players, I played Flavius in *The King of Sorrows* from Dorothy L. Sayer's *The Man Born to be King*. We performed it at a number of venues. There were tremendous write-ups in Asian papers and the *New York Post* had "British Army puts Passion Play before Duty" as a front page headline, one of us having been excused guard duties. I made a number of friends including director Michael ffinch and Andrew Herbert whose father, Anglican Bishop of Norwich, had Kerry connections.

*   *   *   *   *   *   *   *   *   *   *

Contemporary correspondence with my parents indicated that, in December 1957, my father was suffering from gallstones, but the cows were milking enough to supply Cashel as well as to succour three suckling calves. The Electricity Supply Board was shortly to connect the house to the national grid and Meskell was recovering from an operation. The I.R.A. were active in the North and my parents were obviously short-staffed. Guy was about to settle at the vast, rambling wood-surrounded Stradbally Hall in Co. Laois where the Cosbys, having kept home there for generations, were organising education for their children and friends, to help maintain it. I had been to dances there and was later to teach a couple of the younger sons - Julian, was to become an expert in clocks.

* * * * * * * * * *

The following February, I was studying Education at Fanling. We would be leaving Hong Kong in August for a three month's stint in Britain before proceeding to Trieste, between Italy and Yugoslavia. In another letter home, I indicated that "I shall be very sorry to leave Hong Kong . . . . I do not think I'll care for Trieste . . . . it is so small, however there may be some riots to keep us occupied!! The summer is starting to appear again, now". I wrote of large butterflies, frogs like barking dogs, crickets and a tiger in the nearby Tai Tam Yau Mountains. I also mentioned the Communist propaganda-women using loud-speakers to praise Mau. 'Comrades' had been sought to volunteer at Kak Tin town across the border.

Never one to shirk my responsibilities, I often carried the injured or those unable to persevere on my shoulders over difficult terrain. It seems that I was again suffering from a lot of swelling and some pain and was in the Military Hospital in Kowloon. Unable to walk, I now realise that my polio must have been at me. My correspondence to my parents was quite political and I obviously concerned myself in depth with what was going on in the Asiatic sphere. The Huk leader had surrendered in the Philippines, the Straits of Formosa between Taiwan and the Chinese mainland were a battleground and I was to be selected for a special mission to Indo-China, later cancelled. Before leaving Hong Kong, I was entitled to a break. A civilian cargo-passenger boat was offering a round trip to Japan via Taipei and Shanghai for a special rate of $180. Instead, I ended up in Malaya.

We sailed home from Hong Kong around the thirtieth of August 1954, again on Her Majesty's Troopship, 'Devonshire'. Writing from Aden, I expressed concern that customs would demand at least £10 duty on my Welmy 25mm camera and that they would discover my embroidered rugs and ivory carvings. At Colombo, I had bought coconut-wood elephants, and boxes made of ebony, ivory and porcupine quills. Another storm in the Indian Ocean had delayed us for thirty-six hours. On arrival at Liverpool, the battalion would be getting leave. Having studied for my First Class Education Certificate on the three week journey, exams were to be on the tenth of October. Mine would be delayed. At Port Said, the vessel was to be inspected by Mr. Bibby, the owner, which meant extra responsibility to organise cleaning parties. The ship's Indian crew had mutinied as their food, taken on at Colombo, was bad.

In my next letter posted from Egypt, I wrote that we watched enviously as the French troopship, 'Louis Pasteur' overtook us en route from Indo-China. "A lovely boat, she looked more like a luxury liner. Our average speed is 12 knots, hers 26 !!". When we eventually docked there were no problems with the British customs. Many of us wished we had purchased more abroad, for prices were cheap and items inovative, up to date or often the last handcrafted treasures to be made before mass-production overtook the Far East.

*   *   *   *   *   *   *   *   *   *

I spent Christmas 1954 at home. The following January I started a three months' small arms course at the School of Infantry. Training to be a weapons instructor meant talking for so many minutes about a box of matches or a chicken's toe, without gesticulating. Eventually I could deliver an in-depth fifty-minute discourse on any specific weapon. The F.N. rifle and the latest Sterling machine gun were being introduced to NATO forces. With an Ack Pack flame thrower I had a nasty experience. The open-ended pipe-like weapon wouldn't fire as I held it on my shoulder with one hand, so I used two. Suddenly the fuel squirted out and landed over my feet. Luckily it was a 'wet' shot and didn't ignite, otherwise I would have been badly burnt. The Kent seaside weather at Hythe for the duration of the course was appalling and the town very dead. My friend Jan Swartz, who served in the Rhodesian forces, Belfaster Paddy Hull and I would 'escape' to Folkstone for dances held in a local hotel. There was little talent as we waltzed to tunes of an earlier era.

In April 1955, I was a patient in the British Military Hospital at Colchester. Those around me were alarmingly ill, mostly with rheumatic fever. As I lay on my bed, patients on either side of me were wheeled out on stretchers. I didn't like to look for I knew it would be the last I'd see of them. I recovered enough to be discharged and to take up light duties with my Company, now based at Roman Way Camp. Here I was close to my grandmother Minny, and to my uncle and aunt Mick and Pam. For my twenty-first birthday the latter stood me a dinner party at the town's George Hotel. They also invited my friend Celia Chubb, who was working for Liberty's in London. I drove her home but my car broke down. We summoned help from an inebriated party of coloured and Irish revellers, but it was no longer early morning when we reached our destination.

I got presents from a number of relations: Minny gave me her binoculars, Uncle Mick a shooting stick, and my godmother Denise a buckskin waistcoat. Aunt Daisy Ricketts sent me a cheque for a guinea (twenty one shillings, or one euro and thirty-three cents in today's money) and my parents promised me a gold signet ring. I was soon transferred to Norwich where, at Britannia Barracks, I was responsible for training new recruits.

What a relief it was when, the following October, I was on my way to Cyprus. Due to be demobilised within months, I hadn't expected to be allowed to join my battalion for another overseas posting. Although in no way like Hong Kong, Cyprus was an opportunity to be away from 'Blighty', as England was known in military circles. The journey took fourteen hours. We began by flying towards Malta and as we skirted Sicily, we could see Mount Etna erupting to our left. Approaching the 'George Cross' island a mechanical problem developed so Air Control re-directed us to Libya where we were billeted at Tripoli. North Africa was roasting but it was great to have an unscheduled stop and visit the ancient Roman city. The road from the airport was surrounded by desert, and there were even camels. The city centre's Castle Square exuberated a sober air of prosperity with Mitchell Cotts' offices and the Banco di Roma overlooking palm trees and rows of white-topped American taxis. All around were memorials to the Roman past such as the somewhat

crudely restored Marco Aurelio Arch. The white multi-arched royal
palace, approached by wide steps, was guarded by sentries in
domed white kiosks. This was soon to change under Gadaffi. The
engines of our heavy propeller-driven aircraft repaired, we took off.
Flying low over North Africa, we got an excellent view of the desert
and of Egypt before we veered left over the Mediterranean.

Cyprus was quite cool and a bit parched that autumn, but balmy
to us after an English summer. Whisked off to an extensive tent camp
beside the narrow but well-metalled Larnaca road from Nicosia, I
was to be responsible for the guard of several significant places. The
Cyprus Broadcasting Service station, a large single storey building
which wrapped itself round a courtyard, was enclosed by a tall wire
perimeter fence. Headquarters near the entrance was a large tent at
the front of which I sat behind a collapsible table, members of my
guard resting in the cool dark space behind. Turkish and Greek
policemen shared our task. As each sergeant came on duty, I would
be called aside and in a low whisper told "Hello, you Irish, you

good. I Turkish (or Greek); we very good, sympathetic. That other sergeant no good, his people bad . . . . here, a little wine for you." A bottle would appear from under his tunic. Sometimes the gift was a chicken, at others a bottle of Cypriot brandy.

One evening, my duty patrol reported that the wire had been cut along the perimeter fence. A prowler had been seen, so I called the Island security officer. Leaving my second in command in the tent, the rather stout Turkish sergeant of the day and I unsuccessfuly searched. A civilian radio employee had heard noises above his ceiling. When the Security Chief arrived, we climbed into the roof which covered one long side of the building. The sergeant lead the way with a sten gun, I followed with an F.N.rifle and the Security Officer took up the rear. To advance, we had to step on the narrowly spaced rafters to the base of which the plaster ceilings were attached. Suddenly, at the far end of the stretch we could see something. Automatically the Security Officer prodded me with his revolver: "Quick, move . . . . " I over-balanced and stuck the barrel of my weapon into the sergeant's back which meant that he also lost balance and fell feet-first between the rafters. His stomach stopped the rest of his body. All we could do was laugh. The intruder got away but apparently the newsreader was broadcasting an evening bulletin as the two waving legs appeared through the ceiling above. I believe his comments were sensational.

Another of my responsibilities was helping to guard the political prisoners in the Central Prison in Nicosia. It was here that Mikhailis Karaoulis, executed for killing a Turkish policeman, was held. I got to know him and many of the prisoners, and still have a wooden box and a crude notebook made by the carpentry shop and the bindary respectively. They were presented as a gesture of friendship, albeit limited by parameters of loyalty, and of the understanding that we shared. Being Irish

Central Prison,
Nicosia, 1955

I understood their cause, and they were interested in learning more about a country with a similarly complicated history.

An embarrassment at the prison one evening was when my second in command was presented with traditional strong coffee by the Turkish police sergeant. I always enjoyed my cup which, accompanied by water between each sip, was provided as we sat on the sofa in the narrow guardroom. "What shall I do with this muck?" whispered the insensitive East Anglian corporal beside me. I suggested he hid it under the furniture. This he did, but imagine my consternation when it tipped over and a stream of thick black liquid oozed its way to the centre of the floor. "You don't like my coffee? My beautiful coffee which I make specially for you . . . ." Sadly, I too, never got another cup due to my fellow soldier's unacceptable behaviour.

As guard commander of the third of the centres, the Central Secretariat, I was often privy to happenings in other parts of the world, including Ireland, for this was the island's intelligence headquarters. I learnt of the involvement of the Connolly clubs in promoting the I.R.A. and other tidbits which kept me in touch with activities at home. Throughout my tour of duty, I was aware that, unlike Korea, this was terrorist warfare. Eoka, a group which wanted Enosis or union with Greece, was commanded by General Grivas.

A less heroic adventure came about due to a spider. I hate the things which to me are evil and sinister. One day my task was to flush out a cavern where the general was reputedly hiding. I'd be brave and, under cover, approach the entrance myself. Climbing up the cliff-face, with my back against the rock, I edged myself into the opening. "General Grivas, come out . . . . General Grivas, I know you're there . . . . " There wasn't the slightest indication of his presence. All was silent as I listened. Pensively, I looked at the lowish ceiling of the cave and observed a white network gutter with a hole in its side above my head in which, about a metre away, I observed the shape of something slightly weighty making its way towards me. As it reached the hole, a shiver ran up my spine; I was confronted by a large dark spider. Calmly I backed out and announced to those covering me that Grivas wasn't inside. Perhaps that spider saved his life.

Often bombs were thrown at us, or grenades. We usually returned the latter for, once the pin was pulled, thirteen seconds would lapse before the explosion. If they were thrown immediately after the pin had been pulled, we had time to return them, often with disastrous results for the instigator of the action. The homemade bombs were little more than thunderflashes.

In spite of the many hazards, there was still time to spare and places to visit. Much of Nicosia, however, was out of bounds. Several of us outside a basement bar-restaurant one evening, evacuated due to a bomb scare, were to witness the thing exploding. Said to have been planted by Greek Cypriots to target military patrons, it could have killed us. In view of the attitude of the partisans, I never felt comfortable being shaved by Cypriot barbers for fear the razor would 'accidentally slip'.

Famagusta is one of Cyprus' most historic cities. Dotted with ancient mosques and churches, it is now in Turkish hands. Beyond its walls to the south is Varosha, then a mainly Greek resort but now a vacated wasteland. On one occasion I was responsible for overseeing the area around the Greek Central Gymnasium, a huge classical third-level college. Like Portora, there was a central block with pillars, on either side of which were outriders. Four or five bay set-back sections with a low wall in front of each linked the fronts of the three blocks. This building, reputedly a centre for subversion, was supposed to be empty and locked at night. A member of my patrol reported hearing noises from inside, and spyed an open door to the rear of a large lecture-room, behind which shadows moved. The Commanding officer was furious that we had been on private Greek Orthodox church property and was obviously uncomfortable when I took him to investigate. He did nothing, indicating that the situation was a figment of our imagination.

Later that evening, another patrol having seen lights at the rear of the building, I felt obliged to investigate. I chose several reliable soldiers to accompany me. Keeping our backs to the walls, we crept over the low wall and towards the recessed link-building until we were beside one of the ground-floor windows. Mercifully, I instructed all to keep down for suddenly, without warning, a window above us was flung open. A young man looked out over our heads. Those with me ran, leaving me in the crouching position. Their action probably saved my life, for the Cypriot observer obviously presumed that all had fled. He failed to look immediately below him. Eventually the window was closed and after a suitably long pause I returned to my guard tent. That I did not deal with the 'mutineers' with extreme severity denied me the opportunity to report the situation accurately. Attempting to convince higher authorities that something was amiss, I was rebutted.

I was glad to be demobilised in February 1956. I had learnt a lot in the army and had travelled much of the world. I had also gained educational qualifications and had had most interesting experiences. After three years and five days, I was transferred to the Army Reserve for another four years.

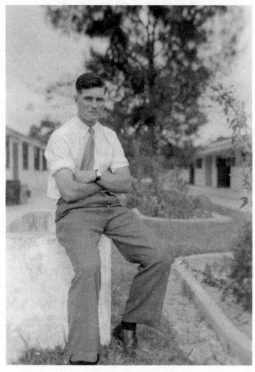

China 1974.

CHAPTER SEVEN

London life begins – a 'Russian' exploit – Harmsworth Press –
Holy Trinity and Sloane Square – a fire alert – Ardmaylebeg is
sold – I return to Ireland.

I had a new grey suit, had attended a demobilisation course on business studies, and was due some leave when I transferred to the Army Reserve. Now on call should war or an emergency be declared, I also had a conviction that I was called to serve God's ministry.

The Army, like any collective organisation where members work and play together, is all-embracing. It is not easy to adjust to civilian life and stand on one's own feet, an adventure in a new world. I sympathise with those clergy, especially in enclosed orders, who leave cosseted if prayerful lives to return to the mundanities of everyday living. There are pitfalls. Relations with other independent people, finding accommodation and work, filling social welfare forms, budgeting for travel expenses or food, and learning how to do everyday chores such as cooking can be stressful.

Home in Ireland after more than three years as a soldier, I had to readjust my life. With the help of my parents and Dean Jackson, friends and relations, I realised that my priorities were to be accepted for the Church's Ministry, to educate myself to the necessary standard for ordination and to raise enough money to pay for it.

I couldn't study at home, even home study courses. Helping my parents was too demanding and the many disruptions made learning impossible. Trinity College was out due to my lack of Irish entry qualifications and I had no money for accommodation and everyday expenses. There was still little available work in Dublin. By now, also, there were no close relations or friends with whom I could stay. London, with its steady stream of Irish emigrants, was my only hope.

* * * * * * * * * *

"No Blacks or Irish" read signs on London boarding houses in 1956. Although I wasn't going to argue the point, I became more adamant than ever as to my Irishness and gained a new-found identity with the underprivileged, especially blacks. I settled for a convenient, if expensive, one-room West-End apartment.

Three Halsey Street, off Cadogan Gardens, was a three storey terrace house owned by the Perrys, an understanding young English couple who lived in the basement. My rectangular room with its screened-off kitchen area faced the street from the first floor and I shared the bathroom across the landing with Milanese Maria, who leased the room behind. Stanley, who occupied the quarters below, other English friends, our attractive neighbour who modelled for an exclusive fashion house, and I spent occasional evenings 'on the town'. At one end of the street was St. Mary's Roman Catholic Church, where I attended the wedding of Arthur Ryan of County Tipperary to his New Zealand bride, and at the other, a popular hostelry. Each morning, as I descended the stone steps to the street, I greeted the same people - few reciprocated.

*   *   *   *   *   *   *   *   *   *   *

Jobless, I went to temporary employment bureaux who provided cheap labour on a non-commital basis. My first assignment was in the East-End Dockland. I remember the underground train travelling for ages to my first civilian job since leaving the army. I worked hard at moving heavy wooden crates with a team of tough Londoners. "Oi, mate . . . . what's the hurry?" The heavily built ganger approached me: "Go and take a rest. . . ." Hard work was not condoned. No doubt union backing ensured that the workload was evenly spread and that time was allotted for each task but I couldn't justify myself sitting around, merely contributing absurdities to the general chatter. Conversation, as with troops, concerned sex, drink and local gossip. I earned a week's pay – no more.

Another bureau, more into clerical workers, offered me a job filing for a Jewish clothing company also in the East End. The other gentile was a large well-endowed Dublin woman with whom I was able to relate. With that firm I learnt how clothing sold in a leading but inexpensive London store chain was made. Huge cutters sliced through layers of felt to produce the shapes necessary to assemble garments. Each would have glue squirted along its edge before being placed upon another and pressed with a vast pneumatic clamp. I don't recall any stitching, but the products looked good. Indeed, as I passed the windows of the stores concerned, I remarked to myself how successful the process seemed to be.

A month or two later I found work which, although still temporary, enabled more satisfaction. The Abbey National Building Society needed account book auditors in their Baker Street front office. This involved taking each customer's book over the counter or receiving it in the post, bringing it upstairs and searching through man-high rotary files. From the customer's card, unrecorded transactions were written up in their account books, and the total totted. There were about twenty of us. The supervisor, Mr. Baxter, a tall thin gentleman with a life of experience, was most helpful, but he became ill and had to take his leave. For some reason, he recommended me, an appalling mathematician, to take his responsibility. I recollect no pay increase and the job was not only temporary, but dead end. However, the Abbey National treated me well and I was given luncheon vouchers for their canteen. Before leaving, I had registered for evening studies at Kings College of the University of London.

Soon I was permanently employed by the Harmsworth Press, a leading London newspaper and magazine publisher. Headquarters was in Stratton Street, a gloomy street between tall Georgian-style buildings off Piccadilly. My L-shaped office, through an archway, across a small yard, and approached up a flight of stairs, faced the first floor of the house in front. I shared it with secretary Joan Hamil-Smith from the West Indies. Initially I took responsibility for small classified advertisements in the *Field*, a glossy weekly dealing with country issues. During my period with the company, our department steadily increased its income through promotions. The Huguenot-connected Marquis de Ruvigny was overall advertisement manager, while Roger Marston and a pleasant young man named Cowell whose parents came from Dublin completed the team. I eventually found myself working longer hours than would enable me to continue my studies and was sleeping a mere five hours nightly. But the work was interesting, I was in contact with customers and communicated with our printers, Gale and Polden of Aldershot. At Christmas, we received gifts of review books at the annual staff gathering. Later, when I had become a publisher myself, I realised that it is the publishers of the books that should have been profusely thanked.

Above the archway leading to my patch was the company accountant's office. The grey-suited middle-aged Scotsman was able to observe the comings and goings of each member of staff. He made himself obvious when one was late, even if we had worked to excess the previous evening. One summer's day he opened up his sash window as I passed. "Mr. Weir, don't you think its time you purchased a decent suit and an umbrella, and maybe a bowler hat for yourself. A gentleman should be properly dressed". I usually wore a cheap and poorly cut jacket and trousers. I couldn't afford a traditional pin-striped suit and besides, the *Field* and our other papers dealt with the country. Later, though, I did buy my first new suit with money my grandmother Minnie had willed me.

A short while later, I boarded an underground train. There was standing-room only. As the doors closed and we began to move, I looked through the glass partition to my right where sat five expressionless bowler-hatted city gentlemen. Each wore an immaculate dark suit, each had a rolled umbrella over his left forearm and each held an open newspaper. Every one of them, however, except the farthest, had his eyes firmly fixed on his neighbour's *Times*. I laughed, but if I did, I was the only one. It lightened my evening as I recalled our accountant's request.

*   *   *   *   *   *   *   *   *   *

Living in Halsey Street, I found myself helping with several London parishes such as Golders Green and St. Martin's-in-the-Fields. St. Martin's included parts of Soho and, as far as I recollect, Buckingham Palace - groups of us would systematically visit the residents of specific streets, or apartments. The poor or foreigners were usually the most welcoming. Often we would have a door slammed in our faces, even before our introductory spiel. Since my time, I understand that this church has expanded its work of accommodating the homeless and feeding the needy.

Parallel to Halsey Street was one of London's most fashionable - lengthy Sloane Street was bounded by posh red-brick Victorian mansions enhanced with Portland stone. One of these, just north of Sloane Square, was the rectory of the Reverend A. B. Carver, an ex-Territorial Army Chaplain. This understanding Church of England cleric was the rector of Holy Trinity Church opposite, the poet John Betjeman's favourite church and, after St. Paul's Cathedral, London's largest. "I'd like to put myself at your service, Mr. Carver" said I, having bravely mounted the steps and rung the rectory doorbell. Ushered in, I explained that I had felt called to the Ministry, that I was already studying, and that I sought pastoral and general experience. He asked would I be prepared to organise a family service on specified Sunday afternoons. With help from such of his parishioners as Lord Cadogan and Mrs. Bliss, an Irish one-time Roman Catholic, we encouraged luke-warm Christians to share in our loosely organised liturgy and, instead of a sermon, split into groups with a leader each. Preceded by a short discourse, a predetermined subject would be discussed at the age level of the participants. It worked well and we had a lot of support. I also contributed to the parish magazine and visited elderly parishioners, activities I continued until I left London.

One Saturday morning, returning from work, my neighbour Stanley and his friend Jimmy were at the door. "We're celebrating, Hugh. Will you join us?" "Of course; hang on a minute and I'll be with you."

In no time, the three of us were in Finch's Pub. This, our local, was crowded out so, after a drink or two, we moved on. At the next 'watering hole' we met up with others including Stanley's girlfriend. Eventually somebody volunteered to lead us to the Bongi Bo, a Polish refugee club, in Fulham Road. "But we're not members . . . . " "Don't worry, I'll get you in" our volunteer boasted. Minutes later, our staggering party staggered down steps into a den of commotion and excitement. Richard Burton and Elizabeth Taylor were exchanging words and I found myself between them. Stanley grabbed hold of me; "Come on Hugh, we've a task over here . . . .". He made me sit down close by a central pillar along with Jimmy and two East Europeans. "We are Russians" said one. Assuming they were refugees, I drunkenly asked when they had escaped from their Communist homeland. They were, however, senior Russian Communist diplomats which Stanley knew, but was determined to get to drop their political persuasion. "Niet, we are representatives of our great motherland . . . . we are proud . . . ." "Have a drink" said Stanley. "Sposiba". Each time the Russians were presented with vodka, they would wait for our backs to be turned and then change their full glasses for our empty ones. Aware of this, we did the same in reverse. As the evening progressed, we drank ourselves sober and the diplomats became extremely inebriated. We got our confessions. "Yes, Communism is terrible. Yes, we want to be Christians . . . . " At seven the following morning, five of us roared through empty London streets in a large Russian car, I think a Zil, and were delivered to our doors. Later, we were invited to the Soviet Embassy. Jimmy and I declined, but Stanley went. As he was leaving, he reputedly slapped his hostess's behind, exclaiming "Thanks, old girl". We weren't asked again.

* * * * * * * * * * *

In September, 1957, at one of our family services, I announced that I would be grateful if any of the congregation had or knew of either a reasonably sized flat for the same rent as that at number three, or a similar apartment for less. My Italian neighbour had grown from one very attractive girl from Milan to four. They would normally have been most welcome but their excitable conversation reached a crescendo every night as I attempted my homework. Stanley had moved out after observing a black magic sex session through a window across the street.

After worship, a delightful elderly lady introduced herself. "I am Mabel Delaforce - I've an apartment in Sloane Square". Horrors! No way could I afford an apartment in this most exclusive of addresses. "How kind of you, but I was considering something more modest" said I. "How much are you paying at present?" I told her my weekly rent. "I'd be delighted to let you have my little flat for that. I could do with someone I can trust. Its only small, you know . . . ."

I made no delay in moving in. Mrs. Delaforce, a great grandmother, was the matriarch of the port wine families of Portugal's Douro valley. They mostly had an English background, just as many of the Jerez families are of Irish extraction. They also spoke English and played cricket. Mrs. Delaforce owned half the balconied second floor of a large residential block between Peter Jones' shop and Sloane Street, nearest the corner with the latter. Retaining the end, she had divided a bed-sitting room and kitchenette off with its own door to the public stair-well. It faced the square and had a french window from the kitchenette onto the balcony. I was in luxury.

Here I was able to entertain friends such as Anne Wilkinson, later with the United Nations in Austria, and Joan Smith, the delightful tall fair Anglo-Brazilian daughter of a wealthy Sao Paulo businessman. Introduced to me by my landlady, Joan later married Peter Brooke, who became Northern Ireland Secretary of State. I was saddened to learn recently that she died in 1985.

At the end of the King's Road which lead through Chelsea from Sloane Square lived Ricky and Gina Jackson's grandmother, Mrs. MacDonald. Ricky was in the British army but Gina was working in London and living south of the Thames; at weekends I would be asked to Cheyney Walk. I can't recall how I was introduced but I would sometimes find myself at parties in Peter Ustinov's nearby home.

My aunt Brenda lived in an apartment off Kensington High Street and her younger daughter, Monica on the far side of Hampstead Heath. I had plenty of friends and was asked to lots of parties, but London can be lonely. Somehow I felt that I couldn't, or shouldn't intrude into their lives, or sponge on their hospitality. Instead, I found myself discovering the secret corners of Knightsbridge, Kensington, Soho and Tottenham Court Road where Foyles, that wonderful and well established bookshop welcomed browsers. I began to know London well. Once a week I would patronise Studio One in Oxford Street, an early multiplex cinema with newsreels, cartoons and documentaries. The ticket for an hour's programme, or for as long as one liked was, I think, a shilling and sixpence – eight euros.

Meals at Sloane Square were minimal. Each morning I would rush a breakfast of toast and instant coffee, or tea. Luncheon vouchers enabled me to eat well in the middle of the day - usually in a downstairs self-service restaurant in Bond Street. I didn't worry too much about supper, perhaps a tin of sardines or baked beans served on a piece of buttered toast before going off to study. I had very little time as the Green Park line didn't go direct. This meant a change at Victoria or South Kensington stations, to a different crowded platform at the busiest time of day. The lectures I attended kept me out until about ten o'clock when I would return, only to be faced with homework. My coffee bill must have been staggering.

Weekends were different. Although I worked in the mornings, Saturday afternoons were for shopping or browsing. Sundays were reserved for entertainment, for walking or bussing around greater London, and for church. Friends and I would make mock conversations on crowded buses, pretending to be film stars as we spoke loudly of our next performances in Hollywood - the babble would hush as other passengers strained to listen.

Contacts with my landlady were amicable. She having asked me to join her extended family at a special birthday party, I remember receiving a glass of port, proffered with great reverence. It was a privilege to be given this sample of the finest product of Oporto and the Douro Valley. Circumstances were to change, however.

My kitchenette, its french windows overlooking the tree-scattered but bustling square, was small. The sole cooking facility was a Baby Belling electric oven with an incorporated grill. Between the two, when using the former, one placed a metal plate so the red-hot element didn't set the roast on fire. One Sunday lunchtime, I bought a small joint of beef. Placing it in the oven, I sat to read the paper but forgot to insert the plate. The cooker burst into flames. With presence of mind, I opened the windows, pulled the plug, bravely picked up the cooker and rushed it onto the balcony to burn itself out. I returned to my chair and continued to peruse the papers. Someone, however, rang Mrs. Delaforce. There was panic outside. The fire brigade was on its way. There was frantic banging on the locked kitchenette door which led from the rest of my landlady's apartment. Using her own, the only, key she unlocked the door and stood, horrified. Words stumbled out: "You're reading the paper . . . . the place is nearly burning down and you're reading the paper. . . ." I disclosed the circumstances and explained that I had taken the safest action. Standing up, I was able to observe that in the square below, the crowd was increasing. Like a Pope from his Vatican window, I leant on the balcony railings and shouted loudly that all was well. The last of Mrs. Delaforce I saw that day was her back as she closed the door behind her, muttering. Some hours later I retrieved the blackened cooker with its minute morsel of charcoaled flesh. From then on, I was greeted fairly but coolly, even having cleared up the mess and having replaced the cooker.

London's smog was in those days at its worst. Sometimes one could see no more than a metre ahead. A nasty sulphurous cloud, it permeated every nook and cranny, and especially one's nostrils, throat and eyes. Rarely could anyone escape. One evening, when Sloane Square was at an almost silent standstill, I emerged from the healthier bowels of the Underground to be almost suffocated. At least I would be able to escape the worst of it in my apartment, thought I. On opening the door I realised that, as a fresh air fiend, I had left the window open.

* * * * * * * * * * *

While I was in London, several of my closest relatives died. A letter from Uncle Mick, to Halsey Street, indicated that my grandmother Minnie passed on peacefully at around 9 p.m. on the seventh of November, 1956. A severe stroke had paralyzed her right side and she had been unconscious since. At her cremation a few days later were quite a few Reid and Gibson relations. The following February, my grandfather Willie Gibson was buried in Mountshannon. He was eighty-two. When I had received the telegram concerning his death from Uncle Mick, then in Limerick, there was a gale in London. Slates and tiles were flying and branches of trees crashed around me as I made for the telephone kiosk in Cadogan Gardens. The only way to contact Ireland was apparently through the United States as cross-channel lines were out of order. I wasn't able to attend the funeral.

In June, Papa wrote that Iva Keane, known for much of my life, had become engaged to Geoffrey de Wilton whose parents I had worked for at Clonoulty. Iva's father Markie who lived at nearby Mogorban was originally from Beechpark, near Ennis. Much involved in Cashel Cathedral parish, he was an active lay reader. His sister Helen inherited the family lodge at Kilbaha in West Clare, near which I later stayed with her kinsfolk. Geoffrey was in India at the time, so he and Iva would spend their early married life there.

The biggest blow, almost a bereavement, was when my parents told me they were selling Ardmaylebeg. Obviously my grandfather's death and the fact that many of their friends, such as the Russells at Cashel and the Lidwills were moving to other parts of Ireland or abroad, made them feel somewhat isolated. Guy was at Castlepark outside Dublin but headmaster Pringle recommended that he be enrolled at a public school in England, rather than at St. Columba's College. Brickwall would enable him to develop his artistic talents, already being encouraged by cousin Kitty Wilmer O'Brien. I had perpetually asserted my hopes of returning to the Ireland I loved.

Having decided to move to England, my father agreed that my mother would fly over and see what properties were available. In no time, she located a secluded moat-surrounded house on a substantial farm in Suffolk. Devastated at the prospect of losing my only permanent home, I flew back to Ireland for a short August vacation and visited old friends, bidding them adieu. With my camera, I snapped the house and gardens from every angle. Crib, my father's Staffordshire bull terrier featured in two of the photographs. Guy, with our cousin Chlöe Gibson who was staying was, as far as I recall, happier at the prospects; he was reaching his teens. I didn't want to know the details of what was happening. What my parents decided to do would be done, it being their decision entirely. I returned to London, disconsolate.

A letter from my father the following month stated "The excitement grows intense! Cows go off to Dublin on Wednesday (less 6 young stock, which we hope to take). They are to be sold on Thursday. On Monday we have the sale of stuff here that we are not taking . . . . Saturday and Sunday (4, 5 October.) we shall be packing up in the house and on Monday 7th October the movers get busy. We plan to leave on Wednesday, 9th".

* * * * * * * * * *

Shortly after my parents settled into Cratfield Red House, I paid my first visit. The house, approached by a longish tree-lined drive, was an 'L' shaped two storey gable-ended building with a three bay front and a central front door, not unlike Irish houses of its size. Surrounding it was a deep moat on which had been left a boat made from an aircraft fuel tank; there were also ducks. A barn and extensive wooden farm buildings stood nearby. Across several fields with no approach road, was a well-maintained but remote brick cottage. Red House had no mains electricity, no water, initially no telephone and a rather crude sewerage system. Beside the drive a wooden hut housed the elder of two farmhands employed by the previous owner. The other employee lived nearby and would follow my parents and their guests. It was claimed he shot at the dogs, and my mother only just avoided him as he jumped in front of her car as she drove to the village. My father was frustrated.

The area where my parents settled was backward and remote. They were not welcomed and were considered outsiders. At the village stores one afternoon, it was made clear to me that locals would be served first, irrespective of one's place in the queue. I think my father was unhappy, but there were faces to see and places to visit. My parents soon made friends and got involved with the local pony club, and the Conservative Club, such were their steadfast political sentiments.

I drove Aunt Brenda on a visit from London. She was delighted at the prospect of having her brother within reasonable distance. As we returned, I drove her Morris Minor. In Witham's narrow High Street, I had to brake to avoid the car ahead which had suddenly stopped. There was a deafening bang as an enormous truck careered into our rear. Half the car was like a concertina and we were lucky to be unscathed. Angrily and frustratedly, especially as it wasn't my car, I approached the driver. "All right mate, calm down. Don't worry, I'm used to this sort of thing . . . . " His comments weren't appreciated but Brenda was soon driving a new vehicle.

Although the sale of Ardmaylebeg had unsettled me and in spite of my sadness and disappointment, I regularly visited my parents. From London, too, I made an occasional trip to France, usually to Berk sur Mer or other places bordering the Manche. For one trip, to Le Treport, I brought my young brother, then at school in Suffolk. We flew to Le Touquet with its local airport linked by small planes from Lydd and other English airports. From Ipswich airport, on the rather ancient Dakota was a scatty woman who chain smoked. The engines roared, the propellers spun for take off and a sign indicated "no smoking", but the lady dropped her cigarette which rolled around the floor of the almost empty plane. As she searched for it under her feet, I looked through the window and prayed. We seemed to only just avoid what looked like an earthern bank as we bouncingly took off. Amazingly we were soon heading for Southend and for France. I preferred travel by sea and land.

That Christmas I spent in London. Relations and friends invited me to parties. Morag Tailyour was a busy senior hospital nurse so I didn't see much of her, Aunt Brenda had lots of visitors and invited some of mine, and Monica and Michael Pine lived in Hampstead Heath. Come New Year's Eve, friends and I joined revellers around Eros in Piccadilly Circus. The inside of a local police cell is vivid in my memory. I was wet and cold and drunk when incarcerated for the night having jumped into the fountain with a crowd of equally inebriated fun-seekers.

Not long into 1958, I found myself a patient in St. George's Hospital near Stratton Street. I remember walking down a busy street on the way to work - that is all. "I suggest you quieten your pace of life; you have been doing far too much", the tactful dark-skinned doctor volunteered.

* * * * * * * * * * *

In early March, having been to Paris and now fully recovered, I was on the boat for Cork. Clerical friends had helped in organising the continuation of my studies in the less urgent surrounds of this Irish city I was to love; they were great. A few days before, I had made one last visit to my Stratton Street workmates. As I returned to Green Park underground station, it was rush hour as people made for their offices after their lunch breaks. I leaned over the railing above the steps as commuters were emerging, half wept and half smiled. "These unfortunate people will spend the rest of their lives doing this every day", thought I. I was glad to be escaping from a life of dull routine - no easy task in a country with a web of bureaucracy, social legislation, tax payments and the like.

Inconsolably lonely, I was the only member of my close but now fragmented family left in Ireland. It was also the first time I had taken the train from Rosslare to Cork. My unhappy thoughts were diverted by the view of the river Lee as the railway came alongside the famous waterway. Railway, roadway and channel were converging on the urban complex, as was I. I had only been through the city on the way to my relatives at Clonakilty. Even my father's cousin Edith Collison, whose house at Rushbrooke overlooked the harbour, was no longer there. I was, however, comforted by recalling that Maurice O'Sullivan of my favourite book *Twenty Years a-growing* had spent time in the place. My recollections of his comments on Cork people and their jibes brought me a warm smile.

Dancing with Rachel Burrows, Cork Grammar School, c. 1958

CHAPTER EIGHT

Cork in the fifties – St. Fin Barres, clergy and teaching – my
father dies – poverty and the pawn shop – drama and radio –
a journey to west Clare – I drive to Dublin.

Cork was exciting; it was different, unsophisticated. After my time
in arrogant London where few people would share the time of
day, this was a simple, warm, untidy, unchanged remnant of the
nineteen-thirties. Her citizens were friendly, if generally poor, and
were curious to know why anybody would give up the comforts and
financial security of the London they knew from their emigrant
relations. It didn't matter if one made mistakes, etiquette was reserved
for Dubs or non-nationals. In the streets there were no neat queues of
Rolls Royces or Jags; cars vied untidily with heavy trucks, horse-drawn
carts with bicycles or even with the trains that crossed the city bridges,
and pedestrians would shout at each other. There was little advertising
hoarding and the houses and shops were generally shabby. But there
was a warm welcome from the poorly-lit interiors. Some of the
women, especially those around the Coal Quay and other market
areas, still wore shawls; many men, even in what we now term white-
collar jobs, wore hobnail boots, uncreased woollen trousers and shirts
without their detachable collars. A few flouted their superiority by
wearing bowler hats and dark pin-striped suits. Most children were
raggedy, a lot of them unembarrassed at having to beg.

Here was humanity in an unorganised, law-free mix-up between
nature and centuries of mainly unplanned buildings. This was
dominated by the Church. Roman Catholicism was represented by its
classical and gothic churches, its black-clothed clergy often
conspicuously perusing their breviaries and busy female incumbents
showing off antiquated convent styles, people crossing themselves
and many Marian statues. Protestants were represented by the

overseeing pinnacles of St. Finn Barre's Cathedral and the crooked spire of the Presbyterian Holy Trinity Church below Montenotte. The names of the streets were evocative. Brian Boru Street, the Mall and Oliver Plunket Street were movingly different - they indicated the city's sense of history, religion and grandeur. The people spoke with that wonderful Cork accent and an idiom gleaned from a mixture of Elizabethan English and translated Gaelic. There were smells, too. Murphy's Brewery smelled of malt, the river Lee of rancid sewerage even though it was full of mullet, and a lot of citizens radiated an indication that few houses had adequate washing facilities.

At seven, the dimly-lit streets would be empty as people went home for their evening meals. Come nine o'clock they began to liven up as men made their way to their favourite locals. Drinking hours were long, so the work-time of the ladies of the night extended well into the mornings. At around 3 a.m. quietness reigned.

*   *   *   *   *   *   *   *   *   *   *

St. Fin Barre's Hostel was a narrow 18th century three storey town house, over a basement, which looked directly across the churchyard surrounding St. Fin Barre's Cathedral. At the rear was a large, long, rather unkempt garden. There were both dormitories and cubicles and initially I shared the former with several budding business and professional men, mainly from west Cork. I later inherited a cubicle with a window to the front. The hostel provided reasonably priced accommodation for Protestant men establishing themselves in city jobs. Some, such as Mr. Kingston, and Manny Sullivan who worked in the flour mills by the docks, had been there for years. The matron, Mrs. Porteous, was the widow of the owner of Templemichael Iron Mills, now managed by my cousin Dermod O'Brien. She was assisted by Annie Cadogan, an always aproned and chatty character from west Cork, with a language of her own, who helped with the cooking and cleaning.

A few metres along Dean Street was the tall Deanery, residence of the Very Reverend Harry McAdoo, later to become Archbishop of Dublin. The Dean, married to Lesley Weir of the Dublin jeweller family, was most helpful and was to teach me much about the

Church of Ireland, anglicanism and liturgical worship. Assisted by his delightful and characterful grey-haired artist-curate, Canon Edgar Mills, he managed a vibrant team which included a mainly male choir, the organist Mr. Horne, and lay workers such as the verger Mr. Perrot, in his magnificent 19th century Cathedral. A copy of that at Chartres in France, St. Finn Barre's was erected as a show of faith in the future of the Church of Ireland following disestablishment. The Cathedral parish, too, was alive; Galwegian Dick Grenham was headmaster of the National School next door where Arthur McAdoo, the Dean's brother, ran the Boy Scouts. The parish stretched from the city to the smart university area and the western suburbs along the south bank of the river Lee.

Round the corner and up a garden-lined drive was the Bishop's palace. This delightful tall and square Georgian building which faced the west-end of the Cathedral across the road, was also a place of activity. Bishop Gordon Perdue willingly received and helped me whenever I called for assistance. Also a Freemason, he once pointed to the two substantial piles of correspondence he had to deal with that morning; "That's Masonic and that's Church stuff. I have to sort through these each day". He was a dedicated, quiet and thoughtful pastor, loved and admired.

Although the hostel was not expensive, I had practically no money. My parents, who were not well off, helped me a bit and I had received a small grant from my home diocese of Cashel and Emly. I would have to raise an income to continue my studies.

At Murlough House in Co. Down, the Bishops' Selection Board for future clerics accepted me for the church's ministry. This meant that I could study for the General Ordination Exam and be given practical training on site. I needed help with theology and Christian ethics, Greek, Latin, church history and general pastoral studies - I was getting the latter, together with liturgical practice, from the Dean.

Some distance east from Dean Street, through a maze of narrow streets, was the Victoria Hospital where I came to know the nurses and staff and opposite, St. John's Church and rectory. This edifice, not fully under official Church of Ireland control, was administered by the Reverend Coslett Quin. A scholarly, kindly, professorial, gentle and pleasantly vague clergyman who spoke Irish as a native, he had an outstanding knowledge of Greek and Latin. Coslett and his wife Doreen had two young sons, John and David, and a daughter, Etaine. In return for my helping out with his Church Services and assisting with the teaching of his children, he tutored me for my exams. We remained friends long after. When at a much later date I was in Dublin, he asked me to help him out by taking services in his then parish of Billis, Ballyjamesduff and the rather remote Munterconnaught in Co. Cavan. I got hopelessly lost one Sunday morning as I sought the latter church but luckily the 'organist' had already decided to get the service going in the little church above Lough Ramor. Another Sunday, I ran out of petrol. The only locatable container into which I could syphon fuel from a 'Samaritan's' car tank was a plastic mug - as I frantically dashed to my car, the stuff melted the frail shell. Eventually I transferred enough to get to a service station.

In Cork, Cosslett spent patient hours helping me to master Greek. He made the language fascinating through his interest and by comparing it with others. For my part, I enjoyed his conversation and taking his Services. There was only a small congregation but I learnt a lot about composing sermons. Sadly, St. John's is now a college and no longer used for worship. I recall one of the first times I conducted Morning Prayer. At the East End was a three tier preaching 'tower'. Behind the altar, curved steps from either side led up to a prayer desk; above this was the pulpit. An earlier pastor, a not very tall archdeacon, could hardly see over the top of the protective wall of panelling. As a consequence, his churchwardens had arranged a small platform on which he could stand. To give my address, I stood on this, even though I had no need. As I gave my introductory words, I inadvertently stepped back and badly twisted my ankle as I landed on the lower level. Tearfully I hauled myself up and confronted the congregation. Their necks were stretched like ostriches as they tried to see what had happened.

Clerical circles in Cork were quite intimate in the 1950s. The city was delightfully provincial. Very few others had returned from abroad, so I was an almost unique phenomenon. I was invited to clerical meetings, my fellow hostellers asked me to their homes, I found myself attending evangelical gatherings, and my cousins the

Grove-Whites who were then in Glanmire, often asked me for meals. Commercial traveller Johnny Haworth, then an active layman employed by the "Aspro Nicholls" pharmaceutical company, felt the need for an inter-parochial fellowship group and asked me to help. Members of numerically diminishing city parishes were encouraged to participate in meaningful activities. One weekend over a hundred people participated in my pilgrimage to Cashel. I still have the group photograph published by the *Cork Examiner*.

A real break-through in my Cork experience was when I was offered the chance to help at the Grammar School. This well-reputed Protestant boys' secondary school had recently relocated from the city centre to Ashton, a pleasant well demesned suburban residence at Blackrock, south of the river Lee.

The headmaster, the Reverend Jerram Burrows, had Fermanagh connections and was previously the head of Villiers' School at Limerick; his wife Rachel, who taught French, was an accomplished amateur actress and artist. The daughter of Clare County Surveyor Peter Dobbin, she was brought up at Kilkishen House.

Jerram was a wonderful schoolmaster; I never heard this saintly cleric raise his voice in anger. Indeed, I recall one incident where a stocky little American boy, whose father was working at the new Whitegate Oil Refinery, belted full tilt down a school stairs and butted head first into the unsuspecting 'Boss'. Winded, Jerram ushered him aside and quietly explained that such activities were "not done" in civilised circles.

Rachel was a very social being. Every spare moment she organised the school staff, her friends and anybody else she could involve, to ensure the success of her many interests. Gradually I found myself under her spell and, in return for acting and doing odd tasks for her amateur drama company, Ashton Productions, meeting all sorts of fascinating people. Jerram was calm, Rachel was the reverse. Each of them were to have a tremendous influence on my life, becoming deep and sincere friends. Their two daughters, Mary, who was to marry Fergus Pyle, a journalist and one time editor of the *Irish Times*, and Margaret, now Mrs. Jim Sides, whose husband is the present rector of Kildrumferton and Ballyjamesduff, were still living with them. Mary was about my age.

The members of staff at Cork Grammar School were accommodating and helpful. One of them, Seoirle MacCuistín, (Sam Mac Cutcheon) became a particular friend. A Gaelic scholar, and a keen fisherman, he had done much to help the Church of Ireland establish the Episcopal Church of Spain as part of Anglicanism; he also translated Irish liturgies into Spanish. Sam was married to a Swedish girl, Barbro. He and I, together with friends would go fishing for bass in the tidal reaches around Monkstown to the south of the city, and to Ballycotton. There we hung passive limpet-baited lines for wrasse (rock fish) from the rocks while we cast our German sprats out to sea, from sometimes dangerous outcrops, seeking pollack and mackerel.

One Sunday, I was taking the bus from Monkstown into the city with my catch of two good-sized bass which I had loosely wrapped, open endedly, in a newspaper - they were laid head to tail. As I boarded the transport, the only available seats were the three-seater benches facing each other just inside the door at the rear. There was one gap between two elderly but plump women on the side I chose. Sitting in the vacant space, my hands held the centre of the newspaper-rolled fish. Disastrously, one shot from the open end onto the lap of my right-hand neighbour and the other slid onto the knees to my left. There was pandemonium; the conductor stopped the bus as I received a tirade of expletives from the mouths of the supposedly 'respectable" ladies. The situation was only resolved after profuse apologies. There was silence for the rest of my journey.

*   *   *   *   *   *   *   *   *   *

On the fourth of June,1958, three months after my arrival in Cork, I received a telegram: "Phone Red House Love Bobbie". I knew that my father had been ill, so I telephoned with an air of trepidation. Bobbie Hardy, my mother's childhood nurse and faithful friend answered: "Come quickly, your father is very ill in hospital".

There being no international airport in Cork, I travelled to England by train and boat. Soon I was holding my father's hand in a public ward at Ipswich Hospital. He was obviously dangerously ill. Doctors and nurses passed to and fro, but I was particularly disheartened and sickened when a seemingly experienced working intern passed. Trying hard, by positive thinking and prayer, to will my father to recover - even though that was unlikely - I felt that I was succeeding. "There's no hope for him, I'm afraid", said the intern. I am sure that Papa heard him, for I sensed him going downhill from thence. He seemed to lose interest in life and whispered that he was unhappy to have left Ireland; things just weren't as he'd expected. He died two days later. I was again devastated.

Papa was buried in Langham graveyard, which had been so familiar to him, following a service in the adjoining church. My mother and Guy, my aunts Brenda and Bryda, and a few other relations and friends were there. There was also, in the background, a soberly dressed lady who didn't seem to wish to make herself known to the rest of us. Respecting her solitude, I wondered was she his first wife? Perhaps I should have spoken to her but, in deference to my mother's sensitivities, I refrained. It was a sombre occasion.

I drove myself back to Cratfield, my mother and brother travelling with invited guests and friends. As I had had no lunch, and was hungry, I stopped at a small store in Stratford St. Mary where I purchased two pork pies. I was late and had to drive fast to arrive before the guests. Leaning over to the passenger seat, I unwrapped one of the pies from its cellophane and, still concentrating on the road, began to devour it. It didn't taste very appetising, but then I didn't feel that good. I ate the first but as I bit into the second, I realised that something was amiss. It was mouldy. Having kept the wrapper, I wrote to the manufacturer explaining where I had bought it, and the circumstances. I gave my Irish address for the reply. Two weeks later, the postman delivered a profusely apologetic letter; apart from being sorry, the manufacturers were enclosing a postal order which well covered the cost of my purchases. They were also forwarding five pounds weight of their 'special' sausages and one of their largest 'special' pork pies. Imagine my embarrassment when, after a further week, I received correspondence from the Department of Customs and Excise: "A Chara, we have at our depot one parcel the contents of which are reputedly five lbs. of sausages and a pork pie. Under government regulations, we are unable to permit the importation of products containing pork. We await your instructions."

The options were limited. I could only consent to the parcel being returned. No doubt some weeks later, the unfortunate Melton Mowbray manufacturer received a package containing very rotten sausages and a pork pie in a similar or worse condition than that which I had devoured. I actually felt sorry for them.

I was now anxious for my mother's welfare. She would be at Cratfield Red House on her own although it was some consolation that Guy was now at a school, Nowton Court near Bury St. Edmunds, only a short distance away. The moat-bound Suffolk house and its land were a basis on which she could built a future, although her money, and the little she had inherited from my father, was tied. She could either sell it and manage a smaller place, or take on something completely different. Some neighbours were kind such as the Luceys who forwent their farm manager Bob Eekhout. My mother, as independent as ever, insisted that I return to Cork. Guy was temporally still at home, so it seemed that she would be able to cope.

* * * * * * * * * *

Although saddened by the loss of my father, I found myself re-absorbed into Cork. Rachel and Jerram Burrows, the Quins, the Grove Whites and my many friends did all in their power to console me. I was made feel very much a part of their circle. In no time I was re-instated a member of 'Ashton Productions', rehearsals for plays taking place in the drawingroom of the headmaster's quarters or in the school's assembly hall. Rachel had a way about her which enabled her to organise all sorts of people. Concert pianist Charles Lynch would give us performances of classical music, Michael MacLiammoir and Hilton Edwards, Paddy Belton and Joan Denise Moriarty, the delightful founder of the Cork Ballet Company, would be amongst the many well known personalities I was to know. I also got an introduction to the bourgoisie of Cork, the media people from the embryonic Cork RTE studios, the school pupils, their multinational parents and a host of other ordinary and less ordinary citizens.

I felt privileged to become involved with so many interesting people. The corner shop, O'Keeffes, welcomed me back, as did the

Bishop, the Dean, the Cathedral staff and my fellow hostellers. The Grove Whites were selling Parklands, their pleasant Georgian residence with its surrounding strawberry fields above Glanmire, and moving to a smaller modern house on the edge of Carrigaline, south of the city; the Newenhams who took over still live in the house and manage the business. Terence Grove White, severely shell-shocked in the war, was married to Claire Fitzgibbon. His second wife, she was a member of the Co. Kilkenny family and also a cousin.

Jerram Burrows had me taking classes at what is nowadays Ashton Comprehensive School. Americans and other non-nationals were establishing the Whitegate oil refinery in Cork harbour and many pupils were their children from a variety of schools. This school work helped my finances. I also taught boxing to those who wished to take up self-defence - I had been quite successful in the army, having been initiated to the sport at an early age. Ex-pupil the Reverend Peter Hanna still tells me that he benefited from my efforts. I also undertook private tuition to individuals who needed help with exams or to keep up with their peers. One of these was a member of the Plymouth Brethren - my student and I would be ushered into a small special 'guest' room, separate from the adjoining house, each morning. There was an eerie sense of exclusivity, but I was well paid and my efforts culminated in success.

Cork was, and still is, a delightful provincial city with an intensely proud population. Indomitable, they put on a bright face even when troubled with poverty, family or other problems. They welcome conversation about themselves and the wider world. As a port its links, unlike the rest of Ireland, are seldom through the capital city. With its own daily paper, its impressive modern city hall, the huge Ford and Dunlop factories and its independent population, it was then very much the capital of the south.

The independence of the city, a hilly water-bound Venice, would often be reflected in its characters. Once, I passed along Bishop Street which ran below St. Fin Barre's Cathedral as an old lady laden with parcels struggled up the steep flight of steps leading to the Dean Street level. Feeling sympathetic, I offered to help. She turned on me as viciously as a cornered leopard. "I'm quite capable of managing my own affairs, thank you. Run off wid yourself, young man, and

mind your own . . . ." Speechless, I continued my journey hoping
that she wouldn't have a heart attack. She dropped a couple of tins
which rolled down the steps behind her, perhaps to be nicked by
less sympathetic kids on their return from school; they, though,
would be of her own.

There were funny sides to Cork life. One night I went dancing at
a National Farmers' Association event in the Imperial Hotel. Most
there were country people from surrounding districts. Even if one
stuck to one's partner for most of the evening, there was usually a
'Ladies' Choice'. This gave an opportunity for the 'wallflowers' to
take the floor. As I, like most of the men, sat on the periphery, a large
strong-looking well endowed farmer's daughter with a shorter-than-
normal flowery dress, made a bee-line for me from the opposite side.
There was no escape. Stunned, I was hauled to the floor with a swirl.
First she flung me, then she pulled me; it wasn't long before she was
squeezing me tight. I had hoped that the attractive little dark-haired
waif a few seats from me would have proffered her hand. As we
waltzed around the floor, my new partner pushed me slightly away
as if to address me: "Have oo a big farrum?" Dashing her aspirations
of marrying a wealthy landowner, I was dropped almost as rapidly
as I had been 'lifted'.

Often I would join fellow hostelers or other friends at a cinema.
There were quite a few in the city, the favourite being the upmarket
Savoy in Patrick Street. The magnificent concert organ rose from
below the centre of the floor as organist Charles Metcalfe belted
popular tunes. This became the main venue for the Cork
International Film Festival. Another cinema was the Lee. Here one
was happier in the cheaper seats - at that time the more expensive
'carpeted' chairs could have been the cause of discomfort as one
itched one's way home. One also had to choose one's neighbours on
the wooden front seats. Shawls were often worn by older women,
especially from poorer districts. The Arcadia was on the other side of
town but we were careful not to disclose our visits. Some people felt
it an inappropriate ballroom for an aspiring cleric.

The parishioners of St. Fin Barre's Cathedral considered
themselves somewhat superior to those of other city parishes. Many
of them were quite self-righteous, especially as regards their

expectations of the clergy. One Sunday, after mid-morning service, a member of the congregation approached me as I clutched the paper I had just purchased. "What have you papers for on a Sunday? Don't you know its the Sabbath, and you hoping to be a minister? You should be ashamed of yourself ". I had great difficulty in explaining that, having worked for a London newspaper, I could guarantee that the producing of Sunday's news was undertaken on the previous Saturday and that it was the purchase of Monday's papers which could be questionable.

Towards University College was a busy pawnbroker's shop. My financial chips were low and as I had inherited some expensively tailored clothes which didn't fit, I decided to pawn them. There were, to my knowledge, no second-hand shops in the vicinity. With no intention of reclaiming them, I chose a large bundle of clean items in excellent condition, convinced that they would be worth at least something. Having wrapped them in strong brown paper, I made my way to the front door and looked up and down Dean Street. There were few people, certainly none that I knew. Awkwardly and embarrassed I almost ran to the shop, opened the door, rushed in, and placed the parcel on the counter. "Phew", thought I to myself, "at least nobody saw me". The owner was dealing with another customer, so I opened the parcel ready to display the chosen items.

"Good evening, Sir. I'm afraid we don't take clothes here".

Stunned and mortified, I had never done this sort of thing before, even when I had been previously on my 'uppers'. I clumsily re-wrapped the parcel and stumbled back to the hostel in the drizzle. Not only was I still penniless, but I had received a blow; thankfully, none of my friends had observed my escapade.

In South Main Street, near Beamishs' Brewery, was a small fast-food outlet which dispensed delicious hot crubeens (pigs' trotters) wrapped in newspaper. There was nearly always a queue after the local residents and University students had poured from the nearby cinemas. Loose sheets of greasy wrappings would be blown around the streets.

One night at about four in the morning, there was an almighty bang outside my window. On opening it, I saw that a car had wrapped itself around an iron lamp-post close to the Cathedral gates. Together with pyjama-clad hostellers and sleepy locals, I rushed over to find the driver slumped over the wheel. His forehead had been bashed and there was blood everywhere. Returning from Dublin, he had fallen asleep at the wheel. The shock helped me to respect human capacities when in control of vehicles.

*   *   *   *   *   *   *   *   *   *   *

Although I was making some money through my part-time teaching, there was certainly nothing to spend on enjoying life to the full. I would join the lads for an occasional 'jar', visit the cinema, or purchase my crubeens, but I was spending more than I was earning. Having had my needs provided by Her Majesty's Government whilst serving with her Forces, and having managed to scrape through on my London salaries, I was feeling uncomfortably poor as a mature full-time student. This was having an adverse effect on my studies but my health dictated that I didn't overdo things. There were no State grants for my education in the fifties.

One day the Dean called me. I don't know if he sensed that I was at a low ebb. "Hugh, I've been considering the re-cataloguing of the Diocesan Library. Would you be interested?" Without hesitation I replied in the affirmative. I loved books and the old Georgian library building was only a short distance to the east of the Cathedral, on the edge of the graveyard. I would be getting £20 for the task. As I blew the dust off ancient volumes, some untouched for decades, I discovered many gems. Some were sold, and the proceeds spent on restoration, but I could keep a number of the modern theological publications to help my studies. Although I had never done book cataloguing before, I did quite a good job. Having finished the task, I was asked to undertake the Cashel Diocesan Library, later to receive sponsorship from Guinness Peat Aviation. It had particularly rare books. Unable to take it on, I successfully suggested a friend, Oliver Langley.

Another venture was the production of monotone postcards and calendars. I still have original pen and ink drawings of Blackrock Castle and St. Finn Barre's Cathedral. 'Special Card Services',

My first postcard; St. Finn Barres.

abbreviated as 'S.C.S.', was founded jointly with a young printer
named O'Leary. I had introduced myself and promoted my drawings
'on spec'. We didn't make a lot, but it was my earliest effort at
postcard production. We discontinued our partnership when I left
Cork.

Passing along Lancaster Quay, I observed a cycle and light
motorcycle shop. Outside were rows of Vespas and Lambrettas, most
of which were beyond my means. I asked what cheap models were
available, and their prices, having convinced myself that it would be
more economical to purchase one of these machines than spending
hours walking across town to Blackrock, or paying bus fares.

"What have you for twenty pounds?" I asked.

"Well, I've this one over here but its not reliable. . . . . This needs
a lot of work on it. . . . . " Recalling my Model Y success at Smithfield
Motors, I told the salesman that no way could I pay more than
twenty pounds. It had to be in working condition, reliable, and I
wanted a guarantee. It worked. I was soon riding a little German
N.S.U. 'Quickly'. It was in good order, had a fifty c.c. engine with a
kick-start, and was reasonably speedy . . . . downhill. It opened new
horizons. I explored minor roads around the city and as far as
Crosshaven and Kinsale where some of the women still wore their
characteristic Kinsale shawls. I rode it to Mariquita Cleeve's wedding
in Clonmel and, stopping near the town, clambered over an iron gate
- in the field I changed into my suit before continuing to the church
on foot. Few detected that I hadn't come by car.

At Myrtleville on the coast south of the city, I swam in a delightful
deserted cove. To my consternation, and theirs, a party of nuns
dressed in long black bloomers made their way down the path
towards me. I can still sense their giggles and innocent
embarrassment. They were so obviously denied the proximity of
semi-clad males.

Another summer's day I undertook a marathon journey, a real
challenge. As I hadn't been to Killarney, I set off early. Before
reaching Macroom, I turned off for the wild Inchigeelagh and
Ballingeary country over minor mountain roads to Kenmare. Having
walked my machine up much of the steep road towards Killarney, I
decided to take a narrow unclassified route through the gap of

Dunloe. There were hostile faces as I noisily put-putted past lines of heavy tourists mounted on docile nags and horrified Americans gaping from outside Kate Kearney's cottage. Already exhausted on reaching Killarney town, I decided not to break my journey except for chocolate and ice cream. The road to Cork was narrow and twisty over the Ballynasaggart mountains and as I passed Ballyvourney, the sun suddenly disappeared over the horizon behind me. Home at around midnight, I shook and shivered for days due to the vibration of my little machine. It travelled about a hundred and thirty kilometres on a gallon of lubricating oil and petrol.

It was increasingly difficult to study. The services in St. John's, and helping at St. Finbarre's Hospital where there were elderly Church of Ireland patients, took a lot of time. Chaplain Fleming at 'Our Lady's' huge mental hospital overlooking the river Lee became ill and I was asked to help by taking services in the little church at the bottom of the hill. There were usually fourteen or fifteen patients, accompanied by orderlies. It was distressing and I would be interrupted during my address by a woman who loudly insisted that whatever I said was heresy. Another would undo her blouse to reveal a gaudy picture of the Sacred Heart. Throughout the services, there would be constant interruption. I was relieved when the task was over. Warned not to become too involved, even psychologically, I had not fully heeded the advice.

One of the events of 1959 was the visit to Cobh of the Italian training vessel, the 'Amerigo Vespucci.' It had been some time since a really large sailing vessel had entered Cork Harbour. Black and white like a chessboard, this three-master was particularly graceful. I took a lot of photographs of her and of Cobh from a touring ferryboat. There were great crowds and flags bedecked every available pole.

Many of my non-working hours saw me at Ashton. Jerram and Rachel Burrows' conversation was enjoyable and worthwhile. Other attractions in their homely atmosphere were their daughters Mary and Margaret. Mary's friends included Marlynne who later married Presbyterian Minister Jim Flack, now a successful professional artist. Sam Mac Cutcheon would often stay after class and, during holidays, Cavan-man Harry Quinlan would visit. Come the evenings, the doorbell would perpetually ring and friends and acquaintances be introduced such as John de Foubert or Kevin Cole. Gregarious Rachel was similar to Lady Gregory. Both encouraged the arts, both were proud of their country, both loved bringing people together and both exuded encouragement. Sometimes visitors from abroad would stay, like American Professor Mendeonez who was booked to give a lecture. Expecting a suited gentleman, those who met the Dublin train waited until there was only a woman and a boy left on the platform. They had not expected a lady, let alone one accompanied by her teenage son. During an evening of classical music by Charles Lynch, the youngster was asked if he liked classical music. "I like anything with a beat", he retorted.

Ashton Productions, Rachel's amateur drama group, was something special. She lived for it and involved most of her friends. If they had no acting ability, they would be given a supportive role. Rehearsals took place in the School Assembly hall, performances in various theatres such as that of the Catholic Young Men's Society. I took part in several plays including *The Words upon the Window Pane* and *The Importance of Being Ernest*. I was also stage manager and painted back-drops. When we won the All-Ireland Drama Festival at Athlone, we hired an Austin A.40 car so that I could drive from Cork with members of the cast and props. Having collected the vehicle from the hire-company the previous day, I parked it in a narrow centre-city street and automatically locked the front doors. I was horrified to find that I had left the key in the ignition. Embarrassed, I had to explain to a patrolling guard why I had climbed through the unlocked rear door and over the seats to release the front door catch. At Athlone the following evening, we celebrated our success. Staying at the garden-surrounded Shamrock Hotel beside the town, I can vividly remember chasing 'frogs' around a goldfish pond in the rain. We almost ended up in the Shannon, too, as I had tried to scare my female passengers by driving down a boat ramp. At many venues, conditions were primitive. Once the lights failed and there was practically no audience when the electricity was switched on again.

The Cork drama scene meant that many of one's friends were connected with the recently established Radio Eireann Studios. I was given several parts to read and got paid substantially. Douglas Gunn later invited me to broadcast on the _Munster Journal_, a programme dealing with local issues and events in the Province. We have kept in touch, and Caimin Jones, who moved to the Banner County where he worked for Clare FM radio, now lives near Ennis.

Once the station needed me to record a piece in a hurry. They contacted the local post office, there being no answer from my number, Whitegate 214.

"Could you help me to locate Hugh Weir. . . . ?"

"Who's speaking. . . . ?",

"Radio Eireann, Cork Studios . . . . "

In no time Post offices on the roads north and south were located.

" . . . . Have you seen Hugh Weir pass?"

Eventually I was flagged down near Gort. Although one welcomes the efficiency of modern telecommunications, in those days everyone was ready and willing to help. I was able to return home, change, and be in Cork just in time to record my piece. At the time lines and equipment were not of a quality where phone-ins could be used.

*　*　*　*　*　*　*　*　*　*

Rachel Burrows, descended from Clare families such as the Pilkingtons and Keanes, had inherited a summer house facing the harbour at Kilbaha on Loop Head. It consisted of an east-facing single storey three room cottage, at the rear of which was a two storey return of nine or ten rooms. Encircling it was a paddock, ablaze with wild flowers in the summer. The road west to the lighthouse ran parallel a few metres from the house and every morning the rattle of churns would accompany the grinding of iron clad wheels as farmers conveyed their milk to the creamery. On the hill across the road, overlooking the Shannon estuary, were the gaunt ruins of Dundalhan, once inhabited by the Keanes of Beechpark, traditional guardians of the Bell of St. Senan. Markie Keane of Mogorban and Iva, his daughter, were also Rachel's kin. Old Mrs. Keane of Dundalhan disliked anybody smoking in the house and caused a special 'turret' to be erected above the nearby cliffs so that those who wished to indulge could retire in private. A swimming pool had been hewn out of a platform of rock below, approached by a cliff-hugging path.

The cottage at Kilbaha had the proverbial ghost. An elderly Keane matron was chopping firewood in front of the house at dusk when she observed a large black dog, its fiery eyes watching her. Scared, she threw the axe at it, rushed into the house and locked the door. The following morning, the creamery cars passing, she flung open a window and called out: "Joe, who owns that big black dog I saw last night?"

"Which dog. . . . ? "

Joe asked her where she had thrown the axe. There, on the grass, was the burnt impression of the iron axe-head.

"That's the devil's dog. He's around all right", said her farmer neighbour . . . . Keep your doors locked at night and stay indoors."

On my first visit to Kilbaha, I had been invited to accompany Rachel for the journey. Others would be making their own way. We boarded a Limerick-bound coach in Cork which seemed to stop at every village or cluster of houses. On reaching the Shannonside city, we had time to spare before the departure of the bus to Kilkee. In an O'Connell Street pub I was introduced to the proprietors and several customers, old friends, mainly in drama circles, of the Burrows when Jerram had been headmaster of Villiers School. Having almost missed our connection, we were soon passing Bunratty Castle. Along the main road, Rachel made observations on the houses and places we passed, and on the people she remembered. At Ennis we were joined by one-time actress Margaret O'Callaghan Westropp of Lismehane, near Tulla - her husband Connor was too involved in his daily milk round to come. At Lissycasey, Margaret and I were told the story of Fanny O'Dea and her fortified egg-nogs. A Justice had been so enamoured by the latter when he had anonymously called that, when the pub proprietress was charged before him for illegal behaviour, he dismissed the case. "From now on we will see no trees" said Rachel; there were, in fact, plenty. Even as we passed Moyasta Junction where the West Clare Railway, made famous by Percy French's song *Are you right there Michael, are you right*, split between Kilrush and Kilkee, there were trees. However, few large ones on the shallow peaty soil could stand the cruel Atlantic westerlies.

As we approached the ocean, we could glimpse the glistening waters of the Shannon Estuary to our left. "That's Kerry over there . . . . and look, there's Mount Brandon . . . . see it ?" The far coast was clear and sun-clad and I could visualise the whole scene on an imaginary map, like those over which I pored as a schoolboy. The approach to Kilkee was exhilarating. Hay was being cut by horse-drawn mowers in small fields where colourful wildflowers were as prolific as the grass. On the left was the little railway station, into which had pulled the diesel-engined bus-like train which had superseded Percy French's steam-driven engine and old fashioned carriages. The scene was unique. This was the real Ireland which, even in Cork, was showing signs of disintegration. As the bus came to a halt outside O'Shaughnessy's, I could hear the rev of the distant engine, and then two loud hoots, as the train pulled its way back to Ennis via Miltown Malbay, Lahinch and Corofin. There was a sense of being deserted, dumped in a wilderness unlinked to the rest of civilization. It was wonderful.

"Welcome back to Kilkee, Mrs. Burrows . . . . great to meet you, Hugh . . . . Miss Gloster (Rachel's cousin who lived at Wellington Lodge) was in earlier and wondered were you down . . . ." Although her kinsfolk, the Protestant Keanes, had not been particularly kind to the local tenantry, there was little visible animosity. One of them, Marcus, agent for the peninsular during penal times had denied the Roman Catholics a church of their own. This resulted in 'The Little Ark', based on a Kilkee bathing hut, being constructed so that Father Meehan could say Mass on the unowned beach, between high and low marks, when the tide was out. This innovative construction is now in Moneen Church. As we were conveyed by taxi from Kilkee towards Kilbaha, the purposeful salutes of those we passed or met reminded me of my old friends in Tipperary.

We pulled in to Haier's public house, and were greeted by proprietor Joe, his wife and a couple of local residents. We then continued up the slight incline, past a small tidal pool, to the house. The caretaker had unlocked the door and opened some windows to air it after the long winter. There was still a mustiness as we entered the damp-pocked hall. I was given the room to the right in which were two ancient iron beds with hair mattresses, a couple of pinewood chairs, a table and some fishing rods and tackle. The whitewashed walls were bare except for a picture frame from which hung a mould-clad print which had slipped from behind the glass. Later, I painted my first mural - a sea angler sitting 'on' the door lintel with his rod extended across the wall and his fishing line leading to the floor in the far corner. My hostess and Margaret went to their own quarters. We met up in the kitchen. There was a buzz of activity as food bags were opened, the larder and refrigerator packed and the taps checked to ensure that the water was flowing from the huge outside tank into which rainwater was channelled.

From day one, I loved the peace and tranquility, the bird and flower-filled sweet smelling countryside surrounded by moody seas, the warmth and friendship of the local people and the rich essence that was all that is best of this solitary outpost. It was so incredibly welcoming. Soon I was brought to meet blind Henry Blake, whose fascinating stories and folklore he related in his native tongue, much to my frustration; I missed so much by not having more than a very basic few words of Irish. Henry and I got on well, he recalling my Gaelic-speaking kinsman Lord Ashbourne's visits to Carrigaholt. I would guide him as he deftly tapped his white wand. Gradually I understood more of our conversation. In the evenings, we would stroll down to Haier's (now Moroney's Lighthouse Bar), or to Johnny's (Keating's), a characterful single-storey bar close to the pier-head. Here, too, would congregate fishermen and visitors from Kerry who had crossed in curraghs. There would be music and singing, some of the participants 'spooning' the rhythm by tapping two dessertspoons on their knees like castanets. Stout would be served in a motley assortment of glasses and jars.

Haier's was usually quieter but in the shop one could purchase daily necessities, even clothes. There was no public television to stifle conversation, even though rural electrification was reaching every corner of the country. The cottage had a gas cooker and there were calor gas mantles throughout and candles for emergencies.

Over the next few weeks of this, my first visit to Kilbaha, came Jerram, the girls, friends and a trickle of visitors from Kilkee and

Limerick. Some would come for the day, more for a weekend or a night, and there was an irregular coming and going which added spice to an already full programme. Some of us would troop over the hill past Dundalhan for a dip in the pool or to put out the lobster pots, these being collected twenty-four hours later and the catch of lobsters and crabs brought back for processing for the table. Afternoons would be spent fishing for mackerel or pollack at Horse Island or what came to be known, because it was one of my favourite stands, as 'Weir's' off the Rehy road a short distance beyond Haier's. Sometimes we would make our way to beyond the Bridges of Ross or to the often dangerous pools on the Atlantic coast. The big bridge at Ross, a natural loop of thick strata undermined by the swirling sea which had worn an inlet some distance further on, has since fallen. I was one of the last to cross it before its demise some years later.

One day, Harry Quinlan, Cecil Lowe who taught in Dublin, and I went fishing on a low-water-only island of rock which sloped down into the Atlantic beyond the Bridges. The sea was calm apart from a slight swell and we enthusiastically hauled in quantities of shoaling mackerel. Cecil was nearest the sea, Harry on the 'summit' and I, because of my inability to balance, had chosen a spot clinging to the steep side nearest the shore. Suddenly Cecil and Harry screamed "GET DOWN!" An enormous twenty metre high tidal wave bore down on us. As it crashed over us we felt the weight of the ocean.

Watching from the cliff were Rachel and Mrs. Michael O'Connor, whose teacher husband from Sixmilebridge had wandered inland. So convinced were they that we had been drowned that they ran to summon help. They were astonished when the three of us, sopping wet and minus our hats and rods and our catch, met up with them along the narrow bohereen. Our escapade taught me to respect the sea and to ensure that someone knew where I would be at any time.

Other activities at Kilbaha included visits to the lighthouse keeper who created intricate scale models of vessels which passed Loop Head. He would take us up the immaculately maintained circular tower and show us the huge lenses which had their own code-pattern so that ships' navigators would know which lighthouse they were passing. Just beyond the lighthouse was the narrow island known as Dermot and Grania's Rock, separated from the mainland by a deep and dark chasm. Cuchulain's Leap was too wide for even a gazelle to jump. Legend has it that a suitor chased the Ulster champion across Ireland to this extremity and, incredibly, leaped to the island after him. Frenziedly leaping back to the mainland he escaped her advances, for she missed her footing and crashed to the white-watered rocks below; hence we have the name Loop (or Leap) Head. Around the turn of the nineteenth century some of the Keane girls had a concrete plinth built into the slope above the chasm. From this, a crude wooden crane was constructed with a seat dangling from it. The young ladies would sit in it and be swung over the roaring sea to the island. A contemporary water-colour picture of this activity hung in the hall at Kilbaha.

Throughout the peninsula were features such as the 'volcano', a puffing hole near the lighthouse and 'the Cabin' which, built like a ship's interior, was once the most westerly private house in Clare. Hanging gardens were created halfway down the Shannon-side cliffs, Horse Island had its cave and souterrains, and there was the 'Little Ark'. There were also Carrigaholt Castle and Cross with its medieval church. Shops stocked bare necessities, but ice creams had been introduced. Milk, of course, came directly from the farmers.

That visit to Kilbaha was to be the first of many. Each guest would make their personal contribution by cooking or washing-up, hammering crab claws and picking out the meat, gutting fish or laying tables. There were also the more permanent activities. I constructed a sittingroom fireplace from circular stones submitted by Rachel (since removed by present owners Margaret and Jim Sides), created a 'coat of arms' of crabs and fishes in a lobster pot and executed numerous drawings and paintings. My hostess, a talented amateur artist, undertook oil paintings of local scenes as also did visiting professionals like John Teehan - lasting records of memorable days. That was also my first real holiday.

*   *   *   *   *   *   *   *   *   *   *

It was drizzling in Cork when we arrived back that autumn of 1959. Being in the valley of the river Lee, there was often a dull misty pall over the city. I didn't notice it this time, however, as I was getting worried. My studies were suffering and I had to get on . . . . and away. Trinity College in Dublin had just introduced a faculty of Biblical Studies and having applied, I had been accepted. On completing my autumn term at Ashton, I was presented with a generous book token on the School Prize Day. I then spent Christmas with the Burrows whose house party included an American artist and his wife and a China Missionary and his child; we had a huge traditional dinner. St. Stephen's Day was spent with the Grove-Whites at Lisheen, their small house at Carrigaline and, according to a letter to my mother, there was such a strong gale that I had to assist the 'Quickly's' motor by pedalling downhill against it. Other seasonal activities included several parties and the launching of the Cork Professional Ballet Company, of which Ninette de Valois was a patron. I also got the loan of a car in which I had driven the owner to Clonmel. While waiting for her, I had visited Kingsmill and Ruth Pennefather at Marlowe, near Clonoulty. I found it depressing passing my old home Ardmaylebeg.

Before leaving the 'Southern Capital', I learnt that a Miss Jennings was selling her Austin Ten. As it was a fairly old car, it would be going cheap. Twenty pounds, which I scraped up from various sources, made me its proud owner. Two weeks after its purchase, on the morning of Monday, 18th January,1959, I left Cork for Dublin. The vehicle barely started as the rundown battery needed replacing and the roads were icy after a snowfall. Negotiating Watergrasshill, some kilometres north of the city, I skidded all over the place as the tyres were bare. After an unpleasant and eventful journey, I arrived in Dublin late and continued south to Bray to take up my appointment at Aravon School. I would be able to attend Trinity and have a small income at the same time.

I was sad to have left a place and people that I had grown to love. I would, however, often return.

CHAPTER NINE

*Schools and studies. Mother re-marries. Buses in Birmingham,
a cottage in Clare, crossroad dances and Erskine Childers.
Language Schools, Russians, machinery and life in the west.*

"Good evening, Mr. Weir".

The 19th January, 1959 was cold and it had been snowing.
Aravon was the epitome of English middle class and Irish
ascendancy primary education. After Cork Grammar School where
we were all on Christian name terms, I was jolted with memories of
my less than happy English schooldays. The school was near the
centre of Bray, still a very 'West British' seaside town inhabited by
retired professionals and returned Commonwealth Servants. The
long two storey building was surrounded by confined pleasure
grounds. While its main entrance entered a thoroughfare of large
resort residences, its back gate faced onto Nóvara road, from the
reverse spelling of which it got its name. Just up the road was the
exclusive 'French School' patronised by the parents of adolescent
girls controlled by a less anglicised staff of delightful, mainly young,
ladies. I enjoyed their company more than that of my rather stiff
colleagues who called the boys by their surnames.

Aravon, established for some years, drew its pupils from
throughout Ireland. It was then run by an English couple, Mr. and
Mrs. Charles Mansfield. He had taught at Clifton College near Bristol,
but did not seem interested that one of my Gibson cousins was a
senior master there; his Cornish wife, Marvina, took a matronly
overview of domestic affairs. Most of the staff, although moulded
into the preparatory school system, were pleasant and got on well.
Brian Studdert, whose forbears hailed from Co. Clare, ensured that
the boys' physiques were developed through an almost military
discipline. Classical teacher Mr. Fisher, who lived nearby, was less of

a disciplinarian. Then there was Miss Moore, Mr. Hitchcock, a young English graduate, arts teacher Miss Price and Colonel Drew. One saw less of other staff members as most came on a daily basis. I was responsible for geography, history, general subjects and, due to it being a boarding school, house duties. These included the supervision of prep (homework) and giving an air of discipline during free time until the last seniors were abed. I would then collect my bundle of exercises for correction before the morning's classes, and make for the separate two storey staff house where I had my own lace-curtained and sparcely furnished second-floor bedroom. Brian Studdert and other resident staff members were also quartered in the stark Victorian building.

Among the pupils were Davidson, now better known as the musician Chris de Burgh, and the Cosby twins of Stradbally with whom, at their own school, my brother Guy had received his early education; Julian, a clock expert, once employed by Aspreys of London, has his own successful business in England. There were quite a few from Cork, the Allens, Haughton and Musgrave, and from the rural south-east, Boyd and Braddel-Smith while most, including the Goodwillies, the two Woodworths and Van Anrooy were from the locality; a few came from Dublin.

Bray was dull after Cork, although nowadays the town is quite lively. The rectory was about a kilometre from the school. Cosslett Quin wrote to me shortly after my arrival: "I think you will find Canon Campbell a nice man to talk to - mention my name to him, or I can write a letter of introduction if desired . . . ." The Canon was indeed delightful, and helpful. I was to see quite a lot of him and Mrs. Campbell. Their son John is now a senior member of the Diplomatic Corps. Cosslett also wrote regarding (boarding) school life: ". . . . as on a long voyage on a ship tempers get very short and frayed at the end of the term! Also meals are eaten often in grim silence which it is better not to break. But some of them begin to thaw and can be friendly and helpful in a shy way or patronisingly so try and stay the course and get on with your work as well as you can in the spare moments if any if you have any energy left." This was sound advice.

Most afternoons I attended the 'Diploma in Biblical Studies' course at Trinity College. The lecturers, especially the characterful

Professor Jenkins who was shortly to become Archdeacon of Dublin and who was almost a hundred when he died in 1998, the Very Rev. Dr. Salmon and Professor Vokes, helped to bring the Bible alive. I soon passed my Old Testament exams. Amongst those also studying were Jack Black, Guy's fellow pupil at Cashel National School who is now the Headmaster of Kilkenny College, Henry Brooks who became the rector of Dunlavin, Tom Corrigan who was, until 1996, Archdeacon of Meath, and the now deceased incumbent of Mohill in Co. Leitrim, Charles Meissner.

It was often difficult to find parking space in or close to Trinity. The Austin 10 was quite long and was giving trouble so I part-exchanged it for a younger Austin A30, a lovely little car. For the first time in my life I made use of hire purchase.

My first holidays from Aravon were spent in Cork and at Whitegate (Co. Clare) where I had negotiated with Mr. Daly, Chairman of the Board of Fishery Conservators, to lease the latter's tiny concrete hut beside Lough Derg at Williamstown. It was a simple building standing amongst bushes of evergreen Japanese honeysuckle. Approached by a short path from the lakeside road, it had bunk beds inside to the left of the central door while on the right was a black pot-bellied solid fuel stove which burned timber or turf. The central window opposite the door faced Williamstown bay over a small boat slip. It wasn't very comfortable, but it was home. Tim Treacy who was now in possession of my childhood haunts, Fred and Nancy Holland and the Burkes of Dromaan, would invite me to join them in the evenings. Harpist Olive Murphy from Cork shared a day's fishing with me on the lake but wasn't catching any fish. In response to her disappointment, I suggested she 'play the (harp) strings' on the line stretching from rod to reel. In no time she caught a large pike which played for some twenty minutes. Other visitors were mainly from Cork.

Come the end of the Easter holiday I was broke. I had overspent and the payments on the A30 were more than I could afford. I sold my car for £200, less than I had paid. My ability to visit friends or travel into Dublin was curtailed. The buses were irregular and it took a long time for public transport to reach the city centre; it was also expensive. I found it increasingly difficult to cope with my studies as well as fulfilling my teaching commitments.

On Sundays I was expected to conduct boring 'crocodile' walks to the Bray Promenade and around the town's streets. With my interest in natural history and the environment, I felt that many of the boarders for whom I was responsible at week-ends would enjoy strolls up Bray Head or to the muddy harbour. Not only did we go on such walks but, with the help of Miss Price, Colonel Drew and other staff members, took motorised excursions up the Wicklow mountains to Glendalough and Lough Dan, and to Holybrook, the delightful estate of Sir Edmond Hodson whose family I had known from childhood days at Williamstown. Such activity was not condoned for it permitted too much freedom in what was to me, a rather straight-laced set-up. Cosslett Quin was so right, especially concerning staff meals. After Princess Margaret's engagement to Tony Armstrong Jones was announced on the Radio Eireann news one morning, I cheerfully entered the diningroom, sat at the breakfast table, and blurted out "I hear Maggie's getting hitched". There was a deathly hush only broken by the headmaster's cryptic "You mean Princess Margaret". Silence reigned until we had finished the meal.

Aunt Lilian, hopeful that I would take on her estate in the Northern Transvaal, wrote regularly. She commented that my lifestyle was not hers; she wallowed in unpredictability and possibly misinterpreted the real 'me' and my true aspirations. The more I gleaned about apartheid, however, the greater was my dislike for a regime which failed to recognise the equality of man. Her letters were newsy and informative and recalled glimpses of her Tipperary youth.

In June, Sean Lemass was elected Taoiseach in succession to Eamonn de Valera. This heralded a new era in Irish politics and in the development of the nation; Ireland and Irish politics were seldom discussed at Aravon.

*   *   *   *   *   *   *   *   *   *

Bobbie Hardy stayed with Mama after Papa's death. Bob Eekhout, who had taken a practical farming course, was spending much of his time helping her. He had served as an R.A.F. Flight Lieutenant and at war's end, was in Germany and at Dover. His mother was a Dunn from Scotland and his father's basically Dutch family had owned an extensive timber business with interests in Baltic and Russian ports. This was confiscated during the Bolshevik revolution and the family financially ruined.

The following January Mama and Bob were married. As it was the beginning of term and my finances were minimal, I was unable to be present. The Registery Office ceremony was held at Saxmundham in Suffolk, after which participants adjourned to Seckford Hall where Guy, about to go to his new school in East Sussex, Uncle Mick and Pam Gibson, Aunt Jean Ayscough, Kenneth and Denise Tailyour and friends apparently enjoyed an excellent lunch. Mick supplied champagne. Papa's sisters and his family were generous too, with their gifts and support. Mama wrote me a long and unusually descriptive letter the following day and thanked me for my present. Bob was to be an excellent step-father, encouraging and generous of spirit.

At Bray I was not comfortable with what I believed to be an out of date educational system which echoed a redundant past. I accepted the offer of a position at St. Stephen's in Goatstown, closer to central Dublin. Due to my lack of qualifications in Irish, I was at the time unable to take a full-time Department of Education post. Incorporated Association of Preparatory Schools' salaries were considerably lower.

*   *   *   *   *   *   *   *   *   *

During the interim between Aravon and St. Stephen's I travelled to England and stayed a few days at Cratfield. There, my mother persuaded me to take my teenage brother on a journey to France to which she generously contributed. We toured the Manche-side resorts west of Amiens, a city I knew from previous visits. The elongated French buses which still had rear-ends extending far beyond the back wheels swayed over every undulation and over-rode the corners. The sun-warm shoreline was uncluttered, and unsophisticated seafood restaurants provided gastronomic delights at reasonable prices.

On my return, the short-lived Institute of Irish External Studies sponsored me to undertake a survey of the Irish in Birmingham. The amount offered would hardly cover expenses, so with the Institute's assistance and a little bluff, I undertook summer relief work for the Midland Red Bus Company. I was billeted in their accommodation at Sutton Coldfield, a suburban dormitory town. Merely tested as to my driving abilities, circumstances ensured only a few local runs. I became anxious that I was running over peoples' toes as they stood at street corners. Also, I didn't know my way around Birmingham: "Oi Luv, yor goin up rong way" commented a customer as she rapped on the dividing window. I spent the rest of the summer as a conductor.

I got useful insight into the conditions of immigrants in such areas as Erdington as they travelled with me, and contacted others at the end of each journey. I also visited Irish ghettoes. Being a bus conductor wasn't easy. One had a ticket machine, and a leather money bag slung over one's shoulder. If fully occupied on the rather awkward metal unit, one would find passengers' hands under the bag's leather flap - handfuls of coins and notes could be extracated. I soon learnt as, when I tallied my takings, what was counted was often considerably less than that taken in. I had to pay the discrepancy, so my left elbow became permanently pressed onto the bag. Often, I would handle a brawl, or difficult passengers, even be threatened by knives. Once there was a running battle and we had to stop at a police station. There were no mobile telephones, only secret signals between driver and conductor.

*   *   *   *   *   *   *   *   *   *   *

St Stephen's was originally located in Dublin's St. Stephen's Green. The martyr was, however, very much its patron. The school's founder was an English clergyman, the Reverend Hugh Brodie. He and his wife Lettice had moved their establishment to a largish park-surrounded two storey house at Goatstown in the south-side suburbs. There was a walled garden and a winding drive lead from the busy crossroads, overlooked by the quaint two storey 'Goat' public house. On a rise across the road was the exclusive Mount Anville Convent girl's school. Behind St. Stephen's stood Dromartin House, an older but once rural residence which, as well as dormitories and classrooms, contained teachers' accommodation, including mine. The staff such as

Colonel Paltridge, Mrs. McCreight, Aileen Finnegan and Paul Guinness, was mainly Irish and I felt more at home.

Just before I joined the school there was a tragedy, for the Brodie's popular only son was discovered dead in his room. This affected both staff and boys. The pupils were, interestingly, quite different from those at Aravon. Most came from the Dublin area, many being the children of businessmen or foreign diplomats such as the delightful Khan family of India. There was also a percentage of Jewish boys.

* * * * * * * * * *

At the end of my first spring term at St. Stephen's I would be driving down to Clare for Easter. A few months earlier, my neighbour Fred Holland, whom I had been visiting in his farmhouse above my grandfather's old home, asked me to sit down - I had got up to leave. "Hugh, you know the old house at the cross below?" "I do indeed, Fred" I replied. "I've been offered £20 by an Englishwoman. If you're interested, I'd much rather you had it. That old hut must be desperately cold." Caught on the hop, and being impulsive, I answered him in the affirmative there and then. So excited was I to own my own property and even though I had not yet paid for it, I slept that night under an awning in a corner, on the turf of the in-fallen thatched roof.

I recalled the White family rearing their twelve children in it when I was a boy. Before them had been Socey Mugavon, noted for carrying a firkin of butter on her head to the Limerick Butter-market every two months. A character, she hailed her neighbours as they passed bringing sacks of corn to the mill on ass-pulled carts. As they stopped to chat, she would flail the cargoes with her heavy stick, as if to emphasise points in her conversation, enough to cause the corn to leak through the holes she created. Her hens would appear from every nook and cranny. In her old age, local children would use bright lights to hunt and capture blackbirds and thrushes at night to augment her impoverished diet.

* * * * * * * * * *

I called my little home-to-be 'Cappaghbeg', due to its location in Cappagh townland and its small size. It then consisted of the two gables and a fraction of the linking walls. It had been a single-roomed thatched cottage. The west gable abutted the narrow unmetalled road as it approached 'Socey's Cross' whereas at the other end was the huge open fireplace, to the left of which was a low doorway. This led into a tiny angular room above a slow-flowing streamlet. To the south was a central door and, on either side, two tiny windows. The small front garden narrowed to where the stream met the road; at the back there was enough space to build an extension and to excavate a space for parking.

Not only had I never attempted to build a roof, but my polio-blighted physique wouldn't permit the effort. However, just over the Galway county border, at Coose, lived a willing and strong craftsman with a delightful disposition. Larry Darcy was to help me rebuild the walls to the necessary height and to cap the cottage with a corrugated asbestos roof. Little did anyone realise the dangers asbestos dust could cause, especially to lungs. I did, though, construct most of the rest of the house myself. I created two minute bedrooms in the road end and fitted bunk-beds. The ceilings were made of hardboard, as also were the partitions.

Having completed the main part, plastered it and given it a concrete floor, I roofed the little lean-to room behind the chimney gable and made it my dining area. I then bought single six-inch hollow blocks for an extension, and sheets of corrugated iron for its roof. From the dining area, steps led up to a small kitchen. I pumped water to the basin tap and to the adjoining bathroom from a well Fred Holland permitted me to excavate across the road. Heating and cooking were initially by bottled gas. Electricity was installed later, as also was the fourteenth telephone in the parish. A larger room approached by a small passage past the bathroom from the kitchen was my bedroom. The front door, protected by a small well-lit porch, was created from bits and pieces of salvage and gifts from friends and neighbours.

Across the front garden I constructed a small corrugated iron roofed guest hut using slobs (thin slabs of bark-sided timber of little use to sawmills). I worked so hard that one night I couldn't understand why the large nail I was hammering wasn't entering the wood. I was holding it with its flat head innermost. Fergus and Mary Pyle were to spend part of their honeymoon here.

Cappaghbeg was fun and my neighbours were wonderful. Once, when I was well settled in, a largish weather balloon fell on one of Fred Holland's fields. My tortoise had also escaped. Having never seen a tortoise, our characterful postman Jack Kelly put two and two together and excitedly greeted me. "They've landed, by God they've landed" said he. "Who Jack?" "Men from outer space . . . ." At the time there was talk of Unidentified Flying Objects.

One Halloween I had driven down from Dublin, opened up the cottage and lit a candle on the windowsill before visiting the Hollands of Nutgrove, towards Williamstown. It was a wet blustery night and my old friend Delia, Mrs. Paddy O'Brien, author Edna O'Brien's aunt, was by herself at Reinskea. Feeling lonely, she decided to visit neighbours and left her new hill-top bungalow for Fred Holland's, or the Burkes beyond. Religious but quite superstitious, she was relieved to see my candle-light at Cappaghbeg. "Obviously", thought she, "Hugh is at home!" Getting no answer as she hammered on the door, she panicked and ran for tree-surrounded Nutgrove. From inside, I heard the tremendous knocking and was called to greet her; at the sight of me, she became an unhealthy grey. Her knocking unanswered at Cappaghbeg, she had assumed that the light was supernatural and that I was still in Dublin.

During summer holidays, there was a stream of visitors. Some of these were old friends from Cashel and Cork while pupils accompanied their parents to see where Mr. Weir lived. Neighbours wanted to know what 'Master Hugh' had done to Socey's cottage. There were others, too, like Eoin (The Pope) O'Mahony from Cork. A family historian and genealogist with an incredible knowledge of people and where they lived, he had a programme on Radio Eireann - 'Meet the Clans'. He would often bank on his friends, including myself, for lifts. As one passed some imposing gateway, he was apt to get one to drive to the front door of the house. Uninvited, he would introduce himself and his 'chauffeur', and accept the hospitality proffered by the unsuspecting owner. I only wish, however, that I had listened to this genius more as he recounted fascinating stories about almost every significant Irish family.

In August, for several years, I hosted my own version of the traditional cross-road dance. As Cappaghbeg was at a crossroads, it was ideal. Crowds would gather from the locality and meet up with friends from Dublin, Belfast, Cork and even Scotland and France. Local musicians played traditional music and I would provide basic food. The bottles brought by guests were generally pooled. Events would begin at around five in the evening. Boats from around the lake would pull in to Sean Conway's neighbouring marl-hole harbour or to Williamstown and their occupants trickle up the hill; cars parked along the roadsides.

Cappabeg would be bustling with those who were staying as they organised the eats and chose their corners for the night. There would be greetings as people hugged and kissed and chatted and laughed with each other. As the evening progressed, more would appear and everyone warmed from the effects of inner refreshment. Occasionally, there would be extra activities such as when Rachel Burrows'dedicated' the cottage by throwing poteen at the front door lintel. For toilets, participants were told "take the first gate on the left (or right), go through it and cross to the second, enter the meadow and you should be able to enjoy some privacy". As the evening progressed though, urgency dictated that the journeys became shorter and privacy harder to accomplish. Eventually most, sober or drunk, local and visitor, would be stepping to the 'Walls of Limerick', the lead being provided by Martin Woods and other local musicians who played for the love of it. Come early morning when others had gone home, little clusters of inebriated friends would finish the remaining bottles. They would then crawl into sleeping bags or lie on rugs or anything else they could find which was soft. I would clamber over the last of them and locate my pad. In the morning there would be groans as each dozy figure would stretch and return to sleep for a few extra hours. None were giddy enough for early morning jogs and there were few for breakfast. As it was usually a Sunday morning, some answered the later morning call to church service or Mass. Those were happy days - I enjoy looking at my visitor's book and recalling those who were there, many of whom are still around.

*   *   *   *   *   *   *   *   *   *   *

My neighbours were delightful and thoughtful. At the end of one weekend, excited at catching a twenty-pound pike, I inadvertently left my fishing tackle on the low wall between the garden and the road. I only realised what I had done when, weeks later, I returned to Cappaghbeg. Shortly after my arrival, I saw from my window that my neighbour John Conway was hesitating at the gate, so I went out to him. "Hugh, you left your fishing gear and rod on the wall when you last went away. I didn't like to move them for a while, but after a couple of weeks I thought there might be visitors around, so I brought them down to my place. I'll bring them up later". Such was their integrity. The O'Briens and the Leahys, old John Tuohy, the various Hollands, the Burkes and Sampsons, the Rogers, Mugavons and Treacys were just a few of the many good friends around me, most of whom had known my grandfather and Dolly. There were also the visitors from further afield.

Canon Young, the rector of Mountshannon, and his wife, had been very close to my grandfather Willie Gibson. I have a wooden bellows with a trout taking a fly which the Canon had carved for him. The Youngs were also kind to me. During the mayfly season the rector would respect his small congregation's angling aspirations by shortening the service. Rather than delivering a long sermon, he would suggest that they should contemplate God's handwork when out on the lake. He was a good unsophisticated country clergyman. When Canon Crowe, the Roman Catholic parish priest died, the Canon walked beside the coffin - long before the popularity of ecumenism. I usually conveyed Miss Farran, an elderly second cousin of my father's, to church. She had been brought up at Tullitra or Fetherstone Lodge near Woodford. We shared Chomley ancestry from Belcamp, Co. Dublin. Lady Talbot de Malahide owned Mountshannon House, and other members of the congregation included the Thompsons, Howes, Flynns, Jamiesons, Hollands, Logans and Mrs. Veller, a Waterstone before her marriage to a German engineer who had been working on the Shannon Hydro

Electric Scheme. There were others, of course, and often there were visitors. I gradually became more involved in parish affairs.

*   *   *   *   *   *   *   *   *   *   *

The suburban South Dublin area around St. Stephen's was really a number of villages linked by large garden-surrounded detached dwellings. Goatstown, at the end of the school's drive, had a couple of rows of low single storey houses, two of which were shops - Shearins being where I bought my newspapers and confectionery. There had been a well in the Mount Anville wall and at the diagonally opposite corner was a garage from which I got petrol. Nearby Dundrum consisted of a bustling narrow main street. On one road from the school to the village was Taney Church while the large Church of Ireland National School was off the other. Headmaster Smyth, a vocal socialist, hailed from Newmarket-on-Fergus where his father had worked at Dromoland. Colonel Considine, of Dirk near Limerick, lived in one of the artisans' dwellings close to Dromartin House, our staff quarters. Opposite were the Misses Overend, one of whom owned an immaculate Rolls Royce; they kept a Jersey herd. Next door was Sir Basil and Lady Goulding's very modern home. Stillorgan wasn't far, but I found myself more inclined towards the city except on Sundays when, if free, I would make for Glendalough or the Dublin mountains.

Not all school holidays were spend in Clare. I went to France too; once to Argentat where the little bus-like train from Tulle careered down the mountainside at an uncomfortable angle before coming to a halt in a grassy open space amongst scattering poultry, and another time to Le Bugue further down the river Dordogne. I also paid visits to England and to friends in Counties Tipperary and Cork.

Term time wasn't that eventful. School policy here dictated that there wasn't a lot of imposed discipline. Once, when I was in charge, the gardai returned a boy who had absented himself. He was reported as having knocked an elderly lady off her bicycle and stolen her handbag. As the inspector handed him over he escaped to the basement, locking himself in the pantry. With visions of crashing china, I tried to reason. Eventually he agreed to come out, provided there was nobody in the adjoining room. Staff members and his fellow pupils watched from a distance as I breathlessly caught up with him on the games field where, brandishing an old badly burned broom at me from the other side of a smouldering incinerator, he kept me at bay. He had been brought from England by his mother following difficult family circumstances and obviously wasn't happy.

Since army days, I was a cigarette smoker, only giving up some time after marriage. Erskine Childers, then Minister for Transport and Power, whose grandson Nicky Moller was one of our pupils, was to present the prizes and give the school's speech day address. He would be greeted by headmaster Brodie at the main schoolhouse and ushered to the assembly hall where staff and boys would be expecting him. We waited outside the door so that we could follow him onto the platform. Several of us nervously puffed at our cigarettes and, as the party came into view, stubbed them out. I had only just lit mine so, rather than waste it, I fingered off the smouldering top and pocketed the almost unused 'fag'. We followed Mr. Childers onto the stage and took our seats, mine being second from the Minister's left. Proceedings were well under way when I smelled burning. I consulted my neighbour Colonel Paltridge who also detected a faint whiff. "Smells like cloth . . . ." Several other staff members whispered similar comments and expressed the fear that the place might have to be evacuated. Suddenly, and with great embarrassment, I realised that it was I who was on fire. The right-side jacket pocket of my new grey suit was gently emitting a hazy cloud of smoke. Without so much as a by-your-leave, I jumped up and dashed across the stage. Making my way through the door, I frantically patted the smouldering cloth. My cigarette had not been fully quenched. The Minister, following a rapidly suppressed general applause, was not amused.

On the staff at St. Stephen's were Trinity College students only a little younger than I. None of us were well paid. Paul Guinness, of nearby Tibradden, and I were offered well-paid parts in an advertising film. Paul, Brook Dowse, Kenneth Knowles and older staff members such as John Falconer and Madge Clotworthy would, with other friends such as Jennifer Gill, Jill MacDougald, Mary and

Margaret Burrows, Heather Crawford, Claire McClenaghan and
Christopher Moriarty (now with a house beside us) visit or stay at
Cappaghbeg. We also had social gatherings at school. At the end of
1962, the St. Stephen's staff was called to headmaster Brodie's
drawingroom. The school would be closing, the owner moving to
England, and the property sold. There were many unsettled parents,
staff and pupils as new schools were arranged. Some parents
withdrew their children. Staff members moved on too.

Early the following year the Brodies, who had sold to developers,
moved to the south of England. Several parents asked me to try and
keep the school going, but I was young and inexperienced and
would have had to seek major financial backing. As the remaining
resident master, I was left virtually in charge. At the end of the winter
term, I contracted jaundice. Quite ill, I should have been a patient of
the Fever Hospital. Instead I recovered at Cappaghbeg. In early April
Norman Lush, a senior master at St. Columba's College, whom I had
approached, wrote : "I am sorry that St Stephen's had to close; with
so many people interested in its continuance it could well have
remained open and prospered, but its knell was tolled last
September . . . ." He also mentioned a circular which had been sent
to parents. "Your heart was in St. Stephen's and you did a great deal
for the place, and I am very sorry for you that you have had to move.
St. Stephen's boys had positive characters, they were real people,
open, and unmoulded along sympathetic lines, they had minds and
attitudes of their own". He then continued his letter with less than
favourable comments on the situation and on those responsible.

The school was finally wound up. I agreed to purchase the worn
tintawn carpet, from my room, and a plywood wardrobe. They were
no bargain, and I found it hard to pay. Brodie had done well with
the sale of the property. "Small sums outstanding in old school
accounts are a bit of a nuisance - I am most anxious to get it all
settled" wrote he ". . . . we miss you all very much . . . ." Brodie did,
however, commend me to Peter Ross who had asked me to join his
staff at Monkstown. "In my opinion, Mr. Weir is a born schoolmaster
- he takes a keen interest in all departments of school life - nothing
is ever too much trouble for him. He is popular with staff and boys
and a most loyal and efficient member of my staff . . ." Although still

dedicated to my Church, I increasingly found that my time was being spent on school problems to the detriment of my studies. My bank account, too, was by no means flush.

*   *   *   *   *   *   *   *   *   *   *

In 1962, my mother and Bob sold Cratfield Red House. There were problems with the roof and the amount raised was not as expected. Bob, a keen sailor, and Mama investigated setting up a yacht chartering business in Spain due to the growing tourist potential. They spent the winter at Benidorm, a "rapidly growing holiday resort with a marvellous climate", where they were sunbathing in December. Guy stayed with them during his school holidays. By March however, they had purchased a small farm at Bedingfield in Suffolk where they erected a Cedarwood house. They also ordered two four and a half ton Bermuda sloops for their 'Seaways Charters' company, but by September that project had been dropped. Instead, they asked me to survey properties on the Dordogne. ". . . . we think you did sterling work in France and I hope it will prove jolly useful to us all . . . ." The Dordogne was then unspoiled and I had a delightful time. My mother, however, set up a successful antiques shop in Debenham and they stayed in that locality for some years before moving to Brockdish near Diss. In 1963 my brother left Brickwall for the Norwich School of Art and Aunt Alice, the second last of my mother's Gibson aunts died.

*   *   *   *   *   *   *   *   *   *   *

Brook House was a large grey detached house over a basement with a central front door approached by a flight of steps and surrounded by dark evergreens. My salary at this school, the largest so far, was £600 paid monthly with annual increments of £20 to a maximum of £1,000. Having been greeted by headmaster Ross, on the first of September 1963, I was taken to my quarters, a semi-detached end-of-the-line modern house built on infill adjoining school property. I had an upstairs room facing over the parking space where I kept my car. Downstairs, I shared a kitchen and livingroom with author and colleague Monk Gibbon, a good friend, even if we occasionally had our differences. The rest of the house was a dormitory for senior boys, our responsibility. They were a great lot and we never had trouble. Some of the pupils, like myself, had come from St. Stephens. There was still a bond between them, their parents and me. Mrs. Clotworthy had also joined us.

Colleagues here were a pleasant lot. The ambiance of Brook House was somewhat between those of Aravon and St. Stephens. Louis de Gardelle, from near Bordeaux, became a good friend and staff-room relations were great. Mary Duggan's husband, later Bishop of Tuam, was the rector of Glenageary while Harry Braddell's people came from the south-east. The matron, Peg Glynn, hailed from near Ardee while others were from Carlow and Dublin. Mrs. Ross handled household problems but willingly undertook other chores. The pupils, more diverse than those at Aravon, came from all walks of life and different parts of the world.

*   *   *   *   *   *   *   *   *   *

The rector of Monkstown, the Reverend Billy Wynne, was a founder of the Irish Samaritans. To encourage my involvement in parish affairs, he had me helping at the nearby young people's home and preaching in his imposing well-attended Monkstown Church. During this Lemass - O'Neill era, efforts were encouraging co-operation between North and South. The country was on a 'high'. The demolition of Nelson's Pillar by subversives however, which I heard from the school, dampened the nation's enthusiasm.

*   *   *   *   *   *   *   *   *   *

At St. Stephens I had been able to take the school on educational trips. Brook House, however, preferred an English orientated in-house education with little parental imput or interference. Amongst my friends were John and Aileen – who had taught at St. Stephen's - Finnegan, Kitty Hassard who was on the staff, Jennifer Gill and June Trotter. Quite often I'd drive Monk Gibbon to his home 'Tara Hall', his normal transport being an elderly bicycle on the carrier of which he would tie a Jeyes toilet-roll box for transporting library books. He was working at Farrell's *Thy Tears Might Cease* and would ask for my assistance or opinions. With 'Monkey', as he was affectionately known, I visited Lady Glenavy - Patrick Campbell, her son, often joined us though most of his time was spent in London and with the B.B.C. - and Dame Ninette de Valois's sister, Mrs. Hornidge. Some parents became good friends, many remaining as such; John Goodbody, our school doctor, has a house near my present home and the Prentices, in Mountshannon.

At Brook House, I had another smoking 'incident'. Smokers often say that they can't "kick the habit"; I learnt my formula by accident, having unsuccessfully tried to give up cigarettes. Come one half-term, I read about nicotine substitute tablets available in Northern Ireland. One of my pupils would be going home to Belfast, so I requested him to get me a packet. An inquisitive youngster, he asked why I wanted them, so I told him. The following week he produced the package for which I paid him. Days later, I having discarded the tablets with little intention of denying myself my addiction, he asked if I had started taking them. "Not yet, but I'll start soon". "When?" he asked. I was so taken aback that I gave him a date. Trapped, I couldn't go back on my word. Within weeks, he was able to congratulate me. It was not long, however, before I was smoking cherootes. I codded myself that they weren't detrimental to my health - smoking only ten a day, I wasn't inhaling them.

* * * * * * * * * *

During St. Stephen's school holidays, I had had two van Beuningan brothers from Utrecht to learn English. They had been recommended by Noelle Clery whom I occasionally assisted with her English language school. In 1964, the Griffiths of Foxrock asked me if I would take on a young Spaniard. As I already had a repeat booking for one of the van Beuningens, I agreed. Mary O'Sullivan and Board Failte were most helpful with contacts and by lending me printing blocks for my 'Cappaghbeg Language Centre'. I was able to farm out, to guest houses and friends, foreign pupils who would assemble at Cappaghbeg each morning for English classes. Thirty minutes would be taken up reading and discussing the *Irish Times*, then on a walk students would learn through the things we'd meet, by interaction. The practical involvement was appreciated, certainly it was successful. That year besides Frederik van Beuningan, I took on his cousin Frederik Hinse from Eindhoven and their friend Daniel Koopmans, two German students, two Cork youngsters with parents in Rome, and Tomás Cologan Machada from Teneriffe, the Spanish boy recommended by Moira Griffith. Tomás's O'Callaghan forebears were from Clare.

The pretentiously-named 'Cappaghbeg Language Centre' thrived on its increasing reputation. Five years after it had started, Hendrick Jan van Beuningen commented in the visitor's book "a nice place to learn English" but Hein, on the line below, wrote "Many successes with your engines". I had decided to discontinue my initiative as a sudden upsurge in popularity for teaching foreigners had lowered standards, and some accommodation was not being checked. It was a pity, as my formula worked, even if based on a small country cottage. I was also a founder member of the first organisation for teachers of English as a foreign language, in Dublin.

Along with Liam de Paor, Maurice Craig, Kevin B. Nowlan, Maurice Manning, Marcus O'hEochaidh and Keeper of the National Museum, Brendan O'Riordan, I was appointed lecturer for the Institute of Irish Studies. At this time, Ireland was beginning to be recognised by non-nationals as something special, a leader of the Celtic world. In promoting this we were perhaps basically responsible for the later title, the 'Celtic Tiger'. Such activities, together with chaperoning groups of foreign visitors on educational tours of Ireland for the Language Centre of Ireland and other professional bodies, brought in necessary income. Radio Eireann's P.P. Maguire also provided me with lucrative radio work.

*   *   *   *   *   *   *   *   *   *   *

One of the most interesting groups I led, in July 1967, consisted of the first official tourists from the Soviet Union. With interpreter Angela McQuillan, early one Saturday morning we left by coach for Lisdoonvarna for a late lunch at the Royal Spa Hotel. An afternoon tour of Galway city was followed by an evening of songs and music and the next day, Connemara. Having visited Clare, and Ardnacrusha Power Station, the following night was spent at Tralee's Meadowlands Hotel where we hadn't been booked in. Unfortunately, the tour organisers had little experience of Irish roads or of the time necessary between venues. We toured Killarney and Cork where, late at night, we found our way to St. Xaviour's University Hall, run by monks. The Russians seemed content with its spartan institutional atmosphere. Father Hurst looked after us well and all were abed early. We visited historical and industrial sites, and also got an insight into 'Trade Union' Cork. The Union Headquarters laid out a red carpet. It was blatantly obvious that I, not a card-bearing Communist Party member, was ignored. About to introduce the leader of the Russians, I was pushed aside while one of the hosts proffered his hand to the wrong person; little did he realise the friction he caused the group, who respected their hierarchy. "Welcome to Cork. Its great to welcome the first Soviet tourists" said he. We uncomfortably followed him to where there were interminable self-congratulatory speeches. Eventually I got cross and forced the release of the group for we were well behind schedule. It was an unpleasant experience - the Russians were sympathetic and obviously uncomfortable. On the way to Cashel the following day, we stopped at Mitchelstown and had a conducted tour of the Co-operative cheese-making plant. Here greetings were also exchanged and each called the other Comrade, but the atmosphere was easier and inclusive. There had been intercommunication between this co-operative and others in the Soviet Union.

Lunch in Grants Old Castle in Cashel was followed by a tour of the Rock and other historic sites. After visiting the Design Centre in Kilkenny, it was later than anticipated when we delivered our exhausted charges to their Dublin accommodation. Later still, as they would be departing for Moscow at six in the morning, we gathered for a farewell. There were speeches, then silence as the Russians widened their circle. Leader Vasily Minayloff and Interpreter Vladimir Pavloff joined us up front. All were poker-faced as the representative of Bord Failte, and then I, were presented with velvet-lined cases each containing a large key. Neither of us was suspicious as cheers and thanks were re-iterated in Russo-English. "We present you with the special freedom of the city of Moscow . . . . may you enjoy the wonderful hospitality that this token implies". Awkwardly, and for my part perhaps pompously, though touched and grateful, we thanked everyone and wished them well. Hugs and kisses were exchanged before we returned to our respective homes.

When I got home, I was fondling my silvery engraved key with pride when I discovered that the oval handle separated from the shaft. Unscrewing and unsheathing it, I revealed a sturdy corkscrew. I could only laugh at the Russian sense of humour and at my own naive interpretation of a gift I still enjoy. Amongst the selected and approved members of the Russian group were teachers, engineers, workers, technicians, students, journalists and Ismailowa Adel Seidali Kisi, Aserbaijan Consultant of the Supreme Soviet. Neither she, nor the nominated leaders were the real bosses. An inconspicuous 'worker', anxious if someone was late or if there was some hitch, reputedly had this role. I was sorry when we said good-bye. In my Cappaghbeg visitor's book, having enjoyed the 'facilities' en-route to Limerick, the Russians wrote complimentary comments such as Adel's "It is wonderful! I enjoy it very much". Two of them did little line drawings.

* * * * * * * * * *

Brook House's owner and headmaster, Peter Ross, took on a bright business-like English mathematical genius as his Assistant Head. As a geographer I had for some time been suggesting that I might have a specially designated geography room. Facilities would include pull-down spring-loaded maps, a projector, a small globe for each pupil and other basics which would have required little expenditure. Mr. White and I had very different priorities and the investment could not be justified. I felt it was time to change professions.

* * * * * * * * * *

The Royal Dublin Society's Spring Show had always lured my family to Ballsbridge. Together with the August 'Horse Show' which was more fashionable, it was one of our major annual events. Farmers and landowners, country people and those from the city would gather at the show grounds. Here we would meet neighbours, friends and those we hadn't seen for ages. Bargains were struck, rosettes pinned and there was an air of professional rurally-based festivity. I was particularly attracted to the machinery. The extensive 1967 show included a display by Beaver Engineering of Bosch and other equipment, including a new machine which Director Cassidy felt wasn't quite in their run of things. The Kyoritsu Power Scythe was a forerunner of the now popular strimmer and brushcutter. "Would you be interested in appointing me agent for these machines?" I asked. Soon I had a contract as sole agent for all but a few eastern counties. The agreement was ideal for, although Beaver would have their 'take' on each of my sales, they would be responsible for the importation and large-scale financial arrangements.

Armed with my contract, I had no commercial expertise apart from a certificate stating that I had successfully passed a military demobilisation course in commerce. With Cappaghbeg as my base and with a secondhand Ford Escort, I was exchanging the secure profession of teacher for the unknown. With a newly purchased secondhand 405 line television, bits of furniture and my personal belongings, Pepino and I drove west. Pepino, a mainly brown Jack Russell terrier, had been given me by the Rosses; he was a brother of one they kept. A great little character, he grew to love the car and to enjoy the travel I was to undertake. Yet another time, I was saying adieu.

Grania, self, Suzanne O'Brien and Maryangela Keane, The Burren, 1977

CHAPTER TEN

Rural business, machinery and overdrafts - a new store, manual telephones, bank strikes, death. Legacy, Dr. Barnardo's and Belfast - a marriage proposal and O'Brien family difficulties.

In July 1967, I settled permanently into Cappaghbeg. I had already got my first Kyoritsu Power scythe from Cassidy's, later re-named Beaver Engineering, and had taken delivery of the Dutch "Mistblower" sprayer I had seen at the Cologne Trade Fair. Over the next four years, I took on other agencies. Alfie Leonard of Ace Heaters in Rush supplied me with Mountfield mowers and his industrial heaters, giving me sole agency for the west together with New Zealand-made Masport mowers. Lenihans of Capel Street in Dublin and O'Sullivans of Cork provided chain saws and tillage equipment, while I bought Skill and Wayne tools from Cunninghams of Phibsboro' and McQuillans. Having no capital, I relied on the thirty days before invoices had to be paid, hoping to sell within that time My manager at the Munster and Leinster Bank's Cashel branch suggested that while he was unable to permit an overdraft, possibly Limerick would. On his recommendation the city's O'Connell Street branch facilitated me .

Once I had started business, I had to keep going and add to my stocks. If I ran out of a machine or spare part, and had yet to be paid for it, I had to find money to replace it. It was imperative to stock quality goods, supply them speedily and ensure that repairs were rapid. The shock absorbers of my comfortable if rather sedate bench-seated Morris Oxford were unable to survive local roads. It was also expensive to run and unsuitable for mowers and agricultural machines. Sheils of Ennis traded it in against a new five hundredweight Ford van, DIE 996.

For many years, I produced letterheadings and Christmas and business cards on my Adana letterpress printer. I have always been fascinated by printing and graphic art. I got my blanks from Masseys in Dublin's Harcourt Street, an exciting shop although, also a chemist's, much of their stock was in the storeroom beyond. My commissions brought in extra finance with little capital expenditure. The Leggs, whose sons Colin and Stephen I had taught, built a bungalow at Mountshannon and Desmond Legg, a senior executive, arranged an agency for me with the Royal Exchange Insurance company. Many tractor customers accepted my recommendation, and I would automatically receive a percentage of annual renewals.

Even with supportive friends and neighbours, Whitegate was not the best place from whence to run a business. The population was small. Rather than machinery, people were interested in boats, fishing tackle, and tools; I did, however, sell outboard motors including the four stroke 'Ocean' from Yugoslavia. My prospects for expansion were restricted.

Since childhood, I have loved travel. I also inherited, perhaps from my maternal grandfather Willie Gibson, a love of machinery and cars. This encouraged me to drive throughout Ireland, mainly the West. I had an affinity with my farmer customers, as much a social challenge as an exercise in money-making. Sometimes I would spend a whole day bargaining, for time was plentiful. Although I disliked whiskey, I swallowed large tumblersful. To have refused would have been impolite. Those who proffered it were perpetuating an inherent generosity. On completion of successful sales I was also offered tea with fresh brown bread.

Lawnmowers and tillers found homes with doctors, widows, at schools and cottages, County Councils and Artificial Insemination headquarters. I sailed to Canon's Island in the Fergus Estuary and out to Aranmore. Near Waterville, there being nowhere to turn my vehicle, I had to back kilometres up a narrow wall-bordered bohereen, well warmed with local poteen. Retailers received regular visits as I built up a network of stockists, mainly for Kyoritsu, Mountfield and various quality tools. I would usually be generously welcomed.

On longer journeys to Kerry or Donegal, I stayed in hotels. This, Beaver Director Jim Kennedy assured me, was a way to make contacts. Even at commercial rates, accommodation for twenty-three shillings at Wexford's Whyte's Hotel in 1968, half-board at the Grand Central in Westport for less than two pounds or, a couple of years later, a bed at Sligo's Yeats County Hotel for seven, sounds ridiculous today.

My regular visits to Dublin to stock-up were time consuming. I only dared invest in a couple of machines at a time. During a good selling week, this meant the loss of a day, and about five hundred kilometres extra driving. Returning from sales missions, I would have to up-date my records - such office work is still anathema to me. I had official looking invoice books, receipts and forms, and an efficient office scene; I also had a typewriter and, with two fingers, made a reasonable job of my correspondence. Because I had worked in advertising, I spent an inordinate amount on publicity. The *Clare Champion* and the *Limerick Leader* were mainly patronised. I also bought stand-space at Limerick and Ennis Shows, and at Ballinasloe Fair. My stall at the Dublin Spring Show in the seventies cost £45 for each of two consecutive years. I later joined Beaver Engineering's at their ample outdoor space to demonstrate Kyoritsu and Bosch tools, and to meet customers. Despite my efforts, I found it difficult to succeed without capital. Since leaving Dublin, I had devoted at least six very full days a week to sales, office work and travel.

* * * * * * * * * *

On Sundays I attended church at Mountshannon. Edgar and Irene Talbot were now in the rectory although, unlike Canon Young, he was Bishop's Curate. My theological studies had been shelved but I still needed a vehicle by which to actively practise my faith. Killaloe Diocese became this. I conducted church services and local people came to me for help. I don't think anyone could have considered me particularly religious though.

Dean of Clonfert Cyril Champ was kind and helpful. Of Huguenot origin, he shared my interest in history; we were both also keen on graphics and printing. Apart from his persistence in introducing me to unattached female parishioners, he often invited me to share his table. Considering the purchase of a small cottage, he asked me if I

St. Caimin's Church, Mountshannon

knew of a place similar to Cappaghbeg. Feeling the pinch and as it
was not suitable for business, we agreed on a figure and I transferred
my abode to his name. Determined to promote the area on the
commercial map, I leased a bungalow in Whitegate from my friend
Josephine Lucas. This enabled me to supervise the erection of a
purpose-built shop, office and workshop on the main road nearby.

At the Whitegate bungalow, I opened a shop. There was room to
display not only small tools but tractors and farm machinery. One of
the machines I displayed outside was a Steyr Daimler Puch four-
wheel-drive truck which, frustratingly, had a maximum speed of
twenty-five kilometres an hour. I bought it from market gardeners
north of Dublin. It was in perfect condition but I was able to observe
every metre of the highway as I drove it to Clare; I sold it to Lord
Blyth. Adrian, his son, had established Rockfield Engineering and
was importing Ursus tractors from Poland, the agency for which I
took for Clare and Limerick. A tough but crude Eastern Block

machine, the popular thirty-five horsepower model retailed at £690. This was approximately doubled, however, when we lost the importation to a larger company from Wexford. I sometimes took delivery at Nenagh, our nearest railway goods station. This meant crawling home for up to five hours. When turning off the Dublin to Limerick road, for Killaloe, I once understeered, hit the bank and almost overturned. A delivery from Whitegate to Labasheeda necessitated seven hours of hitching home; there was little traffic that day, only sympathetic farmers on short journeys. I personally delivered each machine throughout my allotted territory. Mechanical problems were usually due to the "Monday morning" syndrome, then quite common in Communist Poland.

Beaver Engineering were Bosch power tool agents. Thanks to their management, mainly Jim Kennedy, I became a supernumerary local representative, Kevin Synnott being responsible for overall sales. In the summer of 1970, I had attended their instructive Sales Seminar. When I took on Kyoritsu, I had no one to show me what to do if a machine broke down. At my first repair call, I agonised trying to replace the disassembled parts, closely watched by my sceptical customer. Miraculously I succeeded. The course, attended by knowledgeable representatives of large Belfast, Dublin and Limerick companies, gave me a needed insight into the works of electric tools. I now felt competant to undertake the sole Irish agency for Val d'Or from France and to distribute those of Skil and Peugeot.

"You'd best get rid of that van, Hugh", advised friends. "Customers are more receptive if you turn up in a car". In January, 1969, I purchased LIE 990, a robust secondhand Ford, ideal for poor road conditions and less than a year later, with a hire purchase loan, I became the proud possessor of a new Ford Escort. Pepino loved it. He would place his paws on the dash as he stood on the passenger seat, and cringe when we were about to negotiate a bridge or a bump. He knew the roads.

Visitors, including my cousin Chlöe Gibson (later Cockerill) who was studying at Trinity, and her friends, came and stayed. As building progressed at my new store on the Mountshannon road from Whitegate, I tried to keep the bungalow manned, as I delivered throughout the country. In May, 1971, I was demonstrating a rotary mower to a lady in her garden near Castleconnell. As I tipped the Mountfield on its side to demonstrate the rotating blade, I lost balance and thrust my right hand out in a natural gesture to limit my fall. My middle finger was severed. Not fully realising the implications I ran warm water over the stump and blood covered severed finger while Dr. Flynn in Castleconnell was contacted; we were on our way, Mrs. Lind at the wheel. The doctor ordered me straight to Limerick's Regional Hospital where I was ushered down corridors to where a surgeon awaited me. Beside an operating bench, my fingers outstretched on an attached side 'table', the separated portion of my finger was placed in position. A local anaesthetic enabled me to watch it being sewn back. It was an incredible feat and I still have almost full use of it.

On the other side of Jacky Tuohy's cottage from my onetime lakeside hut is Grove Cottage. The Kellys settled here after Buzz (Robert) Kelly's retirement as a civil engineer. Related to the Gleesons of Tinerana near Killaloe, he came from Athlone while his wife Paul was from the North. I was always welcome. After the finger episode they were wonderful and it was through their kindness that I rapidly recovered. Their eldest son Tom now lives in Dublin following a successful business career and his brother Patrick is a Trinity College history lecturer.

*   *   *   *   *   *   *   *   *   *

Life had not been easy when I moved my business into the purpose-built store and headquarters. Having started merely as "Hugh Weir", I spent several years promoting "Weir's of Whitegate", eventually establishing a limited company, Weir Machinery Ltd. This meant a lot of extra work such as Value Added Tax returns, but it legally safeguarded me. Peter Prentice had made a wise suggestion.

The new store was built in a half acre hollow a kilometre west of Whitegate. I filled in the dip between it and the road as a parking area. From the front of the building one entered a largish retail space with an office in one corner. Steps led down to a service area behind. This was approached by a double doorway from outside and off it were two small rooms for spare part storage and tools. Hidden by the level-topped three front walls was the lean-to corrugated iron roof which sloped to the rear and at the back was a grassy area planted with poplar trees and shrubs.

As I was away so much, I gave occasional employment to neighbours such as Peggy Malone. Peggy took charge of the shop and manned the telephone. We were often mesmerised by the amount of pilfering, not only by Irish people but by foreign visitors. The shop was stocked with, besides the goods I sold wholesale, picture-frame kits, toys, souvenirs from Hector Grey, cigarettes and confectionery from local suppliers like Mr. Notley from East Galway.

The Whitegate telephone exchange, one of the last to go automatic, was in the post office. To ring someone, we would turn a handle on the side of our black telephone, pick up the receiver and wait for the operator. Asked for a specific number, the McDermotts would connect us to Limerick. At the end of each call we would ring off by again turning the handle. I needed an answering machine for when Peggy was off-duty and I was away. Problems arose when it was installed. Many customers had never been answered by machine. When playing back the tape there would be comments such as "Mary, Mary . . . . there's some quare fella gabbling on the phone . . . . hello. . . ." or "Jesus, how de ye speak to a machine?" Occasionally, callers would leave an order but fail to give their name or number. This was frustrating.

Rather than manage two premises, I bought a secondhand caravan to sleep in which I parked beside the shop. As it was for summer use and uninsulated, winter nights were often bitterly cold and sleepless.

* * * * * * * * * *

The early seventies brought unforeseen circumstances, especially 1970 when there was a national bank strike. Not only did legitimate businesses suffer, but there were also 'fly by nights'. One German 'gentleman' bought agricultural equipment for his new estate and gave me a cheque. As the strike ended, he sold up and left the country before I had a chance to learn that the cheque had bounced, a blow from which I hardly recovered. This was compounded by the genuine retail customers who, in their own turn, were not paid by their debtors. I felt sorry for these businessmen who, like me, were on a 'tightrope'. We were all in trouble.

*   *   *   *   *   *   *   *   *   *   *

My grandfather Willie Gibson's last remaining sister, Lilian Francis (Tante Lil), with whom I corresponded until the last, died in July 1971. Peter Howorth, my great aunt Alice's son and his wife Val, flew out to Natal; she had left my mother, my brother Guy and me equal shares of her estate. Although I had never met her, I missed her letters and her interest in my future. She was the last link with the Gibson's Rockforest in County Tipperary. After the news, I made a sentimental journey and strolled along roads bordering the estate when I tried to picture it as it had been when my grandfather and his sisters were young. I recalled stories they told me and was able to identify some of the locations. There would be no more. I felt lonesome.

I had no indication as to how much Aunt Lilian had left. I understood that she hadn't done well when she sold Wilton Valley, her large Northern Transvaal farm. The politics of the time were unfavourable to white settlement so far from Cape Town but she had a comfortable house with a beautiful view at Botha's hill. I obtained a small advance from my bank on the strength of correspondence with Barclays Bank, her executors. This enabled me to pay off debts. It was some time before I knew the extent of my fortune; meanwhile, I was penniless and had a living to make.

*   *   *   *   *   *   *   *   *   *   *

As luck would have it, Douglas Gunn whom I had known in Cork, and later in Chapelizod, contacted me. He had been devoting his organising skills to Doctor Barnardo's in the Republic of Ireland. He was, however, leaving the job; would I like it? I was delighted at the prospect of having £1,200 a year, a comfortable roof over my head and the opportunity to be involved with young people. The job would afford me the chance to travel, and to promote my own products during non-working hours. After an in-depth interview with

Assistant Director Mrs. Steadman at Barnardos' Barkingside Headquarters near London, I accepted on the understanding that the job wouldn't be full-time and that I'd be in Clare for weekends. After two and a half decades, I was being drawn to the girl who had attracted me at Limerick Show. Her involvement in Lifeboats and An Taisce, the Irish National Trust, ensured that I'd be in Clare to encourage her, mainly at weekends.

A well-equipped two storey house in Clondalkin, west of Dublin, facilitated access to the road home. I was able to entertain friends and, along with my salary, had generous expenses. Although every move and every expense had to be accounted for, I created my own programme. Barnardo's Irish Headquarters were in Belfast where the organisation, founded by a nineteenth century Dublin doctor, had been operating for some time. I was reminded by my immediate boss, Mr. Vesty, that a hierarchy had to be respected. Following my interview at Barnardo's headquarters, I had to be trained. Putting me through my paces at the Belfast office, Mr. Vesty took me on a tour of orphanages and homes. I was shown what forms to fill, who to send reports to, and who to contact if in difficulty. I would regularly report to Belfast's Antrim Road headquarters. This entailed driving across a city already uncomfortable with itself. I hated the bureaucracy which reminded me of working in England. A Dublin office at Harolds Cross eventually facilitated a southern Irish headquarters - it didn't happen in my time, though.

Circumstances in Ireland were rapidly deteriorating. There was an air of militancy and bombs were going off north and south. I felt my responsibility included giving comfort to those in remote localities who were nervous for the future. This was particularly the case in the drumlin country of Cavan and Monaghan where I mainly visited schools. Barnado's was a Protestant organisation dealing with Protestant people but, although difficult, I made a big effort for its bias to be changed.

Many parishes had Protestant national schools, usually under Church of Ireland management but with Presbyterian and other non-Conformist pupils. Teachers usually managed to impart a wide variety of knowledge but occasionally I would visit a pathetically deprived class, where they weren't able.

On my introducing myself, classes would stand and I'd be collectively greeted, often in Irish. Teachers and their charges welcomed outsiders, especially if expected. Many parents and parishioners, however, were suffering because of the troubles - intimidation being rife. Close to the border, they wondered could they trust the Dublin government. Sometimes the teacher would call me aside or chat over a cup of tea. "Tell me, what's it like over in Scotstown? I hear the O'Neills moved out last Sunday. And there's Billy Fox . . . . Is it quiet down South?" I felt needed in that area and shared a deep sympathy with these small-farming communities, each normally existing without let or harm to or from their neighbours. They were closely knit and not easily upset, but now they were fearful and uneasy. I could sense their despondency as I'd pass a farmer leaning over his gate or a family driving cows. Too often they didn't salute.

The prospect of further well-fuelled pot-bellied stoves, and another batch of enthusiastic kids would encourage me to my next consignment, in spite of sparcely-signed roads which looked alike. At night I'd book in to a nearby hotel. Tourism hadn't arrived, so these hostelries were still very 'commercial', usually with tasteless overcooked food. Muted evening conversations reflected the political situation as participants were careful not to disclose their true sympathies until they knew the circumstances of those with whom they chatted.

It was good to be empowered to cover the whole country. Although I wasn't able to do much of my personal work, I obtained two invaluable insights. The first was into the people and places of rural Ireland, so useful in my later writings and talks. The second was the farm and business opportunities which would enable me to develop Weir Machinery.

I was upset by the individual and family circumstances about which I learnt while with Dr. Barnardo's. These concerned mainly Protestants, but we also had referrals of Roman Catholics. The latter would be recommended to the Society of St. Vincent de Paul which, I pointed out, served generously irrespective of denomination. I felt that their understanding of Ireland by my English superiors was outdated, if unsympathetic. Irish people, especially in the country, stood by their neighbours, irrespective of denomination.

I didn't enjoy my Belfast visits - circumstances north of the border had changed. There were road blocks and firm but nervous soldiers, shattering sounds and sights of devastation, and terror. Suspicions were also festering in the south; familiar members of our gardai could be sympathisers of the I.R.A. Occasional unpleasant remarks about Protestants were encouraging the possibility of a ghetto society. Anonymous telephone calls were received, the republican *An Poblacht* was distributed locally and youngish adult men from outside the parish were playing the heavy and suggesting support for the 'cause' when they visited my shop. Protestants were being branded as un-Irish in spite of Wolfe Tone and Robert Emmet, or indeed of the considerable number of nationalists in the Church of Ireland. These were lonely times, times when one wondered should one keep a gun under the bed for self protection, times when a car-load of strangers could instill fear. Local people were mainly, however, understanding, sympathetic and supportive. North of the border I didn't have neighbours. I was isolated in my car, a Protestant from the mainly Roman Catholic 'Twenty-six Counties'. At road blocks, the authenticity of which was often open to question, I was treated firmly, politely but suspiciously and sometimes with hostility by demented R.U.C or British army interrogators. On examination of my identity, the former would usually categorise me correctly whereas the young English troops would nervously finger their triggers until I was out of range. In some towns and villages north of the Border, I would find myself a conspicuous Protestant amongst hostile Catholics. Eyeing my southern vehicle registration, Protestants could be cool and uncommunicative.

In Belfast, I stayed near the Barnardo's Antrim Road headquarters. Once, on the MI motorway towards Dublin, I learnt on the radio that the pub had been bombed where Mr. Vesty, myself and other members of staff had had a parting drink an hour before. Another time, the room below where I was sleeping had an explosive device thrown through the window. When it went off, the whole floor seemed to lift. Pepino had a fit and ran round the room screaming. It took a long time before I succeeded in calming him. The only damage I suffered, even though my car was rocked when lost amongst a militant crowd near the Falls road, was a bullet hole near the bottom of the driver's door. I was uncomfortable with my British Army background, though I had never soldiered in Ireland.

My Barnardo's travels took me throughout Ireland although I was drawn to where people already knew me. John Howarth had taken Holy Orders and was now rector of Ballymacelligot in County Kerry. I arranged to talk to his parishioners. The storm that night continued through the following day when I was to pass through Cork for Waterford. Starting early I took an almost traffic-free road. Near Ballyvourney, three black-bereted republican supporters questioned me as to my activities and accepted the truth I told them. In Cork city, an angry crowd was attacking a British travel company's office. Several people banged at my car and some tried, albeit rather effortlessly, to rock it. Tempers ran high that day and I was relieved to reach my destination.

I enjoyed working with Barnardo's and experienced some amusing incidents. A parish in Drogheda asked me to speak to a group of elderly ladies. As I talked and showed my slides, one attentive member asked questions, thereby diverting my attention from the rest. They had quietly dozed to sleep. When I finished, one of the awakened ladies stood up with great difficulty and announced: "I'm afraid I don't know what exactly Barnardo's do. Perhaps you'd be good enough to tell us."

*   *   *   *   *   *   *   *   *   *

In 1972, I had to make a choice. Either I would devote time and energy to my business or else concentrate on Dr. Barnardo's. It was a difficult decision. I had invested a lot of energy towards developing the former but now I was devoting almost all my efforts to my salaried employment. I was not though, really happy with Barnardo's interpretation of its remit. I also realised that Aunt Lilian's legacy would enable me to build a house, to restock my shop and to have some financial backing. I decided to put the matter in Mrs. Steadman's hands. "Could I work less days per week?" I requested, through Mr. Vesty. I went on to explain the circumstances and that I couldn't stay on if my request was unacceptable. Barkingside wrote me a very considerate letter. The answer was negative, but for the period of my notice, I could work a three day week: "I would like to thank you for all you have done for Barnardo's, and for your very kind co-operation over the matter of your successor. I do very much hope that your business will continue to thrive, and, from your point of view, I am glad to hear that it is demanding more of your time than it was when you first joined us, with every good wish, yours sincerely, M.E. Steadman."

I closed the house at Clondalkin and handed over the typewriter, projector, screen and keys before driving home to my caravan, and to the continued uncertainty of self employment. I would though, be able to indulge in my increasingly warm relationship with Miss O'Brien.

*   *   *   *   *   *   *   *   *   *   *

In the middle of 1972, I travelled to Paris. Fergus Pyle was the European correspondent of the *Irish Times* when I stayed with him and Mary in their large city apartment. At the Bricolage (Do-it-Yourself) Fair in the suburbs, I met my suppliers and took on new products. La Metalurgie Française confirmed my agency for their huge range of 'Triplex' packaged accessories and tools for all Ireland. Val d'Or was happy with my power-tool sales and I agreed to import lawnmowers from another manufacturer. On my way back I called to Burton on Trent in England, which culminated in an agency for 'Framemaker' instant framing.

Shortly after my return, the European sales director of Triplex came on the first of his promotional visits. He was content to accompany me on my travels in the south, but a visit to Belfast was to be his last during my agency. The road between Cavan and Clones crosses into Northern Ireland twice due to the irregular border with County Fermanagh. I told him this and that we might meet a military patrol.

"What happens then?" he asked. A bit of devilment, which was to backfire, came about me. I told him that he should slip into the passenger foot-well of the car with his hands over his head, and stay there. Before my 'instructions' finished, the inevitable happened. I had difficulty in explaining to my irate passenger that it was a joke, he emerging from the crouched position as the patrol faded behind us. On reaching Belfast, we parked on the Falls Road side of a border line near the Shankhill. As we made for the city centre, I had difficulty in getting him to cross the white-painted indication on the road that Catholics were not welcome, he being one. Relieved - he returned to Europe from Aldegrove.

La Metalurgie Française's rapid expansion necessitated new headquarters at Nangis, south-east of Paris. On the opening day, to which international agents were invited, I sat beside the Spanish representative. Enticed by an assortment of pre-dinner delicacies both of us were hungry as we had travelled without breakfast. Along with the repast were excellent wines. Come the speeches, each of us was inebriated and relaxed as we feigned to understand every word. Suddenly, out of the blue, the 'representative for Ireland' was asked to speak a few words. I can't really remember what I said, but I received hearty applause for my impeccable French. I gained a lot of friends, some of whom later communicated with me and invited me to similar events in their countries. I was also presented with the 'Napoleon' medal I treasure.

In Ireland, business was going well, with sales in all areas. Once I left early for an estate in Donegal where I sold a power scythe. Knowing that I had much to do the following day, I returned in daylight. Reaching home, a message on my answering machine indicated that I'd lose a sale if I didn't call to Lauragh, Killarney immediately. I drove on. "No, there's no Lauragh around here. You don't mean Kenmare?" "Try Sullivans, they may tell you". "I don't know of any Lauragh about Killarney". It transpired that the postal address for this little village beyond Kenmare was, in fact, Killarney. Exhausted, I reached my potential customer around midnight. Having agreed that I would demonstrate the Kyoritsu Power Scythe early in the morning, I drove a few yards, parked in a gateway, and fell fast asleep.

I was beginning to realise that Tante Lil's legacy was quite substantial, so returning from Athlone after a successful day's business, I part-exchanged my Ford Escort for a Peugeot 404. A large comfortable innovative off-white car, it had a leather bench seat and a gear handle which sprouted from the steering wheel shaft. As I drove home, the roads were getting icy. When a stray cow confronted me near Ballinasloe, I braked - as I did so, I spun full circle. I respected power assisted brakes thereafter.

The next day I was parking in Limerick to confirm my insurance. Having pulled behind a large truck, I switched off the engine. I was about to disembark when I realised that the truck was backing towards my beautiful new vehicle. Frantically I searched for the horn, but in vain. Luckily, a passer-by saw my predicament and halted the driver's progress by shouting and gesticulating with his hands from across the street. Only later did I realise that the horn was activated by a large silver circle of metal mounted with the same centre over the steering wheel.

My financial situation now allowed me freedom to pursue the girl with whom I was rapidly falling in love. I also had a social life and would meet up with friends such as Seán Alley, an ex-Colonial vet who was helping to eliminate tuberculosis in Co. Clare. After work he and I would dine at the Old Ground Hotel in Ennis, sometimes with other friends.

Because of my Barnardo's experience, I was asked to join CARE, the campaign to help deprived children. Elected to the Council along with Sister Stanislaus, Seamus O Cinneide and Dermot Gleeson, I was unable to attend meetings as they were held on Sundays. In 1972, I became a member of the Killaloe Diocesan Synod, the Board of Religious Education, the Diocesan Council, the Episcopal Electoral College and was a supplemental for the General Synod. Elected to the latter body was The Honourable Grania O'Brien, also a member of the Diocesan Council. Her father, Lord Inchiquin, had died in 1968 but I used to sit behind them at earlier sessions. Now we eyed each other at our various shared meetings.

Bishop Harry Stanistreet, the father of Jean whom I had known during my Cappaghbeg days, was a delightful and kindly traditional prelate with a genuine affection for his flock. He, and his father before him, had served near Roscrea and in Clare, so he knew both our families. Harry and his wife Ethel were encouraging and helpful. Grania and I and shared many friends, some of whom such as the Ogden Whites at Ballyalla, the Andrews of Knappogue, the Crosbies, Roberts, Immelmans and the Brannigans were citizens of other

countries invited to set up industries, or just reside, in a country
which provided their type of life. There were also the long-
established Clare families like the Tottenhams, O'Callaghan
Westropps, Bloods and Joyces although these, partly due to war and
troubled times, were a diminishing race. We were comforted by such
lovely people, especially as we were both loners, Grania living with
her mother in the large residence her father had built, Thomond
House at Dromoland.

Thomond House

On forfeiting my Barnardo's appointment, I had returned to an
uncomfortable caravan. If I was to successfully woo the person of
my dreams, I would have to feather an acceptable 'nest'. The best
house sites were on the shore of Lough Derg. In a cul de sac, I found
the ideal half acre haggard I purchased from owners Michael and
Davy Eames. It faced Meelick Bay where I had fished for pike and
trout with my grandfather. The first house, as one skirted the bay was
the wooden bungalow built by the Davies family from England.
Apart from the MacMahon's hut further along, houses on the
lakeshore belonged to local families.

I scanned the book of planning designs, *Bungalow Bliss* and
looked at pre-fabricated houses. The latter seemed sound and were
less expensive than conventional dwellings. I settled for a well
insulated Rohfab single-storey three bedroomed gable-ended
construction with a large living room, a kitchen, bathroom,
immersion heater and hot press, and oil-fired central heating. The
Planning authorities, however, insisted that the roof pitch was

lowered due to its highly visible Shannon-side location, a measure which was to cause problems. Further conditions were stipulated to take advantage of a grant for first-time owners. Business was expanding and I needed a self supporting urban base where my tools and machines could be displayed. Premises in Galway, Cork and Ennis were considered, but I settled for Limerick. The O'Connell Street address was good, especially on paper-headings, but for retail sales it was a disaster. The two-roomed basement was at the residential and professional end. Few prospective buyers ventured this far from the busy intersection at the city centre. We suffered theft and other unpleasant circumstances. One lunch break, when I had taken over the shop and remained open, I overheard - on the pavement above - a customer asking where Weir Machinery was. Ascending the metal stairs I found two elderly men telling her she'd do better elsewhere - I was a blow-in, and a Protestant. Stunned, I recalled the city's reputation for the power of its Confraternity. I had, however, lots of Limerick customers and friends such as Jim Marshall, then manager of Boyds Department Store and Jim Kemmy, the delightful socialist politician with whom I was later to share a mutual devotion to history, though our politics were very different.

Courtship was now in earnest. I was at every gathering that Grania was likely to grace; there were charity events at Knappogue and Thomond House, parties in Clare and Limerick and outdoor occasions as well as indoor. The first time I dined at Thomond House, I found my future mother-in-law a little intimidating. Someone had told her I was Lord Ashbourne; I didn't make issue of the inaccuracy. Eventually I consulted Buzz and Paul Kelly at Williamstown, about matrimonial prospects. "Should I go ahead and propose, even though my house wasn't finished?" Encouraged by their affirmation and that of Desmond Fitzgerald from across the lake, I suggested that Grania brought her lawnmower to my shop for repairs. She wasn't there when I arrived but had just left. Horrified at seeing her drive off, I chased down the street. When she stopped, I suggested that we meet at the Stella, a popular and often gossipy news-swopping tea-shop. Grania had by now taken responsibility for two little girls who, the children of an English businessman and his

Northern-Irish wife, were recently orphaned. She was the godmother to Claudia, the eldest. I did not expect, however, that she would appear not only with Claudia and Joy, but with her sister Deirdre. I was flabberghasted. My ruse was rapidly disintegrating. Eventually Deirdre recognised what I was up to, or that I at least wanted privacy, so she offered to take the children to the library. Joy refused, but I decided to go ahead anyway.

"Shall we make our way to the shop?" I suggested.

Grania, Joy in hand, followed me up the street. My intention was to propose marriage in the room I used as an office. I had prepared a letter, in case words failed me. This was just as well for it denied Joy full knowledge of what was happening; Grania bade her stay in the shop. With haste, I reached for the well-mauled envelope in my breast pocket and presented it. I expected an immediate answer, but media interpretations of proposals are seldom representative of the norm. "I'll let you know" was not the desired answer. I was hyped up, nervous and incredibly hopeful.

A day or two later, the awaited letter arrived ". . . . Darling, I will marry you, and I pray so much that we will be happy . . . . I tried to ring you tonight to tell you my mother is very pleased (and says you don't have to ask her permission!). It seems the shores of Lough Derg shut down at 10 p.m. . . . The operator seemed to sense my disappointment and told me very gently." These were the days of part-time telephones. I immediately contacted old friends, Nicholas and Rosemary MacGillycuddy, who were staying nearby. We celebrated into the night before I inebriately wove my way home along the twisty untarred lane.

The next few months Grania and I spent discussing wedding plans and our futures. My Limerick shop was failing so I closed it. Instead, picnics were enjoyed, and tours. As we were drove over mountainous country between Woodford and Killenana, west of Whitegate, I turned to my fiancée.

"Shall we go and look at beds?"

Grania looked astonished. Broderick's furniture store, a motley collection of buildings behind their rural roadside house, was full of furniture at competitive prices. Together with the bed, we purchased other pieces for Ballinakella Lodge, our home to be. Pepino, too, joined in. One evening, when we were dining at Thomond House, he disappeared. Anxious as to his whereabouts, Grania located him. Bored with the dull conversation, he had made his way to the comfortable dog basket in her bedroom, curled himself up and was snoring peacefully.

The Rawsons of Glenwilliam Castle, the Deightons who had once encouraged me to consider Grania as a possible partner, the Cooleys, Brannigans and other friends involved us in a social whirl. On April 25th, Grania and her mother organised a small engagement party but shortly after I had arrived, Anne went to bed with 'flu. Around lunchtime, Grania asked if Bishop Owen would marry us - he would be delighted. After he left we went for a stroll. That evening, Tom Costello sent champagne; his horse, trained at Dromoland, had won the Derby. The Baxters, Ralph was the rector of Shannon, then arrived for the evening meal but Anne didn't feel up to it. My future mother-in-law got worse and Dr. Walsh was called. Sadly, at one oclock in the morning, I helped to carry her gently downstairs to an ambulance for Cahercalla, a hospital near Ennis. From there she was moved to the Regional Hospital in Limerick. Suffering from diabetes, she had had a turn. Eventually she was returned to her beloved Clare as a patient of the dutiful and caring nuns at Carrigoran Nursing Home.

On May Day, we drove to the Dublin Spring Show. En route, Grania and I went to Weirs of Grafton Street to buy her engagement ring. The diamond-surrounded amethyst was set in a coronet-like white-gold framework. Grania gave me a signet ring engraved with our Weir crest and motto. At the Show we met old friends and shared our happiness. The following week, Margaret, Anne's rather intimidating sister, joined us for dinner at Thomond House; apparently I passed her scrutiny. Grania, with her friend Joan MacAleese, had been to visit Anne in hospital.

In Dublin again on May 17th, we had our engagement photograph taken, before a visit to Brendan and Kitty O'Brien. Brendan, descendant of patriot William Smith O'Brien, was the artist Dermod O'Brien's son and a cousin of Grania's; Kitty was, through our common descent from the Bakers, a cousin of mine. An accomplished water colourist, and one-time student of Dermod's,

she had taught Guy when he and her son Anthony were at
Castlepark. We were very fond of them. Brendan was an eminent
medical doctor; Kitty's searching and contemplative eyes caused
others to wonder whether she really approved of them. Kitty took
me to Malahow, Fingal's highest house near Naul, to meet my Baker
cousins. They had bred Arkle, the Grand National winner, and Kitty
later gave us a red rose named after him.

On July 13th, American banker Ogden White and his wife Magee,
who had moved into Ballyalla, once an O'Brien House, kindly gave
us a special party. The O'Dowds, he having been butler for Grania's
father at Dromoland, were now working for them, so old
acquaintances were renewed. Amongst the guests was my mother. It
was the first time that she and Grania had met following our
engagement. Although she had questioned – believing her to be of
a different denomination – Grania's suitability for her son, she now
expressed delight and welcomed her. Audrey O'Brien of Clonmel
whom I had known in my youth was Roman Catholic and due to Ne
Temere, this was still a major concern to her. Also at the sumptuous
repast were Grania's Swedish friends Margit and Öke von Bahr,
David and Geraldine Hely-Hutchinson, my aunt Brenda Bateman
and her daughters Diana Willis and Monica Pine.

*   *   *   *   *   *   *   *   *   *

My wife to be, Grania O'Brien, was the younger daughter of
Donough, sixteenth Baron Inchiquin and of Anne, whose father was
the first Viscount Chelmsford. Their home was Thomond House
which Donough had built overlooking his beloved Dromoland. He
had been compelled, due to escalating costs, to sell the castle in
1962. Near Newmarket-on-Fergus between Limerick and Ennis, it is
now a luxurious hotel. As Grania and I walked the demesne which
had been in family hands for centuries, she exuded devotion for the
place. I too felt a sense of belonging. It was still, although sold to
Bernard MacDonough, much as it had been and the staff would
warmly greet us. Inside, family portraits depicted O'Briens from the
time of Brian Boru, eleventh century monarch of Ireland, to the
twentieth century. There was one of Queen Anne, their English

cousin, and of Irish folklore character, Maire Rua who had three husbands. Close to the castle was the walled garden with stone furniture designed by Grania's grandfather, Elizabethan bee boles, and flowers which had been tenderly nurtured by her mother. Surrounded by ornamental woodland was the Temple – the grave of a favourite family horse, Séan Buidh - the lake and a small lily pond beside which was a grotto. On land retained by the family was the Cathedral Wood of beech trees planted in 1702 following Queen Anne's coronation, and resembling the pillars of a huge church. Various estate cottages included one lived in by the Davins whom I had often visited, the farmyard, Mooghaun Castle of the McGinnises and the separately owned Castlefergus farm beside the river Rine.

Grania's father, Donough Edward Foster O'Brien, had been Aide de Camp to the Viceroy of India, her grandfather, in 1919 and 1920. Lord Chelmsford had two sons and four daughters, one whom was Anne Thesiger. Donough and she had married in 1921. Donough was the direct successor to Brian Boru, inaugurated High King in 1002 and slain twelve years later after defeating the Danes near Dublin. In 1543, his descendant, Murrough, submitted his royal titles and properties to Henry VIII and was in return created Earl of Thomond for life, and Baron of Inchiquin - he was also re-granted his lands. These O'Briens intermarried with the leading families of Europe. Some were loyal to the English, in spite of being denied their monarchy while others, such as William Smith O'Brien, fought for Ireland's freedom. Worldwide, O'Briens are proud of their common heritage. Grania's father had two brothers, Phaedrig and Fionn, and three sisters, Beryl (Gallagher), Griselda (Christopherson) and Helga (Davies).

Anne Molyneux Thesiger was the Viceroy's third child. Her eldest sister, Joan, married Sir Alan Lascelles, while Bridget married firstly Richard Sheepshanks, and secondly, Nello Beccari. The fourth sister Margaret was wed to film director John Monck. Andrew, whose elder brother was killed in action in 1917, succeeded to the Chelmsford title in 1933. The Thesigers originated in Dresden. John Andrew Thesiger born in 1722 had married Sarah Gibson, and their grandson Sir Frederick, First Baron Chelmsford was an eminent lawyer and member of Parliament who became Lord High Chancellor in 1858. Grania's grandfather married Frances Charlotte Guest, daughter of Lord Wimborne and of Lady Cornelia Henrietta Maria Spencer-Churchill, Sir Winston Churchill's aunt.

Educated in England, Grania had been a war evacuee to Canada, her parents having feared that Germany would invade England through Ireland. After the war, she learnt secretarial skills and studied current and foreign affairs at the House of Citizenship, a London-based finishing and secretarial school for girls. She also trained as a ballet dancer with the Royal Academy of Dancing where she obtained honours and a teaching certificate. Secretary to Minister of State Sir Arthur Salter between 1947 and 1952 she was then appointed Social Secretary at the British Embassy in Madrid. The following year she worked for How of Edinburgh, silversmiths in London - who invited her to become a director - but returned to being a Social Secretary in 1954, serving at the British Embassy in Tokyo, the United States Embassy in London and the British Embassy in Lima, Perú.

To assist her parents at Dromoland where they were accepting paying guests to help in its upkeep, Grania returned for the two years before it was sold. Having temporarily resided in a chalet at the nearby Shannon Shamrock Hotel for a similar period, the family moved into the newly built Thomond House overlooking the castle.

In 1966 Donough had a stroke. He died two years later. Grania had succeeded him as President of the Ennis branch of the Royal National Lifeboat Institution. I was at her first gathering in aid of the charity. Soon she became Chairman of Clare An Taisce (The National Trust for Ireland). Also, initially with her father, active in Church of Ireland affairs, she was a member of Synod and of several committees; appointments which, in some cases, we shared. On the death of their mother, she also accepted responsibility for the Harper children, Claudia and Joy.

On July 17th 1973, Grania and I were linking our two proud and ancient family lines. An exciting prospect, it also gave the media plenty to write about. "Bride to be descendant of Brian Boru" headlined the *Sunday Press*; "Society wedding in Clare", the *Irish Press*; "Irish Royal wedding", "Two significant families . . . ." were all to highlight the greatest event in our lives. More important, Grania was intelligent and experienced and we got on wonderfully.

There were problems though. When Grania's father had died, he had left two daughters, Deirdre who had married New York allergist Dr. H. Beecher Chapin, and Grania. He having no male heir, his title went to his next brother, Phaedrig. The remaining Dromoland estate, heirlooms and family portraits were in trust so that they would be kept in O'Brien family hands along with the Inchiquin title. When the castle was sold, so as not to cause a family rift, Donough bought out his brothers'and sisters' interest in the furniture and other non trust possessions. He had also intended and verbally arranged with them that, as he was building Thomond House with his own money on Trust lands, he would exchange a similarly valued section of his adjoining non-trust farm at Castlefergus. Unfortunately, he died before this transaction could be legally confirmed.

Phaedrig, Grania's uncle, along with the remaining acres of the Dromoland estate, the portraits, and items which were his by trust, indicated that he was entitled to Thomond house and its contents. Grania and her mother had intended to move to a new home anyway and were already considering a nearby property. But the situation had changed. I had no desire to move from Whitegate and Grania would be abandoning Thomond House for her mother was now, it seemed, destined to remain at Carrigoran.

A few days before our wedding, we were told that, the house being unoccupied, Phaedrig intended to move in and claim the contents. Friends rallied, sharing my Ford Transit van and their own vehicles, to transfer Grania's belongings to Ballinakella, and Deirdre's to Quinville, her house at Quin. Heirlooms and O'Brien family treasures were meticulously left in the house.

Several of Grania's friends, such as the von Bahrs, were astonished to arrive at Thomond House and find nobody about. The venue for the wedding reception, originally scheduled to be held in her home, had to be changed, the Old Ground Hotel in Ennis accepting the responsibility. To add to our troubles, Grania's elkhound was run over and Patsy Liddy, who had helped as housekeeper, became ill with pleurisy. Anne's confinement to a nursing home meant that we spent time with her, but we had to be very careful not to disclose the less pleasant ongoing events for fear of exacerbating her diminishing health. The days leading up to our wedding were not easy, but this encouraged our support for each other and our love deepened.

Our engagement photograph, 1973.

CHAPTER ELEVEN

*Our pre-nuptial reception and wedding ceremony, luncheon
and Connemara honeymoon. Grania's mother, Anne, dies. Our
real honeymoon in Britain, Holland and France. A rocky future.*

G rania's mother was in Carrigoran Nursing Home and as not
everyone could be with us on the day, we had a pre-marriage
reception at the Old Ground Hotel. Several hundred friends arrived
at the Banqueting Hall at around seven on Saturday 14th July, 1973.
We knew manager Richard Oldfield and the staff of the hotel. There
was always a warm and friendly atmosphere.

The canapés and other delicacies were a delight with all sorts of
savoury and sweet plates; liquid refreshment flowed freely, the décor
and service setting the tone. During my words of welcome, I
requested that we should particularly remember Anne, unable to be
with us. Animated conversation continued well into the night.

*   *   *   *   *   *   *   *   *   *

Three days after the pre-marriage reception, I was alone at
Ballinakella Lodge. As I donned my morning suit and straightened
my tie, the telephone rang. It was Grania's Uncle Phaedrig. I was
delighted and presumed that animosities were over. My
presumptions were shattered when he strongly aired his bitter
relations with Grania. Although this discomforted me on the most
significant day of my life, I was soon off to Kilnasoolagh Church in
my well polished Peugeot. Passing through Mountshannon I had a
second blow: John Tiernan, my grandfather's old friend and
boatman, an expert on Lough Derg and on fishing, had just died. I
was fearful of a third upset, but, thank God, there wasn't one.

Guests were already making their way up the path when I
arrived. The church was beautifully decorated by Mrs. Bridge of

Clarecastle, a delightful character known to us both who was dedicated to the cause of the blind. To overcome jitters, and because of the two body-blows that morning, I acted as one of my own ushers, the others being William Prentice, an ex pupil whose father Peter's company were my Solicitors, Brian Cooley of de Beers at Shannon, Dromoland Farm Manager Robert Blake and my old friend Desmond Fitzgerald of Nenagh.

As guests arrived, some were surprised to be greeted by the groom. A few of Grania's friends were confused when they saw me take my place in the front pew where my brother, then running an antique business in Munich, was already seated as Best Man. Grania meanwhile, assisted by her sister Deirdre, Bets Sparrow, and her Aunt Margaret Monck, was preparing herself at Quinville, Deirdre's house at Quin.

After the traditional wait, organist Jean Gunn, wife of my friend Douglas, resoundingly pounded the strains of "Holy, Holy Holy! Lord God Almighty". A radiant Grania, accompanied by her brother-in-law Beecher Chapin who gave her away, and bridesmaids Claudia and Joy (Grania's wards) appeared in the porch. Having completed last minute adjustments to the wedding gown, they progressed down the aisle. My wife-to-be wore a 'mauve, sprigged, white chiffon gown and a white picture hat trimmed with tulle and mauve flowers'.

Bishop of Killaloe Edwin Owen presided at the Eucharistic Service assisted by rector Noel Young and Mountshannon incumbent Edgar Talbot; Father John O'Donovan, Roman Catholic curate of Whitegate read the Gospel. It was rare for a Catholic priest to participate in a Church of Ireland service but John was before his time; he lead his community with youth projects and social events along with his spiritual commitments. Our guests included four other bishops, family relations and friends known to both of us. After the ceremony, we were touched when greeted outside the door by a guard of honour; local children and their teacher raised the blue and gold Clare colours, once borne by Brian Boru.

After a session with photographers, and greeting guests and well-wishers, Vincent O'Connell drove us in his Mercedes Benz to see Anne. We then proceeded to Ennis for lunch at the Old Ground. The meal was a magnificent fork buffet. Preceded by hot or cold consommé or a terrine, was salmon mayonnaise or prawns a la Russe, a huge selection of red and white meats including stuffed boar's head, and Russian potatoes, beetroot, tomato, coleslaw and egg salads. Our guests were finally offered vacherin glacé, fruit salad and cream, assorted gateaux, fruit jellies or meringue chantilly, followed by tea or coffee. The *piece de resistance* was a sumptuous two-tier wedding cake decorated with Weir and O'Brien family crests created by Betty Smith a friend at Shannon.

After the speeches, we went to private rooms to change. Grania re-appeared in canary yellow while I wore a new grey suit from Fitzgeralds of Cork. A confetti send-off from the steps of the hotel saw us on our way to Connemara for a two-day stay. Because of the children and Anne's illness, we postponed our continental honeymoon. As Cashel House Hotel, once home to the Browne-Claytons, was in Connemara, we had hoped for anonymity.

Journeying north, we stopped at Coole Park, the site of Lady Gregory's old home near Gort. Tired, both of us, due to Anne's incapacity and my mother and stepfather Bob's living abroad, had shared in arranging the day. Only now, we later discussed, did we fully realise how committed we were to each other.

On reaching the hotel, proprietor MacEvilly greeted us. Guests tactfully looked out of the window or at each other as we passed through reception rooms; they had obviously read the newspapers. Our bedroom had been specially chosen, a delightful gesture by the hotel. It was that in which French President General de Gaulle had recently stayed. Later we wandered around the interesting woodland gardens discussing the day's activities. Cousin Liz O'Brien and G.G., the Duke de Stacpoole hadn't realised that we would be staying nearby. Assuming that the Mrs. Weir they expected for lunch the next day was my mother, they were surprised when we appeared at the door. Liz had been at the wedding, but had failed to recognise Grania's new name.

Following our Connemara sojourn, we drove home via Shannon where we collected the girls. They had been looked after by Betty Kavanagh, a teacher in the local Church of Ireland school. Ballinakella Lodge was not the size of house that Grania and they had been used to, and I had had the sole run of it. Grania and I occupied the only double room with a rather narrow bed, while the children each had a bunk in what later became the library. The drawingroom, now our diningroom, was small but had picture windows at the south-east corner of the house and a large one facing the yard. The place is bigger now with a bedroom wing built in 1975, and a new drawingroom and study. We wonder how we managed with four of us - we never seem to have room for two.

*   *   *   *   *   *   *   *   *   *

We were devastated when Grania's mother died. She was a delightfully concerned mother-in-law and I often wish that I had known her and Donough longer. She was buried at Kilnasoolagh on the 13th August, a month after our marriage. We were consoled by the many friends who came to send her off, and that she had been so actively interested in our future, obviously comforted that her remaining daughter was settled. At the funeral, Bishop Owen commended her life as a devoted mother and as a dedicated Diocesan President of the Mother's Union. Shortly after, we spent a long weekend with the Burrows at Kilbaha and later, brought Deirdre and the girls to Co. Fermanagh where we shared my Weir family haunts and my recollections of schooldays at Portora.

It wasn't until September that Grania and I could indulge in our real honeymoon. Claudia and Joy would share our trip to Scotland before we left them off with their grandparents. We would then enjoy our own company. Taking the ferry from Dublin to Liverpool, we made for Macclesfield to stay the night with the Sparrows at Birtles. Driving through Liverpool and its suburbs, Grania quietly commented that I had passed a specific church three times. I had not divulged to her that, as was usual when I was passing through that city, I was lost; I had hoped that if I kept turning only to right (or to left) I would eventually get to the appropriate road, and that she would not have noticed.

After lots of chatting with Geoffrey and Bets Sparrow and a comfortable night's sleep, we continued. We stopped at Carleton Hall near Carlisle where my forbear Anne Carleton's family once lived, now Cumbrian police headquarters, and asked questions about its history. It was late when, having driven through Glasgow, we located a pleasant hotel overlooking the southern end of Loch Lomond at Balloch. The next day's journey through the Grampian mountains towards Glen Mór was enhanced by bright sunshine. At Glencoe we visited the famous monument and chatted to the lone piper as he waited to be photographed with tourists for a fee. Half way up the road north of Lough Ness at Urquhart Castle we scanned the water for 'Nessie', the monster. Although we didn't catch sight of it, I was fascinated by what seemed to be shoals of salmon wending their way a short distance from the shore. The children raced around the ruined fortifications while Grania and I marvelled at the sinister and deep valley. At the southern end of the lake, we had observed an experimental station to generate electricity from wave-power.

It was late when we got to Strathpeffer, a small spa town on the road to Ullapool and the Atlantic fishing ports north west of Inverness. Aunt Bryda and her husband Fitzroy arranged for us to stay in a comfortable little hotel run by Italians where we ate delicious pasta and fish dishes. The following day Fitzroy, kin to the Earls of Cromartie who owned much of the district, and who loved the area, gave us a tour to Loch Luachart and a hydro-electric generating station. En route we stopped for lunch at a pleasantly old fashioned roadside inn and later, amongst Scots pines and rocky bracken-covered terrain, we enjoyed a picnic. This was adder country and we were cautioned to be careful; the serpents could be quite aggressive. We found one of their nests in a rotting tree trunk.

Bryda and Fitzroy had both been at our wedding. He had worn his kilt and the badge of the Scottish Nationalist movement in which he was patriotically involved. This was in spite of his having been Sergeant at Arms in the Westminster House of Commons. They looked lonesome as we bid "goodbye".

In the Cairngorms, the girls' pestering paid them, for I succumbed to a pony-trek. There were apt comments as I mounted a small but sturdy pony. We rode at a snails pace as we had been ordered to keep in line and not to outpace the horse and rider ahead. I found this tiresome but Claudia and Joy enjoyed every minute. Grania patiently waited by the car and caught up with some reading. We also visited a nature park where descendants of Scotland's primeval fauna such as wild pigs, shaggy long-haired cattle with huge horns and wildcats ran almost free.

It would be late before we could reach a major town with accommodation. Crathie was full so we continued to Ballater on the river Dee. Here we found a guest house willing to bed us, I having stressed that I was exhausted. I didn't mention that I had a very sore behind from the pony trek. There was a proviso: we could sleep in the guests' television room, but only when everyone had retired. Neither Grania nor I had banked on the tremendous loyalty of the British people to their queen and her family who were staying at nearby Balmoral. Though it was mid-September, every available bed seemed to be occupied. It was very late when the last viewer left the room, having watched the dullest of programmes. Soon we were asleep in blankets and bed rolls on sofas or on the floor.

I awoke at around five feeling little refreshed, though glad to have had somewhere to rest our heads. Driving down the valley, we sped on to Montrose where my godmother Denise Tailyour lived. From her two storey house near the sea we met her friends, Grania's cousins the Stansfelds, at nearby Dunotter. Denise's house was warm and friendly, but I always feel the North Sea coast cold and unwelcoming. This was to be proved a year or two later when we collected my dear little black pug Bella from Carnoustie where she had been reared beside the bleak Aberdeen to Edinburgh railway.

The Forth bridge was exciting with minute-looking ships passing through the Firth below. Ahead was Hopetown, the magnificent pile of the Hopes, Earls of Linlithgow, from whom my kinsmen the Hope Veres, got their prefix. Approaching Edinburgh, we tried to visit the Vere's ancient seat at Craigie Hall, now a military headquarters. As I took distant photographs, an army jeep passed twice as the occupants observed and re-observed us. Our 'EIR' plate no doubt suggested that we might have caused trouble. We also went to the genealogical department of the Scottish National Library, where I found information on the Veres, de Veres and Weirs, depending on which period of history documents were written.

From Edinburgh we crossed the Southern uplands to Kelso where in the twelfth century, Walter or Rudi de Vere had made a donation to the monastery. Although ruined, it must once have been magnificent. The surrounding town is rather quaint and less Spartan than other places near the eastern seaboard. On a sunny day we continued south over bleak moorland, very harsh in winter. On our left we could see Lindisfarne with its Irish Christian traditions and contemplated St. Aiden and his followers. The area seemed so different and starkly remote from the west. Alnwick Castle towers above its market town. Members of the Heber Percy family from here lived near Nenagh; we were friends when I sold machinery.

Newcastle upon Tyne, some miles to the south, was indeed the industrial city I had envisaged. Even the bridges were samples of industrial revolutionary Victorian architecture, reminding one of the primitive artist Lowry's urban factory scenes. We didn't delay until we reached idyllic Durham with its magnificent cathedral perched above an almost rural river valley, its castle beyond. There is something very powerful, very solid, about this edifice's thick walls with their Romanesque windows and doorways, unlike the more elegant spired cathedrals of the south of England such as Salisbury. The countryside isn't far from its doors and there is tranquillity in its solidarity; the city itself is pleasantly small. I recalled grandfather Willie Gibson's service with the Durham Light Infantry.

We continued our travels inland across North Yorkshire. I was tired and it was raining. If I was to go south from Newcastle today, I would take the coast road and visit Whitby from where my great great grandparents the Chomleys originated. One-time Viceregal Secretary at Dublin Castle, John Chomley (Cholmondeley) married Henrietta Baker in 1805. Sadly, Belcamp, their delightful and unusually shaped listed house north of Dublin suffered major fire damage in 2000.

At nine o'clock we reached Doncaster where we sought somewhere to sleep; the races were on, so there was another premium on accommodation. Eventually we learnt of a woman prepared to take us. Ascertaining that the semi-detached villa on the edge of town was the right one, we parked partly on the pavement and, in pouring rain, lugged our baggage up the long concrete path and into the cosiness of a typical boarding house hallway. Following a warm cup of tea, we climbed the stairs to our room. Grania and I had a double bed and the children, two singles on the other side of the room. Peering between the lace curtains at our parked car, I thanked God that at last we had found somewhere to lay our heads.

Ten minutes later we were in bed and the lights were out, though the municipal lamps shone into the room. I was almost asleep when Grania nudged me: "She's ringing the police". My expletives were unrepeatable but I returned to deep slumber before I had finished my outburst. Soon there was a knock at the door; it was the landlady. "Excuse me, I've just been talking wid police. You'll have to move your car to t'other side of road." I was too tired, indeed astonished, to do anything other than blindly don my dressing gown and slippers and make my way down her fifty-metre path in the pouring rain to move the car to the other side of the road. Had there been a bomb in our boot, the most damage it could have caused would have been to her little wooden gate and the adjoining timber fencing. Exhausted, angry and sopping wet, I returned to bed. The landlady hadn't even had the grace to wait up or thank me. The following morning we left as rapidly as possible.

My mother at that time was living in a cedarwood bungalow she and Bob had erected on a fourteen-acre holding at Bedingfield in Suffolk. There were several outbuildings and the remnants of an old barn. Across a field was the local village stores. The country was flat and almost hedgeless. In nearby Debenham, an attractive Suffolk village with a stream running alongside the main thoroughfare, she had leased a premises in the main street where she ran an antique business. Amongst her friends and neighbours in this fashionable location was Mrs. Shand Kidd, a name associated with Princess Diana, and a leading one-time publisher and his male partner who sold more expensive items. We stayed for two days. Part of the second was a trip to Norwich where I showed Grania my old haunts such as Britannia Barracks, the Cathedral and the Castle.

The day after our Norwich visit we continued to Bournemouth on the south coast and left Claudia and Joy at their maternal grand-parents' large early twentieth century half brick house on the outskirts. The children didn't seem to want us to leave them, but they got a great welcome; there would be plenty of riding and other activities.

Grania and I spent that night on the top floor of a rather bleak guest house at Dover, our car being parked in their steeply sloping park to the rear. During the night we could hear the wind howl, an uncomfortable omen for Grania who is not the happiest of sailors. After a stormy early morning crossing to Calais, we travelled north. We drove through Belgium in appalling conditions to the Hague where Elly and Pim van der Velde O'Breen, while visiting Clare, had pleaded that we stay. Grania told me that there would be no problem when I asked for Floris Grijpstraat; "everyone in Holland speaks excellent English". I chose the only Dutchmen who didn't. Following several unsuccessful requests for directions, I eventually purchased a city map from a murky garage; Elly and Pim's street was around the corner. They were delighted to see us at their comparatively modern house, its garden brilliantly displaying Pim's multicoloured roses. We were shown to a comfortable bedroom which was to be ours for a week. Our host and hostess took us on interesting trips; like most Dutch people, they were devoted to their country and determined to show us as much as possible.

At Sandpoort was Brederode Castle where my mother's Dutch ancestors lived. A large red-brick keep with considerable later additions and a surrounding moat, its adjoining buildings were partly inhabited. We took lots of photographs. That day we also visited Scheveningen, the seashore resort adjoining the Hague; it was bleak, and cold enough for us to wear overcoats. The sands stretched for miles, only occasionally broken by long breakwaters. We passed a purveyor of jellied eels and although I indicated a grá for eels, to eat this sort of food from a seaside caravan was "not done". The smell wafting over the promenade titillated our taste buds and Grania and I hungrily licked our lips. It was not long, however, before we were sitting to a sumptuous feast provided by Elly.

Another day, Pim took pride in showing us magnificent roses in the Kerkenhoff park, not far from his own colourful patch. The lawns were vast and ponds were kept in shape by submerged verge boards, their tops level with the grass. A trip to Amsterdam saw us passing through the flower market to board a tour barge with a perspex roof. We chugged along much of the canal which encircles the city centre, observed historic warehouses and went beneath masses of bridges. We also enjoyed the 'hippy' area. That evening we invited our host and hostess to an Indonesian restaurant near the Parliament buildings. Lots of small dishes with an assortment of mostly piquant delicacies, were placed on the table, a sumptuous risttafel, though we needed lots of water to cool our mouths.

Delft, a smallish town on the road to Rotterdam, is noted for its blue-patterned china. Strolling over the hump bridge, we visited a museum and some souvenir shops before enjoying a traditional tea of poffertjes. We were amazed at how the cook filled dozens of miniature hollows in a hot-plate, similar to but larger than those carved into solitaire boards, with batter. As he finished, and as each was cooked, he flipped it over with a fork so that the other side would be done. He then presented them, sprinkled with icing sugar, piled as a pyramid.

We were also taken to Rotterdam; as we drove beside canals we remarked on the even spacing between herons awaiting tasty morsels. Elly and Pim were wonderful hosts. We had intended to stay only a few days, but Pim had taken a week off and we found it difficult not to remain. On our final morning, following a large breakfast which included homemade 'sauerkraut' and softish Dutch cheeses, we exchanged tender farewells, expressed our thanks and drove via Eindhoven, through the spit of southern Holland, to Heerlen. For the fun of it, we crossed the German border to Charlemaine's Aachen and back on a more southern autobahn into Belgium; I asked the immigration authorities to stamp my passport each time. Traversing the well-wooded Ardennes, we arrived in the Luxemburger town of Diekirke to stay in a comfortable roadside inn but the main road outside our window seemed to be an all-night truck route. The next morning, I almost ended our young and carefree lives as, leaving the hotel precincts, I drove onto the wrong side of the main road.

We intended to motor south to the Dordogne. Time began to run out, so instead we decided at Dijon to go west to Nevers. We knew many Bernadettes and were interested to visit the saint's shrine. Parking outside the city walls, we casually promenaded across the city. St. Bernadette's frail body looked white and delicate as it lay exposed to her adoring followers, in a glass-topped coffin. In the adjoining souvenir store we bought a minute clip of her shroud to present to a devout friend. On leaving the Basilica we returned to where I believed we had left our vehicle, but appeared at a different city gate. We thought that it should be easy enough to locate if we turned right. Had we known, we had parked it only a few metres to the left. We navigated the total of the city's long embracing walls, getting hungrier and hungrier. Late, and when most shops had closed, we found a horse-butcher. Here we bought a hunk of paté to spread on our baguette purchased that morning. Exhausted, we were overjoyed when at last we collapsed into our car's comfortable seats. Towards Bourges and the Loire chateaux, we stopped to devour our purchases. Neither of us like horse-meat but, being famished, we were satisfied with our meal, washed down with wine. That night I was violently sick in our little hotel and had no desire to travel; I just begged a very worried Grania to leave me alone.

Previous visits to the Chateau at Chênençeou, which juts out over the river Loire, encouraged me to share it with Grania. She did enjoy it, but only the outside, it being closing time. When we had left home, she had given me quantities of old francs. They had belonged to her mother. The new franc was now the accepted currency and one shop had already refused payment from our 'collection'. I thought, however, that old francs would still be acceptable by someone with time enough to change them at a bank. Leaving the chateau, I dug into my pocket and handed a fistful to a guide as a tip. A minute or two later, the recipient caught up with us and breathlessly proclaimed the gift to be totally worthless! My laden pocket was back to square one and I had no new money with which to re-emburse him.

After staying another night in a comfortable small-town railway hotel such as is only found in France, and enjoying a delicious menu of the day, we sped north close to the west coast; our time was running out. Falaise, an imposingly sited but ruined castle capping a rocky outcrop, is where William the Conqueror left to war with Britain's King Harold in the eleventh century. As he was an ancestor, we did a cursory tour of the fortress and bought photographs and souvenirs.

Dieppe was our port of departure for Newhaven; there were few direct sailings to Ireland. We parked in a queue, close to the car ahead, and were followed by another almost bumper to bumper. A café faced the parking area, so we sauntered over for a cup of tea. As we sat in the window we observed the drivers of the cars in front and behind conferring. Each then moved their vehicles as far as possible from ours. We presumed that they imagined that we might be carrying bombs. On arrival at Newhaven in the early hours of the following morning, we located a motel with a welcome bed, a self-service tray of instant coffee, tea and biscuits and a kettle-full of water.

An uneventful journey took us the short distance to Bournemouth to visit the children before they went to their English Freemason school. We continued to Newbury for a night's stay with Grania's aunt Margaret where we had a frosty welcome, although we had telephoned and indicated our unforeseen delay.

   Patsy Liddy had cared well for our Labrador Bawn, and Jack
Russell Pepino. Grania was to have her hands full with Claudia and
Joy and, of course, there were to be the problems with future
schooling. In the too near future, legal cases with Phaedrig and
Vickie Inchiquin, including a major High Court judgement, won by
Grania, would demand time and energy. Our marriage was to start
on a rocky path.

The Castle, Falaise

CHAPTER TWELVE

Married life in our first home together - our garden, dogs, cars,
coins, hobbies and saved stones - our own relationships and
friends.

At last Grania and I settled in our small home. Ballinakella Lodge,
named after the townland of Ballinakillew, was erected by
Rohfab, a Cork manufacturer of prefabricated houses on a small
haggard purchased from the neighbouring Eames brothers. My boat
could be moored beyond the end of the garden and the views over
Lough Derg are phenomenal. Soon, however, we found it necessary
to add to the west, and later the east end. This enabled each of us
to have our own study and provided a pleasant guest room as well
as our own quarters.

There were problems with Claudia and Joy's education. Our
finances were at a low ebb and we were unable to pay for their
boarding. Their father had been a Freemason but the English and
Irish orders were separate. Following lengthy communications
however, we received assistance for Claudia at Newtown, a Quaker
boarding school in Waterford, but their grandparents felt that they
would be better with them or with their uncle in Canada, to whom
they eventually went. Claudia has remained in Canada where she is

involved with horses and her young child and Joy, married with a small girl, is in the United States.

Our garden, originally less than half a hectare, was extended by an extra one and a half from another neighbour. Together with the orchard, the area set aside for flowers and vegetables is about one hectare, the rest planted with commercial conifers. We have erected two hundred metres of walls and created a delightful pond with the help of Tomás Porcell. This has settled well and is home to perch, rudd and an enormous eel. We have also planted lots of other interesting trees and shrubs. Many of these were given by friends such as a flowering currant by Lady Ampthill which we call 'Christobella' and a Japanese maple, 'Geraldina', after Geraldine Hely-Hutchinson. Visitors are often astonished when we describe the plants, the true Latin or even English names of which they know, as such. Grania, who once disliked gardening, loves digging away and sowing unusual seeds while, although precluded from involving myself in the physical work, I enjoy landscaping and dreaming of features and plants to be added. Once, whilst working in casual clothes, a car pulled up to the gate. Investigating, I was greeted as the gardener: "Tell me, is this where Mr. and Mrs. Weir live?" I am not sartorially minded but Grania has made me aware that I don't have to use my tatty old jackets, trousers or even shoes until they almost fall off.

Dogs have played a prominent role in my life. Neither Grania nor I could enjoy life without them. Although I was brought up with characters such as Emmy, a Cairn terrier, and Joe, a remarkable Staffordshire Bull terrier with us at the end of the war, I didn't have my own until I was about to leave Brook House. I think the Rosses believed that the ownership of Pepino would help me overcome my growing discontent. Approaching a bridge or bump, when travelling with me in the van, he would remember it and crouch down - I was always forewarned if we had previously travelled the road. The poor little dog came to a tragic end. We had been asked to lunch by neighbours, Malcolm and Muriel Bell. As we parked our car, he slipped out and wandered about the drive. Another friend and fellow guest inadvertently drove over him; we were devastated. He died a couple of days later in our car, his special territory.

Months after Pepino's death, we attended an open air service at Clonmacnoise, the ancient religious settlement on the river Shannon. As we knelt in prayer on a grassy hillside, a beige pug belonging to a nearby family group, made eye contact. We had quite a conversation and I felt he was telling us choose a pug as successor. Grania had her docile Labrador, but Bawn had been mistreated very early in her life obviously by a man, probably in an anorak. She embarrassed us when we went to lunch with our friends the Packenham Mahons, her former owners, at Strokestown House. Entering their diningroom, we were asked to help ourselves to food. As we did so we noticed her squatting on the carpet surrounded by an ever increasing pool. We had forgotten to ensure that she had emptied herself outside.

I mentioned my interest in locating a pug to our vet, Ham Lambert, whose son I had taught, and whom we know well. He indicated that there was a breeder in Kildare. A few weeks later we had a letter from a Mrs. Day implying that she had checked our credentials and, as we had passed muster, she would offer Chlöe. We were on our way. On arrival at her thatched farmhouse, we were shown into her parlour where Grania and she sat on a sofa and I, some distance away, in an armchair. She assured us that Chlöe was ready to be adopted and that the little creature would make for me when the door was opened. She then let in her pack of eleven black pugs. Chlöe was totally disinterested but another, Topsy, made straight for my lap, the beginning of a long and special relationship. On the journey home she sat between my knees and occasionally licked me. Thereafter she followed me everywhere and, like Pepino, loved the car. She would sit astride the backs of the front seats before head restraints were introduced, just like a monkey. It took a long time to overcome the trauma of her death ten years later. As with all our canine friends, we buried her in view of our dressing rooms west of the house.

Grania's fawn pug, Sophia, was introduced following Bawn's death but during Topsy's life. We had agreed to buy her unseen from a breeder near Drogheda. He would await us outside Hueston station, in a red coloured car with a shoebox beside him, Sophia inside it. Embarrassed, I looked into each of the specifically coloured vehicles

Grania relaxes with Sophia and Bella, Ballinakella, 1994.

outside the main entrance before locating them. Devoted to Grania, she blatantly used my lap from which to observe her; she was a faithful little pet. My own next was Bella who was Scottish. We drove to Carnoustie to collect her. Like Topsy she was a delightful and loyal character, but she was burdened by epilepsy and regularly, about once a month, would have distressing fits. One evening, when I was out of mobile telephone range working in Co. Kerry, Grania let her out as usual. Bella who had eye damage, fell into the pond and drowned. Grania was devastated. When she told me the following morning, I raced home to find my dear little canine companion wrapped up, cold in her favourite blanket and in her basket. We embraced ourselves in tears. Perhaps it was because she was so brave and had survived so much ill health that we felt her death so deeply. Sophia felt it too.

Tiggy, given the kennel title of Princess Tika, often corrupted to 'Gita, comes from Wexford. We drove there to check her compatibility and do a deal, but didn't collect her then as I was due to visit France. On my return, I called to her old home where she immediately recognised me. Like Topsy she sat with her head on my lap for the journey to Ballinakella. She got a rather cool welcome from Sophia who was disgusted that I should introduce an intruder into her life. Sophia was, however, lonely for Bella and she and Tiggy became great friends. Gregarious Tiggy is the kindest and most docile of our pets and was, like us, devastated when fifteen year old Sophia gently passed away. Millie, from Waterford where she was to have been bred from, is a characterful little beige bitch with a psychological hang-up. Kennelled with much larger dogs, she had been terrified. This has lead to an excitable, even aggressive nature; attack, to her, is the best means of defence. Although she bullied the long-suffering Tiggy, the two are really great friends. I have always held back a little of my affection for my dogs in self defence for when they end their years. Now, however, I unreservedly cuddle and love them.

*   *   *   *   *   *   *   *   *   *   *

Perhaps due to polio and incapacity, my interest in motor cars has been above average. In rural Ireland, personal transport is essential.

My grandfather, amongst the first to own a car, instilled this interest at an early stage. Another influence was the popularity of dinky toys during school days. I can't recall my parents' earliest vehicles although I do remember a Morris Eight, my Aunt Bryda's Austin 12, and my grandmother Minnie's dark blue Hillman Minx which was laid up on blocks during the war. My grandfather Willie Gibson had succumbed to Hitler's efforts to amass sterling in the late nineteen thirties by purchasing a large Opel for two hundred pounds. I remember the purr of its engine, the smell of its leather and the metal bars at the top of the back of each front seat, onto which I clung as I observed the road over his shoulder. During the war, my mother drove a Baby Austin; it was like a covered bathtub and due to its size, a vehicle with which a small boy could readily identify. Following the world conflict, Papa acquired an Armstrong Siddeley with a Sphinx as its bonnet mascot, and then a Lanchester with a gauge over its front grille. Because of the convenient gear handles on the steering wheel, he was able to handle them with his one arm.

At Ardmaylebeg we had a black Vauxhall with dart-like silver grooves on either side of the bonnet. The doors opened from the front. Once, my mother having stopped to view the river from a bridge near Holycross, our passenger opened a door against the stone parapet before she had put on the hand-brake. As the car moved forward the door got wedged. It took much rocking, pushing, grunting and bad language before it could be dislodged. Two Commer station wagons had been preceded by a 'half timbered' Hillman shooting brake. When I reached sixteen, I was taught to drive on a South Tipperary registered Ford Van, HI 7051. Used almost exclusively for milk deliveries, its rear doors rattled persistently.

Mama and Papa never liked me driving their cars unless for work and I had saved thirty pounds, a lot at the time. I set off for Dublin, my sole aim being to purchase my own velocipede. Unsuccessful, I chanced a last call before catching the return train from Kingsbridge, now Heuston, Station. Smithfield Motors was a main Ford dealer. Locating the foreman, I asked if he had anything for twenty pounds. He very considerately told me that I was unlikely to buy anything for that. Disconsolate, I thanked him as we stood to the rear of the large dark covered area. On my way out, a blue Ford Model Y, with two elderly ladies, entered the garage. "Come back, young fella", called the foreman, "Would that do?" I could have wept with joy. It was late afternoon and insurance companies would be closing. Determined to drive it home that evening, I eventually got a company to issue a short-term policy to get me home - at nearly half the value of the vehicle. I reached almost sixty miles an hour in my anxiety to show off my investment; the cable brakes were appalling but the vehicle was in great condition. As I hummed into our yard, the sash window of my father's bedroom was thrust open: "What the hell have you been up to?" My parents were horrified, but once they realised that I was now independent and wouldn't request the loan of their vehicles, my action was welcomed. In fact my father enjoyed a spin in my carefully polished acquisition, urging me to drive faster. My mother drove it too, usually following a day's hunting when she would ask me to hack her horse home. Each time I returned from abroad, I would push the car out from the harness room, remove the battery and leave it to be re-charged in Cashel. Having cleaned and dried the plugs and re-inserted the battery the following day, I would turn the handle and start the engine. It was easy.

Taking my Model Y to England would have been costly. A net was craned from the mail boat, onto which the vehicle was driven before being hoisted into the hold. Therefore, whilst training at East Anglian Brigade Headquarters, I purchased a Triumph. In Hong Kong my Standard Vanguard was a comfortable car and I recall exciting trips around the New Territories. Having to return from the Far East, I transferred it to a new owner; second-hand cars were cheap as troops and colonial servants came and went.

I posessed no car until I returned to Cork. Having to fund my accommodation at St. Fin Barre's and my theological education, I had little money. To get to St. John's and to the Grammar School to which there was no direct bus service, I had my little 'Quickly'. I hired cars, usually Austin A40s, for trips to Dublin or Tipperary, before owning my Austin Ten.

After three successive Austins, my first purchase at St. Stephen's was a very economical Irish-assembled Heinkel Bubble car with which I had a lot of excitement and fun, and using which I built my cottage, Cappaghabeg. Costing £45, it was a two-seater three-wheel vehicle with a canvas hood stretching from the bulbous rear window to the wide front-opening door. As I carried building materials in my little workhorse, I found that it progressively wandered. To stop, I had to drive into a tree and then, having unlocked the door, push against it so that the Heinkel travelled backwards enough for me to inch my way through the gap. Oil leaked from the sump.

Come the end of the summer holiday I carefully crept my way up to Dublin and back to school. The father of John Brierley, one of my pupils, ran Lincoln and Nolan's garage. He offered to look after and repair the Heinkel. "Just bring it in and ask for the foreman, telling him I sent you". I was most thankful and, the next available day, set out from Goatstown. Keeping my distance from preceding vehicles I drove close to the kerb so I could use it for braking. As I approached the canal bridge, the speeding traffic ahead suddenly stopped and, as there was no kerb, I banged into the rear of a van. Expecting an irate driver to get out and reprimand me or worse, I was dumfounded when he merely continued his journey. As I reached the garage shop floor, the foreman approached, looked at the bubble car, pulled a few knobs and examined it. After a few minutes he stood up, looked at me and asked from whence I had driven. I told him "Goatstown". He turned to face the mechanics: "Come here lads," said he, "this young gentleman has just driven from Goatstown with no brakes, a broken gearbox, faulty steering and a cracked oil sump". Adressing me he continued, "You're a bloody miracle. It's a wonder you weren't killed". When I told him I had come up from Clare a few days before, the assembled mechanics and he were dumbfounded. Following repairs, I was advised to sell it.

Following my advertisement in the *Evening Herald,* a man from Clontarf on the north side of the city agreed to purchase the Heinkel for the same amount I had paid. Receiving the cash, I 'affectionately' but lightly slapped the bulbous rear window. Made of transparent plastic, it left its moorings and tumbled to the ground. The next half hour was spent trying to replace the thing. Eventually, I waved the new owner down the school drive. That night I had no peace. I listened to news bulletins for fear the driver of a Heinkel bubble car had been killed crossing the city. Only the following evening did I comfortably assume that he had reached home.

With the Heinkel money and a little more, I bought a Ford Anglia, not dissimilar to the Popular my grandfather had exchanged for his Opel at Claffeys of Portumna shortly before his death. It had been badly treated. Its headlights were so feeble that one foggy night, towards Birr across unfamiliar midland roads, I had to drive up to signposts in order to read the directions. At Cappaghabeg, Delia, my neighbour Paddy O'Brien's wife, sought a lift to Whitegate. Half way to the village she declared "Hugh, I have a sort of sinking feeling". I interpreted this as possibly car sickness, so sympathetically told her not to worry: "We'll soon be at Treacy's". She persisted however, and held the side of the door. "She must be in pain", thought I as we accelerated over the bumpy pot-holed road. At our destination I pulled the handbrake. As Delia strained to disembark, there was a crunching noise of splitting timber, the seat landing on the road with Delia still on it. It had been mounted on plywood which had rotted around the edge where it was held by the metal chassis. She never asked for a lift again. The battery of that car was nearly always flat, so passengers often had to push. A delightful English colleague and donkey fanatic, the Reverend John Falconer - on a tour of County Wicklow - spent half his time heaving from behind, often up steep inclines.

Coloured white, my first Peugeot 404 was the car with which I wooed Grania and which we drove on our honeymoons. After a couple of years, I was offered a great trade-in. My next 404 was light blue. I also owned the ex-postal service Ford Transit van with which Grania and I moved the furniture from Thomond House.

My 504 was not new, but was even more comfortable. Its successor a less thirsty and smaller Peugeot Station wagon, was bought by a man reputedly repatriated to the United States accused of the ultimate crime; we wondered why he was interested in its length. Since our first diesel, a Citroën ZX. with an opening roof, we have been so satisfied with our local garage, O'Sullivan and Hansbury's at Ennis, that I have kept with Citroën. I am on my second XM.

For delivering postcards as well as books, we purchased a Nissan van, but its engine being under a cover in the cab made driving in warm climates stifling. A Volkswagon Transporter was less popular than my present van, a large diesel Peugeot Boxer. Fitted with over a hundred pockets for cards, and a chest of several drawers for books over which is a mattress-covered platform, it also has a hands-free telephone.

With my machinery business, I was able to undertake most repairs myself and knew a good deal about what to do in an emergency. Now, however, if I have a puncture, I am at the mercy of anyone I can cajole to assist me. This is frustrating, for I delight in machinery and the way things work, particularly cars.

* * * * * * * * * *

Throughout my life, I have enjoyed hobbies. My father, possibly due to his being incapacitated, collected scrapbookfulls of newspaper and magazine cuttings, stamps, stirrup cups, Irish glass, sporting books and prints. My earliest collection was of dinky toys, popular little metal models of cars and vans. As a child, I started to collect picture postcards. Older cards which depicted change were a delight. I hoarded those of the 'City of Cashel', and used my meagre pocket money to buy cards at places I stayed in or near such as Colchester, Dublin or Enniskillen. I must have over a thousand including those we have received in the post, but I often wonder if the stamps aren't more valuable than the cards themselves. My interest and knowledge of postcards has encouraged me to design and publish my own. I regret that I didn't follow my instincts and produce them when younger. I could have been as successful as John Hinde who, for years, cornered the market.

I also collected, due to my father passing me his basis of completed books, cigarette cards. Because each packet contained a card, he had amassed quite a few. His main brand was the small Woodbine, popular with troops. Sporting figures, birds and famous characters were depicted, and there was a write-up on the back of each. While I was at school, the combined collection was passed to my brother along with my stamps. I was not too concerned at the time, but I had collected some magnificent French, Mozambique and other colonial stamps through swapping at school and Irish overprints are now very much in demand.

My coin collection is based on a small boxful, some from my father and the rest from my uncle Mick. There aren't many but I have a medieval groat, an Elizabethan penny and a favourite but worthless Roman coin dating from the occupation of Britain two millennia ago.

The Gibsons, in the yard of their Merrion Square house, reputedly amassed quantities of carved stones and statues collected around Dublin and Meath. I too, have a love of stone and attempt to date ashlar by the way it has been chiselled. Since just before we were married, when I had my first 'patch' on which to display them, I have saved jostle stones, the cylindrical buffers which stopped carriage wheel-hubs from scoring gate piers, and other worked pieces. Owners of ruined houses have been generous but I have usually paid for stone troughs and mill or wheelwrights' stones. They enhance the garden, and are being saved from destruction.

My local histories contain a wealth of information, down to the smallest areas and the humblest of people. Many authors re-hash material about the famous, while ignoring those who are not. Each time I learn of new books which may help me in my researches, I attempt to save for them. I possess most of those produced in Clare, known for its proliferation of published material. It is great to have sources in one's own library. I also have books I will never read.

An ardent armchair traveller, I keep the *National Geographic Magazine*, much to the chagrin of Grania who decries my wall of yellow on the library shelves. I delve into one when titillated by the prospect of a visit to a country written up or having seen a programme on television. I annually collect travel brochures, especially those which advertise places to which I aspire to go. Our collections of the promotional glossy *Ireland of the Welcomes, Books Ireland* about new publications and Irish books in general, and *Irish Arts Review Yearbooks* often come in useful.

Photography is something I enjoy in a very amateurish way. Although I won a highly regarded competition in Hong Kong where the Chinese excel in the art, I only really got going since I started publishing postcards. I treat each photograph, mostly a landscape or townscape, as a work of art in itself and attempt to frame the scene depicted with trees or tall buildings. I have not so far manipulated my photos by computer. Maybe, to keep up with competition, I will have to. The idea doesn't appeal to me.

I would love to spend time drawing and painting; I believe it has a therapeutic effect. When executing my artwork postcards, I feel relaxed and fulfilled. It doesn't require the effort or brainpower necessary for, say, writing regular weekly articles. Perhaps I will eventually slink off to some secret hermitage with brush and palette and let fly with colour and feeling. It would be fun to do the same with poetry too. Although effort is required to perfect it, one needs to be relaxed and carefree as when, forty years ago, I did, in fact, have some published.

Living on the edge of Lough Derg means that fishing and boating have been favourite sports. Unable to sail, I have resorted to using an outboard engine. It is exhilarating to go out on the lake trolling two lines, to breathe in the fresh air, to listen to the silence only broken by the ripple of water on a calm day or the roar of a heavy sea, and to admire a three hundred and sixty degree view of an always changing landscape. Cloud and water effects enhance the sensation, as also does the suspense when a fish bites and the fear that a whopper might unhook itself. I did have a cabin cruiser which I bought from my friend Tom Kelly, but just couldn't manipulate it single-handed. As for shooting, although once a rifle marksman and a fairly accurate wielder of a shotgun, I feel uncomfortable even at the thought of killing a diminishing wildlife. Much shooting is no longer sport, the odds being weighed too heavily in favour of the hunter. I recently witnessed an intruder into our bay, a sanctuary, stand in his boat to aim at a sitting duck only metres away. This disgusts me.

Chess is the only indoor game that I really enjoy. I am no great 'shakes' and get impatient pitting my wits against someone who takes time to calculate each move. Reasonably quick-witted and impulsive, I prefer the gamble of rapid moves, especially responding to a quick-acting opponent. It is the same with draughts, scrabble or card games; in my Cork days, I once won a game of whist. In Hong Kong I had received a thousand Hong Kong dollars at a China Fleet Club Tombola session where symbolic words were used such as 'legs' for eleven. This made the game exciting. Nowadays, because Grania isn't really a 'games' person either and because neither of us have time to spare, I seldom play. I do, however, enjoy opening our games cupboard when we have children to stay; we let them choose.

I enjoy cooking experimentally and seldom use a book. In earlier years I delved into Maura Laverty's Irish Cookery book and others whose titles I've forgotten, but most of my ability to produce a reasonable meal has come through observation. At Ardmaylebeg, Mrs. Meskell and others were willing to share their knowledge and my mother was a dab hand at potato cakes. In London I had to learn as I could only afford to entertain my girlfriends in my apartment. I still recall my first attempt at rashers; they were charred to a frazzle. While I do the cooking, Grania, an excellent cook herself, does the washing up and often points out my easy task as she struggles at the peeling of potatoes and root vegetables or the preparing of onions. My real forte is perhaps my ability to produce a dish in minutes, a challenge. Several times I have given thought to opening a restaurant. I often feel that I could have done better when eating out, and at a reasonable price. Grania brings me down to earth with "and who is going to do all the dirty work?"

There is an old Irish saying "when God made time, he made plenty of it"; for me, he didn't. I would love to spend more time enjoying these interests. Perhaps I need to organise myself, a difficult task due to a full programme of time-demanding activities.

* * * * * * * * * *

Of the variety of people I have mét, there have been few detrimental to my life. I have, rather been blessed with kind, thoughtful and delightful people, many of whom have become friends. During the war, the Polish military underground fighters who taught me boxing were unreservedly kind; I was devastated when told they wouldn't be returning from dangerous flight missions. Miss Chaston in Norfolk used to take me to her little cottage beside the canal near Wroxham. My grandfather's housekeeper Dolly O'Neill, Mrs. Meskell and her husband Batt and so many others in and around Cashel lubricated my evolution. At Whitegate and Mountshannon I was always overwhelmingly welcomed. In the army, or on my travels and as a teacher I have come across lovely people and when I went into business, I found new colleagues co-operative and delightful, even as rivals. Clare people have become special.

Following our marriage, Grania and I realised that many close friends were common to each of us. We lost a few, mainly a tiny minority of wealthy non nationals who had befriended Grania's family when they lived in Dromoland. We were quite content with our lakeside bungalow and our real friends have kept with us. The most touching aspect of my life since marriage has been the lovely way Grania's many O'Brien relations have embraced me into the family circle.

I relish my privacy and have merely a few close buddies apart from Grania with whom to share my life and home. She is my closest companion. She may have interests such as needlework and clothes, but we share eighty percent of what we do. I could not have been as happily married to those to whom I was attracted in my youth, many of them with different life styles. Grania has the confidence to allow me my freedom to do 'my own thing' which, for my turn, I extend to her. We need, however, to keep constantly in touch, even when travelling abroad. We are also wonderfully lucky that our full life together has meant so many other friends; we don't necessarily keep up regular correspondence or visit but share much when we get the opportunity. In hospital or when things have gone wrong, it has been a particular comfort when they have visited us.

On Lough Derg with Alexander, Roxanne and Marianne Rakic, 1979

CHAPTER THIRTEEN

Lay Readers – a new Ministry. Services, Synods and cousins, Dublin Castle receptions, Partners in Mission and Spanish Episcopalians. The General Synod, Standing Committee and Representative Church Body, radio service and commitment.

Already a member of the General Synod, and other Church of Ireland committees, I was unofficially helping those who asked me to take church services. Edwin Owen, Bishop of Killaloe in succession to Harry Stanistreet, who conducted our marriage service, wrote in June 1974. He had been giving thought to the establishment of a Ministry of Readers: ". . . . so I am inviting you, a parishioner of Clonfert, and one in North Killaloe to be the first members of this team". We were to be commissioned to conduct morning and evening prayer, to preach, to assist the ordained priest at the Eucharist by administering the chalice and to undertake various other non-sacramental tasks. Our friend Luke Dillon Mahon was from Co. Galway where his family had lived for generations and Bert Cunningham was based at Shannon. We were commissioned in Killaloe Cathedral on September 1st, twenty-three years before Grania's similar ceremony.

Killaloe Cathedral exudes warmth and a sense of history which for us makes it very special. Founded by St. Flannan, the site's present edifice with its three separated lancet East windows was erected by Grania's forebear, the fourteenth century King Donal Mór O'Brien. Reconstructed and repaired using many of the original stones, its simple cruciform shape carries few pretensions but reflects the local community's sharing in the worship of God, that of a rural people doing their best. It was emotive that our inductions took place within its walls.

In 1974, Ireland had no non-stipendiary ministry. In many areas, clergy were not being replaced due to a shortage of ordained men

and of adequate finance. Although I had put aside training for the full time ministry, Bishop Owen felt that both Grania and I would readily serve at least in the diocese. We joined him for a conference on the Auxiliary Ministry that October. The gathering at Waterville was useful and many of those who attended took holy orders. The Church of Ireland soon accepted this new form of Ministry.

About this time I attended a number of courses and conferences. One was on preaching and during a comprehensive weekend at the Church of Ireland Theological College, aspects of communication such as broadcasting were elucidated. As one of only a few Diocesan Readers, I was in demand. Grania and I found ourselves at Morning Services conducted in such distant churches as Kyle and Corbally, near Roscrea, where the Gibsons worshipped, and Kilkee in west Clare. In the autumn I preached at Harvest Festivals. I was sometimes able to deliver the same address for two venues such as at Templederry and Lorrha in 1975.

I composed sermons and organised services the previous Saturday evenings, even following busy weeks. We would, say, leave home for Bourney near Roscrea at eight o'clock on a Sunday morning. After locating a perhaps unfamiliar church, I would hope – occasionally the keeper of the key was the last to arrive – to reconoitre the layout, spiritually prepare myself and chat to worshippers as they entered. Following the Service, having signed the preacher's book, thanked those present, and said good-bye I'd rush to the next location; sometimes there were three, occasionally four. Having returned home, exhausted after an early start and perhaps a hundred miles of driving, we would open a tin of baked beans and fall asleep. On somewhat rare occasions clergy or parishioners would have arranged a meal. Readers didn't get expenses then, though a mileage allowance and the cost of meals was eventually re-claimable.

On Sunday mornings Mass-goers strolled, chatting, across the highways, to their own churches. They would often park haphazardly, occasionally causing a total blockage , and after Mass would drive into the road irrespective of on-coming traffic. Rarely were we late though, some congregations being surprised to find us there before them.

Many Readers must have been disconcerted at the amount of 'strangers' who have greeted them. People who address large groups must share this phenomenon for their audiences see them, hear them, and know their names. Except for being greeted at the door, the locals often remain anonymous. A few people have a remarkable ability to store names and the faces linked to them; a great man with this facility was Archbishop George Otto Simms.

*   *   *   *   *   *   *   *   *   *

During my Lay Ministry, some experiences have been amusing, others frustrating. A lot of parishioners have a problem with Readers. Where one has a regular commitment such as the taking of services in one's own church there can be smaller congregations. Having spent hours preparing a service and address, this can be disheartening. Later, however, an individual may approach and say "I remember when you were preaching in our church. What you said made a great impact on my life . . . ." Such words, with the help of God, encourage one.

In my early days of preaching, I would read out my addresses. Once a school, Kyle Church near Roscrea was panelled in wood up to about four feet from ground level. The prayer desk was the same height and beside it's restricted surface area was a slit between the panelling and the wall. There wasn't room for prayer books, hymnals and extras. One Sunday I wedged my address in the narrow slit shortly before I would deliver it. Imagine my consternation as all five carefully prepared pages slipped totally behind the panel; they must still be there.

At Killodiernan church near Nenagh, I digressed from the conventional interpretation of the text. There was nothing heretic or incorrect in what I said but as I was saying "goodbye" at the West door, a retired Church of England cleric castigated me for not adhering to tradition. He later confided that my dissertation was a different, but refreshingly acceptable, interpretation of the text.

Another time, I turned up at what, from a distance, I had mistakenly accepted to be the Church of Ireland edifice. Embarrassed, I had to retrace my route to the less conspicuous building I had already passed. Some churches were converted mills such as Bourney, or schoolhouses like that in the Tipperary village of Moneygall. The latter's organist, the Canon's equally delightful wife, ensured that her choral decibels were as significant as their quality; her wonderful enthusiasm shone. Patrick Trench, another keen musician, shared playing the harp and other instruments with his wife Julia at their home near Ballingary in North Tipperary. The hymns he chose for Church services were from several different books and I would get embarrassingly confused as to which to announce. Once I found myself singing the words of a hymn from one book to the identically numbered music of another.

Uncomfortable when there was a cleric in the pews, especially a Bishop, I have found them disarmingly generous and have often been vociferously praised. Microphones presented a problem when not voice-tuned; with my strong delivery, I could deafen listeners. Some congregations were not used to meeting the preacher before or after the service. I felt this necessary, not only to make acquaintance with new people but also to learn who was sick and for whom to pray. Where possible I would thank the singers, the organist, the wardens and others who helped.

Few clergy wrote or telephoned to thank one for standing in, even for them to go on holidays, but there have been some who even sent a small cheque and who did express appreciation. A senior cleric rang one winter Saturday to say he had influenza and was feeling rotten. It was snowing and I was suffering from a severe cold. Believing him to have been considerably worse than I, I agreed to take his service the following morning. With great difficulty Grania and I negotiated the dangerously icy roads to lead his congregation. Afterwards, exhausted and sickly, I suggested to Grania that we lunched in a local restaurant. The same cleric was seated at a nearby table, eating a hearty meal.

I don't believe our Readers have received fair credit for their dedicated efforts as part of the Church's ministry. In our southwestern diocese there has been an uncomfortable gap between clergy and laity, and during the 1990s the Church became distinctly fragmented. Many of us had hoped that auxiliary ministers would pronounce a stronger word on the issue, many having had lay reading experience. Although we have formed an association of readers, a lack of official funding has curtailed our prospects.

Today there are Diocesan and Parochial Lay Readers in most parishes. Once, because most Sundays were spent taking services in other churches, I asked that I take one each month in mine. I ended by sharing with Grania, now also a Diocesan Reader, two a month in Mountshannon and few elsewhere. Following a dedicated quarter of a century I have excused myself of my regular commitment.

*   *   *   *   *   *   *   *   *   *   *

As a member of the General Synod, I shared in the administration of the church, and made many friends. In 1974, in the old Synod Hall attached to Christchurch Cathedral in Dublin, Grania and I got talking with a representative from Co. Fermanagh. Although I had never met Warren Loane, we soon found that we shared similar backgrounds. Warren and his wife, Anne, related to each other, had a large number of blood links with my family. We also had similar interests in genealogy, local history and the countryside. Warren compiled genealogical trees which traced our mutual descent from such forebears as Brian Boru. Both deeply involved in church affairs, the Loanes and ourselves remain close friends.

Some years later Grania and I were invited to the dedication of St. Anne's Cathedral in Belfast. Following the moving choral service we made for the reception in the City Hall. As we approached, Democratic Unionist Party politician, the Reverend Ian Paisley and his followers were vociferously protesting. I turned to Grania and commented "Big Ian is here to greet us".

"Yes, I am 'Big Ian' but I'm not here to greet the likes of you."

The comment was lighthearted and we had little reason to feel animosity towards the reverend doctor.

In 1985, the annual General Synod was held in Belfast for the first time. A pre-session service in St. Anne's was followed by another City Hall reception. When synodsmen were invited to see over the building. Some of us sat in the Council chamber, debating the sentiments of the Lord Mayor should he learn that southerners, some with nationalist sentiments, were 'occupying' seats of power in the North's then strongly Unionist capital city. The welcome we received was unambiguous. The Northern Ireland Office arranged a further reception at Stormont. As we queued in our cars to be scrutinised by security, my passengers and I were ushered ahead to the astonishment of all, particularly ourselves - even past bishops and politicians. Again we were afforded the chance to sit in seats of power within the magnificent purpose-built twentieth century political palace. Two of us were introduced to Secretary of State Douglas Hurd - hardly had we met when his eyes seemed to search for someone of greater significance. I thought him blatantly rude. Who knows?, we could have been politically useful My letter of appreciation to our Belfast hosts was published in the _Church of Ireland Gazette_.

Usually accompanied by Grania, I was privileged to attend other receptions and gatherings. At least three times we went to Dublin Castle. On the appointment of John Armstrong as Archbishop of Armagh in 1980, Taoiseach Charles J. Haughey invited us and six years later, Fine Gael's Garret Fitzgerald had us at a similar gathering in honour of Archbishop Robin Eames. More recently, John Bruton was our host and when the Synod was held in Cork, their Lord

Mayor welcomed us to an evening in the City Hall. These events were enjoyable, dignified and tasteful.

I took my General Synod responsibilities with dedication and spoke on many issues. In 1976, the *Gazette* reported me as saying "Closing of churches hurts, especially when you cannot get rid of them". The media coverage continued ". . . . He appealed for people involved in church extension areas to liaise with those where churches were being closed to obtain furniture and windows for incorporation in the new buildings. In this way the parish would live on!" Three years later, the *Irish Independent* reported me as reminding the Synod that the prolonged postal dispute was causing "tremendous suffering" in the west. The telecommunication and e-mail era had yet to come. I only once suffered the red 'stop' light, to control long-winded speakers, to come on before completing my piece. I also acted as teller, counting the 'ayes' and 'nays' of voting members.

For many years I was a member of the General Synod's Standing Committee. This body of clergy and laity chaired by the Primate discussed ongoing issues of national or churchwide significance such as the re-marriage of divorced persons, the introduction of women clergy, North-South relations and the Liturgy. In 1976, I contributed to *The Churches Response to underdevelopment in Rural Ireland* - a joint Irish Council of Churches and Roman Catholic working party paper. In my various deliberations to General Synod and its Standing Committee, Alan Johnston, the Press Officer reported me as being ". . . . forthright."

*   *   *   *   *   *   *   *   *   *

Most helpful exercises in evangelism and self examination were the Church of Ireland 'Partners in Mission' conferences. As a Killaloe Diocesan representative, I attended the first, held at the Church of Ireland Theological College, in August 1977. Clergy, including Michael Mayes who was appointed our bishop in 2001, and laity from Irish dioceses and representatives of Youth, the Council for the Church Overseas, the Mothers' Union and the Irish Council of Churches joined delegates from other churches in Ireland and abroad, mainly Anglican. Group meetings were shared and relevant issues discussed. Stephen Ambani of Kenya, the Bishop of St.

Andrew's in Scotland and the Reverend Raymond Clarke from Canada were amongst those who, having participated in the soul-searching deliberations, suggested how we could improve the work of the Church. There was a deep spirituality to these conferences, following which representatives reported to their dioceses.

* * * * * * * * * *

In September 1981, following the success of the previous consultation, with Bishop Mehaffey in the Chair, several reverend Canons and myself were elected the organising committee of another 'Partners in Mission' Conference, I being the only layman. We incorporated a number of lay advisers such as Northern Ireland politician David Bleakley, Mrs. Judith May, and Press Officer Alan Johnston. Overseas partners came from various continents and from the Anglican Consultative Council, the Episcopal Churches of the Sudan and the United States being represented, together with the Spanish Reformed Episcopal Church. Constructive criticism and prayerful suggestions culminated in a useful report under the headings of *Ministry, Spiritual Growth, Divisions* and *Structures.* Helpful reading for those concerned with the future of their church, I would love to see it re-issued. Under the heading *Bricks and Mortar,* paragraph three states "More thought should be given to how unneeded churches could be used . . . . " As a member of the Representative Body I soon convened with Bishop Willoughby of Cashel and Mr. Quayle (now a Lay Canon of Armagh), a sub-committee on the "Use, disposal or demolition of closed churches". Any action resulting from our deliberations could only be voluntary, each bishop being responsible for his own diocese unless an issue is subject to the General Synod. Many bishops responded positively.

Sadly, there was little follow-up in some dioceses following this Second 'Partners-in-Mission' Consultation. A lot of hard work went into its preparation and each small working group produced useful ideas but at the time, the Church's leadership was taken up with the Northern Irish situation.

One result of the consultations was the tremendous camaraderie during the four day session. Grania and I offered to help Bishop

Arturo Sanchez of Madrid, and the incumbant of Sabadell, Gabriel Amat, to establish a congregation in Mallorca. The effort failed but we introduced the two delightful clerics to our relations and local contacts. We were unable to join them when they held a service in Port de Andratx, mainly attended by Roman Catholic friends and a few rather disinterested English non-churchgoers. At the time, the Anglican Church in Palma was that of the Church of England and the language English. Catalans being of independent nature and Gibraltar being a Spanish political issue meant that residents had no acceptable catholic option other than Roman Catholicism. Many attended the evangelical gatherings of non-conformist groups.

*   *   *   *   *   *   *   *   *   *

Returning to local events, in November 1974 I was asked to propose acceptance of the Killaloe Diocesan *Board of Education Report.* Bishop Owen in the chair had just appointed Peter Prentice, then President of the Law Society, as Chancellor and had welcomed Luke Dillon Mahon and myself as Diocesan Lay Readers. Nervously, I emphasised the shortage of Church or Ireland teachers; young people should be encouraged to take up the profession.

Social Reponsibility, although practised by individual church members, has seldom received the organised support of the Church of Ireland that it deserves. During Bishop Owen's episcopacy, I was a vociferous member of his Diocesan Board of Social Responsibility. In 1979 he asked me to take the chair. An expensive media personality was invited to talk on alcoholism at an open gathering in Ballinasloe, attended by a youthful audience. Our committee also initiated discussions on divorce, abortion and poverty, and spoke on such topics as coursing, the environment and youth. Due to poor active support and frequent failure to reach a quorum, we decided to disband the Board at the end of 1980. It has recently, under Peter Read's enthusiastic leadership, been resuscitated.

At the 1987 Killaloe Synod I successfully proposed the adoption of a Diocesan Commission on Churches to consider a report on the future of our united diocese - unless the motion was successful, 'ruthless' General Synod action could be taken.

An influential elected group in the Church of Ireland is the Representative Body, colloquially known as the 'R.B'. It was created at disestablishment in 1870 to hold properties on behalf of the Church as an incorporated trustee and to administer funds in accordance with the underlying trusts. Apart from the Bishops and a few co-opted members, each diocese has one clergyman and two laymen. Elected in 1980 on the retirement of Howard Benson, I was to serve for three consecutive three year periods.

As with the Standing Committee, we met once a month in the Boardroom at Church of Ireland House, a refreshingly modern office block at Rathmines, since updated. Howard explained, when I arrived for my first meeting, where I should sit. The Archbishops, Bishops and the Chief Officer positioned themselves at the huge central rectangular table while the rest of us sat around the edge of the Boardroom. Killaloe representatives were behind their bishop midway along the wall opposite the large picture windows. Following prayers, our deliberations usually continued until lunchtime. Sometimes we continued to chat in the room where the Bishops were to have a further meeting. There would be an embarrassing hush as we shuffled out of the door as they took their places.

Membership of the Representative Church Body and of the General Synod Standing Committee was a privilege. It could also be fun and findings were often historically significant. Although we were from both North and South with political leanings from ultra conservatism to almost rabid socialism, and entrenched Unionism to unyielding nationalism, I can't recall any unpleasantness during, before or after debates. Problems discussed concerned the North and South and a deep bond brought us together with one target, the good of God's church and His people. After meetings we would spill down the stairs greeting each other and conversing. Some would queue for the subsidised lunch while others would make for their cars, seek lifts or hail a bus to a railway station. A few would join their wives for shopping sprees. I shared many debates but left those dealing with finance or statistics to the experts. My concern included issues such as the retention or otherwise of redundant churches or Bishop's palaces - I had a major imput into the saving of the Bishop's historic Georgian residence at Kilmore, for instance.

In November, 1986, I proposed a committee to record the contents of churches. Abandoned or de-consecrated edifices sometimes had broken stained-glass windows, damaged pews and Bibles torn and strewn about. In many cases valuable items such as brass lecterns, marble pulpits and carved Holy Tables had been removed; in others, monuments vandalised. Some of these buildings like Clarina were in my own united diocese. With encouragement from fellow Representative Body members such as Corkman T.G.F. Stoney, my proposal, seconded by the Archbishop of Dublin, was accepted. I was to be convener. Walton Empey, then Bishop of Meath and Kildare represented the House of Bishops and Erica Loane, Peter Prentice, Leslie Roberts, T.G.F. Stoney and F.G. Quayle were accepted on my recommendation. Our mandate was to "consider the possible recording of church furniture, monuments and tangible assets throughout the Church of Ireland and to report back with detailed proposals as to how this work might be undertaken . . . ." I had circulated a comprehensive document beforehand.

Peter Prentice was successfully mooted as Chairman. With help from Ireland and abroad, we came up with a skeleton questionaire suitable for recording each church. Dr. Raymond Refaussé, Representative Body archivist, the Very Reverend Maurice Talbot, son of a Dean of Cashel in my mother's time, and Mrs. Lesley Whiteside contributed useful assistance. I was unable to conclude our deliberations as my Diocesan Synod chose a new member of the Representative Body, Howard Benson's son Roy, in my place. Peter Prentice, a co-opted member, had also run his time.

Dr. Refaussé later asked me would I be prepared to be nominated to serve on the Library and Records Committee - I replied in the affirmative. Due to my interest in books and manuscripts and my experience in publishing, even writing, I was delighted. In February 1990, he wrote that he had, with regret, to withdraw my nomination: "Unfortunately, the vacancy on the Committee must be filled by a member of the Representative Church Body . . . . I regret that the Committee cannot have the benefit of your wide knowledge of the cultural and intellectual life of the Church of Ireland. . . . "

The end of my nine years' service to the Representative Body (I had already been superceded on the Standing Committee) allowed me to consider my role in church affairs. Involved in a lot of ecclesiastical and secular charities and committees, my expenditure in unclaimable travel expenses, meals and postage came to almost £3,000 a year and free time was at a premium. Many meetings were held on weekdays. As I was working from Monday to Saturday I was already denying Grania shared marital life. Three years after my withdrawal from the Killaloe Synod and Council, their Commission on churches and the Glebes and Finance Committee, I was happy to be re-elected to the Diocesan Synod and the General Synod; I had missed my friends and the opportunity to debate and support, or otherwise, significant issues.

When local radio station, *Clare F.M.*, was established, Father Rueben Butler invited me to join their mainly Roman Catholic committee for religious broadcasts. Delighted, my acceptance bore the proviso that I would have my bishop's consent. *Thoughts For The Day*, broadcast services, and items of news were undertaken but my diocese was singularly lacking in support. This was elucidated to the Diocesan Synod. Consolation was that Bishop Darling and the Ennis-based station were directly in touch. Martin Browne, once an active member of the Clare Young Environmentalists, and now a prospective monk at Glenstall, was a useful contact and Fathers Gerry Kenny and Brendan Quinlivan were particularly helpful.

Other activities were the dedication of a utility barge in Mountshannon and, when the village won the All Ireland 'Tidy Towns' award, conducting a special 25th Anniversary 'Environmental Service of Commemoration and Thanksgiving'. At the latter there was a large multi-denominational congregation with singing by the Garda Choir. Encouraged by Father Macnamara at his Mass which ended as our service started, an 'extra' crowd of dignitaries and locals joined us, filling spare pews or standing at the rear. The dedication of an Altar Cross for Mountshannon Church in memory of our last resident curate, Edgar Talbot, saw me in the pulpit and I have spoken for the church on radio and television.

During the General Synod in Cork in May 1994, Press Officer Liz Gibson Harries asked me to say a few words for R.T.E. television. The venue was the conference centre's helicopter pad. Each time the elaborate equipment was set up and I was about to speak, a helicopter appeared. It took three attempts before we eventually completed the interview.

One of my few remaining commitments is the contribution of short vignettes and accompanying drawings of churches in the *Church of Ireland Gazette*. I try to visit the edifices and often find them exciting and interesting, especially those off the beaten track.

Delighted to express my appreciation to parishioners of the Chaplaincy of Aquitaine in France for their kindness to my mother, I have preached at services in the chapel de St. Martin in Limieul near Bordeaux. This has enabled me to meet local residents of varying nationality and church practice, thanks particularly to lay chaplain Caroline Brierley. Oak House, an ecumenical organisation founded by Claire Besnyö of Loughrea, with a Celtic bias has recently been spiritually helpful. I was also delighted to lead prayers in Tuamgraney, the oldest continuously used church in these islands, to the 'St. Brendan 2000 pilgrimage' en route from Clonfert to Mount Brandon in Kerry, lead by Father Tomás Ó Caoimh.

*   *   *   *   *   *   *   *   *   *

My commitment to God and my church was reinforced by my experience at the Emmanuel Bible shop in Kowloon in the nineteen-fifties - my interest in Irish church history goes back further. I am often frustrated at the lack of shared dedication and effort amongst Christians. To me, the universal Church is an essential vehicle for the maintenance of spirituality, morality, the perpetuity of stability, and for teaching the Word. A committed ecumenist, I have tried in my small way to bring us together, and am 'at home' with local Roman Catholics. They have been blessed with farsighted leaders in recent years. Bishop Michael Harty was a good friend and Willie Walsh, the present Bishop of Killaloe must be praised as outspoken, generous and gifted. He was amongst those at the ecumenical gathering organised by the Young Environmentalists in 1997, having braved appalling rain. Concerned for his people, he is forthright against injustice. Of course, there are still hurtful divisions such as the Roman Catholic Church's views on acceptance of the Eucharist by members of other churches.

Oak House Retreat, Mount St. Joseph Cistercian Abbey, Roscrea, 1999.

PHOTO: COMPLIMENTS OF OAK HOUSE

I decry political influence on the Church. In Ireland, particularly in the North, Nationalism and Unionism are too often identified with Roman Catholicism and Protestantism. Members of both religious persuasions cross the denominational line, but there are many involved in violence to whom Christianity means little. In the South, the identity of the Church of Ireland with Anglicanism can be, and sometimes is, misconstrued as identity with Anglo-Saxon Britain. I would prefer the American nomenclature 'Episcopalian'. I am also unhappy with the leadership of the Anglican Communion. The politics of its leadership came to mind at the time Bishop Carey, himself no doubt a good choice, was selected as Archbishop of Canterbury. Canterbury traditionally holds the Presidency of the Anglican Consultative Council and of the Lambeth Conference and its Archbishop is Chairman of the Primates' meetings. Because the Church of England is established, its bishops are appointed by the Crown. Their selections may be increasingly forsighted, but I can see many great churchmen who are black, such as Bishop Tutu, coloured or who come from unsympathetic political spheres being unable to serve the Communion's 'figurehead' post. Perhaps we will eventually see the nomenclature changed and the Presidency of an 'Episcopalian' Communion selected on a rotary basis. In this world-community age the post should not permanently rest with the leader of the Church of England. A recent effort to get a seconder for a proposal to this effect received little response. Those asked felt that, at present, any efforts would be unsuccessful. This implies the political influence that I abhor.

Following half a century of active Church involvement I shall continue to do my best with Grania's traditional encouragement and hope that my miniscule efforts will have helped to bring about a better appreciation of God and of his Creation. I yearn to see Christians reconciling their differences and worshipping together, in their own or their neighbour's churches, with equal conscience.

Claire O'Mahony, Martin Browne and myself, following ecumenical gathering, Mountshannon, 1996.

CHAPTER FOURTEEN

An Taisce and the Clare Champion – The Clare Young Environmentalists; their first and subsequent meetings, summer camps, visits to Fermanagh and Mallorca, their awards – and mine.

My father, so much a countryman with a deep understanding of nature and ecology, encouraged me to observe. This enabled me to see the effects of man on his surroundings. My membership of the County Clare branch council of An Taisce (The National Trust for Ireland) enabled an increasing participation in environmental activities. Thanks to the Galvins who own it, and editor Frank O'Dea, I also started a weekly column in the *Clare Champion*. This elucidated my interpretation of the environment as all that influences us on land, in the air and in water.

I felt membership of an organisation based on Dublin somewhat constricting. Environmentalists in the capital, it seemed, were mainly interested in a coastal strip between Malahide and Bray which stretched a mere twenty or thirty kilometres inland. As a teacher, I had attempted to engender an understanding of ecology and life in my pupils, throughout Ireland. Now I felt that too little was being done by An Taisce to involve and encourage young people. I voiced my opinion to the Clare committee, most of whom supported me. Reports sent to Headquarters included accounts of our debates, and there was a request that something be done to rectify the deficiency. Receiving no feed-back, my only course was to resign, hoping that this action might encourage cognisance to be taken. Eventually a number of friends, including An Taisce members, indicated that a youth group concerned with the Clare environment should be considered and that I should give the lead.

In April, 1980, an open meeting was convened in Ennis. Some

forty youngsters aged between ten and eighteen turned up. I had asked that there be no adults for I didn't wish to intrude on An Taisce's membership. Parents and guardians discreetly left their charges at the meeting. I knew a small percentage of these young people, mainly through their families, but the rest were total strangers. Most came because I had written about the event in the *Clare Champion.*

Due to the enthusiasm expressed, I decided to grasp the nettle. The youngsters should feel that they were in authority so, following a vociferous preliminary debate, a committee of twelve was elected. Most were from the Ennis area which made it easier to call future meetings in the County capital. Neil Dargan, now a Cistercian at Mount St. Joseph Abbey near Roscrea, was our first chairman. I knew Neil to be serious and responsible, his father and mother being friends. Most parents became active supporters and were generous with funds and time. The annual membership was a £1 so that no potential participants should be excluded and the organisation was voluntary, the only public funding being a small but appreciated contribution from the Clare Vocational Education Committee. I was asked to preside and Sister Francis O'Dwyer who taught at the local girls school, Colaiste Mhuire, was elected Vice-President. The Church of Ireland and Roman Catholic Bishops of Killaloe accepted our invitation to be patrons; there was to be no discrimination.

Through the Clare Young Environmentalists' member-motivated clean-ups of beaches, public parks, church properties, river beds and streets, visits to wildlife parks and historic sites, walking and cycling trips, public debates, lectures and talks, instruction sessions for photographers or bird-watchers, and exchanges with like minded groups in Northern Ireland, total membership reached about four hundred. The common aim was environmental concern and action. Members produced an excellent magazine which each year bore different titles (for a couple, the organisation was re-named Clare Youth Impact) such as *Todchai An Chlair* and *Hello Clare!* Apart from some sponsorship by advertisers, income came from sales.

Visits to Northern Ireland, mainly Fermanagh, meant that relations and friends such as the Loanes, Brandons, Sides and Elliots helped to make our trips a success. We stayed in hostels and camped at

Crocnacrieve or Monea Castle. An active co-ordinator was Ronnie Hill, headmaster of Enniskillen High School who, caught by a devastating IRA bomb blast at a Commemoration ceremony in the town, remained in a coma until his death in 2001; he did so much to encourage our cross-border relationships.

The enthusiasm of CYE members ensued my regular fifty kilometre drives to Ennis where most committee meetings took place and often on to other places such as Kilbaha, Fanore or Bunratty, for special events. Apart from trips to Northern Ireland, we visited the popular Fota Wildlife Park and Killarney, where National Park wardens took us on night patrols to observe deer, other fauna, and flora. A climb up the valley to Torc waterfall ended in a mid-stream water fight whereas the dormitory in the old church at Muckross was the scene for night-time ghost stories. Connemara and Galway, Dublin with its wax museum, and the ESB's Georgian house in Merrion Square, the Natural History Museum and the Zoo, Tara, and Armagh Observatory were popular destinations. Most of the activities were fun for both members and accompanying adults.

* * * * * * * * * *

After two years of existence, we initiated what became an annual C.Y.E. summer camp. Our field beside Ballinakella Lodge was an ideal site as we had an outside toilet and there were garages for shelter. The lake was within thirty metres and plenty of neighbours were willing to share their expertise at crafts, angling and other skills. Campers included non-members and those who had joined environmental groups we founded in other counties such as Kildare, where the Newbridge College club was active. Each year, we assembled on a Sunday evening in July.

As tents were erected, those who would be sharing the discomforts and excitements of the week acquainted themselves. Occasionally there would be roars of laughter as a canvas would collapse before unsuspecting erectors had had a chance to hammer in the tent pegs. Our yard bell would summon the participants to their initial evening meal, prepared by the first to arrive. The Fortes, who had a restaurant in Ennis were amongst the generous suppliers of extra food, although

I ensured that ample quantities were purchased beforehand with the funds contributed. I would worry that the cooks would burn themselves; I don't think it ever happened. At the end of each exhausting day Grania and I, having seen the youngsters to bed, would attempt to relax. This seldom happened. After we had retired to bed at around midnight, many are the times I had to put on my dressing-gown, or mackintosh, make for the tent village, and read the riot act. The proximity of boys' tents to those of the girls, the strange environment and the off-the-spot supervision was just too much not to be taken advantage of. I am satisfied, though, that the activities were harmless; young people were merely having fun.

Each morning, those brave enough were encouraged to bathe; few refused and many learnt to swim. Even though we were comprehensively insured, I was always nervous of a mishap. After breakfast, some would be delegated to wash up and clear any litter, an unpopular activity. There would then be educational games to encourage observation and environmental knowledge. For 'Kim's' game, an assortment of up to twenty different items such as a button, a stone, a watch or an oak leaf were displayed on a tray for perhaps a minute - each participant would then, within a limited period, write those things they could recall. This would get harder each time as more items were added. There would be quizzes, sensory experiences where, blindfolded, each would attempt to guess what they were smelling or feeling, or hunts for pre-listed selections of flowers, types of rock or leaves. After lunch there were hikes, bus tours, boat trips and similar physical activities.

In the evenings night patrols helped participants to listen, to identify sounds or lights and even to experience walking into lightly powered electric fences. Once a neighbour was quite worried when wheeling his bicycle from his local pub. He was sure he was being followed, but every time he stopped, there was silence. Although he had no light and it was pitch-dark, he would nervously remount and cycle ahead. Nobody disclosed to him that he had been followed by a patrol of hushed children for almost a kilometre. There were ghost stories too, and other games.

On the final Sunday, we would hold an outdoor Ecumenical Service. Father Treacy, a Whitegate man then Dean of Residence at

St. Flannan's College, Ennis, where some of the kids were at school, and our rector of Mountshannon would simultaneously consecrate the Host. Children, parents and friends received their respective Eucharist at a shared Communion, an appropriate preacher being invited to talk. The Reverend Patrick Towers brought a football which he equated to the world and suggested that, as he acted out his demonstration, we were kicking our globe into oblivion. There were often tears as those who had experienced so many facets of life for the first time left for their homes. It meant peace and quiet for us and although I enjoyed it, it was quite exhausting for both of us, especially Grania.

* * * * * * * * * *

The most strenuous activity undertaken by the Clare Young Environmentalists was a visit to Mallorca in 1985. Having experienced the less-known areas of this largest of the Balearic Islands through our visits to Grania's godmother, Brada Paterson, and her daughters, I had begun to love it and its people. Dragonera, a smaller island alongside the south-west coast was in danger of being developed and preventative support was being sought. Organisational correspondence was exchanged mainly with Jacqueline Catalá and Anna Kay, a local politician married to a kinsman of Jacqueline's husband Pepé. Local Spanish and English-speaking residents helped with transport and trips. The Parish Priest of Port de Andratx kindly arranged that Church of Ireland members could partake of the Roman Catholic Easter Eucharist and that we would be involved in a shared singing of Irish, Catalan and Spanish hymns and in contributing Irish prayers.

The collecting of fares and expenses, the arranging of flights – there were no direct planes from Ireland – via London, and accommodation in that city, were nightmares. We ended by taking a Slattery's bus from Limerick to London and a cramped charter flight on to Palma. Sister Francis O'Dwyer, our capable and resourceful Vice-President, and a participating parent helped with supervision. The group also included an older girl from Athenry and two boys from near Ballinasloe, one of whose parents we knew.

We arrived in London on Good Friday and made for our hotel. The place was an embarrassment with dirty rooms, unchanged sheets and even worse. We were relieved to be out of it the following morning. Sister Francis's nephew David O'Dwyer, with whose family she stayed, gave us a tour of Westminster Cathedral, Westminster Abbey, and the Army & Navy stores. Following coffee in a café near Victoria station we caught the train to Gatwick to board the chartered Boeing 757; there was great excitement travelling on the monorail. At Palma we were greeted by a convoy of vehicles, led by Jacqueline, which conveyed us to Son S'Bert, her house. We 'commandeered' her upstairs apartment, the boys in sleeping bags and on beds in one, and the girls in the other. A few also occupied the living room. The following morning we climbed the steep Atalaya, a rocky crag behind the house where I showed them a promontory fort similar to those in Ireland.

The Easter Sunday Mass over, we went to La Granja, an old mill open to the public, where many of the party surreptitiously imbibed

Son S'Bert, Port de Andratx

free Sangria. Several were inebriated as we continued to Santa Magdalena's hilltop monastery. The Dolphinarium was the attraction another day. I had arranged for Brendan O'Regan and Ciara Long to be hauled in a small boat by two dolphins. There was also an aquarium, a zoo, a bouncing castle, miniature motorbikes and remote controlled boats, not all activity being environmental.

A walk through country roads to Andratx market was surprisingly successful. Nicknacks and local souvenirs were purchased and harmless pranks played. We then lunched outside our American friend Nancy Surmaine's casita. A disco that night wasn't successful as most were exhausted or shy but the next day we had a fascinating trip led by schoolmaster Don Juan. Meeting at the little resort of San Telmo, we parked our cars. For the long hike over precipitous rocky outcrops above the sparkling blue Mediterranean, we were joined by a substantial group from Don Juan's Andratx school. In spite of the language barrier, Spanish and Irish participants got on well. It was a tough route, with distant views of Dragonera below, to Sa Trappa, a remote and abandoned Trappist monastery, high in a mountain valley. After touring the terraces and buildings, natives and visitors gyrated the then popular 'breakdance'. It was a great ice-breaker as many made fools of themselves. We returned home from San Telmo by ferry which meant that I had to return for my car that evening.

A day later photographers mingled with friends, supporters and participants when, on the patio above Jacqueline's swimming pool, the Mayor of Andratx attended an official ceremony of welcome and partnership. Letters between his Council and the Chairman of Clare County Council were exchanged as were welcomes and expressions of friendship and support. While this was going on, two or three bored CYE members feasted on party tidbits behind the backs of the audience, a session of Irish dancing scattering them as guests sought seating. Friday morning was spent at fish laboratories on the opposite shore of the bay. There were squeals from the girls at the sight of octopuses and unusual sea creatures. The final day was spent visiting Dragonera, (the Island of Lizards), the endangered island whose anti-development protesters we had come to support. We hired a ferry across the wide channel to the island's quay. As we ate our picnic lunch above, an inquisitive feral pig snatched Sister

Francis's bag. It, and her wimple which had been dislodged, were restored following an exciting chase.

There was heartbreak and tears as our little group bade farewell to Majorquin friends and well-wishers. I still meet people in the Port who recall *los Irlandeses*. We were sad that, although invited, the Andratx children were unable to make a return visit to Ireland. Don Juan indicated that although they would have loved to have accepted our invitation, they couldn't raise the money. The sentiments of Bishop Michael Harty of Killaloe, in his letter to Bishop Teodora Ubedo Gramage, Archbishop of Palma, "In this International Year of Youth, these young Irish people wish to share their yearning for peace and justice with the young people of Spain" were echoed by all.

*   *   *   *   *   *   *   *   *   *

An annual event was the presentation of the Clare Young Environmentalists Annual Environmental Awards. These were allocated to any citizens whom the Committee felt were worthy Clare people, or those with Banner County connections. A number of friends and business associates, asked to donate perpetual shields, were generous. Although we initially had about five, we ended up with nine and a national award given by the directors of Ailwee Cave, including Roger and Susan Johnson. The criteria was 'the person or persons who have done the most to promote environmental concern and action in the field of . . . .'; included were 'community involvement', 'nature', 'history', 'architecture and design', 'industry' and 'education'. Those who, as guests of honour, presented the awards included President Hillery, Ministers Brendan Daly and Síle de Valera, Rita Childers who had stayed with us with her husband President Erskine Childers, author Morgan Llywelyn, Senator Treas Honan, and Chairmen of the County Council. The presentations, once a major feature of the county's calendar, are being revived with Clare County Council, guided by Congella McGuire, thanks to the Chairman. With the young participants, and in co-operation with 'Ennis Information Town' teachers, I have been learning internet conferencing. Modern technology is still a little baffling.

Clare Young Environmentalists with President Hillery, Áras An Uachtarán, 1987

A happy event took place in 1991 when I was nominated for the Nation's primary environmental 'Oidhreacht' award, sponsored by Iarnród Éireann and Radio Telefís Éireann. At Birdhill, our nearest station, Grania, Tomás Porcell and I were greeted early in the morning by the national railway's area manager from Limerick.. Grania and I hadn't been on a train for years, and it was Tomás' first time. From our comfortable seats old landmarks and well-known features reminded me of my youth. As we joined the Cork to Dublin express at Ballybrophy we were appreciative of our red-carpet treatment, fellow passengers enviously eyeing us. At Heuston Station marketing officer Rita Butterly presented Grania with a bouquet of flowers and then guided us over the city. The Saint Stephen's Green shopping centre had just opened and she kindly extolled the virtues of a spree before conveying us to Westland Row to board a Dart metropolitan train for Dun Laoghaire. As we passed Blackrock and Monkstown, she described in detail the recently commissioned train. I again recalled my young days on this line when we would be locked into our small compartments. The scenery had changed little.

Above the fine grey cut-stone station at Dun Laoghaire, the high
class 'Restaurant na Mara' was to be the presentation venue. We were
greeted by Iarnród Éireann's Gerry Mooney, whose family hailed
from Thurles near my childhood home and John P. Kelly, of Radio
Telefís Éireann. Media figureheads, such as Dick Warner whose boat
journeys are viewed by millions, and representatives of sponsoring
organisations were present together with photographers and
journalists. Our own guests were David and Veronica Rowe and, of
course Tomás who had become 'family'. David, who I am sure had
a hand in the proceedings, was later to become head of An Taisce.

Following a delicious five course meal with the best of wines, I
received a framed record of the award and was offered a substantial
contribution towards my environmental aspirations. It was an honour
to have been chosen for such prestigious recognition and a delight
to have shared the day with those dear to me. Newspapers carried
reports of the event, some publishing photographs.

*   *   *   *   *   *   *   *   *   *   *

Having undertaken a vast number of activities, the Clare Young
Environmentalist membership began to wane. We had shown how the
future citizens of Ireland could and should be directly involved in their
environment. The Department of Education, other government
departments, a motor distribution company and corporate bodies now
undertook joint promotions through schools. This excellent campaign
meant that youngsters felt less inclined to participate in voluntary
effort. The organisation is at present dormant, although one-time
members have expressed an interest in promoting its revival.

Founding, stimulating and guiding the Young Environmentalists
was a wonderful and worthwhile experience. Members were a
delightful, dedicated and zealous lot led by their own enthusiastic
committees. Being with them filled an emptiness in life which came
about when I ended full-time teaching. Over ten years we were able
to share experiences, to laugh and occasionally cry, and to feel that
we were all doing something for our environment in a lively and
participatory way.

At Christmas 1997, Brendan Ringrose called a re-union in the Old Ground Hotel in Ennis at which Grania and I were thanked. As we departed, two parents and a number of members and friends bemoaned the fact that there was no record of our activities. Material from newspaper reports, photographs and other sources to write this chapter ran to several times the estimated size, so I was encouraged to publish a small paperback. *The Clare Young Environmentalists – an Educational and Environmental Exercise* was launched by Minister Síle de Valera in 1999 and contains a more comprehensive and illustrated record of C.Y.E. activities. It has evoked happy memories for readers who had been involved. That, to me, was reward enough.

Clare Young Environmentalists' mallorca visit, 1985, with
Dragonera Island in background

CHAPTER FIFTEEN

An early start – my first book. Poems and periodicals, postcards and Christmas cards. Printing and publishing, Houses and harrassment. How we started, recording people, places and homes. Each of our books. Ballinakella Press and Bell'acards in the third millennium.

Most of us have a book in us, and a desire to see it in print. My preliminary attempt at writing and publishing was when I produced the *Haunted House of Haunton* at Glebe House, my first boarding school. It was some time before further efforts. In the Far East, I compiled extensive reports; these were factual accounts of population movements rather than exciting stories of local lore. I first began to write creatively in London. I hadn't the capacity to accomplish more than a few pages on any one subject, so my efforts were limited to short stories and articles. I wrote poems, too, published in digests and London's small circulation periodicals, which did quite well and were also accepted for a number of anthologies. When working for the Harmsworth Press, mainly concerned with advertising, I did quite a lot of editing and writing.

By the nineteen-fifties I found myself chairing school editorial committees and helping to produce their magazines. Some of these were excellent and the standard of contributions outstanding. Looking through them I read significant names, including Patrick Cockburn who is now a 'Financial Times' editor, Irish Senator Shane Ross, an international author, two or three barristers, a public relations expert and several doctors. It was only when I married and wished to spend more time at home that writing became an important part of my life. This led to the professional production of books.

My publishing has also embraced postcards, an interest since childhood. In my teens I created the handcrafted Christmas cards I sold to shops in the Cashel area. I printed them myself when I purchased an Adana letterpress printer and in Cork, shared the production of postcards made from my pen and ink drawings. I also did scraperboard templates sold to customers wishing for personalised cards and calendars. These elements of my life were to be revived in the 'eighties.

* * * * * * * * * * *

In 1979 Grania and I purchased a 'golf ball' typewriter with interchangeable type-styles. Our A.B. Dick offset lithographic press, enabled the production of reasonably good monochrome printed work. Although we facsimiled small books, the machine was mainly for company publicity and for producing letter and billheads, tickets and other lucrative local orders.

The new typewriter encouraged me to write a small book about Hall Craig, the Weir family's Co. Fermanagh home. This twenty-two page account, illustrated with my line drawings, was distributed to family members and sold in a few Dublin and Belfast bookshops. Its production enabled me to understand some of the problems involved in publishing. It was the first of many and, in spite of its amateurish looks, sold quite well. It was also the first book with the Ballinakella Press imprint.

I had often driven down bohereens and along country roads when selling or servicing agricultural machines. Sometimes these routes led to the most delightful, but often dilapidated houses. Many were remnants of ascendancy, uninhabited since their owners, often in a hurry, departed for safer climes during the 1916 Troubles or the Civil War of the nineteen twenties. Others of these usually Georgian-style buildings were still standing and occupied. New owners were living in many but occasionally an elderly descendant of the primary occupants would appear at the door. More were in ruins or had ugly histories. All of them, however, had fascinating backgrounds and I began taking notes on them and their occupant families. Because there existed no comprehensive record, it was felt that the information I was gleaning should be published as a book. This would cover County Clare. I had great fun visiting the seven hundred selected. Some were small characterful cottages, most were medium-sized gentlemen's residences, while a few were exceptionally grand. There were stories of ghosts and murders, subversive activities and threats, many of which I could never pen. Occasionally I experienced hostility but I was usually invited in and offered refreshments and information. Clare people are hospitable.

I seldom wrote up house interiors except with the owner's consent. Near Limerick I was confronted with a shotgun by two elderly bachelors - locals had warned me that they were eccentric and that the legality of their occupation was questionable. Following the Troubles, many properties changed hands for a pittance and a few were reputedly commandeered. Terrible mistakes had happened, but the new Ireland of the seventies was encouraging everyone to overcome differences and look to the future.

Each day selected was spent looking up reference books and noting information on families and their estates, or undertaking field work. On average, I could cover between six and ten properties, depending on the distance. I tried to interview the occupants and neighbouring families and would, when permitted, take photographs. Once or twice I met the proverbial bull. Chased by an irate elderly farmer who didn't like my questions, I also got entangled in barbed wire; fortunately, he became exhausted before he caught up with me. In one ruined house, the opening of a rotten door revealed a stupefied occupant, probably the impoverished owner, surrounded by Guinness bottles, the rain dripping from the open ceiling. I crept away before he awoke.

Whilst compiling *Houses of Clare*, I had to earn our 'bread and butter'. I continued to sell lawnmowers and machinery, write my weekly environmental column in the *Clare Champion* and collect their local "Whitegate notes".

Many of the houses I recorded were O'Brien properties and having married into the family, I felt that a moderately comprehensive book on the O'Briens would give us a little extra finance while still researching *Houses of Clare*. The eighty page *O'Brien - People and Places* is about the whole clan, their arms and titles, castles and churches. It has a useful biography and illustrated one-page chapters devoted to significant individuals such as Brian

Boru and William Smith O'Brien, or places such as the Rock of Cashel and Dromoland. My experience as Heritage Historian for government agencies also helped. When this little book was launched at Bunratty Castle in 1983, Tom Haughey and Padraig Cleary of the Heritage Programme were present as well as Tom Kenny of Kenny's Bookshop in Galway whose family has always been supportive and helpful, and Folk Park Director Christopher Lynch. Iseult Murphy, the tourism-involved daughter of Murrogh and Suzanne O Brien of Foynes Island, whose husband Bryan runs the Dunraven Arms Hotel in Adare, officiated. Several thousand copies have already been sold.

Our friend Eamonn de Burca agreed to do a co-publication on the Burkes using the same *People and Places* format. More substantial than the O'Brien compilation, this was launched by Minister for Education Richard Burke in Kenny's Bookshop. I first met Eamonn at his Castlebar home following his return from England - today he is one of the most successful bookdealers and publishers.

After the publication of *O'Brien - People and Places,* research on the *Houses of Clare* was completed and basically corrected. Most of my pen and ink illustrations were drawn. 'Work experience' assistance from Patricia Roughan whose brother Kieran had been a Young Environmentalist helped, but the major burden of typing up the information fell to Grania. I approached a number of publishers but as the market was limited, none expressed interest.

Our financial resources were stretched. Perhaps my efforts had been in vain and nobody would want the result of many years of research? Grania, however, encouraged me out of my despondency. Eventually we were guaranteed about half the cost of production, the remainder we gambled on. Hopefully, if we had a grand enough launch, initial sales would bridge the gap. The printers might give us extra time.

Botanist and author Charles Nelson and others in the book trade recommended the recently established Boethius Press near Kilkenny. The Hewitt family from England had settled into a small house in a rural field, beside which was their large printhouse. When I introduced myself, they showed me work they had undertaken, much of it books on London and facsimile reprints of previously published works. They agreed to design and print *Historical, Genealogical and Architectural Notes on Some Houses of Clare*, our hefty hardback of over three hundred pages. Desmond Fitzgerald, the Knight of Glin, wrote a helpful and scholarly foreword. Museum Bookbindings in Dublin's Leeson Street added a magnificent cover, cloth bound in green with our arms embossed on the front, and gilt lettering. Dromoland Castle, from one of Grania's old prints, featured on the yellow dust jacket.

We made three journeys to Dublin for the sixteen hundred copies, two in one day. The books were stacked in our drawingroom where they left a long-lasting impression on our newly laid carpet. One day the lot nearly went up in smoke as Grania spilled some hot ashes from our solid fuel fire. Luckily, only the plastic-fibre carpet suffered and had to be covered with mats to hide the large burn marks. Gradually the stock diminished until space was available in one of our outbuildings.

Houses of Clare sold well at its launch by Clare-born diplomat Con Howard of the Department of External Affairs. Colaiste Muire, the large convent girls secondary school in the County Clare capital, allowed us host the 1986 event in their spacious hall. Our friend Sister Francis O'Dwyer who was involved in the Ennis historical scene, and other nuns and staff, helped. The owners of properties in the book, local dignitaries, politicians, clergy, relations and friends ensured the narrowing of the financial gap and we soon felt we would be able to pay off our immediate debts. The gamble succeeded. The Ennis Bookshop, John O'Brien and O'Mahonys of Limerick were then our best customers, but the Mercier Press's retail outlet and other Cork establishments, Kennys of Galway, Fred Hanna's of Dublin and Hodges Figgis also sold considerable quantities. Travelling the country on sales missions, I found that most bookshops took at least one copy. Others were sent to England, Germany, the United States and even Japan.

A great compliment was told me by a lady in mourning. She said that for the months before his death, her father got consolation by reading extracts from *Houses of Clare*, 'it was the loveliest book he had ever read'. Indeed, for many people it revived happy memories. Most like the human element - so many such books concentrate on architecture alone. Naturally there were mistakes and omissions and I got one or two unpleasant communications from those whose houses or family names were accidently omitted. One was quite hurtful, although with some justification.

Ballinakella Press was now established and we felt that while I was calling on retailers with a mere two or three titles, we would be better with more. We decided to expand.

Lloyd's *Tour of Clare*, a small but fascinating description of the Banner County written by schoolmaster John Lloyd in 1780 had been edited and reprinted by Clareman Henry Henn of Paradise in 1893. It was fetching up to £120 on the secondhand bookmarket, so I felt a further reprint could be successful. The same year as the publication of my opus on Clare, we produced a limited and numbered facsimile edition of Lloyd's book to which I added a short introduction. It was also a work of love, welcomed amongst local historians.

Tom Henn, a descendant of Henry's, and an authority on W.B. Yeats at Cambridge University had, before his death, given us one of his favourite books. His nephew Frank Henn, felt that, following publication of the Lloyd's facsimile, he would like his copy of Henry's original edition to be in safe hands and in his family's beloved County Clare. "Would we like it?" Answering in the affirmative, I indicated that on our own deaths, we would hope to leave it to the Ennis Library. He carefully wrapped it and sent it by registered post. After some time he telephoned. We were horrified that we had neither received it nor, naturally, written an acknowledgment. He was likewise bewildered. After much communication with the British and Irish Post-offices, the book was never located. This unique piece of Ireland's history may well be in some thief's book cabinet or worse. There is a remote possibility that it is sitting in some sorting office nook and will eventually be found. Whatever the case, the circumstances have deeply saddened Frank, Grania and myself.

Following the success of Lloyd, we decided to publish two more facsimile reprints in 1987. My mother had sent me *Sketches on some of the Southern Counties of Ireland - collected during a tour in the autumn of 1797 in a series of letters by G. Holmes*. Dealing with an

area of Munster, together with Kilkenny and Wexford, it had been
illustrated with attractive sepia engravings and dedicated to the
Duchess of Devonshire, daughter of the first Earl Spencer. I added
an introduction before sending it, with another book, The Reverend
William Henry's *Upper Lough Erne*, to the printers. We ordered six
hundred and sixty copies, each encased by hardcovers designed by
myself. Henry's fascinating description of the Fermanagh lakelands
had, like Lloyd, been edited before - Sir Charles Simeon King had
written a preface in 1892, and had added extensive genealogical and
historical notes. Our production was to have been launched by Viola,
Duchess of Westminster. Sadly, she was killed in a car accident half
way to Belfast before she could carry out the task she had so
enthusiastically accepted. Instead, at a later ceremony in Enniskillen
Castle, our friend Fermanagh County Librarian Jim Nawn did the
honours.

The next year we published one and a half books. The half was
a co-publication with Sheila Mulloy of her record of the O'Malley
family in what was now to become our *People and Places* 'series'.
Printed in Westport, it was launched by politician Desmond O'Malley
whose Sept had been in the Limerick area for generations; his uncle
had been our family dentist. Co-publishing meant that the author
could share our expertise and link into our series but that we were
exonerated from raising the necessary cash.

Ireland - A Thousand Kings proved to be almost harder to edit
than if I had written it myself. Beautifully and amusingly illustrated
by "Dane", it is a collection of chapters on Irish monarchs.
Contributors include John de Courcy Ireland, Anne Chambers,
Warren Loane, Katherine Simms and Morgan Llywelyn, experts in
their fields. Most facets are covered including the King of the
Claddagh on whom Tom Kenny wrote, Christopher Moriarty's *King
of All Birds* and Grania's piece on the Irish Crown Jewels. Grania's
cousin by marriage, Louis McRedmond also supplied interesting
material and the then youthful Martin Browne wrote an excellent
piece on Daniel O'Connell, *The King of the Beggars*. I contributed the
remaining twenty-five per cent. It was appropriate that our friend
and Clareman, President Patrick Hillery, successor to Irish Kings as
Head of State, should consent not only to write the foreword to

Ireland - A Thousand Kings, but also to launch it. The spectacular event in the Chapter Room at Dublin's Christchurch Cathedral was attended by many heirs to Royal Dynasties such as The O'Conor Don and his cousin Piers O'Conor Nash who lives in the O'Conor family residence, Clonalis, and Grania's cousin Conor. Many friends and academics joined the celebrations as fifteen year old Tomás Porcell pulled a large ribbon at the President's request; a pile of the books was revealed as the parcel opened.

1990 saw four publications. Tomás had now been with us for two years and was showing his talent as an artist. He had gained a knack of simplistic drawing which I felt should be put to use. He accepted that we produce a children's story in Castilian and English and that he would do the illustrations. *Trapa* was a children's adventure taking place on islands off Kerry and Mallorca, based on historical and topographical fact. Tomás's first language is Catalan, however, and although our friend Anne Vera did a great job in arranging the translation of the text, there were linguistic inaccuracies in our own added preliminaries. Although the story is good and we had hoped that the parallel translation would be popular with students, the cover was dull. It did, however, win the prestigious Spanish "Jaime Roca" award. It is a good little book and at the right price.

As well as *Trapa*, we felt that we should contribute to the celebrations of Ennis's seven hundred and fiftieth anniversary. *Ennis 750 Facts* is a thirty-six page booklet with seven hundred and fifty mainly humourous anecdotes I compiled and is illustrated with my drawings. Tomás designed the cover. It sold in local shops.

The real book of the year 1990, however, was Máire Mac Neill's *Máire Rua - Lady of Leamaneh*, about Grania's characterful forebear. Folklorist, author of *The Festival of Lughnasa* and daughter of Gaelic League founder and onetime Minister for Education Eoin Mac Neill, Máire was married to poet John (Jack) L. Sweeney. They lived at Corofin and were good friends. When dining with them, we would admire their paintings many of which they left, including a Picasso, to the National Gallery of Ireland. Indeed, their house at Poulivaun, built on a high bluff overlooking Lough Inchiquin, was quite the loveliest modern residence in the area. Jack predeceased Máire who herself died in 1987. It had been her wish to involve us in the publication of her book. She admired Máire Rua's determination in troubled seventeenth century Clare. Her literary agent, Maureen Murphy, ensured the fulfilment of her aspirations by asking us to accomplish the task. A beautifully produced work with colour photographs, and line drawings by Michael Lenehan, brother of folklorist Eddie, was launched at a ceremony at Dysert O'Dea Castle where 'red-haired Mary' once resided. Another mutual friend, and also a Clareman, Doctor Peter Harbison of Bord Failte, the Irish tourist Board, undertook the launch which was attended by Máire's sister Eilis Mac Dubhghall and other Mac Neill family members, friends and well-wishers. Afterwards we joined many of them at Poulivaun. There was an air of sadness that the author was not amongst us. *Máire Rua - Lady of Leamaneh* has proved its popularity especially amongst visitors to West Clare.

The other publication we produced in 1990 was Dr. Alicia St. Leger's contribution to our *People and Places* series. Out of the blue, I had received a telephone call: "The Bishop of Cork, Roy Warke, has recommended that I contact you." A qualified historian, Alicia had returned to Cork from Canada and needed work. Soon she came to visit us and at my suggestion, undertook to research the MacCarthy Clan. Hopefully the task acted as a stepping stone for she was shortly organising a heritage project at Cobh and later worked on the Middleton Distillery. Her book, *MacCarthy - People and Places*, was launched by Lord Mayor Frank Nash in Cork's delightful Civic Trust headquarters on Pope's Quay. Amongst those present were Alicia's journalist-photographer brother and the Bishop. Most of the illustrations indicate the use of my name in Irish, Aodh de Mheir; this I did in quite a lot of our books, perhaps to incur variety.

The next year, Grania's *These My Friends and Forebears - the O'Briens of Dromoland* was the 'piece de resistance!' She had spent several years researching this work, dedicated to her sister Deirdre and to me. She ensured that, along with a photograph of herself, her beloved pug Sophia should be similarly depicted on the back cover. During the previous years, there had been jaunts to Dublin where she had spent hours in the National Library. There she searched the Inchiquin Manuscripts which her father had left on permanent loan to the State, following the sale of Dromoland. She received valuable help from Assistant Keeper Catherine Fahy and from National Library Directors, Doctors Michael Hewson and Pat Donlon. It is a fascinating well-illustrated and comprehensive account. The printers of most of our previous books, Boethius Press, had now moved to Wales. Although the printing of *Mac Carthy - People and Places* was printed by Colour Books Ltd., an Irish Company at Baldoyle, who did an excellent job, I had agreed with the Hewitts before their departure that we would ask them to print *Forebears*. It was not easy to work with printers that one couldn't visit at the 'drop of a hat'; Kilkenny was only a couple of hours away. The Hewitts did a fair job, though, and employed Belfast binders Robinson and Mornin.

The launch of *These My Friends and Forebears* was held in the National Library, at the invitation of Dr. Donlon. Grania, Tomás and I were to drive up to Dublin in the morning with the books which were to have been delivered to Whitegate beforehand. Consternation reigned when there was no sign of them the day before the event. Phones rang and words stung as we communicated with Aberwystwith and Belfast. At six in the morning, the delivery van arrived at Ballinakella Lodge. This meant all hands unloading, and the re-loading of some, into our own vehicles together with price lists, invoices, food and drink and a range of other books for display. Both of us like to be calm before we speak and Grania as author, and I as publisher, were very much on edge. However, the event proved successful and few detected the crisis. At a second launch at Dromoland, by Grania's special request, I did the honours - a perhaps unique situation where the author's husband, editor and publisher undertook the one task. From O'Briens world wide, Grania has received great commendation.

A friend , Hungarian Raphy Rupert, had lived for some years in Clare before settling in suburban Limerick. A lawyer, sportsman and onetime cavalry officer, he was the son of anti-Nazi Kossuth party chairman Dr. Rudolph Rupert. Collins had previously produced his underground and Soviet experiences as *A Hidden World*. Now the author had lost both legs and was confined to a wheel chair. He and his wife Anne agreed that we should re-publish this valuable work. I took on the task of re-writing the original translation. Our friend Helen Cronin, wife of author to be Risteárd Ua Cróinín, assisted at the computer, as Grania was in Bermuda looking after her ill sister. I designed an evocative cover while Tomás undertook the layout of the text. Colour books did an excellent printing job.

Due to the raising of the Iron Curtain though, few people wanted to read about the unpleasantries of Communist regimes. *Red Wire and the Lubianka* is still available from the pile of over a thousand in our store. It is an excellent story as was confirmed by a young man to whom I gave a lift. "You must be the Hugh Weir who has published those lovely books. I've just been reading the fascinating experiences of Raphael Rupert. . . .". If only retailers and their customers could have overheard the conversation. Raphy died a few years later. He was a delightful character but it was difficult to interpret his rich Hungarian accent.

Ivar O'Brien lives near Grasse in the South of France with his artist wife Patricia. Years ago, when he visited us for the first time, he asked whether there were still O'Brien Castles. He has since written *O'Brien of Thomond,* a major work of which, published by Philimore, we hold most of the remainders. In a similar format to *Máire Rua,* as the second 'in series', *Murrough The Burner - Murchadh na dTóiteán* was his second. It is a life of the provocative seventeenth century Earl of Inchiquin whose line became extinct. I have often visited Ivar and Patricia on my travels to Italy and beyond; they have always been welcoming at their delightful garden-surrounded house.

Sean O'Neill, a noted musician in Dublin, became interested in his family and contacted me with a view to publishing his findings. *O'Neill - People and Places* was launched by a lady politician of the name in the Genealogical Office in Dublin's Kildare Street. A number of prominent Clansmen were present. As with many of the books in the series, I undertook the line illustrations.

We only produced two books in 1992, though we did reprint a small poetic work by Grania's great great grandfather, Sir Lucius O'Brien, *Shooting at Dromoland. Ships in Early Irish History* is a useful hardcover book compiled by Mayo-based Meike Blackwell. Meike, married to O'Malley chieftain Joe Blackwell, was born at Wilhelmshaven in Germany. In Chicago she had got involved in archaeological work and had continued her interests in the history of ships from her Clew Bay home at Ross. She asked if we would publish a number of manuscripts, mainly on Mayo, which we felt too local. We accepted her work on ships, however. This sixty-five page well illustrated account is pleasingly produced. I had been promised a favour by Iarnród Eireann, the State railway company, so it was agreed that they would sponsor the launch in their evocative up-market restaurant at Heuston Station, Dublin. Amongst the publications which wrote reviews was the prestigious *Lloyd's List* of London.

The O'Deas are an ancient Clare family but a Cronin wrote our definitive history of the Clan. *O'Dea - Ua Déaghaidh - The Story of a Rebel Clan* was compiled by Dysert O'Dea Castle custodian and teacher Risteárd Ua Cróinín. Dick approached me on behalf of the O'Dea Clan and asked would we publish this book as a special hard-cover edition, out of the *People and Places* series. *The Clare Champion*, whom we asked to do the printing, did a magnificent job on this little production with its outstanding maps and illustrations. It too, like *Máire Rua* was launched from the steps of Dysert Castle. The task was dutifully undertaken by friend and colleague Frank O'Dea, Editor of *The Clare Champion*. The Clan's Tanaiste Michael O'Dea, Dom. Bernard O'Dea of Glenstall and other bearers of the name witnessed the celebration.

In 1992, we were approached by an academic - Dr. Mary Lyons, was recommended to us by Desmond Guinness. She had made a study of the encumbered estates of which drawings had been undertaken before they had been advertised for sale in the nineteenth century. When we met at a café in the St. Stephen's Green Centre, she indicated that the National Library of Ireland would permit us use their copies of the original engravings provided that we employed their chosen photographer. The result, produced in 1993, is the beautifully printed clothbound book designed mainly by Tomás Porcell and printed by Colour Books. The eight colour lithos are almost perfect reproductions. This book, like Grania's, was launched in the National Library.

Another impressive launch was held at the 'Alliance Française', on the corner of Nassau and Kildare Streets, towards the end of 1993. Stormy October weather failed to prevent a large gathering of French well-wishers, military attachés, and friends of both the publishers and of author Noel MacMahon. Michael MacMahon, with whom I share the Vice-Presidency of the Clare Archeological and Historical Society, outlined the background of the MacMahons and Monsieur Defay, Cultural Counsellor of the French Embassy declared the book available to the public. The event, arranged by Alliance director Monsieur Carrière, was warm, friendly and welcoming for the launch of what many accept as the definitive work on President of France, Marshal Mac Mahon, *Here I am, Here I Stay - Marshal MacMahon 1808 - 1893.* I drew many of the illustrations and most of the maps, ably assisted by Tomás who designed the layout and cover. In 1997, Grania visited the Marshal's descendant, the present Duke of Magenta, at his chateau at Sully as she toured France with the Irish Georgian Society. A lot of interest was shown in the book. Sadly, later that year, Noel MacMahon died.

A book which involved us in a lot of work was historian and friend Tom Coffey's history of his parish. For years Tom had been collecting folklore and history about Crusheen, just north of Ennis. When Ballinakella Press was young I expressed an interest in publishing his findings. I couldn't therefore refuse him when, early in 1993, he presented me with a vast folder of unedited handwritten manuscripts, bits of paper and photographs. His years of research and our compilation of it, culminated in the *Parish of Inchicronan (Crusheen),* launched that July. This event was so different to most

Chateau de Sully

of the previous ones. Parishioners laid on a reception and those present were delightfully unsophisticated. Afterwards we joined David and Veronica Rowe at their nearby house. Tom seemed delighted with the work which, of course, had a limited market; we had undertaken the time-consuming task as a work of love. Too many local histories have been lost or destroyed, especially those by amateurs who continued stockpiling information until they've died. Tom Coffey passed to his reward a few years after publication but his efforts can now easily be resourced. The editing, design and printing by the *Clare Champion* were all undertaken in his own county, an added bonus for one who loved his native Clare.

In 1994, only one title came from our little Press. More money was needed to keep bread and butter on the table than our publishing was producing. I was beginning to concentrate on postcards, the sales of which were increasing This also meant less time for writing. I felt, however, that if possible we should at least publish one book.

Having been Project Historian for the Irish Heritage Programme, my knowledge of the history and genealogy of at least twelve Irish Clans was as comprehensive as any. Due to family connections with the O'Connors of Offaly, I compiled a book on the several different O'Connor Clans. This was stimulating and I recalled my efforts with my O'Brien book. *O'Connor - People and Places* got a low key send-off ; to chose any one of the Clan leaders to launch it at the expense of the others could have been disastrous. It got good reviews, however, and has been one of the most successful publications in the *People and Places* series.

During the following year, we again produced one new book. Valerie Bary, whom we had known for some time, had returned to the area of her roots and had inherited one of the diminishing number of larger properties in Kerry, Calinafercy, near Miltown. While her New Zealander husband Brian was busy on their estate Valerie, who had already contributed work to the prestigious *Irish Ancestor* and other journals, would like to attempt *Houses of Kerry*. The second book in our *County Houses* series proved her capabilities and those of her daughter Stephanie Walshe who undertook the illustrations. Brian compiled an excellent map indicating the locations of each house. It took her two or three years to cover 'The

Kingdom' as Kerry is known, an immense task at any time. Tomás did a wonderful job using the same layout as *Houses of Clare*; most difficult, especially when English isn't his first language. Kevin Myers, who devoted his 'Irishman's Diary' to it in the *Irish Times*, ended his words "It is the purest of pleasures". Much publicity was due to the efforts of Daniel's descendant, Maurice O'Connell who launched the book during 'Writers' Week' at Listowel; it was an appropriate send-off. Another party was held when then Bishop of Kerry, Diarmaid Ó Súilleabháin did a local launch in Killarney's branch Library, attended by many who couldn't make Listowel. Over the years, we have gained a reputation for our generous launches.

By 1996 Tomás had returned to Spain to fulfil his military service obligations and it was unlikely that we could find anybody suitable to fill his place. Grania was spending a lot of time at her computer while mine, due to my lack of expertise and practice, remained dormant. One-time Young Environmentalist P.J. Kenny of Ennis is a computer buff who had been helping us technically. He agreed that he would work on the typesetting and general layout of Joe Dunne's work on his midland-based clan. *Dunne - People and Places* proved his ability. The County Hall at Portlaoise, by kind permission, was chosen for a delightful launch executed by media sports commentator Mick Dunne. Close to clan territory north of the Slieve Bloom mountains, there was an encouraging gathering of Dunnes and a lot of copies were sold. The modern reception area was ideal for the event and those responsible for letting us use it were profusely thanked. Author Joe was co-operative and helpful throughout the production period as indeed have been most of our authors.

About the same time as Joe's book was published, two manuscripts were submitted from Derry. Due to pressure of work, we had decided that in future we would stick to the two or three series' we had established; *County Houses, People and Places* and perhaps that which included *Máire Rua*; *Here I am, Here I Stay; Murrough the Burner* and Grania's book. In refusing these submissions I suggested that as the author had significant journalistic credentials, perhaps he would care to submit a history of his own clan for the *People and Places* series. *O'Doherty - People and Places* by Fionnbarra O Dochartaigh, of eighty-two pages of text and forty-four of genealogical trees, was published in 1998 and launched at a special ceremony in Derry. Clan Herald, Professor Pat Dougherty designed the charts while, as usual, I drew some of the pictures and designed the book. Our friend Anna Maria Hajba did much of the editing.

One of the best researched books in our *People and Places* series is that on the O'Donoghues by Rod O'Donoghue. Rod was an economist and financial director of Inchcape until his retirement. We first met at the Killarney launch of *Houses of Kerry* where I suggested that he might be interested in writing a history of his clan; we have co-operated closely since. Grania and I have become good friends with this delightful resident of London and his family. No stone was left unturned as Rod, often with his sons of whom Richard did the delightful pen and ink drawings, travelled from site to site throughout the country. The result of our combined labours was launched by Chief Herald and National Library Director Brendan O'Donoghue in the Killarney Library in early 1999. Amongst those present was the Clan Chieftain, Geoffrey O'Donoghue of the Glens, and the Barys. A few weeks later I delivered two thousand copies to Rod at his Islington home where he has based the O'Donoghue Clan Society he has established.

Not a few potential authors have looked into the possibility of producing further editions in our *Houses* series. Two are now fully committed and are well into their research. Anna-Maria Hajba is a native of Finland with a Hungarian father, who came to Cork to help in the restoration of Doneraile Court, then in Irish Georgian Society hands. Together with her fiancé Arthur Montgomery, whose family lived nearby, she shared his caretaking and interest in the large St. Leger house. She became interested in its history and that of other houses in this area such as Clonmeen House several miles to the west, where Arthur and she now live. Anna Maria was recommended by Leslie Roberts of Mount Rivers at Carrigaline whom I had asked if he would undertake *Houses of Cork*; he had been on a Church of Ireland committee which I had convened. Now all three, in their own ways, are contributing to her four volume work on some four thousand residences, the first covering north Cork. David Rowe and Eithne Scallon, both natives of the county, are at present hard at work researching Wexford. Eithne has, I understand, done most of the houses in her territory, the southern half; David's many other responsibilities deny him the time he would like to spend undertaking the task he also enjoys. Several others find that shortage of time precludes them from completing their task. Bryn Byrne, a Church of Ireland clergyman who served in Killaloe diocese, is now in Cyprus, so Wicklow is on hold. Across Lough Derg, Hardress Waller has found that maturing years prevent him from fulfilling what had been his ambition for North Tipperary, but competant local historian Nancy Murphy has agreed to see the work to completion. Hardress has done a lot already. Fellow-publisher Eamonn de Burca just hasn't a minute to spare to complete Mayo because, as we know so well, the profession is incredibly time-consuming. Eamonn still has high hopes of covering his home county. *Houses of Galway* may take many years, though I have made a cursory coverage of parts of Connemara and of the Glenamaddy region in the north east. However, Sheila Bagliani of Castle ffrench has agreed to attempt a major portion of the work. She took on the responsibility in eary summer 2001.

During 1999, however, we have been stimulated by the knowledge that two competant and knowledgeable authors have accepted the task of compiling two further southern counties. Melosina Lenox - Conyngham , whose wonderfully amusing stories on Radio Eireann's *Sunday Miscellany* programme captivate so many, is about to start on *Houses of Kilkenny* and Michael O'Sullivan, a professional environmentalist and talented amateur artist already undertaking the illustrations for Anna Maria's book, recently asked to undertake *South Tipperary*. This he hopes to be able to tie in with his assessments of future road-routes for which he and his company are responsible. As with all our publications, I look forward to encouraging them.

Grania and I have come a long way since the days when I would print small books on our A.B. Dick machine. Originally we correlated the pages by hand from up to thirty stacks placed strategically over tables and the floor, before stapling them together by hand. We have evolved a useful working knowledge of publishing and its pitfalls. Many mistakes were made but we now realise such expensive

factors as the legal right of various Irish and British educational and
bibliotechnical authorities to receive free copies. Book design is
more significant than one initially realises. I recall the advice of Miss
Parsons who had a bookshop at Dublin's Leeson Street Bridge:
"Remember, customers want to be able to see and read the title from
a distance. Stick it at the top of the cover." Such retailer customers
have been tremendously helpful from the outset and many have
become good and loyal friends.

*   *   *   *   *   *   *   *   *   *   *

Bell'acards, the postcard section of our business is younger than that
of the printed word. Tomás was able to save little from his meager
expenses or pocket money. Recalling my student days in Cork and
successful experience there, I suggested that we share a postcard
business. We named it partly after our little mascot, my second black
pug, Bella partly because 'Bella' means 'beautiful' in some European
languages and partly as it is not unlike the first five letters of
Ballinakella, the name of our Press and of our house. Initially we
produced cards of Whitegate and Mountshannon, followed by other
local map-based drawings. We also less successfully created A3 maps
of Ireland and of Clare, letter-cards and letter-folds. Today we
distribute my hand-drawn postcards of thirty-one counties, the four
provinces, various local areas such as Lough Derg and the Burren,
and well over twenty different artistic images of Ireland depicting
such subjects as *Irish wildflowers, Irish dogs* and *Irish sea vessels* –
even *leprechauns*. Due to requests from some customers, we also
create cards from my scenic photographs. Although I do the
drawings for the maps and other all-Ireland cards, Tomás - even in
Spain - has coloured some of them. When he left for his military
service, I purchased his fifty per cent interest. Sadly for me, however,
due to health problems and the pressures of a very full life, I may
have to sell off this successful and enjoyable undertaking. I shall miss
meeting my many friends and customers, but I would hope that I
would be able to continue my involvement in a less demanding way
Our type of publishing is not hugely lucrative but introducing
books and postcards is exciting and creative. From a product's

inception, the publisher has to see it through its various editorial stages. Books often have to be read eight times to cover content, historical accuracy, readability, chapter division, grammar, spelling mistakes, idiom and possible legal problems. The publisher has to design them, cost them with different printers and arrange for their printing and binding. Products have to be packaged to prevent damage due to uneven road journeys, or damp, and carefully stored. The least pleasant aspect for me is the selling. Although I love travelling throughout Ireland, waiting until all the retailers' customers are served before presenting one's wares can cause pain and rapid exhaustion if one has to stand for long. Many people make me feel welcome and my goods wanted, thereby making up for those who fail to comprehend my discomfort.

Potential customers, especially of postcards, occasionally make embarrassing comments about my work; they don't usually realise that I am the artist or photographer. "What a dreadful photograph. . . . I could do better myself. . . ." "Why put in that old bridge when you could have used our martyr's monument?" or, in many cases, "No way would I buy that awful looking card. It doesn't even have our parochial house" are some comments, only the language can be less polite. I often find them amusing, but they don't make selling easy. Another problem arises with collecting money. I mainly sell for cash, which is impossible with some of the bigger retailers who insist on credit. Often these, especially the larger multi-national companies, are the worst payers. A lot of time is wasted sending out statements and eventually having to pester their accounts departments by telephone. I prefer to deal with the small unsophisticated Irish retailers in rural towns and villages or such understanding and loyal customers as St. Patrick's cathedral in Dublin or Ailwee Caves - I know I am missing out on a vast urban market.

CHAPTER SIXTEEN

France, Nantuckat and Paul Revere's Massachusetts Inn. A World Trade Centre experience. Edging Eastward – Norway, Sweden, Denmark, Hungary and a marathon to Ankara via Yugoslavia and Greece.

I delight in travel, and seeing the changes in environment. Each area has its specific vegetation and cultivation, its indigenous people and the clothes they wear, their language and smells - even their road conditions. Some people enjoy travel programmes on television or radio, others watch videos, but little beats the experience of actually visiting places.

Air travel is necessary if time is limited or merely to enjoy a particular destination, but it can be boring, even with a window seat. Walking or cycling may be the best ways to enjoy travel, but my favoured mode is the car or, better still, my van. If I get tired and wish to stop I find a secluded site, park and fall asleep as I hit the mattress. In my earlier days I roughed it like most young people. There were few youth discounts, but rail or bus fares weren't expensive. For many trips to France and other European countries I slept under a tree, or in a deserted building. I carried a small one-man tent following the purchase of my first car. Occasionally I slept in the vehicle itself, but this was inevitably uncomfortable. Nowadays I accept accommodation from friends or stay in reasonably-priced hotels or guest houses. Rather than live on baguettes and croissants, pâtés, cheeses, and bottled water, I dine out at least once a day and chat with local patrons or, in the case of 'Les Routiers' restaurants, with drivers from throughout Europe.

During my army years, I travelled to the Far East and Mediterranean. By nineteen seventy-two, I had railed, bussed or driven through much of Europe and had experienced airports at Le

Bourget, Heathrow and Shannon, even Southend and Ipswich. Dover, Stranraer and Harwich harbours had become almost as familiar as Rosslare, Larne and Dun Laoghaire, as I varied my routes. I had camped at Amiens, Cologne, Argentât and throughout Northern Europe. There were, however, many more places to see.

After Grania and I were married, our friends Douglass and Lois Fonda who had stayed at Dromoland as paying guests, felt called to settle in Ireland. Having stayed with us until they had selected their 'dream home' near Mountshannon, they asked me to assist with its development. Just as they were to fly back to the United States before returning to live, Doug slid me an envelope. Enclosed were two return air tickets to Nantucket Island and an invitation to stay with them at their expense. This was totally unexpected. The previous time that Grania and I had been abroad was a visit to Scotland with the Hely-Hutchinsons on a marathon trip to my Aunt Bryda's widowed husband Fitzroy Fyers and to my mother and Bob.

In February 1978, armed with our visas, we boarded a New York-bound Boeing 707. We arrived at Idlewild (J.F. Kennedy) Airport during a crisis. America, especially New England, was getting snowed under. Our flight to Boston was delayed, so we were too late to make connection with the one daily Nantucket departure. Following our remonstrations, Aer Lingus arranged a room at the Hilton, overlooking the Christian Scientists' Mary Baker Eddy Headquarters. Never had Boston been hit by such storms and ours was the first cab to venture through the narrow snow-walled 'gorges'. The city was tense. The taxi-driver gabbled excitedly. He thought we were mad to be travelling as he described landmarks hidden by two metres of snow. President Carter had just declared Massachusetts a Federal disaster area but at our hotel we wallowed in warm luxurious comfort. In the morning a vast American breakfast was brought. Ham, eggs, crumpets and pineapple were accompanied by Danish pastries, fruit juice and jugs of hot coffee.

Our little Nantucket-bound aircraft roared down the snow-cleared runway and over Boston as we identified our hotel below in the brilliant sunshine of the following morning. To our left was Massachusetts Bay and the Atlantic, while to the right the suburbs of Weymouth and Rockland gave way to sparsely populated woodlands.

In the distance Cape Cod hooked to the
north, encompassing the bay. Now
visible was Hyannis of the Kennedys,
Woods Hole, and to the left, Martha's
Vineyard. The Island's dotey airport,
with its small four-storey New England-
style control tower, had several private
aircraft parked beside the runway. We
were met by Doug and Lois who
jeeped us to their home, an elegant
centre-town redbrick mansion erected
by the Starbuck family.

Each of the three five-bay 'Bricks',
in a row, was approached by a flight
of steps leading to a pillared porch. The Fonda's was tastefully
furnished with contemporary portraits and American colonial
antiques. On the roof above, as with most Nantucket houses, was a
cupola. In whaling days, ladies would watch for the return of their
seagoing husbands from these small but comfortable look-outs, their
windows facing all directions. The street below was cobbled and
traffic-free. The capital was friendly, really a small-time New England
town. We were to be wined and dined and shown every feature of
significance from Siasconset village to the rubbish tip where the
wealthy were generous to gulls and scavengers. The sun shone
dazzlingly over piles of rapidly melting snow.

On our first night, Grania and I were overwhelmed by the
tremendous heat generated by the house's central heating system. In
our bedroom we tried to open a window. Alas, each was
hermetically sealed and fronted with a gauze fly-stopper. Eventually
we located the tiniest hole in the frame through which we each took
turns to breathe cool fresh air.

As we were driven over the Island we noted the East-Anglian-style
clapboard houses of the early settlers. We could have been in Essex.
Excellent roads lead us through what had recently been rural
countryside. We visited the Fonda's friends and were shown the
houses of millionaires such as the Johnsons of cosmetics fame. There
had once been a railroad, one of the carriages being preserved in the

town. We shopped and saw how scrimshaw, traditional whalebone ivory etched by sailors on their lengthy excursions, was created. At the museum, Curator Stacpoole, told us his people came from Clare. Doug also showed us his whaling archives. On one walkabout, Grania and I found ourselves behind two ladies strolling on the pavement ahead. So large were their behinds that there wasn't room for both, the outer having to step on and off the road. In a small supermarket, someone seemed familiar - politician Teddy Kennedy was staying in the vicinity. A sign on a small downtown manufacturer's premises indicated that we were 3,746 miles from Paris, 11,124 from Calcutta and 2,740 from the Pole. There was no mileage for Dublin.

We were sad to leave the quaint colonial island, so lovingly preserved. It was bitterly cold as our ferry pulled out from the icy harbour for our journey past several well-known islands. Doug pointed to landmarks such as the homes of wealthy Vineyarders around Edgartown, Oak Bluffs and Vineyard Haven. Woods Hole was a noted marine station.

Back on mainland America, names such as Stoughton - my father's grandmother's surname - and Taunton reminded us of early settlers. Soon we arrived at Paul Revere's Wayside Inn at Sudbury, a colonial-style rural hostelry in tree-set surrounds on the old post road beyond Boston. A classical white church with a stepped steeple nearby was restored by Henry Ford. The place was full of mementos to Longfellow, America's great poet. Excursions to Boston saw us visiting bookstores, the aquarium and 'outlets' from which we bought quantities of discounted clothes and shoes, a new and exciting experience. We also drove to Plymouth and saw the stone onto which the first New Englanders reputedly stepped. There was a replica of the Mayflower, the early settlement and a garden growing samples of plants brought from the Old World. On the way back, we were horrified at the storm damage. Whole houses had been crushed or removed from their foundations and cars buried. It was snowing again and Lois, who was driving, keyed into other drivers as they exchanged weather-language on their radios. In Ireland, we still had to turn a handle to telecommunicate.

Our next destination was New York. Doug drove us in their Jeep stationwagon through Hartford in Connecticut and New Haven. En route we stopped at a 'Friendly' ice cream parlour where Grania and I indulged in delicious ice cream. Unusual for me, I was so stuffed that I suggested that we had just a snack for lunch. For the first time I realised how rural New England is.

At Manhattan, we stayed with Grania's sister Deirdre and her husband Beecher Chapin in their apartment beside eminent allergist Beecher's surgery. They invited us to dinner at the top of the World Trade Centre, then the world's tallest building. In the restaurant, approached through a lobby with an enormous amethyst on show, we sat on the uppermost mezzanine from which we had a magnificent view of Manhattan over the heads of a Jewish wedding party. The post matrimonial celebrations were as fascinating as the view, and reminded us of the Marx brothers - very American, very New York. When we were seated, a waiter appeared: "Would you like to serve yourselves, Ladies and Gentlemen?" Grania and I were hungry

Deirdre Chapin

so, as Deirdre and Beecher ushered us towards an enormous circular table, we felt we should do justice to their generosity. There were platefuls of enticing eats. I had to sample them all and could hardly keep the total amount on my over full plate. Deirdre and Beecher were not great eaters I recalled, as I observed their small helpings. When we had devoured our 'meal', the same waiter appeared: "Now ladies and gentlemen, I presume you enjoyed the hors d'oeuvre; would you like to help yourselves to the main course?"

Following our vast repast we went on to the roof where Beecher indicated the landmarks. I searched for each through the public telescope. Grania and I also commissioned computer portraits of ourselves made of alphabetical letters. It was sunny as we returned to the apartment, but the remaining piles of snow were now a dirty grey. Another day we went to the Harvard Club. At the Metropolitan Club, we joined friends for dinner around a large circular table. I chose clams, having feasted on these small and deliciously delicate shellfish during our time in Nantucket. Imagine my embarrassment when a plate of huge raw shellfish was placed in front of me. I was reminded that in America 'big' is often considered better as I chewed my way through each, continuing well after the others had devoured their chosen morsels. I was careful thereafter in my choice of food.

* * * * * * * * * *

My cousins William and Amanda Tailyour lived in Connecticut. As we were to stay with them, we joined William, who had an office in the Rockefeller Centre, at Grand Central Station. Here we caught a commuter train to Westport. From their local station, William drove us to their delightful four storey wooden home set amongst trees. It was the first time we had met Amanda. Ian and Lillian were small and Alexander had yet to be born.

Our holiday had been wonderful and memorable and we were overawed by the generosity of our hosts and hostesses. My first visit to the United States was an eye opener. It also gave me a basis for my working visits.

That October my mother and Bob were in the north of France; would I join them? I was to take a short Irish Ferries excursion to Le Havre where they would meet me, and I would accompany them to Cherbourg and from whence return.

They were on the quayside when the boat docked. My mother drove their Combi van with Bob beside her, so I sat in the back. After touring the attractive little port of Honfleur we spent the first night in a hotel on the outskirts. The following day we visited La Falaise, the castle from which William the Conqueror had set out before crossing to the battle at Hastings. There were lists of the many families who accompanied him, some well known in Ireland. The journey up the Cotentin peninsula to my port of departure was uneventful apart from my mother's enthusiastic comments about the horses we passed or the areas similar to East Anglia.

* * * * * * * * * *

While still able, I felt I should attempt to see as much of eastern Europe as possible. In June 1989, armed with the excuse that I would write a book about it, I undertook the longest and most exciting of my many journeys. This was to be a fun trip for which I gave myself three weeks. I would sleep in my van which I had equipped with lockers with food, maps, wash-up facilities and miscellanea - a veritable hotel on wheels. I had no mobile but communicated with Grania as often as possible using local phones. The fifteenth was election day, so I cast my vote before driving to Dun Laoghaire to board the Holyhead ferry. The sea was a calm. On arrival in Wales I spent the night in my van; there was a lot of traffic on the minor road beside the Anglesea airforce base, so I arose before daybreak. After a greasy breakfast at Milton Keynes, I drove to Coggeshall where my Uncle Mick and Pam were now living. It was difficult to locate their new home in a quiet backwater but they were delighted to see me. Mama and Bob at Brockdish welcomed me that evening. Following a good nights sleep, a bath and breakfast I bade adieu. There was a seven kilometre queue at the Dartford tunnel and the Sealink ferry from Dover was almost full. On arrival at Calais, I took the road north as the motorway from Dunkirk to Lille is untolled. Near Rheims I located a hideaway surrounded by vegetable plots and small groves a kilometre off the main road to rest my tired body.

I continued my journey over the thickly wooded Vosges mountains, its chalets influenced by their proximity to Germany. Strasbourg was larger than I expected with fine streets and efficient public transport. As I crossed into West Germany, no-man's-land between customs posts was an untidy mess and there were unconventional and unhealthy looking hitchhikers. The traffic was bumper to bumper on the motorway for Stuttgart as its three lanes bore returning week-enders from Switzerland and Southern France. It was intimidating to see several accidents and vehicles stuck in the middle lane while traffic passed them on both sides. I was told later that the drivers and passengers wouldn't dare to move, only to wait patiently for official break-down authorities.

There were signs to Auschwitz, but Bavarians are friendly. The scenery south of Munich began to change. Delightful grassy hill farms surrounded little villages overlooked by attractive onion-domed and well-maintained towers attached to simple barn-style churches. Here were prosperous communities observing simple country lives. Soon, great ice-capped mountains, displayed themselves above the landscape, indicating the Austrian border. Not having eaten a full meal since arriving in Germany, I pulled into the last rest area before crossing. Having parked my van away from the bustling main parking area, I strolled to the self-service restaurant. At the counter I pointed to one of the colourful pictures of laden dishes above a well-built waitress's head and said "Ein, danke". A one-sided rapid-fire conversation ensued. I didn't understand a word, so I smiled, nodded my head and repeated "Danke Schön". Handed a ticket, I was 'commanded' to sit down. When my number came up the waitress shouted the same words several times over the heads of my fellow patrons. She then left her counter and advanced towards me, voicing what I assumed to be expletives. Other customers silently watched as I eventually copped on. I was to go to the counter and collect my pre-paid plate. Apart from the pile of chips, the meal was totally different from that to which I had pointed. I tucked into my vast sausages and lubricated them with plenty of the free mustard sauce.

My appetite satisfied, I made my way to the toilets. I was preceded to the door by a glamourous blonde. Horrified that I had made a mistake and was entering the 'ladies', I checked the sign. On entering I was doubly re-assured when the 'lady' stood at the men's urinals as I took my position beside 'her'. I had never wittingly been in the close proximity of a transvestite. Troops in my regiment used to relate stories of meeting up with them at a pub in Norwich. I felt somewhat uncomfortable if not embarrassed.

Replete, I fell fast asleep in my van but at about three in the morning, was awakened by the shouts of a German-speaking youth at a nearby truck driver. He was soon joined by another but eventually the angry comments of freshly disturbed fellow drivers quelled the row. I couldn't sleep any more, however, and so dressed and continued my journey. I was leaving the then European Economic Community for independent Austria which meant a thorough search by customs at the border.

The road through the Austrian Alps was spectacular. At a well designed and spotlessly clean service area, the tourist shop's counters were full of china maidens and colourfully wrapped packets of sweets, the girls manning them dressed in national costume. I had a coffee and apple struedel. Before reaching the Yugoslav border I stopped at a small filling station. I was flummoxed as the Management wouldn't accept Eurocheques, and I had no cash and no credit cards. Eventually I located enough change in my pockets and from the van's glove compartment to pay my bill. Half an hour later, several vehicles signalled me as they passed. I was slow to realise that my fuel tank cap had not been replaced and I was leaving a trail of diesel fuel. Nestled in a deep valley between mountains, Ljubljana was a pleasant introduction to a country then only recently freed from Communism. However, the roads were appalling and the shops revealingly empty. The only highway to Postojna in Slovenia, and on to the Port of Rijeka, was tolled. Between Posoga and Rijeka, where Marshal Tito built ships, I rested beside a well-maintained war memorial, its communist symbolism depicted in brilliant red.

The Dalmation coast was spectacular. I spent a night in a delightfully situated 'camping' where the level parking spaces were placed amongst apricot trees scattered over the steeply sloping, sheep-inhabited orchard. The Adriatic below was tranquil with little sunbeams sparkling as they hit the water. Sheep bells tinkled in the background. The scenery, although somewhat dull to start with, got increasingly spectacular as I travelled south. Near Obrovac the road crossed a deep gorge, bordered by rich brown cliffs, where an inlet of the sea ventured inland parallel with the mountain range and offshore islands. Beside the towns of Zadar and Trogir, with their bright terra-cotta roofs, children were hawking tortoises on the roadside. Beyond, at Sibenik was the Kika river delta with canal-bordered allotments, like Chinese paddies, little houses and utility buildings pocking the flat landscape.

In Split, a fascinating old city with Greek, Roman and medieval remains, an ancient port and a pleasantly relaxed bustle, I got hopelessly lost. The place is divided by a craggy wooded hill, honeycombed with road tunnels. This played havoc with my sense of direction and I had to ask several people, using sign language, how to reach the Dubrovnik road. Eventually the driver of a family-filled Zatapa bade me follow him; we parted with loud hoots, mine expressing gratitude. Solta, one of the parallel offshore islands looked hot and barren in the haze, its beige cliffs reflected in the still Adriatic water. Colourful wildflowers flourished alongside the road and I took photos of hollyhocks and brilliantly coloured shrubs. Along the south coast towards Dubrovnik, much of the landscape was Burren-like karst with only the occasional parched evergreen bush. To the right, distant fishing boats and ferries plied their way over the sheltered blue waters between the islands.

As one arrives from the north Dubrovnik is not spectacular, although the fortified city walls are impressively strong. They are abutted with massive square towers, with two-tier circular bastions at the corners. I parked facing west towards the moat and strolled downhill and through the city gate. At the time this medieval city-republic was in a remarkable state of preservation and its little harbour was dotted with pleasure boats. There was an air of tradition and grace, unmolested by tourists. The inhabitants were serene and the city exuded an air of confidence. Although tiny when viewed from the surrounding hills, there was a sense of spacious grandeur within. The airport, which I visited to get money changed, was small and unkempt, and the staff not very friendly. German and English tourists had freshly alighted. I sensed the inadequacies of modern air travel - they were missing out on the exciting experiences which could and did happen to those who travelled overland. Armed with a comforting purseful of cash, I drove slowly up the steep incline above the sea, stopped beside the road and sat on a small wall. Here I watched the magnificent deep red setting sun. Looking over the city below, I felt a tremendous sense of history.

Towards Herceg Novi I decided to pull in at a rather expensive-looking but empty restaurant. Its terrace looked out to sea and the cloth-covered tables were correctly laid. A black-tied waiter studied the sea over the far wall with both hands on his hips. He took no notice as I made my way to my chosen place. The wooden chair noisily scraped the tiled floor as I pulled it under me. I sat for perhaps ten minutes, but there was no response from the waiter. I was getting calmly irritated as I raised my hand and gesticulated, hoping for a menu. There was still no reaction. Eventually, a loud party of chattering Germans came and sat. They too tried to get the waiter's attention. The man, having until then had his back towards me, turned round, came over to my table and presented me with the menu. His back was from thence reserved for the Germans, even as he brought me my order. He obviously didn't like tourists, especially German ones. I was served with two courses before he condescended to present the Teutonic party with their menus, even after much noisy attention-seeking on their part. That night I tented on another steeply sloping field beside the sea. I swam in the morning, though nervous of the rock-bordered depth of unobstructed blue water.

Rounding a corner, as I continued my journey, I came to one of the most beautiful pictures I have ever experienced. Boka Kotorska was already familiar from illustrations. This mountain-surrounded twenty kilometre inlet has two low islands near its centre, each bearing churches, one of which is surrounded by tall cypress trees. There was something deeply moving about this tranquil scene. The colourful red roofs of the island churches and the dark green scrub-clad mountains were reflected in the mirror-calm waters. I strolled along the waterfront of a small walled town and took photographs. Reaching Kotor at the eastern end of the inlet, I was reminded of Communist rule for a church stood derelict while cranes nested in its unused romanesque tower.

Near the Albanian border is the attractive island citadel of Sveti Stefan linked to the mainland by a causeway, on either side of which are sandy beaches. Restored as an unobtrusive tourist settlement, many of its houses are leased to visitors while at the north end is a well-disguised hotel. I enjoyed a long swim, for I was about drive inland for Titograd, Pristina and Skopje. Albania blocked my way

south. That intriguing country was still in Communist hands, forbidden territory to all but a few. The road over the mountains was exhilarating and seemed to rest on thin air when bends on stilts bore it over deep ravines. Skardorsko Jesero, over the northern end of which the road crosses a bridge and causeway, is fascinating. Acres of the shallow lake are covered in waterlillies and rushes. In the distance I could discern the Albanian hills. An old castle, over which towered a modern steel electricity pylon, guarded the lake beyond the roadside railway. I pondered about the aristocratic people who built it, and what the Communist regime had been telling the citizens of the sparsely populated district about them.

The entry to Titograd, in Monte Negro, was lined with Cyprus trees, behind which were hillsides of dense mixed forests. The townspeople were undertaking their traditional evening stroll, so I continued up the rugged Moraca valley with its fast-falling rivers whose turquoise waters flow through shallow rocky gorges. I was tempted to swim but the water was icy cold, so I just dangled my toes over a rock and handwashed my face. The top of the range was spectacular and the road twisted into the distance as though the wooded mountains had been scarred with a dagger. Farmhouses with steeply pitched corrugated-iron roofs scattered the hay-cut valleys until I reached Ivangrad and on to Kosova's ugly capital, Pristina. There was a lot of police activity here and I was held up several times. The road south towards the Greek border was not as busy as I had expected and skirted Skopje before its gradual descent

through Macedonia. I chatted with women working in a vegetable plot - they wore their colourful traditional clothes.

Since leaving home, I had had to communicate in several different languages and alphabets. The few words learnt during military service in Cyprus weren't much help to me as I entered the nerve-racking streets of Thessalonika, second largest city in Greece. Having inadvertently got into a central lane, I had to continue with the flow. Eventually I was able to stop at a delightful little Orthodox Church surrounded by a small tree-shaded yard. Parking illegally on the kerbside, I exhaustedly made my way to a stone seat, sat and dozed for ten minutes prior to finding my way to Alexandroúpolis and the Turkish border.

The sea was balmy as I indulged in a mid-day Aegean swim, and I got alarmingly sunburnt within less than half an hour. The harbour at Karála was somehow comforting. It wasn't unlike resorts in the south of France and even had an ancient viaduct crossing the streets. It was obviously a tourist centre as the signs were in the Roman alphabet as well as the Greek. It was a relief to read 'Xanthi 55 kms' and to know that my destination was a correct interpretation of the national language.

On the road ahead were loads of Kurdish refugees. They reminded me of the homebound Moroccans one sees flocking from France or northern Europe to Algeciras in Spain with their well-earned purchases. Children rode on top of a van while others poked their upper torsos out from the side windows. In a low-lying lake beside the road was an island-bound Greek Orothodox church and monastery, but as I continued east, there were Turkish settlements. I felt that these non-Greeks were getting a raw deal. Local roads were in poor condition and a lot of the buildings dilapidated.

At the Turkish border, I perceived the almost aggressive dislike of one nation for the other. The Greeks sent me across the border bridge with a warning. Turks 'escorted' me to their border post. After experiencing much officialdom and a visit to the Bureau de Change, all of which delayed me, I cheerfully sped down a well surfaced "straight" towards Istanbul. Twenty minutes later, a policeman hailed me from behind a cluster of bushes - another stood beside their hidden vehicle as I was politely ushered over and ordered to turn off my engine. My lack of Turkish didn't matter for graphic illustrations using real money made the amount of the fine so obvious that there could be no misunderstanding. That night I left the main road at Tekirdag, drove up a bohereen with huge potholes, and pitched my vehicle amongst the weatherworn sandstone rocks. At five in the morning, half a village was peering through my mirror-clad rear window; I observed men, women and children, but they couldn't see me because of my reflective glass window. Eventually they moved on and I was left in peace to shave and cool myself with water.

I never wish to drive in Istanbul again. Entering the city, such a highway would normally have some five or six lineated lanes each way, but this was unmarked which meant that vehicles of all sizes, including huge American trucks, meandered from side to side as they made rapid forward progress. Occasionally a cow or a brave pedestrian accompanied by a mule would stop the flow. I found it difficult to turn off the road. Hoping to drive to the Topkapi Palace and the historic Mosque area, I found myself in the midst of a market. It was outside a city gate just too narrow for my van to pass through. Shouts and screams and thumps on the sides accompanied those who guided me as I backed the considerable distance to the road and its heavy traffic. My stomach started to cause trouble, I having eaten a delicious kebab and honey-cake lunch in an open roadside restaurant. I couldn't contain myself, neither could I see any chance of pulling to the side of the roadway or of finding a quiet corner in which to rest and rectify an uncomfortable domestic disaster. I was compelled to travel on with the flow of traffic and cross the great bridge over the Bosphorus into Asia. Accompanied by huge trucks and busses, I thundered ahead past the grim shipyards, brown dust causing a hazy road-cap. Eventually, I was able to locate a peaceful country lane, wash, change, and rectify my discomfort. I avoided Izmet, but terminated my journey on the outskirts of Ankara. The prospect of another huge city and the realisation that I would be returning via the same route were daunting . . . . and I didn't understand Turkish. I pulled in to a derelict farm and collapsed in the back of the van with the main door open. It was dusty and very hot.

On my return journey, traversal of Istanbul was easier than expected and I found my way out of the city without too much hassle. There was, though, a lot of oncoming traffic as I entered the countryside. Refugees were fleeing Bulgaria by motorised and horse or mule drawn vehicles, others by foot. They looked sad and bedraggled. My route continued west from the main Edirne to Sophia road, so I lost sight of these unfortunate Turkish refugees from the then political strife. At Kegan, I observed a sign for 'Gelibolu'. My general perception and enough historical knowledge indicated that I was near the battle-field at Gallipoli.

Gallipoli is a bleak spot with few trees, overlooking the straits at the south west end of the Sea of Marmara. Several merchant ships and a tanker were passing as I drove towards the end of the peninsula. I was dismayed to learn that I could have crossed by ferry from Asian Turkey to the port of Eceabat, a journey I had enquired about before leaving home, and to which I had had a negative response. It would have been much more exciting to have made my way through Bursa and along the south side of the Sea of Marmara. Retracing my steps to the main road towards the Greek border, I came across a delightful horsefair, not unlike those of Ballinasloe or Spancil Hill. There were some beautiful animals and a huge assortment of different vehicles, around which crowded hucksters and prospective purchasers.

The return crossing into Greece was less dramatic. Although I was on my journey back to northern European civilisation, it was still exciting. I knew how much time I had, and so decided to visit the vast amphitheatre of Caeserea Philippi at Drama. From here spread the word synonymous with 'theatre'. There wasn't a soul about, so it was a weird experience to clamber over the ancient ruins, then undergoing restoration, in utter silence. Resting at different spots, I would sense the performances which happened long ago. Continuing my journey, I was attracted to a roadside stork's nest perched on the electric wires supported by a wooden pylon - how, I asked myself, could they survive?

Near Thessalonika, I turned south to Lárossa and alongside the inlets embracing Evia Island, to Lamia where I got stuck between two closely parked cars for an hour and a half. Delphi, to its south, is spectacular. High in the mountains above Itéa are the colossal open-air hewn-stone temples and walls of this ancient metropolis.

There are mosaics of people and peacocks, and beautiful classical monuments. Inside the museum are astonishing statues and gold ornamentation. I would have spent longer, but time was short and I wanted to see so much more. The west coast was dull but I bathed in the shallow inland sea near Préveza and had delicious sea-food on the pergola-shaded terrace of a nearby restaurant, totally alone apart from an uncommunicative host. High mountain passes and the spectacular views of Métsavo over its islanded lake as my van laboured above the once Turkish town led me to the surrealist outcrops of Metéora. Carved into or erected on the summits of these landborne stacks of rock, Greek Orthodox monks established their monasteries, the only way of access for some being by rope. More than the various 'mounts' dedicated to St. Michael in other parts of Europe, this city of hermits left a moving impression on me. The place is remote and yet so powerful. It reflected tremendous faith.

Although I would have dearly loved to cross into Albania, then under the control of Communist tyrant, Enver Hoxha, the closest I could get would be near Ohrid. The mountainous road across the Greco-Macedonian border above Flórina led through Bitola and, by a poorly signed route, to the medieval city of the name on the north shore of one of the world's cleanest and clearest lakes, Ohrid. I travelled south alongside the eastern shore. Swimming in the clear warm water was an experience. The colourful fish weaving between and around my legs and pecking at my feet were plainly visible. The night of my arrival, I continued south until I reached the Albanian border and illegally parked under the watchful eye of suspicious-looking dull-uniformed Communist guards. Fireflies buzzed like firework sparks wafting in a wind. A short distance to the east, Prepan Lake divided the three countries of Albania, Macedonia - then part of Yugoslavia - and Greece. The area is beautiful, the people pleasant and the flora and archeology interesting. In spite of the fear of war, the place radiated an incredible peace. I was disappointed that I could stay no longer.

When I reached Skopje and Pristina there was unrest, mainly against the Belgrade government, so I was directed to almost unmetalled and very pot-holed minor roads by Serbian police manning road blocks. The villages were poor, untidy and disorganised - I was reluctantly waived between haphazardly parked vehicles and domestic animals. The people wore colourful folk costumes for both play and work. The Muslim town of Pec, although ugly, was intriguing. More exciting still was the hair-raising hairpin road which climbed almost vertically up the side of the steep mountain range towards Ivangrad. In the Alpine valleys on the plateau above, shepherds guarded straggly flocks of sheep and goats. Scattered hamlets of primitive houses seemed friendly although some locals half heartedly waved as though somewhat suspicious.

When I reached it, huge potholes made the Sarajevo road almost impassable. Oncoming traffic passed me on the incorrect side as each of us negotiated lake-like 'pits'. The Yugoslav government had neglected this road since they started a major new highway, visible along the cliffs of the eastern side of the gorge-like valley, much of it through tunnels. My road eventually levelled over well grazed pasturelands past neat farmsteads with wooden barns and outhouses. Soon I descended towards an increasingly populated suburbia. As I approached Sarajevo a sign welcomed me to the Winter Olympics undertaken a couple of years before.

Lost in a sea of Sarajevan signs I found difficult to interpret, I stopped several people for directions to the city centre. One asked "You Irish?", a statement rather than a question. "Welcome to the tinder box of Europe . . . . it happened here in 1914 and will again". He pointed towards a distant bridge: "That's where Archduke Ferdinand was shot . . . . June 1914" I recalled the start of the first world war as a result of a Bosnian terrorist's attack. Leaving him, I uncomfortably wended my way through the older part of the city, a mixture of nineteenth century elegance and twentieth century Communist gerry-building. The market was bustling with Christians and Moslems, Serbs and Croats, all vying for an array of fresh vegetables. Corrugated-steel public service vehicles conveyed passengers from one end of the city to the other. Their arrogant drivers were a little scary as I shared their streets. The place, if exciting, was tense.

The main road out of Sarajevo was overlooked by massive grim-looking concrete apartment blocks with flat unkempt recreational spaces between. It twisted its way over mountain valleys through Konjic and down the Neretva valley. Moslem Mostar with its beautiful high-arched bridge, now destroyed, had no signposts for Mejerigorje. I wished to pay a visit to the recently established pilgrimage site. When I asked in the nearby town of Capljina, no one would tell me where it was and locals were quite hostile. Eventually I crossed a bridge in the general area and asked some people working on the river's right bank. They were obviously Roman Catholics. "Yes, keep along the road . . . ." An unattractive area of market gardens with recently built 'Bed and Breakfast' homes led to a cluster of stalls selling rosary beads and souvenirs. There was a meditative service in the rather ugly modern church. The congregation were repeating what I sensed to be "Jesus Come" in a mantra-like way, but the atmosphere was spiritually moving.

My journey onwards took me past Trieste and on to Venice, where I slept under the facade of a large eighteenth century church, Ravenna and then to the little republic of San Marino. Small states, like islands, fascinate me. San Marino is a wealthy hilltop fortress above a sea of rolling hills of yellow and green fields and farmland,

Stepfather Bob with my mother, Fontenille, 1994

My mother Suzanne with Guy, Pechbouthier, 1997

its buildings neat and well maintained. The food was excellent but expensive. Retracing my steps through Rimini to Forti, I continued past Florence to Grasse in France where I stayed a night with Ivar and Patricia O'Brien. Their house is erected a-top the canal which supplies the local water, and their swimming pool. After calling on my brother at Pechbouthier and stocking up with wine and Spanish food at San Sebastian, I returned to Ireland on the ferry to Dun Laoghaire.

* * * * * * * * * * *

My next visit to Yugoslavia was not so pleasant. I had driven through Holland, Germany, Denmark and Sweden to Norway and was returning via Czechoslovakia when I had problems getting fuel. The Russians were refusing to supply the newly freed Czechs. There were huge queues at service stations and on reaching Pilzen, I decided to return to Germany in the knowledge that I probably had just enough fuel to do so. I made it.

Near Sopron in Hungary, having crossed a corner of Austria, I located a 'camping' full of Poles and East Germans. Parking my van on a site for the night, I searched for a restaurant - only a bar was open, its tables occupied with hamburger and frankfurter eaters drinking cheap local beer. At the counter I asked, by gesticulating, for food and settled for the only dish available, a long frankfurter sausage in a roll. Beer in hand, I located a seat on a bench facing a table, at the other side of which sat two sober-faced East German couples. I tried to converse but failed. Eventually the barman jauntily bore my supper over the heads of the seated gathering and plonked it in front of me. As I hungrily bit into one end, the mustard-lubricated cylindrical missile of pink meat shot out of the hole at the other end of the roll and targeted the face of the man opposite. Pandemonium ensued but at least I inspired animated conversation.

On the same trip, after I had driven round Lake Balaton, I decided to leave the main road and attempt a short cut. The increasingly diminishing road surface apparently, much to my horror, led to a dangerously radioactive area. 'Skull and crossbones' signs and gesticulative fellow road users had me rapidly renegotiating the route.

Arriving in Yugoslavia, I decided to change some money at Subotica. From there I would drive south to Kosova. As I crossed a major interchange in the town centre, I had observed a bank so parking down the street, I returned to undertake my transaction. There was the usual red tape and a long queue. Reaching the front, I was told I needed my passport which I had left in the van. When I collected it, all was well. After twenty-five minutes, I contentedly returned with Yugoslav money, startled to find my vehicle surrounded by uniformed police. "Is this your van?" I nodded the affirmative. Further questions were put to me in Serbian, a language I didn't know. I was then brought to the police station across the road and told to wait in the cool central hall. A policeman ordered me to sit before making for his glass-partitioned bureau. Every time I attempted to stand, there was a bellow. After five or six hours of twiddling my fingers, an interpreter appeared. A pleasant but experienced sergeant, he spoke reasonably good English. He explained that I had been accused of damaging the rather antiquated Yugoslav-built Zapata car parked ahead of me. My protestations of innocence did nothing to appease the expressionless uniformed police surrounding me. Eventually they agreed that we should leave the building and inspect the damage. I demonstrated that the marks on my bumper, undisguisedly made to coincide with the outriders on the car, were those of studded boots. It was obvious that the sergeant comprehended my plight, but he had to stand by his colleagues. I demanded to see the damage as there was nothing visible. "Its internal . . . . in the engine". The owner asked for £300 in local currency. "No way", said I. The alternative to immediate payment was to spend three days in a police cell until the judge next came to town. As the daylight hours waned, I eventually did a deal for £20, no questions asked. I was freed and as I was about to climb into my driving seat, realised that the owner of the car, wearing a civilian shirt and jacket, wore the same uniform trousers and shoes as the policemen. Thoroughly disgusted, I made for the Italian border to leave Yugoslavia that night. As I angrily footed the accelerator and roared down the road, I was soon flagged down for exceeding the speed limit. The rest of my money went on fines. I was so furious and frustrated when I reached Nova Gorica that I couldn't locate the border crossing-point. Exhausted, I pulled into a lay-by above a narrow lake and fell asleep. Italy was only across the water. In the morning I made my way into Italian Gorizia with ease to spend the rest of my vacation in countries where police were less corrupt.

A journey round Italy and Sicily was another eventful drive, as also have been excursions into East Germany and especially to Spain and Portugal. Citania de Britanica, an ancient Celtic site in north-east Portugal is particularly fascinating but the wide-loaded hay carts of Hungary, Gaudi's archtecture in Barcelona and the characterful scapes of Mallorca, south-eastern Poland, the fortified cities and hilltop towns of Italy and France, the Roman aquaducts and ferryboats throughout Europe and meeting with Norway's King outside his Oslo palace are amongst my many experiences These have opened my life and are to me the equivalent of sport, participatory sport, exciting sport. I love travelling, and I intend to continue visiting new places.

CHAPTER SEVENTEEN

The Irish Heritage Programme – its instigation and initial package. Travels to New York and Washington, to Chicago and Cincinatti, and to Ottawa, Calgary and Edmonton. A hospital visit and a day with Indians. An O'Neill inauguration.

For years Grania and I had known Brendan O'Regan, the originator of the Duty Free Airport concept, a hotelier and an entrepreneur. Brendan, who also founded Co-Operation North, the Irish Peace Movement and Obair, a promotional work-programme in Newmarket-on-Fergus, was always delighted to seek ideas from his many friends and to share them for the development of innovative Irish projects

One day over lunch, Brendan asked me if I had thoughts as to the further promotion of Shannon Airport. I suggested that as there were at least forty million Americans of Irish descent, an interest in finding their roots could be harnessed. He arranged the presentation of my suggestions to Aer Rianta but the time was not ripe.

A year or two later, I received a telephone call. "Is that Hugh Weir? My name is Tom Haughey . . . ." Tom had recently been appointed Planning and Product Development Manager at Shannon and had been searching for new ideas. 'Would I be interested in helping him develop my original suggestion which he felt had potential?' I accepted his challenge to become Project Historian for the new Irish Heritage Programme and in October 1981, Tom, his colleague Padraig Cleary and I met at Ballinakella Lodge. For each of twelve clans we would produce a map of the clan territory, an illustrated clan history, a bibliography, a poster and a family tree. This was later changed to a scroll depicting major clan events and places, their arms, a family figurehead, an early section of their genealogical tree and a prefix such as 'Royal' or 'Brave'. There was also to be a brief history of each clan, another of associated places, a map and gazetteer, a chronology and a bibliography. Each of these was produced separately, but packaged together.

The cost of production, postage, the popularity of each name, and the positive angles such as the value of advertising to the sponsors, was researched. Shannon Development was to take a lead along with Aer Lingus and Bord Failte, the Irish Tourist Board. We also got support from Coras Trachtála (The Irish Trade Board) and from the Department of Foreign Affairs.

My next task was to guide my proposals to a successful outcome, during which Padraig and I would confer. Researching the initial twelve clans, and compiling the information in each package, I gained an insight into unfamiliar people and places such as the O'Dalys of the midlands, the O'Sullivans of Kerry and the north-western O'Reillys. The O'Connors and the O'Briens were particularly interesting due to my family relationships. I sourced reference books such as O'Hart's *Irish Pedigrees*, an essential but occasionally inaccurate work, McLysaght's more recent genealogical books and Burke's *Peerage* and *Landed Gentry* which often contained the leading family trees. Abbeys, castles, major associated homes, and monuments to each family were carefully listed mainly from local histories. As I visited them, I would photograph and record detailed information as a basis for accurate, if basic, guides.

Many times, I would find sites which were incorrectly connected and at others, located places which had lost their identity. Clansmen were usually helpful although in some cases, there was inter-sept animosity. I had to check and recheck my sources and information but was often frustrated at being unable to follow up my researches due to my time schedule.

A difficult task was to identify the correct arms of each family. The O'Connors, for instance, stem from totally different sources, the Offaly clan having little direct blood relationship with the O'Conors of Connacht. Concerning the O'Connor arms, the latter's oak tree was adopted by several of the other septs, which is confusing. I felt that I should be as accurate as possible as to choosing a common escutcheon commercially acceptable to those bearing the same name.

The final draft of each part of my work was carefully typed by Grania who, bless her, is the only person able to read my handwriting. Joe Hartnett, a Shannon Development artist, undertook the final artwork for the scrolls or posters. It was imperative that I ensured the correct dress and depiction of early scenes. The programme was officially launched in September, 1981.

Some forty thousand American-Irish citizens, selected from within a particular income band by a United States based professional organisation, would be sent information on their family name to encourage them to visit the land of their forebears. Each package contained an Aer Lingus discount voucher for travel to Ireland, another for initial research by a reputable genealogist, a guide to Ireland, a cover letter and an application form. These, together with the scrolls and clan information, were pre-addressed and shipped to New York in bulk. There they were posted to the individual applicants.

The response to our mailing programme was excellent. On receiving each completed form and its accompanying cheque, I scrutinised the information and sent a request to an appropriate researcher. A report would be returned, usually indicating the necessity of further work by a professional or by the client. I would forward this, together with a list of local historians, to the applicant.

Soon, hopefully, the Americans would be in Ireland with their families, meeting fellow clansmen and seeing for themselves from whence their forebears came. Many did come, but directors of Shannon Development and the other investors indicated that the returns were not rapid enough. I explained that the programme would take time to mature, but about two years after its launch, funding ceased. The project was terminated but requests for research continued for some years.

*   *   *   *   *   *   *   *   *   *   *

Before the axe fell, a major facet of the Irish Heritage Programme was person-to-person involvement in the United States. Prospective clients should have an opportunity to meet the organisers, genealogists, and historians involved. We would also undertake media campaigns to explain our plans on television, or discuss them on radio. From the 21st September, 1981, I would be spending two weeks in New York, Philadelphia, Washington and Bethesda.

Three weeks before departure, American Tom Lindert of Hibernian Research and I participated in a communications course in Dublin. Initially we were taught the dos and don'ts of television and radio. Derek Davies, a well-known television personality, gave us each a gruelling three minute session. On viewing the play-back, we realised how little of our message we had transmitted. I was corrected for using words such as 'Vietnam' and 'Socialism'. A video presentation depicting an interview with politician John Hume by David Owens was helpful. It showed the relaxed attitude of the interviewee, his ability to impart his message, and that minor mannerisms are acceptable.

At the end of our course, we were congratulated but support from our sponsors' American public relations people would be essential. We needed to know about our interviewers, their characteristics, their audiences, times and locations, and the types of programmes. We should have razors and combs in our pockets for freshening up. On arrival at each media station, we should hand the producer a slip indicating who we were and what we did, together with any visual aids. Our report indicated that only those trained should undertake interviews for if we failed to put over a good image, our project could be doomed. 'Media coverage is important for the success of any promotion, especially ours; practice and total familiarity were essential. The New York Office of Aer Lingus must have back-up information for sending to enquirers who had watched T.V. interviews and communicated'.

*   *   *   *   *   *   *   *   *

Two weeks after the media course, Grania dropped me off at Shannon Airport for the mid-day flight to New York. On arrival in America, we were greeted by Shannon Development representatives Kevin Imbusch and Frank Hamilton who, with Bridie Clarke, did much of the organising. Although we were accommodated in top class Manhatten hotels, we had to account for every penny.

The following day was spent preparing interviews and meeting officials of the Irish Tourist Board. Wednesday was the 'Bloomingdale's' launch. The exclusive store hosted a dress dinner and ball, attended by the Mayor and significant Irish-American politicians and businessmen. During the week they also ran an Irish promotion where we greeted Americans with Irish backgrounds, interesting them in their roots and encouraging them to participate in the Heritage Programme. We were wined and dined in Greenwich village, at an exclusive San Marinan restaurant where the seafood ante-pasta included lobster, and at a Japanese suchi restaurant in Broadway.

On Saturday, I caught an Amtrack Express train from Grand Central Station to Washington, which I had never previously visited. Tom Lindert had been chosen to go to Philadelphia. The scenes of urban Newark, Trenton and the poor districts surrounding Philadelphia opened my eyes to real America. The line south-west of Wilmington crossed wooded countryside and there were glimpses of the Susquehanna river as it meandered through Chesapeake Bay to the Atlantic.

It seemed no time from Baltimore before the train reached a sun-drenched Washington. A large two-roomed corner-suite with every possible facility had been arranged at the Hotel Bethesda Marriott. Nearby, the management of Bloomingdale's White Flint Store welcomed me and facilitated my meeting their wealthy clientele. Fifty per cent indicated Irish blood, many with Munster or Leinster backgrounds and the rest predominantly of Protestant gaelic or planter ancestry.

After two days at White Flint, I moved to Tyson's Corner also in Virginia. At my hotel, my room looked over a vast intersection towards Bloomingdale's, key occupant of a large shopping complex. The following morning I was advised to take a cab to my destination, a ridiculously short distance away. Many of my clients at Tyson's Corner didn't know their names were Irish. Most were wealthy commuters.

At the end of my first day, I was tired. For exercise, and because I could see it in the near distance, I decided to walk back to my hotel. Somehow, I traversed the interstate highway and found myself in a huge grassy bush-scattered 'bowl', central to its confluence with the Washington circuit. There was no way-out. Each time I climbed to the margin of a roadway as it crossed a bridge over another, I found no pedestrian pavement and vehicles drove frighteningly close to the parapet. After almost an hour I decided to take my life in my hands. As luck would have it, it was closing time and traffic had slowed down. Stepping off the narrow curb I dashed between cars and trucks. Drivers opened windows and shouted obscenities. I was an "idiot", a "f . . . . . . imbecile" and was told "you'll be killed". Never again will I attempt to cross a major United States highway on foot.

While at Tyson's Corner, the Embassy arranged an introduction to a senior representative of the State Department, the President being too tied up to welcome even visiting Heads of State. The Los Angeles *Twin Circle Catholic Magazine* contacted me and Bill Maxwell of Aer Lingus sent them publicity. I later became a regular correspondent to their widely circulated paper.

The fall sun shone as, on Sunday 4th October, I was conveyed by cab along the spectacular Potomac river drive past the Pentagon, to Washington National Airport. In eight days I had seen the White House and the city's sights whilst I had also been astonished at the poverty of the black community; I had met leading parliamentary and business personalities and I had worked hard. 'I should have stayed longer' I thought as my plane departed for New York. Tom Lindert was already waiting at J. F. Kennedy Airport. I had completed my first American promotional tour.

*   *   *   *   *   *   *   *   *   *

At home I had a lot of catching up to do. People I had met at Bethesda, Tyson's Corner, and New York were already contacting me, and I was receiving their completed forms for processing. I also had to write reports and detail my expenses. Due to the antiquated telephone system in Whitegate I was given an office at our Shannon Airport headquarters.

The 22nd October edition of the *San Francisco Examiner* carried a large Hearst Feature Service article headlined "A Big Boost for Irish Genealogy". It started: "New York - About 40 million Americans,

almost one in five, have a measure of Irish Ancestry . . . . ". It went
on to suggest that the estimate was not guesswork but was based on
diligent investigation by two of Ireland's most respected
genealogists. "Even Weir and Lindert, who practise their speciality for
the Irish Government were surprised . . . ." We were indeed.

* * * * * * * * * * *

At the beginning of 1982, I received a letter from Bord Fáilte's
Publicity and Public Relations manager, Paul Larkin. He was
delighted that I had agreed to participate in their United States Media
campaign in March. ". . . . you have been chosen because we feel
that you will be able to do a good job simply by talking, not only
about your own area of expertise, but in a warm and knowledgeable
way about any aspect of Ireland . . . . " Two briefing sessions were
planned, one for Dublin and one on arrival in New York. The Dublin
session, in the Irish Tourist Board's boardroom, was followed by a
television teach-in at Carr Communications.

Departure for New York would be on the eighth, with a final two
day briefing on arrival from the Department of Foreign Affairs, the
Irish Trade Board, The Industrial Development Authority and Aer
Lingus. There would also be United States-orientated TV/Radio
training. We would be returning within a fortnight, but were
welcome to stay on at our own expense. Amongst my colleagues
were Pyers O'Conor Nash, economist and nephew of then The
O'Conor Don, Director Joe Dowling of the Abbey Theatre, Vonnie
Reynolds who was then one of Ireland's leading couturiers, Joycean
expert David Norris, Director of the National Stud Michael Osborne,
Nora Owens, John Doyle of Seafood fame and Blathnaid Reddan of
the Crafts Council.

From our arrival in New York, we received red-carpet treatment.
Staying at the Waldorf Astoria Hotel, we were special guests at a
reception by the Irish Tourist Board. The following day, 9th March,
public relations company Thomson Monroe put us through our
paces. American television and radio techniques, Public Relations
manager Pat Tunison warned, were very different to those at home.
We had to be aggressive and forget about reputations or dress. The

conference was enjoyable with plenty of humour. Irish Tourist Board Executive Vice President for North America, Donal F. McSullivan, hosted another great party that evening. The next day, after final comprehensive briefings, we were on our own.

After landing at Indianapolis on a flight from New York, I was conveyed to the Sheraton Hotel. A bath and a change of clothes was followed by an enormous Mexican-style dinner. Early on Thursday, my chauffeur collected me for the first of my television programmes. CBS gave me an excellent fifteen minute slot but my next assignment was a ten minute phone-in on leprechauns. I told of the early Irish being small, hence the low doorways in our castles and abbeys "maybe leprechauns were their ghosts". _The Jim Gerrard Show_ had already started when I took my seat, but I enjoyed my hosted talk with the young President of the Ancient Order of Hibernians. Three interviews later, I departed for Cleveland. The plane was delayed because of thick fog, so I chatted with Farm Conventioners and travel agents.

The metropolitan train pulled into the station at the base of Cleveland's Stouffers Hotel well after midnight. In the 1930s Art Deco foyer an all-black jazz band played tunes from early films. Complaints that my door wouldn't lock ensured a change of room, but the second, with an outstanding view of the icy Lake Erie, had a problem too, for someone had also forcefully entered it. A temporary bolt made me feel slightly more secure. Leaving my belongings in the hotel's safe, I felt uncomfortably out of place as I strolled along Euclid, a lengthy streetway. The Erie-side docks to the north with their overbearing dark-painted cranes made an industrial backdrop to an Afro-American streetscene and astonished shopkeepers commented as I entered their premises. Television producers later expressed horror - nobody could accept that I hadn't been mugged or assaulted. 'White men just don't go such places!'

Following an uneasy night's sleep, I underwent successful news programmes and chat shows. When not on a media pitch, I was expected to arrange other interviews to get extra coverage. ABC's taped _Morning Exchange Show_ with Fred Griffith was relaxed as was Dorothy Fieldheim's five minute taping for the _Noon News_. Next, I contracted a series of five short radio programmes with Jodi

Fairchild. Rather than use a cab, I had walked the fourteen blocks. Jodi was delighted at my achievement and we warmed to each other immediately. One o'clock was a downtown N.B.C television taping of their *Sunday Magazine* with Tom Haley and Mona Scott - the Twigg band from Offaly played Irish music whilst I commented on slides of Ireland. A fifteen minute radio programme, and a long interview with Elaine Rivera of the *Cleveland Press,* followed by a photo-session, demanded stamina.

Before departure on Saturday I had a ten o'clock interview in my hotel with Mike McNulty, Editor of the *Sun Newspaper.* An excellent, almost poetic, four column article with a useful message proved his detailed knowledge of Ireland.

The Hopkins International Airport at Cleveland was ultra modern and carpeted in blue. On arrival at the multi-storey Cincinnati Stouffer's Towers Hotel I was allocated the penthouse Manager's Quarters. I kept back from the windows though, as my floor overhung the building and the extra width had a glass floor through which I could view the distant street below. Removing a dressing gown, slippers and chocolate from the pillow, I plomped onto the bed, exhausted.

A short while later Bernie Farrell, Marshall-to-be of the St. Patrick's Day Parade the following day, telephoned. 'Would I be ready in fifteen minutes to go to an American Irish Meeting in Kentucky, across the Ohio river?' After a bath, I descended to the lobby. At the hotel entrance a large Cadillac awaited me with its front passenger door open. At the Kentucky gathering, I elucidated my Government's abhorrence of terrorism. Some supporters of Noraid were unpleasantly provocative.

I liked Cincinnati with its similar air to Dublin or Boston and its Trollope literary connection. The Saint Patrick's Day parade, at which I was to be Guest of Honour, took place on Sunday, 14th March. I rose early as I had to meet a group of travel agents and prospective tour operators over breakfast. Around one o'clock, I arrived at the parade's television and media stand. There had been a mix-up regarding my schedule for the following day, so I agreed to an interview during the parade. Closely followed by a television camera crew, I walked alongside and chatted with participants. Having completed this, I boarded the official rostrum and was ushered to a central front-row seat beside Commissioner Murdoch. The huge parade of over seventy-five floats and bands, many of them arranged by the Shriners, an influential charitable organisation of fezz-capped professionals and businessmen, took an hour longer than expected. Their elephants left nature's messages, soon cleared by an orderly with a scooper. The event was fun and I blew kisses to semi-nude beauties on the larger floats; I don't think that gesture was particularly popular though.

In the evening I met John O'Regan, a member of the Irish Georgian Society, who arranged a meal and an interview with his sister Mary-Anne of the *Cincinnati Post*. After a phone-in on Radio Chicago's *Floyd Brown Show*, I was given a grand tour of the city by the Carr family. Ray told me that the only Weir he knew of came from Whitegate, Co. Clare! Mrs. Carr was the local Irish Georgian Society president, and Ray has a T shirt business in Ireland. That night I was lavishly entertained in a mid-town restaurant. I was not sober when I retired to bed.

A heavy night's sleep was followed by a huge breakfast to fortify me for my first Monday television session with WKRC. The station's news crew was covering the Indiana floods so I met my inverviewer at the Shriner's Children's Burns Hospital. John O'Regan then collected me at Stouffer's for the session with his sister who was creating a St. Patrick's Day editorial based on our chat. I had a great fifteen minute live interview with Norman Mark at 11.15 a.m. and an hour later was on CBS channel 9 with the *Hugh Dermody Television Show*. I couldn't keep my 1 p.m. appointment with Debbie Connor, so I arranged a phone-in from Chicago the following morning.

My visit to the Children's Burns Hospital, one of the world's most advanced, was a privilege. Shriners' Recorder Settle entertained me to lunch in the organisation's Temple before I was taken on a tour of their headquarters and met the Grand (Chief) Potentate. At the main hospital, doctors explained their work. I spoke to many of the children, some of them frighteningly badly burned, and from my roll presented a sticky machine-embroidered shamrock to each. The fear of infection was so great in one ward that I had to wear special clothing and a nose and mouth guard, and be disinfected at each of the sealed glass security doors. One young black boy had been fuelling his motor-bike when the gasoline ignited; he was so badly burned and raw that one couldn't tell the colour of his skin. Although his face was skeleton-like with no protruding nose or ears, no lips and his body delicately bandaged, the staff hoped to eventually repair him enough to give him an almost normal life. There was also a young Vietnamese, a similarly burned casualty of war. Each recognised what I said and made appropriate retorts. I was also shown skin cultivation where specialists could nurture even a minute piece to expand and then graft it to a child's tormented body, little by little. This was unique at the time.

One child asked me what Ireland was like and was there any possibility of her being able to visit? Touched by her request, I came up with a suggestion for the Tourist Board. "It would be a wonderful gesture if one or two of these children could be invited for a holiday and would pay Aer Lingus and Bord Fáilte to provide transport and accommodation because of publicity". They were most receptive to the idea. In June, however, I received a letter from Pat Tunison saying that, having pursued the Shriners' Hospital idea for several months ". . . . we ran into problems with insurance and responsibility . . . . All in all, while a marvellous idea, it fell into the pitfalls of bureaucracy".

In the multi-storey foyer of Chicago's luxurious and ultra-modern Hyatt Hotel, a band played as water tumbled from pool to pool. My fabulously equipped apartment had a magnificent view over Lake Michigan. I was, however, too tired to enjoy it. My first Tuesday interview on AM Chicago was shared with delightful local hero Tim MacCarthy who had saved President Reagan from assassination. He would be the leader and honoured guest of the city's St. Patrick's Day parade the following day. We had a long chat while waiting to be called. Next, WJJD-AM's Reese Richards gave me thirty minutes on his *Chicago Viewpoint.* He asked sensible questions and had obviously prepared his programme. Ushered into a small waiting room beforehand, I sat beside a well dressed and attractive black lady. She was founding a new church. When told what I did, she informed me that I should meet her partner, soon to join her. The door opened and another glamourous and magnificently dressed black lady appeared. "Meet Mr. Weir, he's from Ireland and promoting heritage", said my friend. "Gee", said the newcomer enthusiastically, "My Moma was a Weir". Sadly, I was called to perform before we could continue our conversation. Perhaps my forebears were not as perfect as I was lead to believe, or maybe the lady's mother's people were called after a kindly benefactor. I would love to know.

Mark, my chauffeur, took me to each destination by sumptuous Cadillac but, after this last interview, we found ourselves in a mighty traffic jam. Having missed the Debbie Connor Show I decided that I would be better off walking, for most stations were within a close radius and, anyway, the limo was costing the government $33 per hour.

At the Irish Export Board I met Pat Walsh of Aer Lingus, and Anne Byrne. We toured their impressive set-up and had several photograph sessions with directors and visiting personalities, following which we adjourned to O'Leary's restaurant at the Hyatt for lunch. I rang my bosses in the afternoon and was told I was free for the rest of the day. After telephone chats with our friends the Murphys, Evanston residents who own the Old School House at Corofin, and the Raclins who used to stay at Dromoland, I went sightseeing.

Below a central city bridge, the river was dyed green. I had already been proffered green beer on camera and there were shamrocks, green leprechauns and people dressed in green. I was chuffed when, as I entered a large bookstore, two teenage boys held the door: "Gee, isn't that the man we saw on T.V. this morning?" The magnitude of Chicago and the significant rôle played by Irish names in its development is impressive. It was, however, living up to its reputation as the 'Windy City'.

On St. Patrick's Day, Chicago showed up contemporary Dublin's efforts as an embarrassment. The whole city was 'Irish' and the population greeted each other with "Top of the morning to you" or "Have a nice Irish day". I had no time for an introduction when Claude Webber hosted me on WIND radio at 8.15 a.m. The enjoyable two hours live interview on the popular _Bob and Betty Sanders Show_ was shared by the married couple and myself. I then undertook

several phone-ins including one to Detroit and another to
Milwaukee. My television interview with Smiley Harris live on
"*Chicago Today*" was another success. I ended at 4.15 p.m. live with
Eye Witness News on ABC's T.V. channel 7. . . . Phew!

My final event in Chicago was to attend the sumptuous St.
Patrick's night ball. Black tie was necessary again for this grandest of
events, with attention focussed on leading American and Irish
dignitaries and the Lord Mayor. Chicago-born actor Donald
O'Connor got special recognition at this most Irish of events. An
uncharacteristically arrogant Catholic nationalism was represented,
but the evening was magnificently organised with symbolic serviettes
and place mats depicting Irish family names. I eventually tottered
back to my hotel and to bed.

*   *   *   *   *   *   *   *   *   *

Sharing our experiences back at the Waldorf in New York, members
of the campaign felt that we had served our country well, and had
had the experience of a lifetime. We ate a great dinner that night and,
after a de-briefing session on the Friday, collected our baggage for
the journey home.

Donal F. McSullivan wrote "Your professional contribution to our
St. Patrick's Day P.R. thrust was of immense value. Your energy and
enthusiasm, coupled with the preparation applied by Pat Tunison
and her associates, ensured us a winning formula from the outset"
and thanked me for my "professional and invaluable imput". In
Ireland, Jim Larkin wished, in a similar communication, to formerly
record "Bord Fáilte's gratitude and appreciation". He ended "Once
again, many thanks for your help and for all your very hard work
which I assure you is much appreciated." I was delighted with this
endorsement.

*   *   *   *   *   *   *   *   *   *

A report had to be written up on this latest American visit and piles
of research applications had arrived at home during my absence. It
was assumed I was a genealogist, and both American and Irish

citizens asked for advice on their grandmothers and close extended families. As a clan historian the overall identity of people and their surnames is my main interest but I did relay genealogical enquiries, so it was natural that clients couldn't distinguish the difference.

In September 1982, six months after the United States media tour, I was en route for Canada to a very different Irish population, many with an Ulster Protestant background. Mr. and Mrs. Ron Lewis, owners of O'Shea's 'Market Ireland' in Ottawa had invited me to give five minute consultations at their stores.

Owning no decent camera, I purchased the latest and best Canon which I was told would be cheaper than in Ireland. It was not, but I was able to take terrific photographs. The afternoon of the twenty-second, I was interviewed by Margaret Trudeau of the political family. Monica Pine (née Batemen), my first cousin, greeted me the next day and at four in the evening we drove across the river to Quebec. On an island en route we watched chipmunks scattering up and around trees before making for the Gatineau Park and its lakes. The autumn leaves were incredibly beautiful. That evening I met Monica's two daughters and enjoyed catching up with family news.

During my four days in Ottawa, my hosts also wined and dined me. Like so many places in the city, my central hotel was named after General Sir Guy Carleton, later Lord Dorchester. He was the uncle of Anne Weir (née Carleton) who, with her husband Robert, built Hall Craig, their son John being his equerry in 1779. Magnificent books on my Governor kinsman were presented to me. I was also shown the Rideau Canal where hundreds of Irish navvies had died of malaria.

Each day, visitors from as far as Toronto and Montreal queued to learn about their Irish forebears. One lady with an uncommon name challenged me on her husband's origins. She didn't know that we had been to Portora together and that his unusual family history was familiar to me. I had great fun in unabashedly telling her that 'the present senior bearer of his name was born in Cork around 1934 and was educated in Northern Ireland', together with other reasonably intimate facts. She was astonished. I eventually had to admit to the truth.

I always had an interest in how the 'West' was 'won' and jumped at the opportunity to learn more when authorised to fly to Calgary.

The exciting seven hour daylight journey crossed the width of Canada. As I looked down from my window seat, I marvelled at how pioneers had negotiated the myriad lakes and wetlands of Ontario and Manitoba. On board were Inuits on their way to the Northern Territory and Europeans heading for the oilfields, or on to Alaska. It was difficult to understand the cabin crew's Quebequois French. The vast flat cornfields of Saskatchewan reminded me of Dean Jackson's suggestion that I consider ordination for that diocese, and that Ralph Baxter, one-time rector of Shannon, was ministering as an Archdeacon somewhere below. Saskatoon, the state capital, looked bleak as we refuelled; some indigenous Canadians disembarked.

As we lost height, the lights of Calgary twinkled in the dark. From my ultra-modern multi-storey hotel in the city centre, I could view some of the huge high-rises then being built; one added two storeys during my short visit. Here were more recent Irish settlers, mostly from Munster and Leinster, helping to develop this hundred year old metropolis. I was dumbstruck when visiting the original stockaded fort erected within memory at the Bow and Elbow river confluence.

Asked to lecture at the University by the local historical Society, I was dined in a tower-top moving restaurant. From it could be seen the Rocky Mountains to the west and to the east, the Alberta grainfields. Before sitting at our window-side table, I placed my coat and camera on the sill. As the restaurant circled, my possessions stayed where they were. Embarrassingly I solicited the aid of the kitchen staff to locate them - they had 'disappeared' behind a long blank wall

Having finished greeting and meeting potential clients in the Bow Valley Centre and undertaking radio and television interviews, I walked through the city. The metropolitan railway wended along the streets, only pulling in to raised-platform stations to load or disembark passengers. Pedestrians, apart from the many sad-looking and often drunk Indians propping street corners, flowed across covered walk-ways linking the second floors of warm, brightly lit commercial blocks. I was reminded of pioneering adventure stories read to me in my youth when shopping in the Hudson Bay Stores. It was like being on the edge of the world. Souvenirs included miniature seals of genuine sealskin, and miniature totem poles.

'Edmonton really will be a last outpost', thought I, as I sought consent to travel overland by bus rather than by air. Leaving my hotel, I was surprised to be greeted with heavy snow. So was everybody, for it usually waited till October. I had hoped to go via the Rocky Mountain resort of Banff on the Vancouver road, but due to the change in weather conditions my Red Arrow coach would instead be going direct via the township of Red Deer. Built for long distances and Canadian weather, the vehicle was comfortable and warm, not unlike an aircraft. Headsets were provided and there was ample foot room between the seats. At the rear was a toilet and a self-service kitchen. I was embarrassed when I had to be shown how to pay for the automatically dispensed ready-packed food and drink, and how to heat my meal in the micro-wave oven.

Fellow travellers told me we were on the main highway from Canada and the central United States to Anchorage in Alaska or, a little nearer, Yellowknife in the Canadian North West Territory, depending on the branch taken. There was little traffic, merely an occasional supply truck or a similar southbound coach to ours. Set back from the highway on either side were the clapboard houses erected, and often already abandoned, by twentieth century German, Lithuanian or Russian immigrants. There were few trees, although scrubby birches surrounded some homesteads. Villages such as Olds, Lacombe and Leduc were pretty bleak.

Edmonton is a hilltop city of rapidly rising office blocks. My hotel was on newly developed land to its south. A view of the distant airport gave me a certain comfort in knowing that the outside world was a mere plane journey away from this remote urban settlement. On the morning of the 29th of September, we circled the city by car to a most modern shopping complex, a world leader of its time. The central two-storey foyer was a veritable jungle of trees and succulents, no doubt unaware of the freezing outside weather conditions. Wealthy oilmen and geologists, clients at O'Shea's newly established emporium managed by the Lewis's daughter, told me they would welcome a roots-searching Irish vacation.

Fascinated by ethnic people, I asked to visit an Indian reservation, but had no desire to be a tourist at a specially provided visitor amenity. Eventually, with Irish diplomatic assistance, I was invited to a reservation some sixty kilometres away. Here I was feasted on buffalo meat, berries, wild salmon and wine made from local plants, while dancers wove around me in comparative darkness. How intimidated early pioneers must have been when confronted by such war dances. The gyrations to music with the dancers' long feathered head-dresses swaying to the rhythm instilled a nervousness and thrill. These Indian people, now left with only a portion of their lands, had a deep cultural and spiritual ancestry very different to that of Europeans. I was thanked vociferously for requesting my visit, and asked to convey greetings to the people of Ireland. My hosts didn't perhaps realise how small a cog I was in our multi-faceted society.

My stay in Edmonton was all too short before I was flying back to Ottawa where the next three days were spent at O'Shea's, viewing the city and visiting an Indian gallery with cards and toys, models and even a book by an Inuit Weir. My cousin Monica introduced me to her friends - one of her daughters being close to the Prime Minister's aspiring 'right-hand man'.

On one of my internal flights, I was booked onto one of the tiny jets which ply between cities. On either side of the central aisle were single seats, the pilot fully visible up front. I commented to my heavily-built neighbour, whose bulk almost met mine across the divide, that there was no hostess. "Its a fact; no self-respecting hostess would risk going up in one of these things." It was a relief to sit in a comfortable Aer Lingus seat for the journey home to Grania. My first visit to Canada had been a delightful experience.

*   *   *   *   *   *   *   *   *   *

The O'Neills were one of the twelve clans chosen for our Heritage promotion, so I took up the suggestion to attend the Inauguration ceremonies for the Chieftain of Clan da Buidhe; Grania could come too.

It was dull when we arrived at Shanes Castle, Lord O'Neill's family seat beside Lough Neagh. A platform with microphones and a large oak chair under a canopy was approached over a narrow red carpet. At four o'clock, Portuguese 'Prince' Jorge O'Neill and his Iberian supporters arrived. He was wearing a green cape on the back of which were sewn the O'Neill arms; others, in black academic gowns, bore wooden shafts with pointed tops. Irish airs were played as a group of young dancers, dressed in red, added colour. Photographers and pressmen were a major portion of the three hundred who witnessed the event. Afterwards we chatted with Lord and Lady O'Neill and the Portuguese Prince's son. It was an interesting and useful experience.

Economists responsible for funding tourist promotion expected rapid returns. Professionals involved in the Heritage Programme were transferred to other spheres and there would be no further financial support. My efforts, however, were not unrewarded. For years afterwards, I was contacted by those following up their personal searches and many visited us. Tom Haughey is now a senior executive at Dublin Airport and Padraig Cleary runs his own Public Relations business.

Pug mad! Topsy, Sophia and 'Marty', c. 1980

CHAPTER EIGHTEEN

Silver Wedding celebrations – Bermuda and frog-hunting.
Presidential visits and an Archeopiscopal blessing. A dedicated
television programme, Tomás, a family tragedy. Launching
books. Hong Kong and changing times.

Grania and I celebrated our twenty-fifth wedding anniversary with
a garden party. Over a hundred guests joined us on our lawn for
a buffet on 17th July 1998. Tomás, about whom later, volunteered to
help organise the event, before which he and his cousin Joan Miguel
Ferrer sent us off for a delightful week staying with Grania's sister in
Bermuda. We flew from Shannon via New York. I had had trepidations
about visiting this small Atlantic island and had surmised that I would
be bored. From our arrival and welcome, we were both fully and
enjoyably occupied. The friendly black Bermudian driver who drove
us in his taxi from the airport pointed out features between
conversations on his mobile phone. Approaching his girl-friend's
house, he arranged for her to greet us as we passed. Sure enough,
there she was, running down her garden path, with arms flailing.

Deirdre's residence, part of an exclusive condominium, overlooks
the Great Sound, a small inland sea embraced by the low thirty
kilometre island. Directly in front, beyond the tennis courts and
swimming pool, are several mostly inhabited islets and in the
distance, the naval dockyards beside the gap through which cruise-
ships make their way to Hamilton. When shopping between the
capital's quaint colonial houses and modern high-rises, one can often
see their huge bulks towering above or 'blocking off' the ends of the
busy streets. The city, visible across the bay, is linked by punctual
ferries which operate like urban bus services.

Deirdre was wonderful and drove us to St. Georges, the old
capital, which has Tucker family connections and to the Naval

The Tucker House Museum, St. George's, Bermuda

Dockyards, each at opposing ends of the island territory. We wined and dined in exclusive clubs and restaurants and met her friends, some of whom invited us to share their hospitality.

At one dinner party, hosted by Glenys Stephenson whose son wrote a book of his experiences in the Himalayan foothills, I couldn't contain my curiosity. From the time we landed in Bermuda, there was each evening a tremendous cacophony of chirping. Informed that the noise was made by tree frogs, I searched for one. To make such a loud din, I was convinced they must be a reasonable size. Much to the amusement of everyone, on our hostess's pristine balcony, a chirping started from the succulent plant behind me. I sought the perpetrator, diligently but unsuccessfully examining both sides of each leaf. Eventually Glenys suggested I look for another in a plant in her fireplace. Watched by fellow guests, I carefully lifted the pot and there, underneath, was a miniature light-green creature the size of my little finger-nail. I apologised for my disbelief when told its likely size.

Deirdre also hosted a party attended by most interesting people including Andrew Trimingham of Trimingham's Store and president of the island's Historical Society. We visited the Astwood family who live on one of the earliest estates and the Cox's colonial home still resided in by the family, with its quaint furnishings and memorabilia. I now knew why Deirdre sold her house in Co. Clare, and settled in Bermuda, her Atlantic paradise.

* * * * * * * * * * *

At Ballinakella Lodge, the sun shone as our friends assembled on the lawn. We had rested the previous day while Tomás and Joan-Miguel erected our canvas awnings, for it had rained heavily and was to continue the following day. Eats were organised and we concocted a sangria-like drink which friends and relations doled out from large containers. Three girls, including the daughter of Risteárd Ua Cróinín who wrote our book on the O'Deas, played traditional music in the background as Grania circulated, able to enjoy uninterrupted conversation. It was a lovely day. We had felt that rather than expecting our guests to give us expensive silver, we would ask for scrapbook reminiscences, or plants. Throughout the garden and in our library are these reminders of our happy life together, and of our friends and relations.

* * * * * * * * * * *

During the previous twenty-five years, Grania and I had shared so much. Having started married life with a newly erected prefabricated bungalow, we were now living more comfortably with an added drawingroom and an abundantly windowed bedroom with views over the lake. Our garden had been extended and had matured and we used it for strolls, and to entertain.

There had been many highlights, the first being the visit of President Erskine Childers in December 1973. Erskine, a good friend of Grania's parents and related with families of mine, had been invited by Father O'Donovan to open Teach na Feile, a small general purpose hall in Whitegate. Father John, a great organiser, promoted

With Bermudian Frog, Silver Wedding anniversary, Ballinakella, 1978.

the parish with regattas, marquees and pony races at which I often undertook the announcing and sometimes commentated. In order that Erskine and his wife Rita would enjoy a degree of comfort, we forwent our own bedroom. The house was guarded by gardai and security officers. The day after the festivities, Erskine and I took a scenic drive over the hill country behind us. With his aide-de-camp, Commandant Leo Buckley seated in the back, we left home followed by a stream of official cars. My Peugeot was well able to take the potholes and bumps of roads I alone knew. Deep in conversation, I failed to ensure that the vehicles behind were in sight as I turned up a remote bohereen. Imagine my horror as, looking in my rear mirror, I saw the fleet of official cars roar along the better road which we had left, ignoring the turn. They got embarrassingly disorientated and nobody was amused. Erskine was great company though, and we discussed a wide variety of subjects.

In October two years later we had the Archbishop of Armagh and Primate of All Ireland, George Otto Simms, to stay. Not only had he always been most helpful to me especially during my student days, but his wife Mercy was related to Grania. We had invited him as Grania, secretary of the Friends of St. Flannan's Cathedral in Killaloe, had asked him to talk on the Book of Kells. This was during the height of the Troubles and Dutchman Teide Herema was held hostage at Monasterevan. Gardai, fearing that subversives could target senior Protestant clerics, were concerned for the Archbishop's safety. He arrived driving his own car but with a garda escort which had collaborated with the local force. The police detailed to protect both Erskine and George Otto thanked us profusely for the use of our facilities. Following the Primate's stay our local guard made a heartfelt plea: "Please, Hugh, don't bring any more important people". I could empathise with him for I don't think there had ever before been so many senior police officials in the area. However, it wasn't long before Mountshannon won the Tidy Towns Competition, and later saw the closure of the last Irish manual telephone exchange. For these events, there were helicopters, boats, and even more security.

My cousins William and Amanda Tailyour stayed with us from Connecticut in 1979 when their elder two children, Ian and Lillian

Alexander, Amanda and William Tailyour

were tiny, and before my Godson Alexander was born. The two children stood in front of a portrait of my Gibson grandfather and his sister Daisy, which had been painted when they were about the same age. The two pairs were incredibly alike. William Tailyour's grandmother was another of Grandfather's sisters, Molly. Through his father's mother, a Cooper from Co. Limerick, he is descended from Grania's forebear Máire Rua and is a kinsman of author Robert Graves. William and Amanda's third child, my Godson Alexander turned out to be a thoroughly delightful person, a keen sportsman, extremely clever and of a generous disposition. In June 2000, to the dismay of his parents and so many of us who knew and loved him, he tragically terminated his life aged seventeen, the day before his graduation from his exclusive American Academy. Sadly for me, I was unable to be present when over four hundred shared a service in celebration of his life at his family's Episcopalian church at Westport. Only a couple of years before, I had been privileged to join them there for his confirmation.

David Hicks, son-in-law of Lord Mountbatten, whose parents lived near my Gibson grandmother's Feering Bury, and who had known Grania in her youth, arrived in his large logo-adorned car. He had a world-wide reputation for his designer goods and his logo was famous. As he got out of his vehicle he presented us with a delicious pot of jam. On his next visit, while staying at Dromoland, he asked us to dinner where he chose the best and most expensive wine to accompany a delicious meal. Sadly, he was to die a few months later.

In August 1988 we hosted President Francesco Cossiga of Italy. A keen historian, he had seen my book *Houses of Clare* and was interested in meeting us. Accompanied by three Irish and three Italian detectives, his entourage included his diplomatic envoy Signor Carrachiola, his Irish chaplain, Father Michael Hayes, his doctor and his aide de camp. Dromoland Manageress Elizabeth O'Mahony guided them to Ballinakella. The day was spent in deep conversation, not only about houses but about politics and other subjects. He invited us to stay at his Quirinal palace in Rome but we were unable to accept the offer before he ended his term of office.

Other Italian visitors were Degna Marconi Paresce who came in 1986, and her sister Gioia Marconi Braga, daughters of the famous inventor Guglielmo Marconi and close cousins of Grania. Although we had met at her home at Alpine in New Jersey, I was away when Gioia stayed. However, four years later we entertained Degna's granddaughter Donata Paresce with her American friend, Tom Courtney. Jerram Burrows, my Head at Cork Grammar School has been welcomed almost annually with, until she died, his wife Rachel.

Since Cork and Dublin days, I haven't joined any amateur drama groups. In 1989 however, Douglas Gunn asked me if I would do a solo performance as Dean Swift for the Mental Health Association of Ireland. His ensemble and the Patrician Consort, Frank Dunne as soloist, would be providing the music. With trepidation I accepted; the Dean's works are crammed with inuendo and satire, so I knew the task would be difficult. I was in stitches of laughter, as were those witnessing the activity, whilst donning the heavy garments of the time which I had to wear. There was a packed audience in the Royal Hospital at Kilmainham, including the Minister for Health, and we were congratulated on an 'excellent performance'.

I live Here, a series of hour-long television programmes by our national station, Radio Telefis Eireann, depicted the activities of individuals based on their homes. In 1989 I was chosen, but there was a problem. My multi-faceted life has taken place mainly away from Ballinakella Lodge which had only been my home for some fifteen years. The producer had to arrange two separate weeks of filming to cover both Ardmaylebeg and County Fermanagh, shots while boating on Lough Derg, and visits to Ennis. The July weather was fairly good. As it was 'my' programme, I had to give the lead and interview others rather than be asked questions.

In front of the house I introduced myself and my background from a comfortable chair. Next there were interviews with longstanding friends such as Jackie Tuohy who built my first clinker-built boat, Peg Burke who accommodated my language students and Peter Levie, now of Williamstown Harbour and owner of the Shannon Castle Line. A visit to Ardmayle had me sharing reminiscences with our old neighbour T.J. Maher, shortly to retire as a member of the European Parliament. In the North, a party of Clare Young Environmentalists re-enacted previous experiences and shared activities with young people from Irvinestown, Co. Fermanagh. My old school, Portora, and other special places were visited such as the Lough Navar Look-out with its views of Lough Erne and the distant Atlantic, and Florencecourt where Deirdre O'Brien Vaughan of Newmarket-on-Fergus had her talented pupils playing traditional music. A Sunday service in Mountshannon was taped too, and an interview with the Franciscan Father Guardian during the Fleadh in Ennis. The exercise was fun; the directors and the camera and sound people had been delightful and very professional. A lot of old friends from my past, with many of whom I had lost touch, contacted me and recalled happy times.

Quite a few students have stayed with us in recent years. From France came Gael du Jonchay, Philippe Nivlet and other paying guests, whereas Celina, Justo, Joan Miguel and other young people from Spain have helped at home and with our business in return for their fare and the opportunity to learn English. Staying with Jacqueline and Pepé Catalá in the seventies, we had attended a family christening. Introduced to Juan and Jomita Porcell and their two small children, Maria Rosa and Tomás, little did we know that we would become Tomás's 'Irish parents'.Years later, Grania was on

*Jacqueline and Pepé Catala with son José and Jacqueline's first pike.
Lough Derg, 1983.*

a solo trip to Port de Andratx. As Justo Romero had returned to Spain hoping to become an airforce pilot, we would welcome a replacement. Anna Kay, a local politician married to Pepé's kinsman, told her that she knew the perfect person.

Tomás had no English, and had never travelled outside Spain, so in November 1987 I met him at London's Gatwick airport, there being no direct flights to Ireland. After greeting each other, we made for the car park where I had left Grania's car. I searched and located what I believed to be the number of the parking lot but there was no sign of the vehicle. After a frustrating half hour, Tomás nervously volunteering suggestions such as "are you sure you have the right number?", we located it elsewhere. Having accepted my credibility Tomás bombarded me with questions as we crossed an autumnal England with its heavy traffic and bright lights. He hadn't, however, consulted me before misinterpreting the word 'ladies' - he re-appeared from the female toilet at a Welsh service station.

Over a period of eight years, as Tomás grew from a fourteen year old boy into a confident, authoritative and delightful young man, he developed expertise in computers, the English language, salesmanship, and just about anything except the outdoor tasks we had originally expected of him. Although each year he went home for his holidays, he became 'family'. Tomás was and still is popular with our friends and, as he often accompanied me at work, with business colleagues. Amazingly, for a person with no formal instruction, he learnt to design, type-up, print out and help with the editing of our books. To facilitate Spanish tradition, we adapted our hours to eat a noonday lunch, followed by a short siesta, before resuming work from two in the afternoon. His interests in television, music, and the theatre encouraged us also to enjoy musicals and concerts in Limerick, Ennis, even Dublin. Sheila, a kind friend in R.T.E. obtained a ticket to the Dublin rehearsal of the annual European Song Contest which enabled him to see the first live "Riverdance" performance – he was ecstatic. Each St. Valentine's day he would produce a special dinner for us with a delightfully designed menu and trappings.

Tomás had to make his own way in life. We encouraged him - difficult, for he had become so much a part of our lives. Each year he makes one or two visits 'home' to Ireland, and he regularly

Tomás and bride
Consol, Palma 2001

telephones. He has established a successful bookshop and office servicing company in downtown Palma. In May 2001, Grania and I shared in Tomás' marriage celebrations to Consol Pinya Gallego, a delightful native of Palma. She was known to him whilst he was living at Ballinakella and they became re-acquainted some years later. The custom in Spain is that not only is the bride given away by her father, but the groom by his mother. He asked especially that Grania undertake this task. In the church Grania and I were privileged to sit at the special 'Prie Dieu' up front. The following month the couple flew to Clare for their honeymoon.

* * * * * * * * * *

An interest in archaeology and history has found me being elected Vice-President, along with National Heritage Council member and friend Michael MacMahon, of the Clare Archaeological and Historical Society whose President is traditionally the Franciscan Father Guardian of Ennis. Grania and I are also members of other Clare groups and contribute to the Shannon Archaeological Society's journal, *The Other Clare*. The Clogher Historical Society, the Friends of Enniskillen Castle, the West of Ireland Family History Society and the Irish Genealogical Research Society also receive our support. I have lectured to some and have conducted tours for the Irish Georgian Society, of which Grania was a founder member. Like her, I am also a director of the Hunt Museums' Trust and share an oversight of one of Europe's leading private museums. Established by the John Hunt I knew in my youth, it is still actively supported by his son John and his daughter Trudie. I am also a director of the Christian Training Institute which, amongst its aims, encourages reconciliation with its multiplicity of opportunities both in Ireland and beyond.

It is always a privilege to launch other people's books. Professor Desmond Roche promoted an excellent two-volume history of the Woodford area in County Galway, the second volume of which, *Clanricarde Country,* I launched in 1988. Three years later, Grania had me undertaking the events for her family history, *These my Friends and Forebears.* Other publications include a racy novel *The*

Rage of Galway by Patrick Cleary, and a general history of Co. Clare by Brian Dinan, both in Ennis. The Feakle and Flagmount areas of Clare were written up by local author Joe Noonan. Introducing me at its publication, chairman Billy Loughnane chuffed me when outlining my involvement with the area, by identifying me as "one of our own". *Schools in Ogonnelloe* got a send off at a parish party as I was about to sail to France, whereas *Stair agus Béaloideas Páirtín agus Miliuc*, a record of an area near Limerick, I launched in a hostelry at Ardnacrusha.

Opening picture exhibitions for the *Clare Champion* and for artist Phil Brennan whose delightful nature paintings have become so popular has also been a welcome task. Such activities invite one to share an appreciation of the efforts authors or artists put into their work.

At my talks and lectures to both academic and non-academic groups on Ireland's history, her clans and the evolution of Irish names, audiences have been both youthful and mature students under programmes organised by the University of Limerick, Elderhostel and other specialist convenors . My life has been and still is, very full.

*   *   *   *   *   *   *   *   *   *

I had never returned to Hong Kong when Tomás and Deirdre suggested that Grania and I should have a holiday, so, in 1993, we flew to London for a flight via Bangkok. Above north-eastern Europe it was exciting to observe the Russian topography and later, over India, the Himalayan foothills. A day and a night in the Thai capital were crammed with a visit to the Royal Palace, shopping and jaunts in Tuctucs, the cheap motorised tricycles. We then flew to a very changed but still colonial Hong Kong where we were met at Kai Tak Airport by our Tuohigs Travel representative. Organised, by a local Chinese company, a trip to Macao by hydrofoil followed by a bus journey over an area of China east of the Pearl river to Kwangchou, and a return by rail to Kowloon were highlights; on this we were accompanied by a delegation of Scandinavian medics, an Australian couple and New Zealanders. Passing through the passport check from Macau into China, we proffered our visas which had been organised through the Chinese Embassy in Dublin, while the others were on a collective card. Our identities were embarrassingly scrutinised; perhaps the authorities hadn't processed Irish visitors before. The bus journey was terrible but the driver did his best to negotiate vast potholes and higgeldy-piggedly traffic, mainly bicycles. A miniature Guelin near Foshan with caves and swinging bridges, a 'typical' rural village, a snake farm, and the sights of Kwangchou city were fascinating, as was a canal journey with a scenario unchanged for centuries. Our hotels included the famous White Swan, from the balcony of which, as dusk turned to night, we watched busy shipping on the river below. In Hong Kong we climbed the Peak by cable-car, travelled by bus to Repulse Bay and, from our hotel in Kowloon, visited a Chinese market but a train journey to Fanling in the New Territories was shattering. The countryside had been developed and the town swamped by a vast 'centre'. I am glad we went when we did but I have no great desire to return, the place I had once loved was so changed.

Certain items which I have accumulated during my lifetime are special. My first copy of Maurice O'Sullivan's *Twenty Years A-growing* and R.M. Lockley's *I Know an Island* are amongst the books I still possess. The *Bible* I received at Confirmation is near my bed but the '*Revised Standard Version*' I acquired in Cork in 1958 is still my favourite. The little matchbox of Australian gold nuggets and the polished axehead which Mr. Baynham gave me, a box on which my mother painted a hunting scene, my father's curio chest and the box and book presented to me by prisoners in Nicosia are amongst the things which, of little monetary value, I lovingly cherish.

Proud of my roots, I often find myself in County Fermanagh. Recently too, I organised an historical tour of Ardmayle. Unknown to me, pictures by local artists were on display in the church. As we made our way through the graveyard, I was totally taken by surprise as I was warmly greeted by old friends. Here also, I was 'one of our own'. I recalled so many happy times amongst them.

I often feel lonely for my family. Their members are dwindling. My mother, so vibrant, hard-working and gregarious, now lives with my brother at Pechbouthier, east of Bordeaux. She sold her delightful

Fontenille

house at nearby Fontenille in 1999. Guy's prime occupation is his paintings. He has not been to Ireland since 1980 but following her move, my mother spent two months at Ballinakella recuperating

With Axel and Ebba Hamilton (3rd and 5th) and Malcolm Ross-MacDonald, Banagher, 1995

PHOTOGRAPH: INGRID ROSS-MACDONALD

from illness while he was on his annual visit to the Americas. Sadly, she has had to spend several lengthy periods in hospital since. My father's generation has passed, though my mother's brother Mick's widow Pam constantly keeps in touch. Their daughter Chlöe and her husband Tim occasionally visit from Cambridge, and we regularly communicate. My other (Weir) first cousins share news at Christmas and Diana and Dick Willis came to Ireland in autumn 1999. We met in Dublin and enjoyed dinner together at Portlaoise where we talked for hours, catching up with family news. Their daughter Lucy stayed a few years ago but the other members of this talented family and their children seem to gravitate eastwards. Amongst the many other friends and kinsfolk to stay with us or visit are Warren and Anne Loane whose daughter Erica, now Lady Fairfax Lucy, stayed with us for a year while she was organising Limerick University's Self-Portrait Gallery and whose brother Charles is married to Sarah Mahon of County Galway. Anne and Warren keep in touch by telephone and we often visit each other. The Weirs of Dromard near Enniskillen, the Elliots, and Dick and Joan Brandon who lived at Castletown Manor

Captain Mackey, daughter Anne Loane, granddaughter Erica, County Donegal

near Hall Craig, together with Chomley cousins such as the Blennerhassetts and Bennetts of County Limerick have all been to Ballinakella. Douglas Graham was a keen genealogist and we spend long hours discussing family connections when, with his wife Ann, he stayed. There have been even more of Grania's people, and lots of other friends from all over the world. We love having them.

* * * * * * * * * *

Amongst my earliest memories is sitting on my father's knee in the orchard at Peldon with the dogs licking my face, and climbing the snow-clad moat at Ardmayle with Dolly O'Neill. I am glad my life has taken the course it has. Only in recent years has my polio made its presence uncomfortably real. Had I been encouraged to develop my early efforts at card design and writing, I might have become a leader in one or both these fields. This is conjecture, however, and I am satisfied that when my days come to an end, I shall have at least tried my best to make my small world better. If spared, I intend to continue my efforts for many years to come, for I still enjoy a privileged and happy time.

I am glad when I enter a local shop, to be addressed as just Hugh, the name with which I was baptised and one of my parents' first gifts to me. This is in keeping with my sense of equality. I feel nostalgic, however, when, say, no longer does the little spring bell warn the owner that a customer is entering. Few today are the cluttered characterful manned emporia with counters, in front of which one waited to be served from shelves behind. Cold storage has superseded tins of food and salted bacon, but adequate transport ensures a variety of fresh unfrozen vegetables in the remotest convenience stores. Old names persist, as the families of previous owners continue business tradition. We buy our papers at Treacys in Whitegate, and Keanes in Mountshannon where still hangs a photograph of my grandfather's record catch of trout. Shops such as these supply bread, milk, vegetables, tinned foods, ice-cream, the more recently introduced videos and the basic needs of the community. For more specialised foods or magazines, customers make for larger towns and multipal stores. Tuohys of Coose, who supply building materials and hardware, continue to expand, though some customers go where they think they may do better - they seldom consider the cost of travel, the valuable time wasted, or after sales servicing. Decimal coinage, rather than the twelve pennies to a shilling, and twenty shillings to a pound make transactions easier, especially as the Euro becomes accepted throughout the European Union. Weights and measures also being decimilised, calculators lighten the burden on our now idler brains.

On Sundays, rural churches are still well attended although Saturday evening Mass has been introduced for Roman Catholics. Pope John XXIII ensured increasing interdenominational fellowship as services and community events are shared, but much clerical leadership has been superseded by "democratically" elected committees, in some parishes a regressive step. Perhaps circumstances will change, hopefully with a return to a realisation that man is not in control of his destiny, and that religion is important. Christian fellowship has been harassed by ill-considered and hurtful statements such as the "Dominus Iesus" document of Cardinal Ratzinger in 2000, the rantings of certain non-conformist clerics, the sinful behaviour of a few 'religious', the identification of religion with politics and the turmoil in Northern Ireland. No longer are the local civic guards occupied with the elimination of noxious weeds, but rather with curbing the spread of heroin and ecstasy, or preventing violence. In cities, anonymity breeds problems such as car theft and joy riding, house break-ins, muggings, teen-age drinking and drug sessions, sexual crimes and vandalism; no longer can one leave one's home unlocked. Government scandals are necessitating costly tribunals, while politics and politicians get a diminishing reputation.

Irish-owned airlines link small regional airfields and Irish shipping, Swansea ferries, Stena and other lines have regular car ferries to Britain and France. People used to be excited when told of adventures in Hong Kong or Paris - even Dublin was an experience denied to many. Today, many have crossed the border to the 'North' to take advantage of the ongoing cease-fire and there are few who haven't travelled beyond Ireland. Motorways are being constructed across the island, other roads are improving and most families have a car. Public transport has been updated, and pensioners are conveyed free although rural railway and bus services are scant. Telephones are to a universal standard and electricity is available to all. Even remote homes are linked to water schemes and there is public waste management. Due to the recent economic boost there has been an upsurge in new housing and an increase in pride for both personal and public property with colourful gardens and landscapes being created.

Living conditions have changed, too. No longer do home-dwellers sit in draughty stone-floored kitchens huddled over turf fires where most of the heat rises into open chimneys. No longer are there the large scrubbed wooden tables at which one sat on wooden benches to enjoy bacon and cabbage or soda bread and butter, accompanied by strong tea. Most people have entrance halls, livingrooms with carpeted floors, walls with decorative pictures, and kitchens with built-in cupboards and electric fridge-freezers, washing-up machines, liquidisers, toasters, cooker-hobs, ovens and other facilities. Cosy bedrooms have comfortable electrically-heated beds, well-constructed chests of drawers and wardrobes and there are bathrooms with the latest 'white' furniture. Computers are given pride of place where until the nineties, television sets stood. No longer do radios crackle. Most people have video recorders, so there are few cinemas, and then mainly in towns. Homes are electrically warmed, or have oil-fired or gas central heating. Double glazing helps to keep the winter cold at bay. Nearly everyone has hot water and sewerage or if in the country, septic tanks. Chairs are comfortable and there now is adequate electric interior lighting, some of it by halogen lamps. Internet correspondence means that postal deliveries linking lonely outposts are diminishing, though there seems to be plenty of 'junk' mail. The busy housewife increasingly purchases ready-made foods, rapidly reheatable in microwave ovens. Country people can now live almost as conveniently as those in cities, but are moving to where the jobs are. This is at the expense of their communities.

Farmers struggle to make ends meet and tourism concentrates on activity holidays and city tours, many enterprising housewives enhancing their incomes through 'bed and breakfast'. Rural Ireland still remains comparatively unspoilt and tourist opportunities do remain. Wind farms, interpretative centres and electricity pylons may be necessary, but not in most people's 'back yards'. Educational facilities have improved beyond comprehension. There is also a new-found maturity in the Irish State. An influx of settlers, many of them New Age Travellers or refugees, is possibly uniting a once divided people. Politics in the Republic can now be discussed openly with little fear of reprisal. It is a more comfortable and positive country for most. Hospitals and medical care are now of a standard comparable with the world's most advanced while banking, commerce, industry and the facilities and opportunities they offer make Irish life in the twenty-first century the envy of much of the world's population.

Like my contemporaries, I have witnessed incredible changes over more than half a century. Although many of these cause me sadness, I reflect on the improved living conditions and happier state of those who were born less privileged than I. Membership of the European Union, the United Nations and efforts for world and local peace on an ever widening scale indicate an improved future for those who will be entrusted with our planet. I am happy to be 'one of our own', amongst my own, my wife Grania being the real mainstay of my life.

With Noel Crowley, Clare County Librarian, Veronica and David Rowe at launch of 'Intimations', Ennis 2000

PHOTOGRAPH: COURTESY VERONICA ROWE

FACES INDEX

Aborigines, New World, 47
Adrian IV, (Pope), 98
Aherne, Father (Franciscan Guardian), 341
Alamaki, Toyni, 78
Allen family, (Cork), 179
Alley, Séan, 213
Alliance Française, 287
Amat, Gabriel, Reverend, 258
Ambani, Stephen, Reverend, 256
Ampthill, Lady (Christobel) (née Hart), 237
An Taisce (National Trust for Ireland),
    207,221,265-6
Anderton, Peter, Captain, 25,27
Anderton, Mrs. Peter, (Sheila) (née Dwyer),
    27
Andratx, Mayor of, 271
Andrews family, (Knappogue), 213
Anglican Consultative Council, 257,263
Aquitaine, Chaplaincy of, 262
Armitage family, (Noan), 73
Armstrong, John, (Archbishop), 255
Army Reserve, 140,141
Arthur, King, 42,43
Ashbourne, 1st Baron, 14,15
Ashbourne, 2nd Baron, 16,174,215
Ashbourne, Lady, (Frances Maria Adelaide)
    (née Colles), 14
Ashbourne, Lady, (Marianne) (née
    Conquerré), 16
Ashton Productions, (Cork), 162,170
Ashtown, 4th Baron and Lady (Oonagh)
    (née Green-Wilkinson) 69,
Astwood family (Bermuda), 336
Atlee, Clement (parliamentarian), 57
Atwater, M.M. (author), 97
Ayscough, Aunt Jean (alias Reid), 182
B.B.C., 21,194
Bagliani, Mrs. (Sheila) (authoress), 292
Bagwell family (Tipperary), 72

Baker family (Malahow, Co. Dublin),
    217,218
Baker family, (Lismacue, Co. Tipperary),
    22,
Barnardo, Dr. (philanthropist), 207
Barnes, Frederick, 15
Barnes, Mrs. Frederick (Morag) (née
    Tailyour), 15,153
Barrett, Master (Tipperary), 78
Barry family (Tipperary), 67
Barton family, 123
Bary, Brian (cartographer), 289
Bary, Mrs. Brian (Valerie) (authoress), 289
Bateman, H.M. (artist), 18,19,99
Bateman, Mrs. H.M. (Brenda) (née Weir),
    18,19,99.100,147,152-3,161,182,218
Bawn, Colleen (labrador), 235,238
Baxter family (Shannon), 217,330,
Baxter, Mr. (Abbey National), 143
Baynham, Mr., Reverend, 5,57,346
Beccari, Hon. Mrs. (Bridget) (née
    Thesiger), 220
Beckett, Samuel (author), 102
Belfast, Lord Mayor of, 255
Bell, Mr. Malcolm and Mrs. (Muriel), 237
Bella (pug), 229,240,293
Bellamy, (Bellingham), Mr. (murderer), 46
Bellassis, Sir Henry's regiment, 11
Belton, Paddy, (actor), 162
Benson, Howard, 259,260
Benson, Roy, 260
Bermuda Historical Society, 336
Besnyö, Mrs. (Claire) (née Burke), 262
Betjeman, John (poet), 4
Bevan, Aneurin (parliamentarian), 57
Bianconi, Charles, 37,69,70
Bibby, Mr. (shipping magnate), 133
Bishops' Selection Board, 157
Black and Tan Hounds, 75

Black Knight (pekinese), 58
Black, Jack (now Reverend), 180
Black, Mrs., 74
Blackwell, Joe, 286
Blackwell, Mrs. Joe (Meike) (authoress), 286
Blake, Henry, 174
Blake, Robert, 224
Bleakley, David (politician), 257
Blennerhassett, Bennett etc. families, 123, 349
Bliss, Mrs., 145
Blood family, 214
Blyth, 3rd Baron, 202
Blyth, Adrian, Hon., 202
Bord Failte (Irish Tourist Board), 194,196, 317,322,326
Bosanquet, (army officer), 122
Bosnian Terrorist, murderer of Archduke Ferdinand, 311
Bosun, Springer Spaniel, 32,37
Boy Scouts, 157
Boyd family, (Wexford), 179
Braddell, Harry, 193
Braddel-Smith family, (Wexford), 179
Braga, Mrs. George (Gioia) (née Marconi), 340
Brandon, Dr. Richard and Mrs. (Joan), 266,348
Brannigan family, 213,217
Breadon, L. S. (schoolmaster), 116
Brehon Law Commission, 14
Brennan, Phil (artist), 345
Brian Boru (Ard Rí), 218,219,221,225,255,278
Bridge, Mrs. (Joyce), 223
Brien, John (Fermanagh), 114
Brierley, Hon. Mrs. (Caroline) (née Gordon-Walker), 262
Brierley, John (Dublin), 243
Brierley, Mr. (father of John), 243,
Brody, Reverend Hugh and Mrs. (headmaster), 183-4,190-1
Brook, Rupert (poet), 22
Brooke, Mrs. Peter, (Joan) (née Smith), 147
Brooke, Rt. Hon. Peter, 147

Brookeborough, 2nd Viscount, 105
Brooks,Henry, Reverend, 180
Brown, Floyd (media host), 325
Browne, Martin (environmentalist), 261,264,282
Browne-Clayton family (Galway), 226
Bruton, John (parliamentarian), 255
Buckley, Joe (merchant), 80,91
Buckley, Leo, Commandant (Aide de Camp), 338
Burke family, (Cashel), 80
Burke family, (Dromaan), 36,180,186,188
Burke, Michael (newsagent), 80,92
Burke, Mrs. Peg (Dromaan), 341
Burke, Reverend Curate (Cashel), 74
Burke, Richard, (Minister), 279
Burke, Sir Bernard (genealogist), 317
Burke's Stationery Shop, 92
Burrows Jerram, Reverend, (headmaster), 159,162,169,172,177,227,340
Burrows, Mrs. Jerram (Rachel) (née Dobbin), 159,162,169,170-77,187, 227,340
Burton, Richard (actor), 145
Butler family, 61,66
Butler, Father Rueben, 261
Butler, Mr. (Portora Bursar), 116
Butterly, Rita (Iarnród Éireann), 273,
Byrne, Anne (Irish Export Board), 327
Byrne, Bryn, Reverend, 292
Cadogan, 7th Earl, 15,145
Cadogan, Annie, 15
Cairns, Gill, 75
Caldwell family, (Cashel), 95
Camier, James, Reverend Canon and Mrs., 253
Campbell, John (diplomat), 179
Campbell, Mr. (tutor), 20
Campbell, Patrick, 3rd Baron Glenavy, 194
Campbell, Reverend Canon and Mrs., 179
Cappabeg Language Centre pupils, 7
Carden, Sheila, 343
Carey, George, Archbishop, 263
Carleton, Captain, (Fermanagh), 12
Carleton, George, (Fermanagh), 102
Carleton, Lancelot (Fermanagh), 102

Carleton, William (Fermanagh), 102
Carr, Mr. and Mrs. Ray, 325
Carrachiola, Signor (Diplomat), 340
Carrière, Monsieur (Alliance Director), 288
Carrigan families, 72
Carrol, Alice Caroline – see Howarth,
Carrol, Egerton, (great-uncle), 45
Carson, Edward, Sir (politician), 66
Carson, William, The Reverend, 66
Carter, Billy (farm manager), 78
Carter, Jimmy (President of United States), 296
Carver, A.B. Reverend, 145
Cassidy, Captain (Director, Beaver Engineering), 198
Catalá, José (Mallorca), 342
Catalá, Mrs. Jacqueline (née Paterson), 269,341
Catalá, Pepé, (Mallorca), 269,341,342
Catalans, 258,342
Catchpool family, 22
Catchpool, Edward (Essex), 22
Catchpool, Rebecca (Essex), 22
Catholic Young Mens' Society, 170
Cavan, Major (schoolmaster), 51,54
Chambers, Anne (authoress), 282
Champ, Cyril Very Reverend, 201
Chapin, Hon. Mrs. H. Beecher (Deirdre) (née O'Brien), 216,221-2,224,227, 286,299, 334,336,345,
Chapin, H. Beecher, Dr. (allergist), 221, 225,299
Charlemaine, The Emperor, 233
Charles, Bonny Prince, 10
Chaston, Miss (teacher), 40,248
Chaucer, Geoffrey (author), 21
Chelmsford, 1st Baron, 220
Chelmsford, 1st Viscount (Viceroy of India), 218,219,220
Chelmsford, 2nd Viscount, 220
Chelmsford, Viscountess (Frances) (née Guest), 220
Chicago, Lord Mayor of, 328
Childers, Erskine, (President), 190,272, 336,338
Childers, Mrs. Erskine (Rita), 272,338

Chomley family, 188,230,349
Chomley, John (Vice-Regal Secretary), 230
Chomley, Mrs. John, (Henrietta) (née Baker), 230
Chopping, Richard (artist), 44
Christian Brothers, 109
Christian Training Institute, 344
Christopherson, The Hon. Mrs. (Griselda) (née O'Brien), 220
Chubb, Celia, 135
Churchill, Sir Winston (statesman), 220
Claddagh, King of, 282
Clare Archaeological and Historical Society, 288,344
Clare County Council, 271-2
Clare F.M., 171
Clare Young Environmentalists, 8,261-2, 265-7,269,272-5,341
Clarke, Bridie (U.S. Representative), 319
Clarke, Raymond, Reverend, 257
Cleary, Noelle (educator), 194
Cleary, Padraig (Shannon Development), 279,316-7,333
Cleary, Patrick (author), 345
Cleeve family, (Clonmel), 72
Cleeve, Harry, 75
Cleeve, Mariquita –see Hichens,
Cleeve, Mrs. Harry (Olive) (née Penniman), 75
Clifton-Brown, Mrs. Peter (Petronelle) (née Grubb), 67
Clogher Archaeological and Historical Society, 344
Clopton, family, 21
Clotworthy, Mrs. Madge (musician), 190,193
Cockburn, Patrick (editor), 276
Cockerill, Mrs. Tim (Chloë) (née Gibson), 26,56,101,150,203,348
Cockerill, Tim (lawyer), 26,56,348
Codner, Maurice, (artist), 99
Coffey, Tom (author), 288-9
Coffin family (Cornwall), 42
Coghill Brothers, (teachers), 47
Coghill, Mr. (headmaster), 49
Cole, Kevin, 170

Cole, Old King, 5
Cole, Sir William, 102
Colles, H. Johnathan Cope, 14
Collier, Mr. (schoolmaster), 51,54
Collison family, 18-9,21
Collison, Albert, 19
Collison, Mrs. William (Caroline Annette)
    (née Frost), 19
Collison, Edgar, 19
Collison, Edith (Cork), 4,18-9,40,101,153
Collison, Francis, 19
Collison, Henry, 19
Collison, Henry, Reverend, 19
Collison, John, 19
Collison, Mrs. Albert (Eugenia) (née
    Montague), 19
Collison, Mrs. Francis (Phoebe) (née
    Watts), 19
Collison, Mrs. Henry (Kate) (née Collison),
    19
Collison, Mrs. John (Elizabeth) (née
    Middlemas), 19
Collison, Mrs. Nicholas Cobb (Elizabeth)
    (née Stoughton), 19
Collison, Nicholas Cobb, 19
Collison, William Thomas, 19
Collison, William, 19
Cologan Machada, Tomás, (Tenerife), 195
Combined Cadet Force, 103,116
Commons, House of, 46
Connaught, Duke of, 18
Connolly family (Tipperary), 68
Connor, Debbie (media host), 325,327
Considine, Colonel, 189
Convicts, Spike Island, 14
Conway, John (Whitegate), 188
Conway, Sean (Whitegate), 187
Conyers, Dorothea (authoress), 21
Cooley family (Shannon), 217,224
Cooper family (Killenure), 73
Cooper, Mrs. Austin, (Ethel) (née Leahy),
    95
Coras Trachtála, (Irish Trade Board),
    317,327
Corby, Miss Ethel (Tipperary), 95
Cork Ballet Company, 162,177

Cork, Lord Mayor of, 255
Cornwall, Duchy of, 46
Corrigan, Tom, Reverend, 180
Cosby family, 133,179
Cosby, Julian (clockmaker), 133,179
Cossiga, Signor Francesco (Italian
    President), 340
Costello, Tom, 217
Couchman, Walter, Admiral Sir, 25,44
Council for the Church Overseas, 256
Counihan, Mr. (Tipperary), 78
Courtney, Tom, 340
Cowell, Mr. (The Field), 143
Cox family (Bermuda), 336
Crafer family (Norfolk), 30
Craig, Maurice (author), 195
Craik-White family, 71
Crawford, Heather, 191
Crib, Staffordshire Bull Terrier, 150
Cromartie, Earls of, 228
Cromwell, Oliver, (tyrant), 65,68
Cronin, Mrs. Dick (Helen), 285
Cronk, the raven, 106
Crosbie family, (Ennis), 213
Crowe, Reverend Canon, (Mountshannon),
    188
Crozier family (Fermanagh), 9
Cuchulain (legendary figure), 176
Cunningham, Bert (Shannon), 250
Curry (fellow student), 55
Cyprus Broadcasting Service, 136
Daly, Brendan (Minister), 272
Daly, Mr. (fishery conservators), 180
Darcy, Larry (Galway), 185
Dargan, Neil, Father, 266
Darling, Edward, Bishop, 261
Davern family, (Cashel), 80,90
Davidson, Chris – see de Burgh,
Davies family (Meelick Bay), 214
Davies family (Pembrokeshire), 42
Davies, Derek (Radio Telifís Éireann), 319
Davies, The Hon. Mrs. (Helga) (née
    O'Brien), 220
Davin, Derek and Elizabeth, 219
Davis, Thomas (nationalist), 13
Day, Mrs. (Pug breeder), 238

de Burca, Eamonn (publisher), 279,292
de Burgh, Chris (musician), 179
de Foubert, John, (Cork), 170
de Gardelle, Louis (teacher), 193
de Gaulle, General, 226
de Mamby, Count, 29
de Paor, Liam (archaeologist), 195
de Ruvigny, Michael, Marquis de, 143
de Stacpoole, (George) Duke , 226
de Valda, Richard, 27
de Valera, Eamonn (President), 72,116,181
de Valera, Síle, (Minister), 272
de Valois, Dame Ninette, 177,194
de Vere, Baltredus (Radulphus), 9
de Vere, Walter or Rudi, 229
de Vesci, Mrs., 18
de Vilmorin, Mrs. (June) (née Paterson),
    269
de Wilton, 'String', 75,119
de Wilton, family, 6,22,69
de Wilton, Geoffrey, 150
de Wilton, Mrs. ('Han'), 75,119
de Wilton, Mrs. Geoffrey (Iva) (née
    Keane), 75,150,171
Defay, Monsieur (Diplomat), 288
Deighton, Colonel John and Mrs.(
    Maureen) (née Hunt), 217
Delaforce, Mrs. (Mabel), 146-9
Delahunty, Mick, (musician), 75
Delany family (Tipperary), 59,67
Denny family (Fermanagh), 123
Dermody, Hugh (media host), 325
Dermot and Grania (legendary figures),
    176
Devane, Jimmy (Tipperary), 59,70
Devitt family (Tipperary), 59
Devonshire, Duchess of (née Spencer), 282
Dillon-Mahon, Luke, 250,258
Dinan, Brian (author), 345
Dobbin, Peter (county surveyor), 159
Dobbin, Reverend Canon, 94
Donegall, Marquess of, 100
Donlan, Pat, Dr. (National Library), 285
Donoughmore, 7th Earl and Countess, and
    family, 72,75,76
Dorchester, 1st Baron, (Sir Guy Carleton),
    329

Dougherty, Pat, Professor (Clan Herald),
    291
Dowling family (Cashel), 80,94
Dowling, Joe, (Abbey Theatre), 322
Dowse, Brook, 190
Doyle, John (Restaurant owner), 322
Dragoons, Inniskilling, 11
Drew, Colonel (teacher), 179,180
Druce, Mrs. (Kathleen) (née Howorth), 45
du Jonchay, Gael, 341
Duffy, Gavin (nationalist), 13
Duggan, Bishop Jack and Mary, 193
Dunbar family (Fermanagh), 9
Dunbar, Sir John, 9
Dundrum, (champion horse), 68
Dunlop, Colin, 117
Dunn family, 181
Dunne family, 290
Dunne, Frank (Soloist), 340
Dunne, Joe (author), 290
Dunne, Matty (Tipperary), 91
Dunne, Mick (media comentator), 290
Durham Light Infantry, 23
E.O.K.A., 138
Eames, Michael and Davy, (Clare), 214,236
Eames, Robin, Archbishop, 255
Edward VII, 2
Edwards, Hilton, (actor), 162
Eekhout family, 182
Eekhout, Bob (stepfather), 181-
    2,192,226,296,300-1,311-12
Eekhout, R. Suzanne – see Weir, R.
    Suzanne
Elizabeth II, 228
Elliot, Mr. Jack and Mrs. (Meta) (née Weir),
    266,348
Emmet, Robert, 209
Emmy (cairn terrier), 237
Empey, Walton, Archbishop, 260
England, Church of, 14,118,258,263-4
England, Church of, Commissioners, 22
Episcopal Electoral College, 213
European Parliament, 59
European Union, 352
Evans family (The Ennis Bookshop), 280
Fahy, Catherine (National Library), 285
Fairchild, Jodi (media host), 323-4

Fairfax Lucy, Lady (Erica) (née Loane),
    260,348
Falconer, John, Reverend, 190,244
Farran, Miss Edith, 188
Farrell, Bernie (Parade Marshal), 324
Farrell, M.J. (Molly Keane) (authoress), 21
Farrell, Michael (author), 194
Fascists, Italian, 16
Feehan's Stores, Cashel, 91
Ferdinand, Archduke, 311
Ferrer, Joan Miguel, 334,336,341
Fetherstonhaugh, (fellow student), 55
ffinch, Michael (army officer), 132
Fieldheim, Dorothy (media host), 323
Finnegan, Mr. John and Mrs. (Aileen),
    184,193
Fisher, Mr. (teacher), 178
Fitzgerald, Desmond – see Glin
Fitzgerald, Desmond (Nenagh), 215,224
Fitzgerald, Garret, (parliamentarian), 255
Fitzgibbon, Gerald (lawyer), 16
Flack, Jim, Reverend, 169
Flack, Mrs. Jim, (Marlynne) (née Kingston),
    169
Flavius, (Roman soldier), 132
Fleming, Reverend (chaplain), 169
Flynn family (Mountshannon), 188
Flynn, Dr., (Castleconnell, 204
Fonda, Douglass Jr. and Mrs. (Lois), 296-8
Fontleroy, Little Lord, 3
Forbes, (fellow student), 55
Ford, Henry (industrialist), 23,87,298
Forde, Paddy (doctor), 122
Forte family, (Ennis), 267
Fox, Billy, Senator, 208
Fox, Charles (politician), 46
Francis, Mrs. (Aunt Lilian) (née Gibson),
    4,7,15,101,181,206,210,212,
Freemasons, 157,
French, Percy, 172-3
Friends of Enniskillen Castle, 344
Fyers, Fitzroy, Colonel, 18-
    19,100,182,228.296
Fyers, Mrs. Fitzroy, (Bryda) (née Weir), 17-
    19,100,161,182,228,241,296
Gadaffy, (President of Libya), 136

Gaelic League, 16
Gallagher, The Hon. Mrs. (Beryl) (née
    O'Brien), 220
Garda Siochana Choir, 261
Gaudi, (architect), 314
George IV, 46
George V, 14,17
Gerrard, Jim (media host), 323
Gibbon, Monk (author), 193,194
Gibson family, 12,61,149,206,246,251
Gibson Harries, Mrs. (Liz), 261
Gibson, C.B., Reverend, 13,15
Gibson, C.E., Reverend, 46
Gibson, Ernest Victor, Hon., 16
Gibson, Fanny, 14-5
Gibson, John George, 15-6
Gibson, Michael W., 15,26,56,96,101,135,
    149,182,246,301,348
Gibson, Mrs. C.B. (Margaret) (née Justice),
    13
Gibson, Mrs. Michael W. (Pamela) (née
    Chard), 15,26,56,101,135,182,301,348
Gibson, Mrs. William III (Louisa) (née
    Grant) (1st m.), 13-6
Gibson, Mrs. William III, (Charlotte) (née
    Hare)(2nd marriage), 14-5
Gibson, Mrs. William IV (Emily Rachel)
    (née Tucker)(1st.m.), 14-5,45
Gibson, Mrs. William IV (Sophia Charlotte)
    (née White) (2nd m.)14-5
Gibson, Mrs. William V, (Evelyn R.E.) (née
    Reid), 15,22-4,28-9,48,55-6,135,144,
    149,241,339
Gibson, Violet Albina, Hon., 15-7
Gibson, William I, 13,15
Gibson, William II, 13,15
Gibson, William III, 13-6,
Gibson, William IV, 14-5
Gibson, William, V, 4,5,9,15,22-4,27,31-2,
    35,37,44,55,59,61-2,68,100-1,149,
    150,188,206,214,230,241,244,339,349
Gibson,Mrs. (Marianne) (née Bagnall),
    13.15
Gill, Jennifer, 190,193,200
Gleeson, Dermot, 213
Glenavy, 3rd Baron (see Patrick Campbell)

Glenavy, Lady (Beatrice) (née Elvery), 194
Glin, Knight of, 280
Gloster, Miss Elinor, 173
Glover , B.K., 117
Glynn, Peg (matron), 193
Goodbody, Dr. John, 194
Goodwillie family, Wicklow, 179
Goodwin, Robert, 10
Gore, Sir Paul, 11
Goulding, Sir Basil and Hon. Lady (Valerie) (née Monckton), 189
Graham, Douglas, Reverend, 104,106,113,116-7,349
Graham, Mrs. Douglas (Ann), 349
Grant, Joseph (lawyer), 13
Grant, Mr.(barber, Cashel), 95
Graves, Robert (author), 339
Greek Orthodox Church, 307
Green, Mark, Reverend, 132
Gregory, Lady (Augusta) (née Persse), 170,226
Grenhan, Dick (teacher), 157
Grenville, 1st Baron (parliamentarian), 46
Grey (fellow student), 55
Grey, Hector (merchant), 205
Griffith family, 194
Griffith, Fred (media host), 323
Grivas, General, 138
Grove-White family, 18,159,162-3,177
Grubb family, 22,67
Grubb, Brian, 67
Grubb, Louis, 67
Grubb, Mrs. Sam (Phyllis) (née Hutton), 67
Grubb, Sam, 67
Grubb,Mrs. Louis, (Jane) (née Jobson), 67
Guinness, Desmond, Hon, ., 287
Guinness, Paul, 184,190
Gunn, Douglas, 7,171,206,225,340
Gunn, Mrs. Douglas (Jean), 225
Gurney family, 40
Hackett family, 67
Haier family, 173
Haier, Joe, 173
Haier, Mrs. Joe, 173
Hajba, Anna-Maria, (authoress), 291-2
Haley, Tom (media host), 324

Halpin, Mr. 'Buddy' (teacher), 116
Hamil-Smith, Joan (secretary), 143
Hamilton family, 9,12,102
Hamilton, Count Axel, 347
Hamilton, Countess Axel (Ebba), 347
Hamilton, Frank (Shannon Development), 319
Hampson (fellow student), 48
Hanley, Bill (Lanespark), 59
Hanna, Fred, (bookshop), 280
Hanna, Peter, Reverend, 163
Harald V, King of Norway, 314
Harbison, Peter, Dr.(archaeologist), 284
Harcourt-Wood, Barbara, 50
Hardy, Bessie (Bobby), 44,160,181
Hardy, Reverend, Canon, 59
Hare (O'Hehir) family, 16
Harmsworth Press, 6
Harold II, 234
Harper, Claude, 215
Harper, Claudia, 7,215-6,221,225-8,230-1, 234-6,
Harper, Joy, 7,215-6,221,225-8,230-1,234-7
Harper, Mrs. Claude (Joan) (née Harvey), 216
Harris family (Tipperary), 22,107
Harris, Bobby, 75
Harris, Smiley, (media host), 328
Hartnett, Joe (Shannon Development), 318
Harty, Michael, Bishop, 262,272
Harvey family, 227,231
Hassard, Kitty (teacher), 193
Haughey, Charles J. (politician), 255
Haughey, Tom (Shannon Development), 279,316,333
Haughton family, Cork, 179
Haworth, John, Reverend, 159,210
Hayes, Michael, Father (Presidential Chaplain), 340
Healy, Mrs. Tim, (Patricia) (née Williams), 25
Healy, Tim (doctor), 25,44
Heber Percy family, 229
Hely-Hutchinson, David (naturalist), 218,296
Hely-Hutchinson, Mark (banker), 75

Hely-Hutchinson, Mrs. David (Geraldine) (née O'Brien), 218,237,296
Henn, Frank, Colonel, 281
Henn, Henry, 281
Henn, Tom, Professor, 281
Hennessy family, (Tipperary), 59,70
Henry II, 98,
Henry VIII, 219
Henry, William, Reverend, 282
Hepworth, Barbara (actress, 100
Herbert, (Bishop of Norwich), 132
Herbert, Andrew, 132
Herema, Teide, (industrialist), 338
Heritage Council, National, 344
Hewitt family, (printers), 279,285
Hewson, Michael, Dr. (National Library), 285
Hibernians, Ancient Order of, 323
Hichens, Mrs. Robert (Mariquita) (née Cleeve), 75.168
Hicks, David, 339
Hicks, Mr. and Mrs., 339
Hill, Ronnie, (headmaster), 267
Hillery, Patrick, Dr. (President), 272-3,282
Hinde, John (photographer, etc.), 245
Hinse, Frederik, 195
Hitchcock, Mr. (teacher), 179
Hitching, Mr. George and Mrs. (teachers), 274
Hitler, Adolf (dictator), 241
Hodges Figgis (bookshop), 280
Hodson family (Wicklow), 37,181
Hogan, Willie (gardener), 36
Hogg, Reverend, Canon, 73
Holland family, (Nutgrove), 36,186,188
Holland, Fred, 36,180,184,185,186
Holland, Mrs. (Nutgrove), 38
Holland, Mrs. Fred (Nancy), 36,180,184
Holmes, G. (author), 281
Honan, Tras, Senator, 272
Hong Kong Police Department, 125
Hope Vere family, 229
Hope-Lang, Keith, 55
Hope-Lang, Mrs. (Ella), (née Weir), 50
Hope-Lang, Mrs. Peter (Nan), 96,97
Hope-Lang, Peter, (headmaster), 50,55, 96,97

Hope-Lang, Reverend Mr., 50
Horne, Mr. (organist), 157
Hornidge, Mrs., 194
Howard, Con (Diplomat), 280
Howe, Reverend Canon (Fermanagh), 105
Howe family (Mountshannon), 188
Howlett, Mr., 48,
Howorth, Henry Hoyle, Sir, 45
Howorth, Henry, 45
Howorth, Mrs. Peter (Val) (née Morris), 45,206
Howorth, Peter, Colonel, 45,206
Howorth, Mrs. Godfrey, (Alice Caroline), (née Gibson, alias Carrol) 15,45-6, 192,206
Hoxha, Enver (Communist tyrant), 310
Hughes, (headmistress), 44
Huk leader (Philipines), 133
Hull, Sergeant Paddy, 134
Hume, James, 11
Hume, John (politician), 319
Hume, Sir John, 11
Hunt family (Tipperary), 70
Hunt Museums Trust, 344
Hunt, John ,Senior, 94,344
Hunt, John, Junior, 344
Hunt, Mavis, 34
Hunt, Pat, 34
Hunt, Trudie, 344
Hunt, Vere Robert Vere, 34
Hunter Blair, David, Colonel, 25,44
Hunter Blair, Neil, 25,45
Hurd, Douglas, (N. Ireland Secretary of State), 255
Hurst, Father, 196
Hussars, 15th , 26
Hyde, Douglas (President), 72
Hyde, Timothy, 269
Imbusch, Kevin (Shannon Development), 319
Immelman family , 213
Inchiquin 13th Baron, 286
Inchiquin, 15th Baron, 219
Inchiquin, 16th Baron, 7,71,213-4,216,219, 221,226
Inchiquin, 17th Baron, 220-3,235
Inchiquin, 18th Baron, 283

Inchiquin, 1st Earl of, 286
Inchiquin, Lady (Anne) (née Thesiger), 71,214,217,218-20,223,225,226-7,
Inchiquin, Lady (Vickie) (née Winter), 235
Indians, Red, 47
Ireland, Church of, House, 259
Ireland, Church of, 16,98,99,130,157,192, 207,209,221,251,253,258,260,263,269
Ireland, Church of, General Synod Standing Committee, 260,
Ireland, Church of, General Synod, 213,250,258-9,261
Ireland, Church of, Representative Body, 250,257,259
Ireland, John de Courcy, 282
Irish Council of Churches, 256,
Irish Evangelical Society, 13
Irish Genealogical Research Society, 344
Irish Georgian Society, 45,70,291,325,344
Irish Republican Army, 132,138,209
Irish Studies, Institute of, 195
Jackson, Gina – see Meares Malone,
Jackson, Ricky, Colonel, 75,101,106,117,147
Jackson, Robert Wyse, Bishop, 73,75,94,141,330
James I, 102
Jamieson family (Mountshannon), 188
Jenkins, Reverend Professor, 180
Jennings, Miss, 177
Joe, (Staffordshire Bull Terrier), 237
John XXIII, Pope, 350
Johnson, Mr. Roger and Mrs. (Susan), 272
Johnston, Alan (media officer), 256
Joyce family (Newhall), 214
Joyce, James (author), 109
Juan, Don (teacher, Andratx), 271-2
Justice, Dr. (Cork), 13
Karaoulis, Mikhailis (nationalist), 137
Kavanagh, Betty, (teacher), 226
Kay, Anne (Anna) - see Vera,
Keane family (Clare, Tipperary), 171,173,176
Keane family (Mountshannon), 349
Keane, Marcus (agent), 173
Keane, Markie (Tipperary), 150,171
Keane, Mrs. Nicholas (Helen) (née Molony), 150

Kearney, Kate, 169
Keating, Johnnie, (publican), 174
Kelly, Jack (postman), 186
Kelly, John P. (Radio Telefís Éireann), 274
Kelly, Mr. Robert and Mrs. (Paul), 204,215,
Kelly, Patrick, Professor (historian), 204
Kelly, Tom (businessman), 204,247
Kemmis family (Tipperary), 69
Kemmy, Jim, (politician, historian), 215
Kennedy family (United States), 297
Kennedy, Basil, 118-9,
Kennedy, Fred, 118-9,
Kennedy, Jim (Beaver Engineering), 200,203
Kennedy, Mrs. (Rose Mary) (née Studdert), 119
Kennedy, Surgeon and Mrs., 95
Kennedy, Ted (politician), 298
Kenny family (bookshops), 280
Kenny, Gerry, Father, 261
Kenny, P.J. (computer expert), 290
Kenny, Tom, (Kenny's bookshop), 279,282
Kerr, John (Fermanagh), 112
Khan family, 184
Kidd, Brian, 117
Killaloe Diocesan Board of Religious Education, 213
Killaloe Diocesan Commission on Churches, 258,261
Killaloe Diocesan Council, 213,261
Killaloe Diocesan Glebes and Finance Committee, 261
Killaloe Diocesan Synod, 213,258,260-1
Killaloe Docesan Board of Social Responsibility, 258
Kinane family, 59
Kinane, Dan, 32
King family (Castletown), 114
King, Archbishop, 102
King, Charles Simeon, Sir, 282
King, David, 10
King, Mrs. (Anne) (née Weir), 10
King, Thomas, Reverend, 102
Kingston, Lord, 11
Kingston, Mr. (Cork), 156
Kipling, Rudyard, (author), 21
Kisi, Ismailowa Adel Seidali, 197

Knowles, Kenneth, 190
Knyvet family, 21
Koopmans, Daniel, 195
Kurdish Refugees, 307
Lambert, Ham, Mr. (veterinary surgeon),
    238
Lambeth Conference, 263
Langley, Oliver, 166
Larkin, Jim (Bord Failte), 328
Larkin, Paul (Board Failte), 322
Lascelles, Alan, Sir, 220
Lascelles, Hon. Lady (Joan) (née Thesiger),
    220
Laurel and Hardy, (comedians), 54
Laverty, Maura, (authoress), 248
Leahy family (Whitegate), 36,188
Lear, Edward (poet), 21
Legg family, Colin and Steven, 200
Leinster Regiment, 44
Lemass, Sean (parliamentarian), 181
Lenihan, Eddie (folklorist), 284
Lenihan, Michael (artist), 284
Lennox, Colonel, 26
Lenox-Conyngham, Melosina (authoress),
    292
Leonard, Alfie, 199
Leprechauns, 327
Levie, Peter, 341
Lewis, Miss (Edmonton), 331
Lewis, Mr. and Mrs. Ron (Ottawa), 329
Librarian, Cork University College, 13
Lidwill family, 150
Lind, Mrs. (Patricia), 204
Lindert, Tom (Genealogist), 319-22
Lindsay, David, Sir, 27
Linlithgow, Earls of, 229
Lipizzaner horses, 62
Litwack, Mrs. (Julia) (née Pine), 18-9,332
Lloyd, Colonel, 11
Lloyd, John (author), 281-2,
Llywelyn, Mrs. Morgan (authoress), 272,
    282
Loane, Charles, 348
Loane, Mrs. Charles (Sarah) (née Mahon),
    348
Loane, Mrs. Warren (Anne) (née Mackey),
    254,266,348

Loane, Warren, 254,266,282,348
Lockley, R.M. (author), 42,346
Logan family (Mountshannon), 188
Long, Ciara, 271
Longfellow, Henry (poet), 298
Lords, House of, 16
Loughane, William) (lawyer), 345
Lowe, Cecil (teacher), 175
Lush, Norman (teacher), 191
Lynch, Charles (musician), 162,170
Lynch, Christopher (Bunratty Folk Park),
    279
Lynch, Martin (Mountshannon), 23
Lyons, Mary, Dr., (authoress), 287
Lyte, Henry Francis (hymn-writer), 102,104
Mac Cutcheon, Sam and Barbro- see
    MacCuistín
Mac Dubhghall, Mrs. Eilis (née Mac Neill),
    284
Mac Neill family, 284
Mac Neill, Eoin (patriot), 283
Mac Neill, Máire, (folklorist), 283,284
MacAleese, Mrs. (Joan), 217
MacCarthy, Tim (hero), 326
MacCuistín, Mrs. Seoirle (Barbro), 160
MacCuistín, Seoirle, 160,169
MacDonald family, (Cashel), 80
MacDonald, Mrs., 147
MacDougald, Jill, 190
MacEvilly, Mr. (hotelier), 226
MacGillycuddy, Mr. Nicholas and Mrs.
    (Rosemary), 216
Mackey, Captain, David, 348
MacLiammoir, Michael (actor), 162
MacMahon Clan, 288
MacMahon family (Limerick), 214
MacMahon, Marshal, (President of France),
    288
MacMahon, Michael (historian), 288,344
MacMahon, Noel (author), 288
Macmanaway, Dean, 106
MacMaster, Anew (actor), 80
MacMathuna (O'Mahony), (Cashel), 80
Macnamara, Tom, Father, 261
Macnamara, Mr. (O'Briensbridge), 119
Magenta, Duke of, 288
Maguire, Mrs. and Miss (Fermanagh), 105

Maguire, P.P. (R.T.E.), 195
Maguire, Rory, 9
Maher family, 59
Maher, Albert and family, 59,65,77
Maher, T.J. (member, European Parliament), 59,82,84,341
Mallow Town Council, 13
Malone, Peggy, 7, 205
Manning, Maurice, 195
Mansfield, Captain, 11
Mansfield, Mr. Charles (headmaster), 178
Mansfield, Mrs. Charles (Marvina), 178
Marconi, Guglielmo (Inventor), 340
Margaret, Princess, 181
Maria (from Milan), 142,146
Mark, Norman (media host), 325
Marston, Roger, 143
Martley, Elizabeth, (née Gibson), 14
Martley, Francis, 14
Marx Brothers (comedians), 299
Masefield, Charles (poet), 21
Mau Tse Tung (Chinese patriot), 133
Maxwell, Bill (Aer Lingus), 321
Maxwell, Celina, 341
May, Mrs. Judith, 257
Mayes, Michael, Bishop, 256
McAdoo, Arthur, 157
McAdoo, Harry, later Archbishop of Dublin, 156,163,166
McAdoo, Mrs. Harry (Lesley) (née Weir), 156
McCarthy family, 284
McClenaghan, Claire, 191
McCormick, Mrs. (Clodagh) (née Grubb), 67
McCreight, Mrs. (matron), 184
McDermott family, (Whitegate), 205
McDonough, Bernard P. (Dromoland), 218
McGinnis, Mr. Frank and Mrs. (Patsy), 219
McGuire, Mrs. Congella, 272
McKenna, (fellow student), 102
McLysaght, Edward (genealogist), 317
McNulty, Mike (editor), 324
McOstrich, Mr. Wilfred and Mrs., 101,330
McQuillan, Angela (interpreter), 195
McRedmond, Louis (author), 282

McSullivan, Donal F. (I.T.B. Vice President N. America), 323,328
Meares Malone, Mrs. (Gina) (née Jackson), 147
Meehan, Father, 173
Mehaffey, James, Bishop, 257
Meissner, Charles, Reverend, 180
Melbourne (fellow student), 55
Mendeonez, Master, 170
Mendeonez, Professor, 170
Mental Health Association of Ireland, 340
Mercier Press (bookshop), 280
Meskell, Bat, 32,68,78,132,248
Meskell, Mrs. Bat (Molly), 32-3,61,63, 68,248
Meskell, Peter (historian), 85
Messel, Oliver (designer), 39
Metcalfe, Charles, (organist), 164
Millie (pug), 240
Mills, Edgar, Reverend Canon, 157
Minayloff, Vasily, (Russian visitor), 196
Minogue, Mr., (caretaker 'The Rock of Cashel'), 94
Mitchel, A.J., (fellow student), 102,117
Moller, Nicky, 190
Monck, Mr. John, 220
Monck, The Hon. Mrs. (Margaret) (née Thesiger), 217,220,224,234
Montgomery, Arthur, 291
Mooney, Gerry (Iarnród Éireann), 274
Moore, Jimmy, Bishop, 117
Moore, Miss (matron), 179
Moriarty, Christopher (author), 191,282
Moriarty, Joan Denise (dancer), 162
Mosley, Sir Oswald, 28
Mothers' Union, 256
Mountbatten, Earl, 339
Mugovan family (Whitegate), 188
Mugovan, Socey (Whitegate), 36,184
Mullins, hardware shop (Cashel), 91
Mulloy, Mrs. (Sheila) (authoress), 282
Munnings, Alfred, Sir (artist), 4,58
Munnings, Lady, 58
Murdoch, Commissioner, 325
Murdock, Iris (authoress), 21
Murfet, Michael (teacher), 116

Murphy family, 67-8
Murphy, Bryan (hotelier), 279
Murphy, Eddie, 68
Murphy, Mr. Steve and Mrs. (Meredith), 327
Murphy, Mrs. (Nancy) (historian), 292
Murphy, Mrs. Bryan (Iseult) (née O Brien), 279
Murphy, Olive (harpist), 180
Murphy, Professor Maureen, 284
Murray Moore family, 72
Musgrave family, (Cork), 179
Muslims, 311
Mussolini, "el Duce", 17
Myers, Kevin, (Irish Times), 290
Nash, Frank, Lord Mayor, (Cork), 284
Nash, Piers O'Conor, 283,322
National Farmers Association, 59,164
Nawn, Jim (Librarian), 282
Nelson, Admiral, 45
Nelson, Charles (Botanist), 27,
New York, Mayor of, 320,
Newbridge College Young Environmentalists, 267
Niven, David (actor), 20
Nivlet, Philippe, 341
Noonan, Joe (author), 345
Normans, 70,98
Norris, David, Senator, 322
Notley, Mr. (distributor), 205
Nowlan, Kevin B. (professor), 195
O Brien, Mrs. Murrogh (Suzanne), 279
O Brien, Murrogh (Foynes Island), 279
Ó Caoimh, Father Tomás, 262
Ó Cinneide, Seamus, 213
Ó Dochartaigh, Fionbarra (author), 290
Ó Súilleabháin, Diarmaid, Bishop, 290
O'Brien family (David), 72
O'Brien family, (Sir John), 72
O'Brien, Anthony, 218
O'Brien, Audrey, 75,218
O'Brien, Dermod, 156,217
O'Brien, Donal Mór, King, 250
O'Brien, Dr. Brendan, 217
O'Brien, Edna (authoress), 36,186
O'Brien, Fionn, Hon., 220
O'Brien, Ivar (author), 286,313
O'Brien, John (bookshop), 280

O'Brien, Peter, Lord (lawyer), 16
O'Brien, Michael, 36
O'Brien, Mrs. Brendan (Kitty) (néeWilmer, 150,217-8
O'Brien, Mrs. Conor (Maire Rua) (née McMahon), 219,284,339
O'Brien, Mrs. Eddie, (Liz) (née Acland), 226,
O'Brien, Mrs. Ivar (Patricia) (née McLoughlin), 286,313
O'Brien, Murrough, King, 219
O'Brien, Paddy (Rienskea), 36-7,188,244
O'Brien, Mrs. Paddy (Delia) (née Tully), 36-7,186,188,244
O'Brien, Sir Lucius – see 13th Baron Inchiquin
O'Brien, William Smith (patriot), 109,217,220,272,279
O'Callaghan family, 195
O'Callaghan Westropp family, 214
O'Callaghan Westropp, Conor, Colonel, 172
O'Callaghan Westropp, Mrs. Conor (Margaret) (née Blaauw), 172
O'Casey, Sean (playwright), 109
O'Connell, Daniel (parliamentarian), 70,109,282,290
O'Connell, Maurice, 290
O'Connell, Vincent, 225
O'Connor, Donald (actor), 328
O'Connor, Mr. (butcher), 89
O'Connor, Mr. and Mrs. Michael (Sixmilebridge), 175
O'Conor Don, The, 283,322
O'Conor families, 288,289,317
O'Daly family, 317
O'Dea family, 287,336
O'Dea, Dom. Bernard, 287
O'Dea, Fanny (publican), 172
O'Dea, Frank (editor), 265,287
O'Dea, Michael (Tanaiste), 287
O'Doherty family, 290
O'Donoghue family, 291
O'Donoghue of the Glens, Geoffrey (Chieftain), 291
O'Donoghue, Brendan, Dr. (Chief Herald), 291
O'Donoghue, Richard (artist), 291

O'Donoghue, Rod, (author), 291
O'Donovan, John, Father, 225,336
O'Dowd, Mr. Patrick and Mrs. (Kathleen), 218
O'Dwyer family (Nodstown), 70
O'Dwyer, David, 270
O'Dwyer, Francis, Sister, 266,269,270-1,280
O'Faolain, Sean, (author), 86
O'Hanlon, Dr., (Minister), 340
O'Hart, John (genealogist), 317
O'hEochaidh, Marcus, 195
O'Kelly, Sean T. (President), 72
O'Leary, Mr. (printer), 168
O'Mahony family (bookshops), 280
O'Mahony, "the Pope", 12,186
O'Mahony, Mrs. (Claire), 264
O'Mahony, Elizabeth (hotel manageress), 340
O'Malley family, 282
O'Malley, Desmond (Politician), 282
O'Meara family, 38
O'Neill family, 332
O'Neill, 4th Baron, 332
O'Neill, Dollie, 32,35-7,61,188,248,333,349,
O'Neill, Jorge, Prince, 332
O'Neill, Lady (Georgina) (née Montagu Douglas Scott), 333
O'Neill, Sean (author), 286
O'Regan, Brendan (Broadford), 271
O'Regan, Dr .Brendan (Shannon etc.), 316
O'Regan, John, 325
O'Regan, Mary-Anne (journalist), 325
O'Reilly family, 317
O'Riordan, Brendan, 195
O'Sullivan family, 317
O'Sullivan, Mary, 194
O'Sullivan, Maurice (author), 4,42,154,346
O'Sullivan, Michael (artist, author), 292
Oak House, 262-3
Old Shuk (the ghost), 172
Oldfield, Richard, (hotel manager), 223
Ormonde, Earl of and Duke of, 11,66
Osborne, Michael (National Stud), 322
Otter Hounds, Eastern Counties, 20
Overend, The Misses, 189
Owen, Edwin, Bishop, 217,225,227,250-1,258

Owens, David (interviewer), 319
Owens, Nora (politician), 322
Packman, Mrs. (Emily Charlotte) (née Gibson) (alias Storey), 15
Paisley, Ian, Reverend, 255
Pakenham Mahon, Mr. Stuart and Mrs. (Olive), 238
Palmer, Mary, 75
Palmer, R.J.B., 117
Palmer, Reverend Canon and Mrs., 75
Paltridge, Colonel (teacher), 184,190
Paresce, Donna (Donata), 340
Paresce, Donna (Degna) (née Marconi), 340
Parnell, Charles S. (patriot), 109
Parsons, Miss (bookseller), 293
Partners in Mission Conference, 257
Paterson, Mrs. Jack, (Brada), 269
Patton family (Fethard), 59
Pavloff, Vladimir, 196
Peggy, (my mother's mare), 86
Pennefather family, 69,73,177
Pentyrch Fox Hounds, 41
Pepino (Jack Russell Terrier), 198,203,209,216,235,237-8,
Pepys, Samuel, (diarist), 21
Percival family, 100
Percival, Rt. Hon. Spencer, (parliamentarian), 46
Perdue, Gordon, Bishop, 157,163
Perrot, Mr. (verger), 157
Perry, Mr. and Mrs. (London), 142
Pertwee (fellow student), 55
Phillips family, 22
Piggy, Miss, 39
Pilkington family (Clare), 171
Pine, Michael (architect), 18,19,100,153
Pine, Mrs. Michael (Monica) (née Bateman), 18,19,99-100,147,153,218,329,332
Pitt, William (parliamentarian), 46
Plunket, David (lawyer), 16
Plunket, Lord, 13
Plymouth Brethren, 163
Pocock family, 107
Pocock, John, 75
Pocohontas, Princess, 48

Police, Yugoslav, 8
Polish Airmen, 1,40,248
Ponsonby, Harry, 75
Porcell Calafat, Tomás, 237,273-4,283, 285,287-8,290,293,334,336,341-345
Porcell Calafat, Maria Rosa, 341
Porcell Palmer, Juan, 341
Porcell, Señora de (Jomita) (née Calafat Vera), 341
Porcell, Señora de, (Consol) (née Pinya Gallego), 343-4
Porteous, Mrs. (Cork), 156
Pratt, Archdeacon, 105
Prentice family, 194
Prentice, Peter (lawyer), 204,224,258,260
Prentice, William, (lawyer), 224
Presbyterians, 14
Price, Miss (art teacher), 179-80
Pringle, (headmaster), 150
Pull (fellow student), 48
Pullen family, 29
Pyle, Fergus (editor), 159,186,211
Pyle, Mrs. Fergus (Mary) (née Burrows), 159,169,186,190,211
Quaile, F.G., Lay Canon, 257,260
Queen Anne, 218-9
Queen Boadicea, 5
Quin, David, 158
Quin, Etaine, 158
Quin, John, 158
Quin, Mrs. Coslett (Doreen), 158,162
Quin, Coslett, Reverend Canon, 157-8,162, 179,181
Quinlan, Harry (teacher), 169,175
Quinlivan, Brendan, Father, 261
Raclin, Mr. Robert L. and Mrs. (Ernie), 327
Radio Éireann / Radio Telefís Éireann, 21,162,170,181,186,195,261,272,340
Radley, Miss, 44
Rakic family, 248
Raleigh, Sir Walter, 45
Ratzinger, Cardinal, 350
Rawson, Colonel Aubrey and Mrs. (Wendy) (née Worledge), 217
Rea brothers, (Portora), 103
Read, Peter, 258
Reade, Constance, Miss, 112,114

Reade, Mrs. John (Mary) (née Weir), 114
Reade, Arthur George, Reverend, 114
Reagan, Ronald, (President, U.S.), 326
Reddan, Blathnaid (Crafts Council), 322
Refaussé, Raymond, Dr. (archivist), 260
Regan, Larry, 82
Reid family, 96,149
Reid, Mrs. Hugh (Beatrice) (née Lucas), 25
Reid, Geoffrey, 25
Reid, Hugh, Captain, 23,25,27
Reid, Mrs. William (Louisa) (née Barkly), 25
Reid, Percy, 22,25-6,
Reid, Mrs. Percy (Rosa Jane) (née Catchpool), 22,25-6
Reid, William, 25
Revere, Paul, 298
Reynolds, Vonnie (couturier), 322
Rhodesian Forces, 134
Richards, Reese, (media host), 326
Ricketts, Captain Theophilus, 44
Ricketts, Mrs. S.L. (Aunt Daisy) (née Gibson), 15,44-5,84,101,135,339
Ringrose, Brendan (lawyer, environmentalist), 274
Rivera, Elaine (media host), 324
Roberts family (Ennis), 213
Roberts, Leslie (Cork), 260,291
Robertson, June O'Carroll, (authoress), 45
Roche, Desmond, Professor, 344
Rogers family, 188
Rogers, Mrs. (Carol) (née Pine), 18-9,332
Roman Catholics, 98-9,155,173,208-9,218, 258,262-3,269,312,328,350
Romero, Justo (Mallorca), 341,342
Ross, Mr. and Mrs. Peter, 191-3,197-8
Ross, Shane, Senator, 276
Ross-MacDonald, Malcolm (author), 347
Roughan, Kieran, 279
Roughan, Patricia, 279
Rowe, David (also "Dane"), 274,282,289,291-2
Rowe, Mrs. David (Veronica) (née Hardy), 274,289
Rowlette, Frankie, (schoolmaster), 116
Rowse (fellow student), 48
Royal Air Force, 40

Royal Dublin Society, 72
Royal Geographic Society, 131
Royal Norfolk Regiment, 20-1,120
Royal Ulster Constabulary, 209
Rupert, Mrs. Raphael (Anne), 285,
Rupert, Raphael (author), 285-6
Rupert, Rudolph Dr. (politician), 285
Russell family (Cashel), 22,95,150
Russell, George, 73
Russell, Wilfred, 73
Russian Tourists, 195,196-7
Ryan families, 70
Ryan family (Bawnmore), 68
Ryan family (Inch), 69
Ryan, Mr. and Mrs. Arthur, 142
Ryan, Commander, 69
Ryan, Denis (Ardmayle), 59
Ryan, Mrs. (The Moat), 58,70
Ryan, Peg (The Moat), 58,70
Rynd family, 105
Sally, Staffordshire bull-terrier, 40
Salmon, Dean (lecturer), 180
Salter, Sir Arthur, (politician), 220
Samaritans, Irish, 193
Sampson family, 36,188
Sanchez Arturo, Bishop, 258
Sanders, Bob and Betty (media hosts), 327
Saorstat Éireann, 32
Sergeant at Arms, House of Commons, 228
Sayer, Dorothy L. (authoress), 132
Scallon, Mrs. (Eithne) (authoress), 291,292
Scott family, 116
Scott, Kenneth and Mrs. (Hazel), 116
Scott, Mona (media host), 324
Sean Buidh (favourite horse), 219
Selwood, Major-General, (fellow student), 55
Settle, (Shriners' Recorder), 325
Shanahan, Mrs. Paschal (Patsy) (née Liddy), 222,235
Shand Kidd, Mrs., 231
Shannon Archaeological and Historical Society, 344
Sheehan family, 70
Sheehan, John, 78
Sheepshanks, Richard, 220
Shepherd, Mr., 57

Shine, Eileen (nurse), 95
Shine, Mrs., 95
Shriners, (Charitable organisation), 325
Sides, Mrs. Jim (Margaret) (née Burrows), 159,169,174,176,191,266
Sides, Jim, Reverend, 159,176,266
Simms, George Otto, Archbishop, 252,338
Simms, Katherine, Professor (historian), 282
Simms, Mrs. George Otto (Mercy) (née Gwynne), 338
Skittles, (courtesan and horsewoman), 62
Smith family (Caher), 72
Smith, Mrs. Eric, (Betty), 225
Smyth, Mr. (headmaster), 189
Snowdon, Earl of, (Armstrong Jones, Tony), 181
Soldiers, General Sarsfield's, 11
Soldiers, King James', 11
Solms Braunfels family, 232
Somerville family, 9
Sophia (pug), 238,284
Spain, Reformed Episcopal Church of, 160,257
Sparcely Populated Areas Commission, 71
Sparrow, Geoffrey, 227
Sparrow, Mrs. Geoffrey (Bets), (née Wilbraham), 224,227
'Spot Tobacco', 73
St. Aiden, 229
St. Andrew's, Bishop of, 256
St. Bernadette, 233
St. Brendan, 262
St. Flannan, 250
St. Leger family, 291
St. Leger, Alicia, Dr. (archaeologist), 284
St. Martin, 262
St. Michael, 310
St. Patrick, 326
St. Vincent de Paul Society, 208
St. Vincent, Lord, 46
Stacpoole, (Curator, Nantucket), 298
Stanislaus, Sister, (social worker), 213
Stanistreet, Jean, 213
Stanistreet, Mrs. Harry (Ethel), 213
Stanistreet, Reverend Mr., 213
Stanistreet, Harry, Bishop, 213,250
Stanley (of Halsey Street), 142,146

Stansfeld family, 229
Starbuck family, 297
Steadman, Mrs. M.E, (Barnardo's), 207,211
Steele, Mrs. William B. (née Reade),
    112,114
Steele, William B., Reverend,
    104,110,112,115
Steele, William, Senior, Reverend, 104
Stephenson, John, (author), 335
Stephenson, Mrs. Glenys, 335
Sterne, Laurence, (author), 104
Stoker, Bram (author), 39
Stoney, Mr. T.G.F., 260
Studdert, Brian (teacher), 178
Studdert, Mrs. Loftus, ('Loffie') (née La
    Touche), 35,37,118
Sudan, Episcopal Church of, 257
Sullivan, Manny, (Cork), 156
Sullivan, Sergeant (lawyer), 16
Supi Youlet, (Siamese cat), 64
Surgical Congress, International, 17
Surmaine, Mrs. (Nancy), 271
Surtees, Robert S. (author), 4,21
Swartz, Jan, 134
Sweeney, John (Jack) L. (poet), 283
Sweeney, Mrs. John – see Mac Neill, Máire
Swift, Dean (Dublin, author), 340
Synnott, Kevin (businessman), 203
Tailyour family, 100
Tailyour, Alexander, 15,300,339
Tailyour, Mrs. Kenneth, Denise (née
    Whitridge), 15,27,100,135,182,229
Tailyour, Mrs. William (Amanda),
    15,300,338
Tailyour, Ian, 15,300,338-9
Tailyour, Kenneth, Brigadier, 15,100,182,339
Tailyour, Lillian, 15,300,338-9
Tailyour, Mrs. (née Cooper), 339
Tailyour, William, 15,300,338-9
Talbot, Reverend Edgar and Mrs. (Irene),
    201,225,261
Talbot, Maurice, Dean, 260
Tausch, Paul, 45
Tausch, Mrs. (Rosaleen) (née Angus), 45
Taviani, Dr. Ugo, 17
Taylor, Elizabeth, (actress), 145

Teehan, John (artist), 176
Templemore, 4th Baron, 100
Thackarey, Charles, 21
Thackery, William Makepeace (author), 4
Thesiger, John Andrew, 220
Thesiger, Mrs. John Andrew (Sarah) (née
    Gibson), 220
Thompson family, (Mountshannon), 188
Thompson family, (Ardmayle), 59
Thorington, James, 269
Thorne, (later staff officer), 122
Thurles and Kilshane Foxhounds, 31
Tiernan, James (Illaunmore), 38
Tiernan, John (Mountshannon), 38,223
Tiggy (pug), 240
Tito, Marshal, 303
Todd brothers, J.H. and W.H., 117
Tone, Wolfe, (patriot), 209
Topolski, Felix (artist), 97
Topsy (pug), 238,240
Tottenham family (Mount Callan), 214
Towers, Patrick, Reverend, 268
Treacy, Father, 268
Treacy family, 188,349
Treacy, Honor, 21
Treacy, Mick, 58
Treacy, Mike, 58
Treacy, Tim, 180
Tree Frogs (Bermuda), 335
Trench, Mr. Patrick and Mrs. (Julia), 253
Trimble, Mrs., 104
Trimingham, Andrew, 336
Trollope, Anthony (author), 324
Trotter, June (nurse), 193
Trudeau, Margaret (interviewer), 329
Trustham, Mrs. J. (Harriette) (née Collison),
    19
Trustham, J. (lawyer), 19
Tucker family, 46,334
Tucker, Admiral Benjamin, 46
Tucker, Admiral John Jervis, 14,46
Tucker, Mrs. John Jervis (née Young), 46
Tunison, Pat (U.S. public relations), 322,328
Tuohy family (Coose), 349
Tuohy, Jackie (Williamstown), 36,204,341

Tuohy, John (Reinskea), 36,188
Turkish Refugees, 309
Turner, Lady, 26
Tutu, Bishop, 263
Twigg Band, (Offaly), 324
Ua Croínín, Risteárd (author), 285,287,336
Ubedo Gramage, Archbisop, 272
Umfreville-Moore, Nigel, 117
United Nations Organisation, 120,352
United States, Episcopal Church of, 257
Usher, Reverend Mr., 30
Ustinov, Peter (actor), 147
Van Anrooy family, (Wicklow), 179
van Beuningan brothers, 194-5
van Brederode family, 232
van de Velde, Pim, 231-3
van de Velde, Mrs. Pim, (Elly) (née O'Breen),
    231-3
Vaughan, Deirdre O'Brien, (musician), 341
Veller, Mrs. (née Waterstone), 188
Vera, Mrs.Anne (née Kay), 269,283,342
Vesty, Mr. (Barnardo's), 207,209, 210
Vokes, Professor, 180
von Bahr, Mr. Öke and Mrs. (Margit) (née
    Roempke), 218,222
Wade, Tommy, 68
Wakehurst, 2nd Baron, (Governor of N.
    Ireland), 103
Wallace family, 59,70
Waller, Hardress, Colonel (author), 292
Walsh, Dr. (Newmarket-on-Fergus)., 217
Walsh, Pat (Aer Lingus), 327
Walshe, Mrs. (Stephanie) (née Bary), 289
Walshe, Willie, Bishop, 262
Walton, Isaac, (author), 66
Warden, Air Raid, 41
Warke, Roy, Bishop, 284
Warner, Dick (media figurehead), 274
Warrington, R.D. (fellow student), 102
Wass, Gwen, 41
Watney, Mrs. Sanders, (Biddy) (née Weir),
    18,26
Watney, Sanders, (brewer), 26
Watson, Mrs. (Molly O'Connell Bianconi),
    70
Webb, Timothy, 117

Webber, Claude (media host), 327
Weir Robert I, 10,11
Weir, Alexander I, 9,10,11
Weir, Mrs. Alexander I, (Anne) (née
    Dunbar), 9,10
Weir, Alexander II, (Sandy), 9,10
Weir, Mrs. Alexander II, (Sarah) (née
    Goodwin), 10
Weir, Charles, Sir, 18,26,99
Weir, Clive, Sharon and family, 348
Weir, Edmund, Captain, 18,20,112
Weir, Mrs. Robert (Elizabeth) (née Gore),
    11
Weir, Enid, 18,19
Weir, family, 9,18,21,96,120,277
Weir, George, 10
Weir, Guy Anthony, 5,6,15,18,19,25,57-8,
    61,74,79,81,101,112,127,132,150,152,
    161-2,180,182,192,206,218,224,313,
    346-7
Weir, Mrs. Hugh, (Grania Rachel) (née
    O'Brien), Hon., 7-8,15,18,25,71,211,
    213-4,217- 240, 244,246-7,249-51,
    254-5,261,268-9,273-4,277,279,280,
    282-3,285-8,290-1, 296-7,299,318-9,
    332,334,336-8,340-2, 345,347,349,352
Weir, Jane, 9,10
Weir, John I, 9,10,18,329
Weir, Mrs John I, (Caroline) (née Chomley),
    18
Weir, John II, 10,11,18
Weir, Mrs. John II (Clara) (née Sadler), 18
Weir, John III, 10
Weir, Mrs. John III (Frances) (née Dickson),
    10
Weir, John IV, 10
Weir, John V, 18
Weir, John VI, 18
Weir, Mrs. Terence J.C. (Katherine) (née
    Lennox), 26
Weir, Lady (Margot), 99,100
Weir, Lydia (née Hill), 10
Weir, Mary (née Kygard), 10
Weir, Octavius, 17,18,19,29
Weir, Mrs. Octavius (Flora) (née Collison),
    17,18,19,100

Weir, Mrs. Terence J. C. (R. Suzanne)
(néeGibson, alias Eekhout), 2,4-6,9,
15,18-9,22,24-6,28-9,32,41,49,63,68,
78-9,81,83,85,101,106-7,133,141,152
157,161-2,181-2,192,206,226,231,241-2,
281,296,300-1,311-13,346,348,
Weir, Robert, 18,329
Weir, Mrs. Robert (Anne) (née Carleton),
10,12,329
Weir, Terence J. C., 2,-4,6,9,15,18,19-22,
25,28,49,61,63-4,68,77,79,81,85,
95-6,106,112,133,141,150,152,157,
161-2,181-2,241-2,255,265,348-9
Weir, Wilhelmina Ruth (née Brien), 114
West of Ireland Family History Society, 344
Westminster, Viola, Duchess of, 282
White family (Ballyalla), 213,21
White family, (Cappaghbeg), 36,184
Whiteside, Mrs. Lesley, 260
Whitridge, Mrs. (Mary Albina) (née
Gibson), 15,27,339
Wilde, Oscar (author etc.), 102
Wilkinson, Anne, 147
William I, The Conqueror, 233,300
William IV, 46
Williams, Evan, family, 71
Williams, Mrs. J. (Hughie Thelma) (née
Reid), 25,27,44,45

Williams, J, Major, 25
Williams, Jacqueline (see Healy, Mrs. Tim),
1,44
Williams, Mr., 46
Williamson, Henry (author), 4,21
Willis, Edward, 18
Willis, Henry, 18
Willis, Lucy (Anderson), 18,19,348
Willis, Mrs. Richard (Diana) (née Bateman),
18,19,99,218,348
Willis, Richard, 18,19,348
Willis, Tilly, 18
Willoughby, Noel, Bishop, 257
Wimborne, Viscount, 220
Wimborne, Viscountess (Cornelia) (née
Spencer Churchill), 220
Wingfield family, 123
Woods, Jack, Father, 130,131
Woods, Martin, (Mountshannon), 187
Woodworth brothers, (Wicklow), 179
Wynne, Billy, Reverend, 193
Wyse family, 72
Yeats, William Butler (poet), 109,281
Young, Canon and Mrs., 188,201,225
Yugoslav Police, 310,314